Azerbaijanian
Poetry

Азәрбајҹан поезијасы антолокијасы

AZERBAIJANIAN POETRY

CLASSIC
MODERN
TRADITIONAL

Edited by Mirza Ibrahimov

PROGRESS PUBLISHERS
MOSCOW

Compiled by OSMAN SARYBELLI
Designed and illustrated by NAZYM BABAYEV

ПОЭЗИЯ АЗЕРБАЙДЖАНА

Антология

На английском языке

Printed in the Union of Soviet Socialist Republics

Contents

5

7

Modern Poetry

13

14

15

16

Folklore

ASHUG HUSSEIN DJAVAN

The People and Literature

Dear Reader,

The writer of these lines is firm in his belief that art must always remain true to its native roots, both socially and aesthetically, and must never sever its links with the people and the land that gave it birth.

I remember how, far back in 1915-18, when my family lived in the village of Eveh, in the Sarab Province of Southern Azerbaijan, we children would sit by the stove when the winter evenings were long and cold and listen with bated breath to the fairy tales our mother told us. We were madly excited when the hero of the tale came to grips with the *devs*, and we squealed and jumped for joy when he killed the seven-headed dragon who had blocked the way to the only forest stream whose icy water kept the village alive in the sultry heat of the southern summer. Our mother Zakhra told these tales in her own way, putting into them her own dreams, hopes, joys and sorrows. We were not the only ones who loved those tales. The adults needed them too, for the tales comforted them, helped them to bear up under life's trials, and taught them how to fight for their happiness.

Everything in those tales was dear and familiar to us. In them we saw our villages, our mountains, forests, springs and rivers. In them we heard the enchanting strains of the *tar* and the *saz*. And our mother invariably concluded the stories with the words: "May our tall, snow-topped mountains never collapse! May our fruit trees never wither! May our streams never run dry! Glory to the brave, my children! Eternal joy to friends!"

Years later I read something like that in our *dastan,* in our most ancient epic poem *Dede Korkut.* Its heroes ponder on the purpose of life, they analyse the deeds of their forefathers, and sternly judge their own actions. I think this is one of the distinctive aptitudes of the Azerbaijanians, cultivated and assimilated through many long centuries and naturally reflected in our proverbs, sayings, *bayat,* folk legends and, finally, in written literature.

21

Let us recall Nizami Ganjevi who lived in the 12th century, and his remarkable "Quintuple". The heroes of this poem often pause to review the road they have traversed, to put their attitude to life and events to the exacting judgement of conscience, and sometimes to contemplate the starlit sky and muse about the secrets of the Universe.... Nizami wrote about the rulers and warriors of ancient Greece and Iran—about Alexander the Great, Darius, and others—and about the great philosophers Aristotle, Socrates and Plato. In his poems one hears, alongside the clanging of swords, the measured sound of the pick wielded by Farkhad, a stonecutter and a man of the people. Nizami's genius brings the world's greatest philosophers together, and at their symposium they hold a debate on the purpose of life, on the secrets of the Universe, and on the rights and duties of man.

The thoughts and feelings of Azerbaijanian writers and of the anonymous authors of folk legends and songs have always been with the people, whose lot they dreamed of improving. The Azerbaijanians love life, and they also love knowledge. The poetess Mekhseti-Khanum, who lived in Ganja in the 12th century when religious dogmas compelled women to cover their face with a veil and turned them into domestic slaves, went about with her face uncovered, convened meetings of writers and musicians, and wrote her rubaiyat which rejected scholastic dogmas and extolled the right of human beings to enjoy the pleasures of life. The fanatics proclaimed Mekhseti-Khanum an infidel and banished her from the country.

The humane philosophic traditions of Azerbaijanian poetry have very deep roots which were neither severed nor weakened even in the most tragic periods of Azerbaijan's history.

And there were many of such periods, indeed. The territory of Azerbaijan was time and again the arena of major historical events. We know from the writings of the ancient historian Herodotus and the Greek geographer Strabo that on this territory the Medes—the remote ancestors of the modern Azerbaijanians—built up one of the mightiest kingdoms in the ancient world with a flourishing economy and culture. Zoroaster's *Zend Avesta*—one of the oldest works of science, literature and philosophy—was written in ancient Azerbaijan. Our ancestors were fire-worshippers. The temples and palaces built by them were masterpieces of architecture. A temple of fire-worshippers has been preserved in the village of Byul-Byuli, not far from Baku. As we know, one of the most interesting features of human thinking—the struggle between good and evil, between light and darkness—is embodied in Zoroastrian religion. Our remote fire-worshipping ancestors believed in the power of light and its ultimate triumph, and took a very optimistic view of man's life and struggle. All injustices and vices were personified by Ahriman, the spirit of evil and darkness, and the forces of evil were doomed because sooner or later they had to be vanquished by Ormazd, the spirit of good.

These views and beliefs, eloquently expressed in folk oral art as well as in the pictorial and the applied arts, were very widespread, and that is why other religions, including the Islam, met with a strong opposition in Azerbaijan. According to historians and eyewitnesses, Azerbaijan was an object of constant concern and worry for the Arabian caliphate. This land was ever in a state of unrest which, in the 9th century, found an outlet in the mighty movement of the Hurremites, which shook the rule of the caliphate and demanded a number of progressive social reforms. The culminating point of the movement was the armed uprising of the people, headed by Babek. The struggle went on for twenty years and ended in bloody battles at the foot of Mount Savalan, where Babek met his tragic death.

Let us recall the 13th-14th centuries. The hordes of Tamerlane invaded Azerbaijan. They ravished the towns and the villages. People fled the country in their thousands. Culture went into decline, fanaticism grew stronger than ever, and pessimism, Sufism and asceticism spread wide. The people countered asceticism with their inherent love of life, and this found its reflection in the work of great poets and philosophers. Suffice it to remember the feat of Nasimi, the Giordano Bruno of the Orient. His poetry is infused with philosophical thought and expresses the ideas of pantheism, the teaching which in the Middle Ages came closest to materialism. It elevates man, proclaims him omnipotent like Allah, and extolls him as a treasure of great ideas, feelings and creative powers.

For his progressive ideas, for his desire to rescue man and his mind from the snares of fanatical dogmas, Nasimi met a terrible death. The fanatics, who held a stranglehold on freedom, caught Nasimi in Aleppo and, in broad daylight, skinned him alive!

In this ever-changing world, where life never stands still, the means of reflecting it in art change too.

The Azerbaijanian people is lucky in that the chief milestones in its life and history have been described in literature with great exactitude. There was Fisuli in the 16th century, and Vagif in the 18th—two great poets, each of whom started a new chapter in Azerbaijanian literature. In their poetry the reader will find an expression of the people's spiritual life in a different age from that of Nizami and Nasimi. The lyrical hero of both Fisuli and Vagif is extremely responsive to life's phenomena, to Nature, he strives to cognise the beauty of the world and the secrets of being, he despises social vices, ignorance and backwardness which poison people's existence, and he stands up for the freedom and dignity of men.

Azerbaijanian literature reflects in greater or lesser measure all the stages of the thorny path, with its sharp ups and downs, travelled by its people. As in the literatures of all other peoples, expression is given not only to the social aspects of life, but also to the lyrical feelings of man, to his inner world, his hopes and dreams. Azerbaijanian poets left us romantic

23

descriptions of the landscape, finding beauty even in the desolate plains and steppes that may appear dead and bleak to strange eyes, even in the winds—cold and cruel in winter, and parching and hot in summer. The Azerbaijanian reader thinks it only natural that his native mountains should hold such an important place in the Köroglu epos and in *ashug* poetry. The scenery in Azerbaijan is full of contrasts and is amazingly varied. In August, the temperature rises to plus 35-40°C on the western shore of the Caspian Sea, in Baku, and in the steppe regions of the Muganskaya and Milskaya plains, while in the mountains of the Small Caucasian range the weather remains cool. Here everything bursts into flower at this time of year. Herds of cattle graze on the green mountain slopes and in the alpine meadows. The water in the countless springs is cold, sweet and clear. There are places very high above sea level where agriculture flourishes; there are vineyards, orchards producing apples, almonds and apricots, and livestock-breeding farms. In the lowlands cotton, wheat, water-melons and musk-melons are grown. I should like to make special mention of the juicy pomegranates grown in Geokchai, and the delicious, fragrant musk-melons and quinces for which the Milskaya and Muganskaya plains are famous, because all of them will be found in Azerbaijanian poetry as symbols of beauty. The Astara and Lenkoran districts in the south-eastern part of Azerbaijan have a subtropical climate, and yield great crops of lemons, tangerines and tea. Azerbaijanian tea, the "Bouquet of Azerbaijan" especially, is considered one of the best and most fragrant in the world.

Ganja, Tabriz, Ardebil, Baku, Shemakha, Nakhichevan, Urumiyah, Shusha and other ancient towns, mentioned in medieval historical literature, are situated on Azerbaijanian soil, and it is these towns which gave Azerbaijanian culture its splendid poets, musicians, artists, architects and sculptors.

An acquaintance with our oral and written literature will give the reader some idea of Azerbaijan.

Literature is above all else a chronicle of the spiritual life of society. Progressive Azerbaijanian writers always tried to discharge their duty to the people with honour in spite of all the odds and obstacles. The great Nizami complained in his works about the court poets who cheapened and stultified poetry by depriving it of thought. The same bitter plaints can be heard in the work of Nasimi and Fisuli. The struggle between the different literary trends in Azerbaijan became especially intensified in the 19th-20th centuries. That was the time when the part of Azerbaijan north of the Araks withdrew from the socio-political sphere of influence of Iran and Turkey and, becoming part of the Russian Empire, entered the orbit of European relationships. It was a great turning-point in the history of Azerbaijan which strongly affected the entire life of the people and, to a certain extent, renovated it. And that was the period (19th century) when revolutionary-democratic ideas were voiced most powerfully in Azerbaijanian literature. The realistic trend appeared and it was promoted by Mirza-Shafi Vazeh, A. Bakikhanov, Mirza Fatali Akhundov, Najafbek Vezirov, Nariman Narimanov and other prominent authors. The central themes of their writings were social struggle, progressive ideals and the needs of the people. Their cause was to bring enlightenment to the people, and they dedicated themselves to the struggle against social oppression, fanaticism and ignorance. They made translations of the classics of Russian and West-European literature, of humanist philosophers, enlighteners and revolutionary democrats, and disseminated their ideas in Azerbaijan. Naturally enough, this new, realistic and democratic literature encountered the vehement opposition of backward and reactionary circles.

The struggle reached boiling-point at the beginning of this century. The Russian Revolution of 1905, which dealt the first shattering blow at the tsarist autocracy, gave this struggle a new scale and a new purpose. Literature acquired a new content. Jalil Mamedkulizade, a fervent propagandist of revolutionary-democratic ideas, began publication of a militant satirical magazine *Mollah Nasreddin* in which he printed the wrathfully trenchant satires of the great Sabir. Baku, which was already making headway in its industrial development and whose oil riches had attracted the attention of foreign imperialists, became a centre of revolutionary struggle and also a centre of struggle for the national freedom of the Azerbaijanian people, for a new culture and art. All these complex developments and their even more complex reflection in the spiritual life of the country left a deep imprint on the Azerbaijanian literature of those years. Twelve years later, in 1917, the Great October Socialist Revolution was accomplished in Russia, ushering in a new era in the history of mankind. In 1920, the people in the northern part of Azerbaijan took the reins of power into their own hands, set up a Soviet state, and proceeded to build up their new life and new culture.

The Soviet epoch has witnessed a tremendous upsurge in Azerbaijanian culture and economy. I must emphasise the scale on which the general cultural development of the people was launched. Illiteracy was eliminated, a complete emancipation of women carried through and they were drawn into public life, a compulsory seven-year school education in towns and villages was introduced and thousands of specialists were trained to work in the different branches of the rapidly developing industry and science. Today, Azerbaijanian literature is flourishing. The works of J. Jabarly, Samed Vurgun, M. S. Ordubadi, Mekhti Hussein and many others are popular with readers everywhere in the Soviet Union.

Gifted young writers have now entered the literary scene. Working in close contact with our experienced, veteran authors, they experiment with

25

new forms seeking to best render the inner world of our people, their life and their creative endeavour.

The poems collected in this book are only a drop in the ocean, of course. They are too few to give the reader a full idea of the involved historical past and the present life of the Azerbaijanian people. But we trust that these samples of our literature will conjure up a picture of Azerbaijan, of our wonderful land.

Azerbaijan belongs to those countries whose culture and literature are little known in Europe to this day. The publication of this anthology was inspired not only by our love for our culture and national literature, but also by our sincere wish to contribute our share to the cause of strengthening mutual understanding and friendship between nations. For our part we translate Homer, Dante, Shakespeare, Balzac, Tolstoi, Pushkin and Byron into our own language. We read them and admire them as much as we do our own Nizami, Nasimi, Vagif and all the other poets represented in this volume.

Mirza IBRAHIMOV

March 5, 1969

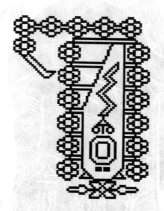

Classic Poetry

Nizami Ganjevi

(Gassida)

My ghazals reach the ear of the people in a wave of
harmonious sounds,
My ghazals are the colour of poppies and, like wine, lull
the heart-beats to sleep.
All that moves in the far starry heavens, all is put into
motion by me,
And in Fortune's gold cup I'm the water, while the sky
is the scoop of the deep.

**Mekhseti-Khanum
Ganjevi**

(Rubaiyat)

A world there is for those in love with mines of precious
stones,
But bards select a different world as setting for their
thrones.

Fisuli Muhammed Suleiman-Ogly

("The Shah makes uncommonly free, with his moneys and land...")

Though a sultan am I, yet no conquering sword do I wield;
With my conquering pen do I force all and sundry to yield.
Every word that I write serves, relentless, the truth to advance;
'Tis a weapon, I swear it, as mighty and sharp as a lance.

Mollah-Panakh Vagif

("In this world there is nothing in which to believe...")

In this world there is nothing in which to believe.
All things are distorted I clearly perceive,
And friends' declarations are meant to deceive.
Fulfilment of promises I can't perceive,
While for falseness in love my whole being must grieve.

Mirza-Shafi Vazekh

("Though every time you utter words both true and wise...")

Though every time you utter words both true and wise
A thousand storms break out and countless dangers rise,
Pay little heed to that, whatever may befall.
Mirza-Shafi Vazekh, prize honour above all.

Gatran Tabrizi

GATRAN TABRIZI, a poet of whom his contemporaries wrote: "All poets are drops in the ocean, and Gatran is the ocean." He lived at the end of the 10th and the beginning of the 11th centuries. Details of his life story are not known. All the information we have is that he was born in Shadiabad near Tabriz, that as a young man he went to Ganja where he earned fame at the palace of the Shahdadides, and then returned home and died there.

Tabrizi wrote in Persian, although his contemporaries insist that there were also works in Azerbaijani. We have inherited his Persian-language legacy, the most noteworthy in which are his historical poems about the wars fought in the 11th century, his poetry describing the earthquake in Tabriz, and his love and philosophical ghazals.

The Earthquake at Tabriz and an Ode to the Emir Abunasr Mamlan and His Son

(Fragment)

Gaze on the might of Yezdan.[1] Gaze on the mighty work
of his hand.
Such deeds seem as little or naught to the hand of Yezdan.
No man can comprehend in its fullness the power of God.
No man can comprehend in its fullness the valour of God.
He makes gardens into barren hills and plains—such is his
power.
He converts barren hills and plains into rich gardens in
flower.
If contemplation makes you aware of humility—that is but
fitting. . .
If you are cast into confusion by his might and his
mystery—that, too, is fitting.
You who would reach to the innermost sense of these things,
You who would master the innermost motive of all of
these things,
Make your way to Tabriz, learn how God's mighty had cast
it down,
Make your way to Tabriz, learn the tale of that most
tragic town.
The city through the centuries raised its head to the sky,
Through the centuries men raised its walls up on high,
The town where men stretched out their hands for a star,
The town that raised towers to Saturn on far,
Lost its pride and was crushed in the space of one hour,
Death took a great toll in the span of one hour.
Many women of beauty, like Kashmir's most fair,
Died in gardens of paradise—still they lie there.
The departed, entombed, shall rest evermore
In once lovely homes in the earth's ghastly maw.
Men whose homes were once filled with rich goods of all
kinds,
Men whose stores were once filled with good things of all
kinds,
Have been felled by misfortune and roll in the dust.
They perforce sold their sons for the sake of a crust.
People starve though the city is bursting with bread.
People thirst though the waters have everywhere spread.
In penury people put value on wealth,
But, death being near, on life and on health.

[1] Yezdan—God.

39

Those who perished were saved from misfortune and
                                               badness,
While the living are plunged in a sea of deep sadness.
All men knew misfortune. For children they keen.
The death of their brothers and sisters they've seen.
In mourning they bloody their cheeks with their nails.
They gnaw at their fingers to stifle their wails.
In the night-time disaster enveloped the town—
You have heard how the towers and walls were cast down.
Helpless children were left by their more helpless mother.
Inconsolable lovers forgot one another.
Till that day of doom none shared woe with another.
Till that day no man had to comfort his brother.
Today in disaster men lack clothes and bread,
And every one feels he were better off dead.
Since God in his wisdom created the world,
And the planets that whirl beyond our own world,
Such tremors on earth there never had been,
A calamity such as mankind had not seen.
This misfortune is fruit of our own wicked acts,
For we did not repent for our unworthy acts.
To bring comfort to those who were not taken by death
The Emir, and his son were saved from sure death.
The elders rejoice when they set eyes upon them.
The young men rejoice, for they now gaze upon them.
While Iran's Emir and his dear son still live
No cause for a Moslem to weep shall they give.
The Emir is a sun that shall never burn low,
Like unto a moon forever aglow.
Thanks to him far more lovely this town shall arise
Than the towns of Iraq to delight people's eyes.
Let there be no more grieving, Tabriz of well-wishers!
Let there be no exulting among our ill-wishers!
Those who love you, Mamlan, have not one heart but
                                               hundreds,
Those in love have not one soul but every one hundreds.
Far dearer are you than vast riches or gain
For the country's well-being is the child of your brain.
All the world's Padishahs are the friends of this crown,
Abunasr the victor casts enemies down.
Under victory's banners he routs every foe.
May his enemies' troops be companions of woe.
May his honey be venom for those who wish ill,

And may poppies be vipers and evil men kill.
Since for him gold means gifts and not riches to hoard,
And since silver's so common at his festive board,
Silver desires to return to the earth
And gold to its vein, since it feels of no worth.
His hand and his sword in peace and war burn,
But extinguish great fires like water in turn.
The gold from his coffers to pilgrims' hands flows
And his sword paints the fields with the gore of his foes.
No riches by him are detained for one night,
Or hidden in dungeons away from the light.
More dear than his soul to him is a guest,
To treat guests with honour is the Emir's behest.
High above Khorasan the moon rises bright.
There the moon does not set, but shines through the night.
Mamlan and his deeds make the sun's face seem dim,
And the sphere of men's doom is reduced thanks to him.
Mamlan bows to none. The world's held in sway.
He takes orders from none—the world waits to obey.
Men grieve when a fortune finally ends,
He grieves for a fortune not given to friends.
In truth and in courage he stands quite apart.
He believes in humaneness and greatness of heart.
He keeps every promise. He never breaks one.
He will never abandon a task once begun.
He makes great what was small, on what's hidden casts
                                                light.
He makes poverty riches and sadness delight.
His name's like the sun that shines forth in all parts.
And his goodness a great and warm wind for all hearts.
The steppes become seas at one wave of his hand,
And the sea by his will becomes dry desert land.
No man in the world is as faithful and true
In fulfilling what Allah told men they should do.
At banquets the Emir is noble and grave.
And in war he surpasses the bravest of brave.
An anvil for him becomes pliant as wax,
For his foes wax becomes a stone wall, or an axe.
While the deep sea holds pearls his crown to adorn,
While men prefer poppies to thistles and thorn,
May he live and rejoice in thousands of ways,
And count in their thousands such fine festive days.

Translated by Tom Botting

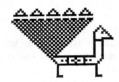

Mekhseti-Khanum Ganjevi

MEKHSETI-KHANUM GANJEVI was an outstanding 12th-century Azerbaijanian poetess—a rare phenomenon in medieval Moslem East. No details about her life are known except that she was born in Ganja and was highly esteemed at the court of Sultan Sanjar of the Seljuk Dynasty. It is also known that Mekhseti-Khanum Ganjevi was persecuted for her courageous poetry condemning obscurantism, fanaticism, the dogmas of the Shariat and the Koran. Her only works that have come down to us are philosophical and love quatrains, glorifying the joy of living and the fulness of love.

Each columned arch within your house, each brick, that
you see here
Depends on the head of shah or finger of vizier.
But every inch of earthen sod whereon your cattle plot
Is as the lovely hair that hides the cheek of your beloved.

* * *

From when we climbed that pinnacle—love's minaret, my
dove,
We both have known no other words but passioned words
of love.
Best no one cross the threshold of this love, our dwelling-
place,
Whose heart is cold as ice, unkindled by love's burning
grace.

Rubaiyat

* * *

Don't ever wait from others any help when you're in need—
O Heart, they scarcely would proffer a dried and withered
reed.
Stinginess makes each a beast, but thriftiness sustains at
least,
So when your means are rather poor, watch with care
expenditure.

* * *

A world there is for those in love with mines of precious
stones,
But bards select a different world as setting for their
thrones.
The bird who eats love's magic grain lives on another
plane—
His nest beyond both worlds, ignoring riches, scorning
fame.

* * *

Ah this then is my heart, and this—what true love means!
Like unto others, love but brings me torments unforeseen.
And my poor heart's the primal source of every sigh and
bitter cry.
Ah this then is my heart, and this—what true love means!

43

* * *

Though you should be the lord of all, the people's crowned
head,
One day you may be forced to cry from poverty instead.
For people let your heart be moved, grow close to them and
dear;
And fear the day you'll need their aid—in kind is payment
made.

* * *

Should Egypt, China, Byzantine, belong to you alone—
It follows then, you know, you may call all the world
your own.
Still. . . Make your life a merry one! For your predestined
lot
Is thirty feet of winding-sheet, a nine-foot burial plot.

* * *

Museum of the Brave is Kharabat—the Hall of Fame.
Here none ignoble, mean or low, a place may ever claim.
And who but sets his foot within must pay respect, esteem:
Here none through sophistry, deceit, a place may ever claim.

* * *

A man is joined to woman when they tie the marriage knot,
And this is right in Allah's eyes—his law forbide it not.
For me, the knot of marriage joins me to my Rubaiyat—
Is there ONE Faith that would comply to such a marriage
tie?

* * *

No force can bind us: pull of moment, arrows flying home,
Nor any wild nostalgia that seized our hearts whilom.
Though my soft braids turned chains of steel and anchored
in your heart,
Could any chain keep me at home if I should wish to
roam?

* * *

44

As in a daze reposing by the field-canal, you dream,
O moon-faced Angel, slim as willow bending o'er a stream!
I come down the embankment bathed in sunshine straight
                                    to you—
That I come down for water, Lovely Creature, do not deem.

* * *

The pleasantest aroma is set drifting from your hair,
The morning breezes catch it up and breathe it everywhere.
Should some ascetic pilgrim see your charms as we
                                    embrace—
Could he again religious turn, asceticism bear?

* * *

O come, my love, and press your lips, your tender lips to
                                    mine:
Restore me once again to life, so from your love like wine
In blind intoxication I be clay within your hands,
And of the world's great weal or woe I'll never even know.

* * *

Thus said the Rose: Before I'd time to open up my eyes,
Before I plucked Joy's berry from life's Earthly Paradise—
Myself was plucked, for pressing out the essence of my
                                    scent.
O may those hands be plucked off, too, from life in just
                                    reprise.

* * *

On grasses green a flower glows in tender ecstasy,
The nightingale pours out his trilling scales in rhapsody.
Both in enchantment dwell, forgetting what invoked the
                                    spell—
The rose that life is brief, the bird his lonesome grief.

* * *

I came across a man upon the road but yesterday—
He wielded well the stick he held, and all along the way
In fury he was beating some poor woman, wifely slave.
All passers-by drank in the sight with no sign of dismay.

* * *

Translated by *Gladys Evans*

Khagani Shirvani

KHAGANI SHIRVANI (Afsaladdin Ibrahim ibn-Ali Nadjar) (1120-1194), a great Azerbaijanian poet and thinker, was born into the family of a carpenter in Melgem, a village near Shemakha. He was brought up by his uncle Kafietdin Omar ibn-Osman, a Shirvanshah doctor and astronomer. In his youth Khagani wrote under the pen-name of Khakaiki, which means a seeker for the truth. After he had been invited to the court of the Shirvanshahs he assumed the pen-name of Khagani ("regal"). The life of a court poet palled on him, and he "fled from the iron cage where he felt like a bird with a broken wing", and set off on a journey about the Middle East. His travels gave him material for his famous poem Tohvatul-Irakein (A Gift to the Two Iraqs) in which he described his impressions of the Middle East, and also his philosophical gassida The Ruins of Madain. On return home, Khagani broke off with the court of the Shirvanshahs, and Shah Akhsitan I gave the order for his imprisonment. It was in prison that Khagani wrote one of his most powerful anti-feudal poems called Khabsie (Prison Poem). Upon release he moved with his family to Tabriz where fate dealt him one tragic blow after another: first his young son died, then his daughter, and then his wife. Khagani was left all alone, and he too died in Tabriz. He was buried at the Poets' Cemetery in Surbakh, a suburb of Tabriz.

Khagani has left a remarkable Persian-language heritage which includes some magnificent odes—distiches of as many as three hundred lines with the same rhyme, melodious ghazals, dramatic poems protesting against oppression and slavery and glorifying reason and toil, and elegies lamenting the death of his children, his wife and his relatives.

I read to the savant some works of my art
And praise for my verse welled up from his heart.

Pure mother-of-pearl his mouth seemed to be
That with jewels and pearls could fill all the sea.

Pearls always have come from deep in the brine,
But the savant found pearls in verses of mine.

He told me, "Two things I would that I knew—
In what land were you born? And whose son are you?"

"A student am I, a man of the arts.
From my town of Shirvan I came to these parts.

A Meeting with Jamaladdin of Mosul[1]

Excerpts From
the Poem
TOHVATUL
IRAKEIN[2]

"My father served the true God on high,
But a carpenter by my trade am I.

"For many a year in calamity's cave
I would suck from my thumbs the wisdom they gave."

He asked how I came to be in Iraq.
For what cause on my land had I turned my back.

"Great famines swept through our land without halt.
Where wheat once grew tall, now waters run salt.

"The countryside there is rich and delightful,
Yet the life that men lead is bitter and frightful.

"Cool waters well up from many a spring,
But the mountains spit fire, standing by in a
ring.

"So my land had suffered at Fate's ruthless hand
There is now an inferno where once was my land.

[1] Jamaladdin of Mosul—the emir that reigned in Mosul in the days of Khagani.
[2] "Tohvatul Irakein"—"A Gift to the Two Iraqs".

47

"A Damocles sword hangs over the town,
How can men fight volcanoes and rocks raining down!

"In my land I bore torture far worse than the rack,
So I shook off its dust and came to Iraq.

"Pray hie to the palace. Enlighten the Shah—
And say to his gates I come from afar!

"A hearing I crave. The Shah shall know all!
Be my guide to the Royal Audience Hall."

The savant replied, "Unworthy you are
For an honour as great as greeting the Shah!

"Your 'I, only I' sounds boastful and vain.
You should learn to be brief, more modest and plain.

"The emptiest barrel makes the most sound,
But a wise man won't talk or look too profound.

"The folk who hear fools find their interest
                                        flags,
Even lions' hearts crack when anyone brags.

"A flood of vain words can not put to flight
A man who is brave and ready to fight.

"To spout without logic any fool can,
It's the sign of a petty, ignorant man.

"Go preen like a pheasant, if such is your wish,
Then be plucked like a pheasant and served on a
                                        dish!

"When a mirror reflects a fool-cockatoo
He will ask with surprise: 'who on earth are you?'

"But after such birds are nonplussed by the truth,
They will parrot refinement much worse, forsooth.

"Our Shah favours praise well rounded and ripe,
But he knows men and words—put that in your
                                        pipe!

48

"True wisdom he loves, that never will fade,
But to callow words little heed shall be paid.

"A great many men the Shah's sherbet drink,
Yet the ones who forget it are more than you'd think.

"No sane man small drops by oceans would measure,
Nor you and your mite by shahs and their treasure.

"Do not be too eager great riches to take,
Lest the noise make the guardian dragon awake.

"Be modest and brief in all of your phrases,
Don't beat your breast, don't sing your own praises.

"Pay heed to your master. Drink in each word
Like a boy who is seen, but seldom is heard.

"If an evil-tongued knave full of malice you are,
Know, you won't be let near to the gates of the Shah.

"Your speech lets you down when your tongue's like
                                        a flail,
Let the mouth hold the tongue as tight as a jail.

"The tongue is the sharpest of swords, it is said.
Have a care lest that sword should cut off your head!

"The tongue is the doorman of hell's deep abyss;
Whereas silence can lead to heavenly bliss.

"The fish found the strength to make its mouth close.
It was guided by signs the zodiac shows.

"The serpent of Eden showed its forked tongue—
When the Lord cast it out the world was still
                                        young.

"A man may be sure his soul he can save
If his tongue will lie still as if in a grave.

"So hurry off home for all you are worth.
And don't stop till you reach the land of your birth!

49

"In schools study arts and crafts, learn them all
And the lessons you learn forever recall.

"Since you are a Türk, and because you are young,
You should learn, while you can, the Arab's great
                                            tongue!

"Today far too much in culture you lack.
When you finish your schooling return to Iraq."

I said, "I have come from afar, as you know,
So I cannot return with nothing to show.

"What a gift shall I bear when I go again
To my home that lies under famine's stark reign?

"When the neighbours ask me what should I say
About teachers that speeded me on my way?"

He said, "Take this ring back home from Iraq,
Men will know you are studious, not one to slack.

"I give you this ring. Let that be your prize.
Forever it should be the light of your eyes.

"To reset this sapphire craftsmen were bid
From the chalice men call the eye of Jamshid.[1]

"As long as you wear this ring on your hand
You have nothing to fear on sea or on land.

"The most sacred names engraved on this ring
Have endowed it with force—a magical thing.

"This seal breaks the spells that Ahriman cast.[2]
It was worn by Jamshid in days now long past.

"And if in your country famine should linger
You'll be saved if you wear this band on your finger.

---

[1] According to the Iranian legend the Shah Jamshid had a chalice
in which he could see the whole world.
[2] Ahriman, in the Zoroastrian religion the god of evil and darkness.

50

"Now that you own this most precious band
Make sure you don't let it out of your hand.

"The seven wide bands of earth[1] knew this ring
For Jamshid would wear it when he was their king.

"Though you are no doctor men's wounds you shall
dress
And through your own land bring the balm of redress.

"This ring can detect all venom and bane,
And what cunning would hide to you shall be plain.

"To take and possess it many men dream,
But you never should yield to any man's scheme.

"On your ring inscribe words by which men will be told
That it cannot be bought, borrowed or sold.

"The true worth of what by right you now own
I'm afraid by its owner can never be known.

"So here is your ring. And now you must go. . . ."
On taking his gift I bowed very low

And answered, "May Allah lengthen your days!"
I expressed my deep thanks in thousands of ways.

I bowed down before him, kissing the ground—
The most grateful of souls that ever was found.

I knew I was helped by Allah's firm hand
On the road from Iraq that leads to my land.

I crossed the boundary of Kukhistan
And the gossips soon saw me enter Shirvan.

I found that each moment people had free
They would fill by discussing my ring and me.

[1] The Seven Bands. According to Islam, the Universe consists of seven parts (belts or bands).

51

Each one who had seen, or not seen my ring
Would expound on that wond'rous magical thing,

The news of my gift from mouth to ear flew.
Very soon it had reached the Khagan's palace, too.

So soon to the royal court I was called.
The great ruler breathed threats, he'd swear and he'd scold,

"To please me is all that you can expect.
Give your ring to your ruler. He'll gladly
                                    accept!

"That ring has cost lives and fabulous wealth.
Don't you dream you can keep it all to yourself.

"Unworthy your hand is of such a fine ring—
A cheap iron band for you is the right thing.

"Don't treat Jamshid's jewel like some silly toy
Or you'll find yourself deep in trouble, my boy!"

I said, "But I trust our Shah won't begin
By abandoning justice, for that is a sin!

"If evil prevail at any king's court
Then his rule shall be cursed, his life shall
                                    be short.

"If God did not build with justice for all
The blue dome of your court would shatter and fall."

The Shah spoke again, "That ring you can trade—
And a town is the price that to you shall be paid!"

I said, "Sell a gift? Such acts I despise!
That would sully the sun that shines in the skies!

"My ring has no price. It could not be sold
Though you offered the world and all of its gold!

"By wearing my ring I can dominate space.
Right off to the Moon and back I can race.

52

"The deepest blue seas by Khizir once known
Would be no more than pearls to set off my stone.

"When I trim my nails the heavenly sphere
Seems to see many moons with light silver-clear.

"The Sun found my ring such a splendid sight
He believed it the North Pole gleaming white."

When troubled or ill, when my spirits were low,
I would gather new strength from that magical glow.

The ring in my turban's folds I would hide,
Or concealed in a pocket, deep down inside.

I kept it so secret because of its worth
Far beyond any treasure down here on our earth.

Then fear of the tongues that wag night and day
Made me keep it at home well hidden away.

So great was my fear with my ring I might part
A great pain in my head seemed to split it apart.

Transgressing all bounds, the devil of gain
Split open my mind and lodged in my brain.

My rage made me lean towards Tugan Shah,
But selfishness drew me towards Tekin Shah[1]

Like a paralysed beggar dumped on the street
I could not go ahead and I could not retreat.

Since bread one must eat, at feasts many times
I would chant for the riff-raff flattering rhymes.

I often felt horror, stricken with shame—
For their gold I had let them sully my name.

When a lamb meets a dragon it freezes with fear
So my heart always cringed as if danger were near.

[1] Tugan Shah, Tekin Shah—rulers of opposing tribes.

53

A cup I became for the wine rascals drank
From the touch of their hands my inner soul shrank.

All bibbers of wine love to pass round the cup
To drink it and then to break it up.

The cup of my soul was soiled, but not broken—
Though a chattle for years by wastrels bespoken.

Jamshid's magic chalice I never became—
I was just a cheap goblet for knaves, to my shame.

*　*　*

One night I saw dreams as if I were cursed,
Till it seemed that my head most surely would burst.

My mind walked beside me, then, seizing my ear,
It showed me a world where oneness shines clear.

With one hand I held onto reason, my brother,
And the staff of my faith I grasped with the other.

With reason and faith to guide and support me
I found the true way as the savant had taught me.

My eyes found that seven dark veils had grown bright
While another nine veils were blazing with light.

At dawn clear horizons delighted my eyes
With the hues of silk raiments adorning the skies.

I gazed at the glorious heavens above
And my heart overflowed with ineffable love.

I saw a great tent of white move up and rise—
And it trailed ropes of fire as it swept to the skies.

It set all the heavens blazing that morn
While the Moon changed its tint in the circle of dawn.

Miraculous scenes I saw all around
And I heard many voices rise and resound.

54

The wonderous dawn redoubled its might
And infinity's secrets I learned from the sight.

What Adam once witnessed in forty long days
Was revealed in one morning to my startled gaze.

As day raised its banner someone drew near
And I saw that my guest was none but Khizir.

His face glowed with glory splendid to see.
With respect and affection Khizir looked at me.

His crescent-shaped mouth had uttered no word
Yet I knew all his thoughts as if I had heard.

His lips exhaled light, illuming his head
And a new sun was born with each word that he said.

Then thirty-two stars formed in once lambent row—
Gleaming mother-of-pearl by the sun set aglow.

Like an intimate friend, the most precious on
                                                      earth,
He spoke words that proved of infinite worth.

He saw that my life had been bitter and dreary
And he knew that my heart was wounded and weary.

He shouldered my load and drove away pain
From my head, and I found I was well once again.

Like rose-scented myrrh, his words, full of grace,
Annointed my head and sprinkled my face.

Sweet attar of roses, camphor and balm
Soon had soothed my vexation leaving me calm.

The one who such pain from my shoulders could
                                                     lift
I longed to repay with some marvellous gift.

The voice of clear reason had set my mind free,
The breath of Khizir was sweet unto me.

My inner voice said—The ring I should give
To Khizir, for it's thanks to him I still live.

I kissed the dear ring my mentor gave me,
Then I laid the gift down for my saviour to see.

He hardly could trust his eyes any more,
Astounded he gazed and whispered with awe:

"How came you by Jamshid's marvel unique,
This miraculous thing?—I beg you to speak...."

I said, "In Iraq, that land on afar,
A wise man I met, a famous khodja.

"The straight way of truth by him I was shown,
And he gave me this ring to keep as my own."

But Khizir extended a generous hand
That held a new ring, a rainbow-bright band.

The gift that he offered where iris arcs burned
He placed on my ring and my own gift returned.

"This ring", he said, "wear on the right hand
                                        alone,
On the left—the magnificent one of your own.

"The two will give aid in your most dire plight—
That ring on your left hand and this on your right."

He added, "I've seen some good friends of mine,
Men with crystal-clear souls, the finest of fine,

"At a hunt in the hills for the bravest of brave.
They indulged in that sport for which manly hearts
                                                crave.

"Our company made a very fine sight,
So yesterday's hunt was a day of delight.

"I recited your poems while we took rest,
And your work underwent a most astringent test.

"They drank in your poems. They savoured each word,
And said, 'It's the first time such verses we've
heard!

" 'Say, who is this poet? What is his name?
In his land do they sing his praises and fame?'

" 'Khagani of Shirvan he's called,' I replied,
'Both his name and his verses are known far and wide.

" 'A master of learning, both genial and wise,
His knowledge and skill should be praised to the skies.'

"I lauded your learning, its depth and its range.
Then my friends said to me, 'Indeed it is strange,

" 'Such attainments should earn Khagani a high place,
And that they have not is a shame and disgrace!

" 'The worth of this poet and men of his kind
Is not understood by the evil and blind.'

"They spoke of your fate and they said in the end,
'Khizir, go to him—be the poet's best friend.

" 'Support him and guide him on his road through this
life.
Protect him from foes, from hardships and strife.'

"Those noble souls bade me to speed on my way
And now I have come here to do as they say.

"So pay great attention, remember right well
The advice that I give you, the tale that I tell. . . .

"Of a honey-hued life you cannot be sure,
It is fickle and you must trust it no more.

"Chameleons and turncoats—keep them at bay.
Don't let double-faced monsters hold you in sway.

"Don't heed wavering colours that seem the most bright,
Don't trust scented beauty at dawn or by night.

"A man is made splendid by arms that he bears—
But a woman by paints and silks that she wears.

"Though seventy centuries be Adam's age,
It must seem but one day to the righteous and sage."

Khizir's exhortations, though graciously told,
Were barbed and my face went as yellow as gold.

To use this great moment my mind was inspired.
I stuttered and blushed, but made bold and inquired,

"You came like an angel, I listened to you,
You say that our world has a honey-like hue,

"You say it's exalted, yet also it's low,
Tell me, when to our doom with our world must we go?

"How long must men live in hope and in sorrow?
How long must we live in fear of the morrow?

"Will some men escape over bridges that blaze?
Or must hell-fire take all at the end of their
days?

"From mankind's five senses can there be relief
For us here on earth, be it ever so brief?

"A canopy covers our little home,
Tell me, is it a stage with a black-painted dome?

"Will peace ever come to this circle in space?
When will this little spot be dislodged from its
place?

"Beyond the equator, what could I see?
What lands and what peoples are waiting for me?"

I put many questions to him in my haste,
But I saw that my manner was not to his taste.

He frowned and then spoke, "I see for a start
That the spirit of evil has entered your heart.

58

"Introspection," he said, "leads away from the truth
You dream of the cosmos like some callow youth.

"Thus never would reason the learned and wise,
For a grave contradiction within your words lies.

"How long will you gabble with hardly a pause
Philosophical rubbish and theories of yours?

"Such studies we call by the name 'felsafeh'[1]
Which is just like the word meaning foolish—'saféh!'

"The words of the Koran no sophism hide,
Nor do facts it expounds; that can't be denied.

"The wise men well known—and to them you may
                                              speak—
There's taught in philosophy preached by the Greek.

"Abandon vain thinking, don't be so foolish
All your philosophies are not worth one phylius.[2]

"Turn your face to the Kaaba and give up your vice.
You've no need for six facets like gamblers' bone
                                              dice!

"Find the meaning of life. You never should be
Like an empty old cage for a bird long set free.

"Don't be double-faced, without body or head,
Like a tambourine's vellum, whitened with lead.

"Don't squander your time for moments of bliss,
They are fleeting as joy obtained by a kiss.

"In faith your support you always must find,
And not in Euclid and Greeks of that kind!

"Don't pay too much heed to their empty word—
Justly forgotten as soon as it's heard.

[1] Philosophy.
[2] Phylius—copper farthing.

59

"Would you order the nightingale—'Trill till you faint'?
Or the spider to make you a picture with paint?

"So busy's the spider, so by spinning diagrams neat,
That like geometricians he's no time to eat!

"About Islam's doctrines and scholars please ask...
I shall answer, for that is a genial task!

"A man who the turban of true faith can wind
Has no need of the crown of kings and their kind.

"If you don't have a diadem you should not frown,
For the lack of it may prove your most precious
                                              crown.

"The finest of heads is the head still uncrowned,
For no better in this or the next world is found.

"Should a head that is crowned lose the love of the
                                              mass--
It will find that uncrowned it looks sorry and crass!

"The tricks of this world do the strangest of things—
Jamshid becomes slave and monsters are kings!

"The demands of the epoch have such a wide range—
Like the skins that hold water they vary and change.

"A waterless skin will be parched as with thirst,
While a skin with too much will swell up and burst.

"Now say, Khagani, will you always be able
To gather up crumbs from the new-rich man's table?

"At times, beyond doubt, you may break a long fast,
But how long do you think such a blessing will last?

"By people's portals don't hang around,
Or you'll be like the crooked tail of a hound.

"Those stupid, ignoble men fear honest work
Like base cringing curs, any duty they shirk!

60

"The chains on a dog that is guarding a gate
Are better than tawdry gold crowns of the great.

"Don't serve the unholy—don't let them come near—
But fling open the gates of the truth without fear.

"From the gateway of evil your soul you must thrust.
Go your way, Khagani, in your God put your trust."

Translated by *Tom Botting*

The Ruins of Madain[1]

My soul, come, draw lessons from life, look around...
A mirror to help you in old Madain can be found.

Beside the Dajla[2] lie the ruins of great Madain.
The river's long banks with bitterest groaning resound.

More blood flows than water from Dajla's suffering eyes.
No tears touch its cheek, dried by flames that from
                                    smouldering ruins arise.

See—the Tigris is foaming—foam curls on the lips of each
                                    wave....
How mournful those ruins burying hearts and their sighs!

The heart of the Tigris is burnt by sorrow and fear.
Can flames be so intense that the water itself they sear?

The river great tribute must pay every year to the sea,
So add your small part with a drop of your blood, not a
                                    tear.

Heave a sigh and the flame from your heart will divide the
                                    Tigris' great stream—
Then one river of ice and another of lava will gleam.

The river enchained had to witness the end of this
                                    place,
It twisted and turned like a chain when it heard the last
                                    scream.

May their hearts draw men here! May the voice of the
                                    ruins prevail!
Let every heart hear at least one whispered word without
                                    fail!

It seems that those jagged-toothed ramparts hold precepts
                                    for men,

[1] Madain (Al Maidan)—the Sassanid capital Ctestiphon, plundered
by the Arabs who built Bagdad nearby.
[2] Dajla—the Tigris.

That they soon must be granted a tongue and will tell their
own tale.

The owls' endless hoot makes my head ring as if with mad
cries.
To sooth my discomfort the tears will soon start from my
eyes.

All songs here are elegies. Nightingales here are all owls.
The cry Madain raised to heaven throughout the world
flies.

This place speaks of chambers of justice once ruined by
hate.
The throne fell to tyrants who rose unaware of their fate.

Was fortune or God's retribution the force that could
shatter
The towers and bring down in ruins a palace so great?

Don't laugh at my tears in this dead place enveloped in
palls—
A man would look foolish if he did not weep in such halls.

As mighty as Kufa was great Madain in its prime.
As lofty its towering fortress, as strong were its walls.

Though pity burns hot in your heart, if your judgement is
cold,
You will see Madain in its beauty like Kufa of old.

Yes, once long ago Madain was a work of great art.
The palace had gateways that blazed with mosaics and
gold.

Here Babylon's king fulfilled orders that other men gave.
At Madain's court Turkestan's mighty khan was a slave.

From this spot was launched an attack on the lion of
fate,
By that lion whose statue is standing here noble and brave.

Imagine this place that once held a whole land in its sway,
The fort as it was, not the ruins that lie here today.

63

The walls would say, 'Weep! for you, too, have good reason
for sorrow.

To dust all must crumble and you, man, are just living
clay!'

Dismount from your horse, for your lips to this earth you
should press.
Here an elephant's foot crushed Ne'eman,[1] the great
master of chess.

Now elephants' castles by monarchs are no longer won,
For the elephant time marches on and brings kings to
distress.

Time was when the shahs could bring elephants under their
sway.
Now time checkmates shahs, they're like elephants gone
far astray.

Here Nushiravan's blood was drunk by Ormuz from his
skull.
The drink was so strong that it made Ormuz stagger and
sway.

A moral was carved on the rim of the crown on his head.
In mine are now surging a thousand as yet still unsaid.

For mandarins Kesra was famed, for his splendour was
Parvis.
They have long been forgotten and lie with the most
humble dead.

For banquets great Parvis had greenery beaten from gold—
A golden-green garden! A wonderous sight to behold!

That ruler has gone and his plants made of gold are no
more.
Proclaim "Kemtaraku".[2] His fate shall no longer be told!

You ask where such rulers have gone, since today there
are none—

The earth has embraced all these kings, every shah and
khagan.

[1] Ne'eman (Numan)—Persian king.
[2] "Kemtaraku"—"Many such came and went". (*Koran.*)

64

Now pregnant with life, she conceived with the greatest of
ease,
But bearing new life she now finds is not easily done.

The wine pressed from grapes here is blood of Shirin
dripping red.

The peasants make pots from the body of Parvis long
dead.

How many a despot and tyrant this earth has embraced!
Yet still she is yearning for more to recline in her
bed.

That black-hearted earth with a snowy and mountainous
head—
She rouges her cheeks with the blood that her children
have shed!

Teach men, Khagani, how fickle is fortune and life
And let the khagans come to you and by wisdom be led.

Though dervishes wait at the gates of the shah for a
gift
That shah one fine day like a dervish may have to make
shift.

From Mecca come presents, but I sent my gift to Shirvan
From old Madain, may its moral men's spirits uplift.

The beads many count come from Jamra[1] near Kaaba
today,
But yours should be made from the flesh of Salman[2] turned
to clay.

These vast flowing waters hold lessons—so drink while you
may
Where two rivers[3] unite as the Shatt—then set off on your
way.

[1] Jamra—place near the temple in Mecca.
[2] Salman—sage sold as a slave to Mohammed.
[3] The Euphrates and the Tigris.

65

From journeys on far one should bring back a fine
souvenir—
My friends, let my gift be the verses I offer you here.

Though seeming disordered my words have made mysteries
clear,
Thus Isa[1] also taught, half deranged by a single idea.

Translated by *Tom Botting*

[1] Isa—Jesus.

A Love Song

As long as my heart is still beating
　　　　the one that I love shall be you.
As long as I hold something dearer
　　　　than life, it shall always be you.
Affection within my soul burning
　　　　lent strength to my heart in the past.
The impulse to keep my heart beating
　　　　forever, my dear, shall be you.
Whatever the wound I may suffer
　　　　the balm for my pain shall be you.
Whatever disorder afflicts me
　　　　the cure for my ill shall be you.
I always shall be at your service
　　　　whatever your heart may desire.
One sultan in life I acknowledge,
　　　　and that one shall always be you.
If ever I write about faith
　　　　and ingratitude, now I proclaim
The title shall start with the letter
　　　　which begins my beloved's first name.
In matters of state, or of faith and apostasy you can't
　　　　deceive me. . . .
For you are my Khan, my Belief, my idol—all one and
　　　　the same!
Who is Khagani? Oh, my sloe-eyed sweet beauty, approach
　　　　me and claim
To be Khagani's khagan, be my monarch demanding
　　　　acclaim.

Translated by *Tom Botting*

Nizami Ganjevi

*NIZAMI GANJEVI (Ilias ibn-Yusif) (1141-1209), a great
Azerbaijanian poet and thinker, was born in Ganja, where he
lived all his life and where he died. Nizami is the pen-name of
Ilias ibn-Yusif, and it means "one who strings syllables".
Nizami has left us an enormous legacy which we can only call
a heroic accomplishment. His most famous works, which are a
worthy contribution to world literature, are the five long poems,
of 30,000 distiches, known as* Khamsa *(Quintuple); the didactic
poem* Storehouse of Mysteries *(1173) containing twenty chapters
and "talks" with preachings and parables woven into the fabric
of the narrative; the lyric poems that sing glory to purifying,
ennobling love—*Khosrau and Shirin *(1181),* Leili and Medjnun
(1188) and Seven Beauties *(1197)—widely known in the Middle
East; and the historico-philosophical poem* Iskander-Nameh
*(Book of Alexander the Great) (1203).
Nizami was not a court poet and he criticised those who were in
the service of the rich and powerful and extolled their masters'
virtues for money. However, Nizami himself was obliged to
dedicate poems to rulers and eminent people, driven to it by
poverty and the need to find protection. Thus, his* Storehouse of
Mysteries *was dedicated to Bahram-Shah, who liked it so much
that he sent Nizami a young slave girl as a gift. This girl, whose
name was Afrak, became Nizami's first and only wife, and the
mother of his son Mohammed. She died young, in 1180, and
Nizami poured out his love for her and his grief in the poem*
Khosrau and Shirin.
*Many poems were written in imitation of Nizami, and some of
them—like the works of Amir Khosrov Dehlevi, Alisher Navoi,
Djami and Fisuli—were completely individual, original writings
which made milestones in the history of the literatures of the
Middle East.
The 800th anniversary of Nizami's birth was celebrated in the
Soviet Union in 1947.
People coming to Azerbaijan for the first time always make a
pilgrimage to Nizami's mausoleum near Ganja, to pay a tribute
to this great poet.*

The Contest Between Khosrau and Farhad

Khosrau asked once: "Where do you come from,
                                        say?"
Farhad replied: "From regions far away."
Khosrau: "In what crafts does your land excell?"
Farhad: "We purchase grief and souls we sell."
Khosrau: "By selling souls what do you gain?"
Farhad: "Our bards this custom don't disdain."
Khosrau: "Your soul from love is well nigh
                                        fleeing?"
Farhad: "My soul? I love with all my being."
Khosrau: "Shirin's affection do you prize?"
Farhad: "O yes, I prove it with my sighs!"
Khosrau: "Is she the moon that shines at night?"
Farhad: "Though drowsy, still I see her light."
Khosrau: "When will your heart forget her glow?"
Farhad: "When I am buried, lying low."
Khosrau: "When she appears, you trembling,
                                        sigh?"
Farhad: "To please her in the dust I'd lie."
Khosrau: "But if she wounds you in the eye?"
Farhad: "I'll give both eyes without a cry!"
Khosrau: "If someone offers her his heart?"
Farhad: "My sword of steel will do its part!"
Khosrau: "She never will become your own!"
Farhad: "A glimpse of her is joy enough alone!"
Khosrau: "If all your chattels she demands?"
Farhad: "I'll give her all, as she commands."
Khosrau: "But if she orders—go away!"
Farhad: "My head then at her feet I'll lay!"
Khosrau: "Forget this friendship, do you hear?"
Farhad: "Can friendship be destroyed by fear?"
Khosrau: "Be calm, it is a day-dream, see?"
Farhad: "Nay, calmness was not made for me!"
Khosrau: "Give up your love, and bear your lot."
Farhad: "For me life without love is nought."
Khosrau: "With patience men condole for sure."
Farhad: "Some men endure, I can't endure."
Khosrau: "By what great sorrow are you torn?"
Farhad: "Our parting makes me weep and mourn."
Khosrau: "Would you desire to have a wife?"
Farhad: "Alone I can no more bear life."
Khosrau: "Give up Shirin, you must obey!"
Farhad: "Shirin is mine, that's my last say!"

69

Khosrau: "Her name to mention do not dare!"
Farhad: "You see and hear Farhad's despair!"
Khosrau: "And if I come to love Shirin?"
Farhad: "The world will burn to ashes clean!"

Khosrau could give Farhad no fair reply.
And thought it best to stop with him to vie.
Confused, the Shah had surely to admit
Not having ever met such ready wit!
The Shah proposed of gold a heavy sum,
To this proposal proud Farhad was dumb!
The Shah's sharp spoken word was firm and sound,
Instead of gold he tried a stony mound:
"Upon our roadway stands a mountain tall,
With pain men cross this giant stony wall.
Your work will be to dig through stone and lay
For people's easement a convenient way.
No man can undertake this work; they say
That you alone can do it, so I pray.
In honour of Shirin you do the work,
My promise to reward you I'll not shirk.
Fulfil my cherished wish, and ease my load—
Through these great mountains dig a well-paved road.
You will be worthy of my gratitude,
I'll grant you all that vainly you pursued.
You will be housed with honour at my place,
You'll be promoted owing to my grace."
Farhad stretched iron muscles: "I obey,
The obstacles I'll duly clear away,
But if in this great labour I succeed,
There's one condition that the Shah must heed:
Tomorrow, if you wish, I can begin,
But on condition—you give up Shirin!"
The Shah, enraged with what Farhad had said,
Was just preparing to chop off his head—
Then thought: "Khosrau is not on terms with fear,
Farhad will hew not earth but stone rock sheer,
If it were earth to dig and cart away—
Then that alone would take him many a day."
So: "I agree," said Shah Khosrau with heat,
"To compromise it is meanness and deceit.
Well, start to work and show your perfect skill—
And we will watch you boldly dig and drill!"

Farhad, provoked by this insulting speech—
"Just Shah," said he, "how this high mount to reach?"
He showed the mountain looming far away,
That mountain's name is Bisutun[1] today.
The mountain was of mighty granite stone,
To be of utmost hardness it was known.
He hoped the promise of the Shah held good,
And toward the mountain ran as whirlwinds would.
He left the palace, flying like the wind
Toward Bisutun, and never looked behind.
He reached the mountain, without cry or moan,
And with his pick began to break the stone.
So, bit by bit, he hewed some figures fine,
Most beautiful, of wonderful design:
He made the sculptured figure of Shirin—
As with a sculptor's chisel, firm and keen.
Then with the pick's sharp point he drew alone
Khosrau, Shabdiz, upon the mountain stone.
Before these busts you see the sculpturing man
Who died, according to a villain's plan:
Khosrau betrayed his vow, his word he broke,
Sent to Farhad a hag who dealt the fatal stroke.

Translated by *Olga Moisseyenko*

[1] Bisutun—legendary mountain on which Farhad carved the image
of his beloved Shirin.

Ghazal

O radiant-face beloved, whose cherished bride will you be?
Whose dignity will you raise, whose honour and pride
will you be?

You are shaded this eve by the awning your master has
spread,
Whose queen with your odorous tresses and grace will
you be?

You are sweeter than honey, no sherbet is sweeter than you,
Whose rill his course with love's wavelets to trace, will
you be?

In the darkness of night you're a lamp with bright light,
God guard you from evil eye,
Breath of life—o whose love to caress and embrace will
you be?

You are gone, how can poor Nizami live alone with his
grief?
He is down now, whose healer his pain to appease will
you be?

Guit'a
(fragment)

Near the garden, too shy to go in, I was burnt by a flower,
How I trembled... She laughed with her laughter of
resonant power,

And the emerald garden, it echoed the sweet rolling
laughter,
She, smiling, exceeded in beauty the flowery bower.

In the morning, at dawn, fleecy cloudlets shed tears on
the garden,
And the jasmine laughed, and the violets smiled, revived
by the shower.

Translated by *Olga Moisseyenko*

Gassida

It is I who am peer of all knowledge, my renown of
                perfection is great,
My genius is vast as the heavens, for I dominate earth, time
                and fate.

My breath fills the earth, it resembles the resonant chimes
                of a bell,
My pen is a banner of glory called to conquer the earth
                and create.

And my proud, lofty brow has attained in its power
                Keigubad's regal crown,
Nay, compared to this height and this grandeur his palace
                is of far lesser weight.

In the sky rose my wonderful sun to shine for the whole
                universe,
While my body can breathe and give life, its power will
                never abate.

In the world of the bards has my name reached immortal
                and glorious fame,
And my genius is here, of this palace, where the Shahs
                reign—the master innate.

Magnanimous and large is my heart—a vast storehouse of
                nobleness pure,
It is sealed with the seal of deep truth, and the truth
                therein lying is great.

If, with pride overwhelmed, the works of Zabur I peruse,
His tongue for the reading of thoughts I wish to cut out,
                for sheer hate.

Generosity often breeds pity, gentle words are bred daily
                by me,
My gift shows freshness and beauty, sweet youth seems
                forever its mate.

My ghazals reach the ear of the people in a wave of
                harmonious sounds,
My ghazals are the colour of poppies and, like wine, lull
                the heart-beats to sleep.

All that moves in the far starry heavens, all is put into
                motion by me,

73

And in Fortune's gold cup I'm the water, while the sky is
                  the scoop of the deep.
I'll not strike tambourines to no purpose; with drums comes
                  a wedding for sure,

When my word sounds, music is worthless, and all
                  instruments silence keep.
If my writings have flaws in their wording, they are still
                  of an exquisite style;

If my syrup has dregs—still with pleasure, for its taste,
                  you will drink of it deep.
My new style has begun a fresh epoch, and now naught of
                  old values remains,

If a new word is coined it is useless, for compared to my
                  word—it is cheap.
With my writings of beauty mysterious, I have conquered
                  the heart of the world,

And from all this success and this glory—admiration and
                  love do I reap.
When I write, my great writings are such, that Ibni-
                  Mugla[1] covets my pen,

Where my word is of clearness astounding, there his poise
                  Ibni-Khani[1] can't keep.
When my lips part to utter wise sayings, then all people
                  in gladness exult,

And the buds of the flowers open, by my spring from their
                  winter sleep freed.
If my word is not heard in its glory, and no gladness or
                  joy light the scene,

Then no bard will you witness whose singing to the advent
                  of springtide would lead.
I have cause to be proud of my writings, of the beauty
                  sublime of my pen,

And you notice the exquisite wording, when my wonderful
                  verses you read.

[1] Ibni-Mugla, Ibni-Khani—poetic rivals of Nizami.

I am mother-of-pearl, I am virtuous, I am clearer than
crystal-clear gems,
But am troubled that, causeless, some harm me, and deprive
me of things that I need.

When my breath comes out freely and deeply, it resembles
a light-floating mist,
And it warms me and makes my fine verses string like
pearls on a thread, bead by bead.

I am truly the star that is shining, making nought of my
enemies fierce,
It is greater than art and the Muses, and makes poets and
thinkers recede.

Nizami's style resembles a charger with a bridle—a light
leather strap,
And my grief is a hard, heavy stirrup, but how perfectly
gallops my steed!

Translated by *Olga Moisseyenko*

The Story of Sultan Sanjar and the Old Woman

A poor old woman, harassed and in pain
Came to Sanjar the Sultan to complain:
She said: "You have no justice, you offend,
Your club-law and your cruelty has no end.
Your drunken steward came to me, the lout,
Kicked, knocked me down, till he was tired out.
He seized me by the hair—an innocent old crone,
And dragged me, heeding neither cry nor moan.
A crowd flocked round, he swore at me, the brute,
Abused, reviled me, hard blows following suit.
He yelled: 'You hunch-backed hag, you'd better tell
Who killed a man quite near to where you dwell?'
He searched my house in hope of finding there
The murderer. . . . O master, is that fair?
The reason was the steward's drunken state,
But why to torture me? O what a fate!
If subjects of the king ransack his land,
Can an old woman answer for the band?
The steward wished his false rights to assert—
Are not your justice and my honour hurt?
The blood flowed thickly from my wounded breast,
I have no strength to bear this cruel test.
O mighty Shah! I writhe with dreadful pain,
To God you'll answer should my cries be vain.
You have no mercy, you're unjust, unfair,
Your club-law is a torture, hard to bear.
A shah should grant his people bounty, grace,
Whilst you defile your honour with disgrace.
To rob poor orphans—that's no valiant. deed,
I see the sequel to your acts, indeed!
Don't rob old crones that hunger they should bear,
And be restrained, at least, by their grey hair!
You are no shah—a knave, and nothing more,
You cause great sorrows on our homes to pour.
If you but strove with love your land to bless,
Your subjects would rejoice of your caress.
They would respect and honour you, no end,
And would consider you their greatest friend.
Your criminal acts created chaos here,
What valorous deed was yours, of conscience clear?
This state used to be famous for its might,
Its kings were praised for being just and right.
Now homes and hearths are ruined here by you,

76

The empty barns present a desolate view.
Recall the dreadful deaths you caused around,
Your turn will come! Yet you'll be safe and sound
If justice you adopt as guiding star;
Today is yours more than tomorrow, Shah!
Be kind and just to crones, infirm and old,
Attend to them, their words are more than gold.
Refrain from ruining homes of innocent folk,
They may take vengeance with a fatal stroke.
From your vile bow-strings swarms of arrows sped,
But starving men may rise and strike you dead!
This bear in mind: you are the key to peace,
Is mankind born disaster to increase?
You were made king to keep your folk from harm,
To treat their wounds with vivifying balm.
To what your subjects say, o Shah, give ear,
To what their hearts demand, give heed sincere.
No heed to words!... Though taking Khorassan—
Your loss was great, when everything was done."

Of shame today remains not even a token,
Loyalty's done away with, vows are broken,
Justice and conscience to the winds we fling,
They've fled, found refuge under Phoenix wing!

O Muse, your poet's words now stop their flood:
For Nizami has steeped his soul in blood!...

Translated by *Olga Moisseyenko*

Fragments from "The Arrival of Iskander-Nameh[1] in Bardaa and His Encounter with the Queen Nushabaa"

(From the poem
ISKANDER-NAMEH)

Oh, wine-bearer, bring me a cup of your exquisite wine,
It is for the thirsty a spring giving water divine.
I feel all aflame and my thirst rouses terrible pain,
O bring me some wine, let me drink till no remnant
remain.
Bardaa!... what a beautiful country! a wonderful sight:
In spring and in winter the flowers are fragrant and
bright,
In summer the tulips and poppies with scarlet tints glow,
In winter the breezes of spring-tide caressingly blow.
The verdant and soft rustling forests are numerous here,
Surrounded by springs that are welling, melodious and
clear.
The fields are adorned with thick willows of emerald green,
The gardens resplendent—a fairy-land never yet seen.
The pheasants have built for their brood in each cypress
a nest,
The ptarmigans coo, and the partridges sing there with
zest.
And flower-beds slumber in silence, perfuming the air;
The lands of this country are free from all worry and care.
The sweet smelling greens in all seasons here sprout and
abound,
Here flourishing nature is bountiful all the year round.
The birds to this country flock always to nest and to
feed,
Here all, even pigeon milk, is to be found, if you need.
The soil of this country is verily nothing but gold—
As if the saf-flowers were blooming, so fair to behold.
Wherever you pass through the verdant and prosperous
places
You witness the ease of existence and bright, happy faces.
A garden as lovely as this one is not to be found,
Nor also a land like Bardaa, where these riches
abound.
An eminent narrator tells us a wonderful lay,
A lay that in eloquent wording survives to this day:

The fair Nushabaa reigned here—queen of this land
superfine,

[1] Alexander the Great.

78

A patron of feasts rich in delicate sweetmeats and wine.
This female jeyran would have none of the masculine race,
And rivalled the gorgeous pheasant in beauty and grace.
An eloquent talker, unyielding, and wise and sincere,
In figure a goddess, with temper of kindness and cheer.
A bevy of comely young maidens surrounded the Queen,
They stood in a round and created a picturesque scene.
Besides them, the Queen had trick-riders and many a
                                                    knight,
Great numbers of warriors presented a marvellous sight.
Although they were men in attendance, the prop of her
                                                    reign,
Yet none of them ever set foot in her private domain.
The kingdom was governed by women with masterly
                                                    skill,
To men she would never in person give word of her
                                                    will.
The women were able and clever in action and plan,
And managed affairs by themselves with the help of no
                                                    man.
Men housed in the outskirts, ne'er settled to live near their
                                                    Queen,
And chose for their homesteads vast meadows, delightfully
                                                    green.
In fear of her wrath none would venture to enter the town,
They loved Nushabaa for they knew of her wondrous
                                                    renown.
Whenever she ordered to corvee the men would forsake
Their homesteads to labour, all ready to die for her
                                                    sake.
When King Iskander with his legions appeared in the land,
The tents of her warcamps were countless, her army well
                                                    manned.
He saw here a country of luxury, joyful and free,
The crops were amazing, the rivers a wonder to see.
He questioned the people: "Whose country of beauty is
                                                    this?
And who is the sovereign who reigns in this country of
                                                    bliss?"
They answered: "These riches, these confines you hardly
                                                    can span,
Belong to a woman, in courage exceeding a man,
A beautiful woman, in fearlessness resting secure,

Surpassing in beauty the pearls of the sea, and as pure.
No person can equal this woman in wisdom and might,
The support of her subjects in times of disaster and blight.
Arrayed in the masculine armour, her foes she defied,
She comes of the House of the brave Keyani, that's her
                                                    pride!
She wears no Caucasian hat, but the crown of a queen,
A chieftain is she, though her soldiers she's never once
                                                    seen.
Her numerous slaves are undaunted, the best of their race—
But none of these soldiers caught ever a glimpse of her face.
The Queen is surrounded by women, full-bosomed and fair,
With them she is apt to take counsel where men have no
                                                    share."

.   .   .   .

The Shah Iskander was surprised and well pleased with the
                                                    story,
And wished to set eyes on this woman of beauty and
                                                    glory.
He witnessed the wonders around him that made him aware
That this was a country unique, of prosperity rare.
The King Iskander thought it pleasant to stop here and rest,
They stayed and made merry—the sovereign himself and
                                                    the rest.
The Queen was informed that an alien army was here,
That King Iskander had come down as a friend to her
                                                    sphere.

.   .   .   .

The soul of the Padishah burst into bloom with desire
To meet this wise woman, to study her country entire,
To learn from the Queen of her secrets that made her
                                                    great land
Yield fruits of the choicest, her forests and pastures
                                                    expand,
And what were the bounds of this kingdom so vast to the
                                                    view,
And whether the stories of all that he learned here were
                                                    true.
They brought Shabdizaa, golden-shoed and the best of his
                                                    breed,
'Twas morning. The Sun of the Universe mounted his steed,

80

And all was prepared in advance for his trip to the Queen,
He went as an envoy the news he so longed for to
glean.
As soon as the fane came to view with its walls tall and
wide—
He stopped and dismounted to rest from his tedious ride.
The palace with towering arches appeared to his eye
So tall and so mighty, they seemed to be kissing the sky.
The maids of the Queen saw the envoy sent here by the
Shah,
And ran to inform of this startling event Nushabaa:
"The camp of the eminent Shah has emitted a ray—
He honours our country by sending his envoy today!
He comes to Your Majesty, worthy and handsome and wise,
With news of his King that would make him sublime to
your eyes.
Himself oh! so clever, polite and exceedingly fine,
He looks like a lamp that was lit by our Maker Divine!"
The Queen gave the order to clear and to deck her domain,
To clean and to straighten the roadways that led to her fane.
Her ladies in waiting put on their most gorgeous array,
The palace was smothered with flowers, voluptuous and
gay.
The maidens of honour wore jewels, had musk-scented
curls,
Their gowns were of silk decorated with diamonds and
pearls.
The Queen, like a pheasant tripped lightly, with infinite
grace,
And wondrously bright, as a lamp, was her pure, smiling
face.
She mounted the throne and sat down, like a goddess
arrayed,
And held a fine orange, tradition most strictly obeyed.
She ordered her servants, as custom demands, to
invite
The envoy of note to present himself now to her sight.
Her faithful attendants were ready the Queen to obey,
They hastened her will to the envoy at once to convey.
The "envoy" walked fearlessly in, without any constraint,
He mounted the throne—this brave lion, devoid of all
taint.
Contrary to custom he kept on his belt and his sword,

81

And made no low bows as an envoy, this eminent lord.
He noticed the wisdom and grandeur, and fathomed their
price,
A picturesque palace, built really to daze and entice!
He noted the stir and the bustle, the court maidens'
grace,
The perfume of amber and musk, the content on each face.
The glittering jewels that decked them so dazzlingly
bright,
Reminded the Shah of the stars on a dark moonless night.
The brilliant reflection of jewels on maiden and dame
Seemed likely to crown Iskander with a halo of flame!
It seems that the ocean itself, and each diamond mine
Had sent their best valuables here in her palace to shine.
The envoy's unseemly behaviour had outraged the Queen,
Who became very angry at what she had seen.
She thought: "He knows nothing of what our customs exact,
No notion has he how an envoy's expected to act!
This poor ignoramus should duly be kept in his place,
His negligent manner toward us is perfect disgrace!"
But, watching attentively, suddenly doubt stirred her mind,
She probed him like gold to find out what was hidden
behind.
She looked at him, guessed that himself Iskander Shah
was there,
Made place for the King on her throne, glad her honours
to share.
She guessed Iskander had behaved so by way of a joke,
And, wishing his presence beside her, Her Majesty spoke:
. . . .

"Be welcome, a chieftain, be welcome, o great Iskander!
How quaint, you yourself are your envoy, come here from
afar.
My sensitive heart has divined it. I see it this way:
Your royal demeanour and manners a sovereign betray.
No envoy are you, but a king, am I right, I demand?
No envoy are you but a sovereign to rule and command!
Your proper informant—your sword is the enemy's fear—
Unsheathe it before me, no other would dare, that is
clear!
But if in my presence you draw it—your rights you exceed,
It means violating the bounds of convention, indeed.

82

Your sword will not help you, speak not of its valorous
                                                    might,
Find other excuses to make yourself fine in my sight.
You come as a guest, but my nets draw around you secure,
Just think of it, think and reflect—you are not yet mature.
My luck brought you here, to my throne, to my land rich
                                                and gay,
Long live this fair Luck that smiles down on my people
                                                today!"

. . . .

Her words were sincere, and her heart beat with joy in her
                                                breast,
Her throne, decorated with crystal, she left for her guest.
"My throne is your own, famous Shah, on this throne take
                                            your seat,
No place for two rulers to sit thus enthroned, 'tis not meet!
From chess you must know that two kings with each other
                                            contest,
Their conflict is painful, of wit and endurance a test."
The beautiful Ruler stepped down from her sumptuous
                                            throne,
And honoured the Shah with the offer to make it his own.
Like somebody's bride, on a plain golden chair she sat
                                            down,
And said: "I am surely your slaveling on whom you may
                                            frown!"
The heart of the giant was thrilled by the speech he had
                                            heard,
He flushed and he paled, was excited by gesture and
                                            word:
He thought: "The sly queen, though a woman, has thought
                                            out her plan,
She seems to be able, and brilliantly wise, like a man!"
. . . .
He mused, and reproached himself now for the fault he had
                                            made
Of putting himself in the power of this royal maid.
If ever a knight made attacks on her land—'twas in vain—
The dragon would capture him duly, and that was quite
                                            plain.
If ever a singer sang songs no composer had made,

83

The gay *kamanchah*[1] would make fun of his voice thus
                                                    displayed.
So plunged in a reverie grievous, deploring his fate,
He scolded his nature, his conduct, his error so great.
Deep grief overwhelmed him; with patience this grief
                                                would he meet,
He bowed the proud head held so high, and acknowledged
                                                    defeat.
The Queen gave the word to her maidens to honour the
                                                    guest
By gracefully decking the tables with all that was best.
The feast should be worthy in food and in wine of the King,
Most savoury dishes the maidens were ordered to bring.
Her servants obeyed her, their bustling about never ceased,
They ran to and fro, and prepared a most wonderful feast.
They brought in great dishes of mutton and lambmeat of
                                                    choice,
The bread was in loaves, newly baked, for the heart to
                                                    rejoice.
The tables were laid near the palace and reached to the
                                                    gate,
The dishes were flavoured with saffron and ambergris.
The pies, richly covered with sesame, buttered and sweet,
And everything seemed as most fine and delectable meat.
And bullocks, well roasted, and all kinds of delicate fish,
A bull with the sphere on his horns, lying low on the dish,
And lambs settled gracefully, seeming so glad, beyond
                                                    words,
As if they grew wings in their strange exultation, like birds.
And jams most delicious and syrups with lemon, made
                                                    sweet,
The almonds, pistachios, nuts were a pleasure to eat.
Some food smelt of ambergris; the taste of such savoury
                                                    wealth
Could help a poor sickening man to recover his health!
And almond khalvah in great blocks; so much food all
                                                    around,
That vessels enough to contain it could hardly be found!
The sherbet was flavoured with rose water, fragrantly fine,
You took just one sip and it tasted of ambergris, like the
                                                    best wine.

[1] Oriental fiddle.

84

Besides this the Queen placed in front of her throne, made
of gold,
A panel, exceedingly polished and rich to behold.
Four cups were displayed on the panel before Iskander:
One cup held red rubies, the second gold ore, bar on
bar,
The third cup held pearls, in the fourth glittered sapphires
rare,
Thus showing her riches, she honoured her guest with her
care.
As soon as the people were brought to a sociable mood,
And mouths were preparing to swallow the excellent
food,
The Queen murmured thus: "Oh, I beg you, most eminent
Lord—
Partake of the viands that are spread on this welcoming
board!"
He answered: "O beautiful woman, I blush at your word:
For all that you told me just now is so very absurd:
Here, lying before me, are stones of a value most rare,
But can you digest them? Why offer uneatable fare?!
And man with a mind, can he eat of the stones here
displayed?
His stomach will never accept them, if even well paid!
But treat me to food that would flatter the stomach at once,
To victuals that, temptingly, offer the hand to advance."
The Queen was amused, and she laughingly said to the
Shah:
"If valuable stones cannot nourish a being so far,
Then jewels are useless, and really of very small need,
But why all the efforts to own them, with fever and greed?
If really these glittering jewels as food cannot serve—
Then man, due to them, cannot rise in the world with much
verve.
I duly acknowledge the fact that a stone is no food—
But why do we labour to get it? This must be tabooed!
We clear away stones from the road, a good pass to afford,
Then why all the stones that are precious so well do we
hoard?
We try to collect them, we dig with avidity great,
But eat them we cannot, they lie in a quite useless state.
If you, mighty Shah, have no love for a rich precious
stone—

85

Reduce what you have, and thereby you will safeguard
                                          your throne."
The words of this woman so lovely impressed him with
                                                  force,
The athlete agreed with her wise explanation, of course.
He said: "Oh, Khanum, your true words contradiction
                                                   defy,
With words of your judgment no masculine judgment can
                                                    vie.
Your lips spoke the truth about jewels, for each precious
                                                  stone
For lost health and happiness, surely can never atone.
Be praised, lovely Queen, for your wisdom and cleverness
                                                   rare,
Thus showing the way I must go to be honest and fair.
O clear-sighted maiden, your words have sown wonderful
                                                   seed:
No coinage of gold shall I have, no advice shall I heed,
The gold I shall throw on the ground for it comes from
                                              the earth,
Where mines are its cradle, the primary place of its
                                                  birth."
Her ruby-red lips smiled in hearing the Ruler applaud,
They seemed to illuminate nature, approving the lord.
She ordered her maidens to serve him with exquisite
                                                  meats,
And treat Iskander to the relish of delicate sweets,
She tasted each dish with a tender, benevolent smile,
Her guest was amazed at her grace as he watched her the
                                                  while.
The Shah was uneasy at this unexpected strange turn,
When dinner was over, he rose to depart, with concern.
But when he was leaving the Queen made him vow not
                                               to hurt
Her subjects, her land, and no rights in her realm to assert.
Then Shah Iskander duly published a royal decree,
And left the great Queen and her country well governed
                                               and free.
And when Iskander left the city the Queen breathed relief,
From God she expected great help and from fortune but
                                                  grief.
To guard from the wrath of the Shah her dear country
                                             she prayed,

86

And thanked her Creator for saving her land from the raid.
And when the dark night overpowered the sun and the day,
She kindled a lamp while the candle extinguished its ray,
And high in the heavenly sphere with the coming of night
The stars lit in legions their galaxies, twinkling and
bright.

Translated by *Olga Moisseyenko*

Hassan-Ogly Izzeddin

HASSAN-OGLY IZZEDDIN was one of the first Azerbaijanian poets to write in his native language. He lived in Asfarain, a town near Khorasan, at the end of the 13th and the beginning of the 14th centuries. Investigations show that his poetry in Azerbaijani and Persian (his verses in Persian were signed "Pur-Hassan") enjoyed great popularity. Only two of his ghazals—one in Azerbaijani and the other in Persian—have come down to us.

My mistress is a heartless flirt—
      O, woe is me!
I think of her with fevered brow—
      O, woe is me!
All say of me that I eat dirt—
      O, woe is me!
My burning heart knows no rest now—
      O, woe is me!
My bright-eyed beauty stays away—
      O, woe is me!
And all night long I count the stars—
      O, woe is me!
The day we met I'll ever rue—
      O, woe is me!
O, tell me why she keeps afar?
      O, woe is me!
Is there for love a remedy?
      O, woe is me!
My love consumeth all of me—
      O, woe is me!

Translated by *Arthur Shkarovsky*

Nasimi Imadeddin

NASIMI IMADEDDIN, an outstanding poet and philosopher, was born in 1369 or 1370 in Shemakha. The country was invaded by Tamerlane, and Nasimi's work naturally reflects the hardships suffered by the people under his grim rule. One of the forms of protest against the Timurides and Islam was "khurufism", a sectarian movement headed by Nasimi's teacher Faslullah Naimi (1339-1396). Nasimi adopted khurufism, the doctrine that man and deity are one ("Allah is myself"), and as a sign of solidarity with Naimi assumed the similarly sounding pen-name of "Nasimi" which means "a pleasant breath of air". After the death of Naimi, who was murdered by Timur's son, Nasimi set off on a journey about the Middle East to preach knurufism. In 1417 in Aleppo, he was seized by the fanatics who, on orders from the town's ruler, skinned him alive for his "blasphemous" poetry.
Nasimi established Azerbaijani as a literary language, although he also wrote in Arabic and Persian. His ghazals were philosophical love poems, and the theme of his mathnavi *and* rubaiyat *was the purpose of life, love and the beauty of Nature.*

* * *

Framed by its dusky locks, your face my heart ensnares;
I burn with passion's hopes, its yearnings and despairs.

Of eyes that glow like stars I am the helpless prey—
Torment me, sweet one, not thus cruelly ere you slay.

But rarely to the end the cup of bliss is drained;
Yet think what pain is mine who is by you disdained.

Count not your beads, I beg, hide not in prayer from me;
A lover is no bird to cage thus mercilessly.

Your beauty night and day I praise in sheer delight.
If I desist, o Lord, turn not my day to night!

You promised I might drink of Eden's gushing spring—
To me not wine—a cup filled with its waters bring.

While you repel my love, there is no peace for me.
Spurn not, o houri mine, your faithful Nasimi!

Translated by *Irina Zheleznova*

At love's most sumptuous feast was I with love made
                                                    drunk—
Is not this why to me besotted seems the monk?

Of love I took a draught, I worship at its shrine;
Think not, a pious one, that I am drunk with wine.

Love leaves me dazed and sick, I stagger, overcome,
Whene'er to its embrace, enchanted, I succumb.

I am a drunkard, aye, but wine to me seems weak;
Upon the couch of love sweet solace do I seek.

When man, by Nature's will, did first appear on earth
A dram of love did he receive from her at birth.

Wind, water, fire and flame, the world is drunk with love,
The devil and the ghost, the serpent and the dove.

The earth, and heaven too, this would I say on oath,
So trust my words, I pray, are sots and drunkards both.

The sky reels drunkenly; the stars, half-swooning, wink—
Of love's sweet-scented wine a cupful did they drink.

And so in paradise did Eve, and Adam too,
Men, angels, houris, sprites, the faithless and the true;

Kings, prophets, holy men, Mukhtar and Suleiman,
And Noah of the Ark, and Jesus—everyone;

The Shah Mardan, Kerrar, the heathen, the devout,
Those who are firm of faith and also those who doubt;

Apostles, saints and seers, the scorned and the
                                                    extolled,
The sages and the fools, the young, the very old.

The zealous Mufti claims his share in open glee;
The Ghadi,[1] holy one, joins in the revelry.

The tavern-keeper drinks, the tavern haunter too,
The dervish and the priest wax maudlin o'er the brew.

The infidels, the giaours partake of love with zest;
All lovers are alike, none differ from the rest.

The outcast Angel drinks who waits at Heaven's door;
The mystic tries a sip and, thirsting, calls for more.

Love's fumes are wondrous strong, and though the cup be
                                              small,
He who doth fill it full, may reel and, stumbling, fall.

A drop will make one faint, one's limbs to wax 'twill turn,
With passion's melting fire one's heart 'twill sear and burn.

The voices in the inn are hoarse and shrill with wine;
The flute and tambourine, carousing, moan and whine.

There is a city where love reigns and lovers dwell;
Come, knock upon its gate, and enter for a spell.

No man who there abides, the morning sober meets:
The city walls are drunk, the market-place, the streets.

Alone the drunkards leave upon this earth a trace.
Mansour[2] was right, for love doth all of life embrace.

Our hearts reflect the glow upon Mount Sinai;
We who are drunk with love can happy live and die.

The Universe is drunk, for drunk 'tis meant to be—
Thus holds the keeper of both time and destiny.

The sun itself is drunk, else would it give no light;
'Tis clear to Nasimi, no veil obscures his sight.

The secret has he probed of love's mad drunkenness,
And now in flaming words his knowledge doth confess.

Translated by *Irina Zheleznova*

[1] Mufti, Ghadi—high Moslem officials.
[2] Mansour—Oriental poet and philosopher.

Two worlds within me fit, existing side by side,
Yet narrow is for me this world where I abide.

The heavens and the earth within me are confined
But what I am but ill in words can be defined.

From nature I derive, of her I am a part,
And when of me you speak from this do not depart.

Conjectures lead astray, to guess is but to err;
Be guided by the truth and put your trust in her.

Part form and content not if you would have me whole:
I am the body, aye, but too I am the soul.

No treasure-house contains the riches that are mine,
The pearls, the precious stones, the silks of rare design.

Great, shining, wondrous gems within me lie concealed.
So heavy are my crops that none can count the yield.

Man is my lofty name. I am Mount Sinai,
Life and eternity, the world, the boundless sky.

I am the universe, the spirit, and the dream,
The banks I overflow of time's unending stream.

The stars, the silent orbs, and fate are part of me.
Be mute. No tongue can paint my image truthfully.

I am the golden Sun whose glory never wanes;
Describe me not in words, for I will burst their chains.

I am a man of weight to whom respect is due;
I am a sweet too hard for children's teeth to chew.

I give off sparks like flint, I can be set aflame,
Yet fire cannot devour this that to be I claim.

I am a fount of love; life I beget and mould,
But there is more to me than life's short span can hold.

Both youth and age am I in all their riches decked;
My treasures are too great for mirrors to reflect.

Though famed is Nasimi and noble is his name,
Yet is the man in him far greater than his fame.

Translated by *Irina Zheleznova*

Need I my throne, need I my crown, my lands and castles,
                                        tell me, love,
Need I the heart within my breast if you and I be parted,
                                        love.
You are the fever that consumes—I waste away beside you,
                                        love.
You are the balm that heals my wounds—I live anew beside
                                        you, love.
Love is a joy, a priceless gem—no Moslem dares deny it,
                                        love.
What need have I of life itself if you and I be parted, love?
I offered vows, I sent up prayers, I knelt before my Maker,
                                        love.
But if my dreams go up in smoke, then truly prayers are
                                        futile, love.
My love is dead—what use to weep, what use to mourn,
                                        O Nasimi?
If love is dead, and I can live, then tears are vain,
                                        O Nasimi!

                                Translated by *Irina Zheleznova*

*   *   *

The sweetness of reunion will he know and bless
Whose heart was cruelly wrung by parting's bitterness.

He only who did see the moon by arrows rent
Will watch it rise anew in joy and wonderment.

The nectar of your lips he who has tasted not
Is doomed to die of thirst and share a beggar's lot.

To touch that mole of yours, I would give up my sight;
The fool who scorns my choice exists bereft of light.

Beside you precious stones are naught but clods of earth;
He will deprive himself who would deny your worth.

You are a cypress, aye, but not a full-grown tree;
A sapling's grace is yours, its tender modesty.

The sun obscures the moon, so dazzling are its rays;
But you defeat the sun—your beauty dims its blaze.

O doff these silks, I pray—your loveliness they mar:
They fade, and you remain a never-fading star.

Translated by Irina Zheleznova

S hah-Ismail Hatai

SHAH-ISMAIL HATAI (1485-1524) was the founder of the shah dynasty of the Sefevides (1502-1736). Writing under the pen-name of Hatai, he produced a large volume of lyric poetry in Azerbaijani, and also a number of didactic and philosophical works, among them the poems Ten Letters *and* The Book of Morals. *In the reign of Shah-Ismail Hatai, Azerbaijani was promoted to state language on a par with Persian. Hataï's poetry is graceful and polished and his language closely approaches to folk idiom.*

Winter's shaken off, and spring arrives!
Rosebuds waken, garden plot revives,
Birds all trill in aching harmony,
Love's a thrilling flame, disturbing me.
Earth is dressed in furry, downy green,
Whispers press the silence once serene,
Water rills lap at the cypress root,
And turtle-doves coo plaintive notes that flute.
Nature's budding smiles on meadow-grass
Flash through dew-drop miles like beads of glass.
Seaward rain clouds . . . rare as precious stones,
Wings a crane and circles azure zones—
Taloned falcon brings it down to earth.

Bakharia[1]

To silken blossom, apple-trees give birth;
Playful, flees the Moon from clouds in vain,
April showers drench the earth with rain,
Nightingales in trilling song repine,
Tulip petals hoard the dew's sweet wine,
Steppe-quails deep and bookish thoughts pursue,
Turtle-doves keep cooing, loo-a-loo. . .
Drunk a mite are violets, unaware.
Swans alight like feathered moving air:
Preens with pride each bird his curven breast,
For cygnet-peep is heard from hidden nest.
Earth's a filigree of rainbow flowers,
Trees make jubilee in leaf-green bowers,
Bindweed seeks relief by river-bed,
Cowling shirt in reefs above his head.
Linden boughs display their dancing grace,
Praising spring the rose lifts tender face,
Rivers top their banks: a flood terrene,
Garden trees put on their mantles green.
Moonlight boon is pure on cherry-tree,
Mute the moon, lost in a starry sea.
Over meadow lies a flowered throw,
Veils of snowy bloom on lilacs show,
On flower petals rime of silver down.
Narcissi rise and mime in paper crown,

[1] Spring song (Azerb.).

Argavan[1] is vain of buds that blush,
Doves would fain be near a blooming bush.
When first sighs the early, pre-dawn breeze,
Buds veil eyes in sepal-curl to tease.
Orion spears with light a purple sky,
A cypress rears in giant pride on high.
Saucy flirt, the rose her power knows,
Deeply hurt, the nightingale's love flows
In notes as dour as any mullah knew.
Meadow flowers cherish rime and dew,
Morning finds Narcissus sleepy-eyed,
The tulip, crowned and throned, in solemn pride
Scorns the right of other suzeraine.
Combs its spritely curls the wheat-ear vain,
Distilling ambergris upon the air,
In murmured glee streams circle gardens fair.
To mountain tarn gazelles come from the heights,
Poppies turn their red lamps off at night,
Blinding lovers so they lose their way.
Peacock Ruler of the Garden sways
His trailing swathe, his diadem askew;
Rose petals bathe in cool and crystal dew—
A Mecca spring of water, chastely clean.
Gardens fling on togas red and green,
A snowy turban wears each mountain crest,
The Iris bears a dagger, in protest,
To stab the eye that joylessness denotes.
Whistles rise from flocks of starling throats,
That answers find in bill and coo of doves.
Cool the wind and fragrant as it moves
All undeterred to shake the leaves to foam.
Migrating birds fly far away to home:
Raven, crake, and stork and wild goose clans.
Green-headed drake now stills its stroking vans,
Planes oblique to landing on the lake.
Owls shriek and hollow echoes wake,
Through mountain glade is partridge laughter blown,
Cypress shade at rooted feet lies prone
With leaf-curl rim sun-dappled to a frieze.
Birds sing hymns pitched in a thousand keys,
The open lips of primroses pink stains,

[1] Mountain flower.

100

Young foals skip and shake their growing manes,
Their shrilling neigh the whistling Kite-scream feigns.
Lambkins play, it's lambing time again:
Sheep drive to the mountains has begun.
Sun-beams cut till blood-red streamlets run.
Gaily gambol partridges with zest
Before they settle in the family nest.
Cypress, metal-green, lips folds of sky,
Left and right it gazes, towering high.
The rose-child plights its troth, becomes a bride
And wears a veil of crimson on her head.
Chamois frail her fawn has fondly fed,
Bounds away to feed on meadow-grass;
Gazelle musk perfumed through the steppe-lands pass,
The sweet musk seeps the black earth through and through.
Wild herds come down to feed on meadows too.
Flying cranes lament high in the sky
Wind sustains for miles their anxious cry.
The raven's heart one second misses beat
At plunging dart of falcon's raking feet.
Birds entice their nestlings to take wing.
Sun—paradise for every scaly thing.
Dews hang like pods on meadows, strung in rows.
The bull's horn prods the earth with vicious blows.
Each flower bears a thrusting bumblebee.
Ants with care drag loads in company,
Their damp eggs bring, to dry them in the sun.
The rainbow swings its veil of prisms spun,
Leaves consign their tremors to the air,
Arrow-shaped, graceful beyond compare
The Parrot speaks in beaten silver tongue—
Oration all with sweetened words is strung.
Swallows found again their former nests:
Birds homeward-bound have reached their native rest.

Translated by *Gladys Evans*

Stone

Stone, how did it come to be:
Who is certain of his view?
Ask of stone how, openly:
Only silence answers you.
Neither tongue nor soul has stone—
But when dawning breath of man
Touched it, then and then alone
The history of both began.
Close associations so
Often link up stone with man,
That stone itself may often grow
Into a statue of a man.

Translated by *Gladys Evans*

Bayat

Hatai's of a special school—
Pedant, dot my i's to rule;
Sect—a Sufi: they know much.
Yet truth to tell, I'm but a fool.

Hatai, business may ordain
That you call, a loan to gain.
Don't bite off more than you can chew—
Or little friendship will remain.

Translated by *Gladys Evans*

Life must have a lodestar, dear—your love's the only one
for me,
The light that gleams in your sweet face—the only sun
that shines for me.

Shall I—about the heartache sore in every vein I have—
complain?
No, nor seek relief at all: my pain becomes a salve
for me.

Ghazals

This earth I picked up near your door, for all the world
I would not trade—
From earth one foot of yours has trod—a Solomon's temple
built could be.

The radiance of your face once seen, the moon's a wan
and worthless thing—
Your praises ever on my lips might truly Koran
verses be.

O Hatai! Love's torments are a sign to show that
you love true—
And torments from a loved one's absence—Heaven's
blessings, you'll agree.

* * *

My heart loitered in a temple of idols—idolater
became;
Urgent the nightingale's singing—but I know the promise
he proclaims.

I razed the temple of my being to ashes—all over first
love:
O only among the ruins the young lover may nurse his
flame.

They are thirsting for my blood—your inebriate, languorous eyes:

104

Your brows where these inebriates couch—altar for each
devotee.

Joseph the Chaste to the dimples that dance in your cheeks
would succumb—
Caught in the net of your curls, would awake where only
madmen be.

"O Hatai, where is your bed, your turban?" asks the
Hermit, stern—
I gave them up as pledge for wine—my sorrows only
taverns see.

＊　＊　＊

Your face, the full moon, are the same—or are they not?
Temptation-like, your curls enflame—or do they not?

Her beauty, o unhappy me, her graces—all
The riches of our age proclaim—or do they not?

Your silken lashes and your brows, like crescents, are
As thin as bowstrings, so you claim—or do you not?

When the ascetic curses the young lover, are
His curses foul blows and shame—or are they not?

Hatai, when he weeps on leaving you, then have
His tears a river's semblance—or have they not?

Translated by *Gladys Evans*

Fisuli Muhammed Suleiman-Ogly

FISULI MUHAMMED SULEIMAN-OGLY (1498-1556)—this greatest of Azerbaijanian 16th-century poets was born in Kerbela. He wrote in three languages—Azerbaijani, Arabic and Persian—and used all the genres and artistic forms known in Medieval Oriental literature. He was celebrated as one of the major poets of his day for his ghazals, his romantic poem Leili and Medjnun *written in Azerbaijani, his* Book of Plaints—*one of the first prose works in Azerbaijanian literature, his poetry condemning feudal despotism, and his allegorical poems. Fisuli's philosophical poem* The Rise of Religions *gives an analysis of the teachings of ancient Indian, ancient Greek, Arabic and Azerbaijanian philosophers. We shall never cease to marvel at the depth of understanding in his love ghazals, at their melodiousness, perfection of form and clarity of thought. Many of them have been set to music.*

Fisuli lived in constant need, which we know from his numerous complaints against the times which brought nothing but ruin, chaos and destitution.

The poet died of cholera in Kerbela.

The 400th anniversary of Fisuli's death was marked in the Soviet Union in 1958, and a monument to him was unveiled in Baku.

From the Poem
LEILI AND MEDJNUN

As graceful as a cypress-tree was she,
This beauteous maid whose face could only be

Compared to some exotic, dainty bloom,
So fair, so fresh and tender as to doom

A poet's pen to vain meandering.
In short, she was perfection, and to sing

Her loveliness is futile. Yet I dare
This to attempt. . . . Her soft and flowing hair

Curled to her waist. . . . She was a rose-bud. . . . Nay,
A daffodil, a fragrant lilac spray.

Medjnun and the Dawning of a Great Misfortune

Her cheeks gave off a golden glow, her eyes
Were dark, deep pools. . . . It was as if the skies

Had to the earth surrendered her, a moon
Whose brightness never dimmed, not e'en at noon.

Her ruby lips, her plaits, her youthful grace
All drew him to Leili. To him her face

Seemed quite beyond compare. He never knew,
For he would not consult his glass, that few

Were there with features that could match his own
And that in beauty she, Leili, alone

His equal was. By fortune's will these
                                        two
Loved one another deeply and did rue

The hours they spent apart. Drink did they
                                          full
Of love's sweet brew, a potion wonderful

But dangerous withal, for overcome
Were they, and soon. . . . A mad delirium

107

Seized upon both. All difference was gone;
Their beings merged, and they became as one.

If someone spoke to Geis[1] it was Leili
Who answered, and, contrariwise, 'twas he,

Geis, who replied whene'er she was addressed.
This fond attachment filled them with unrest.

As time went on in strength it grew; no love
Could be so overpowering; they strove,

To no avail, to seek diversion in
Life's small pursuits. Leili need but begin

Upon a book, and lo! the letters fade,
And Geis is there before her, and the maid

Smiles fondly at her lover; nor can he,
Howe'er he try, from her dear image flee.

Yet willingly a poem together they
Might scan, and even argue o'er the way

'Twas written; this detracted not from their
Affection in the least. Indeed, to share

Each thought and feeling but enhanced the more
The touching love that for each other bore

Leili and Geis. . . . But tender passion is
To peace of heart a stranger, and gives rise,

Too oft, to dark anxiety and pain. . . .
They loved so well that they could not remain

Serene as once they were. Instead, in gloom
Now were they plunged at times, and to assume

A look of ease became a wearing task.
Of one another they dared hardly ask

[1] Original name of Medjnun.

108

How 'twas they fared. . . . Nor did they even try
To speak their hearts, so awkward and so shy,

So chained of tongue were they become. Their eyes
And brows now spoke for them, and all disguise

Was thus abandoned. Soon the household learnt
Their ill-hid secret, and the love that burnt

Deep down within them was to all revealed
And could no more, alas, be kept concealed.

The veil was lifted, and the mischief done;
Whatever peace had still been theirs was gone.

They were exposed to undeserved rebuke;
Each sigh of theirs, each fond and loving look

Was taken note of. Now were they compelled
To practise stealth. And though their hearts rebelled

At this, and discontent did rule the day,
Yet was there nothing else to do, and they

Were forced to search for pretexts ere they
                                        might
Hold ordinary converse and delight

In one another's presence. Oft did Geis
Resort to cunning and a plan devise

That he might win the cherished company
Of her he loved. "Come, help me out,
                                    Leili,"

So would he say. "I fear I have forgot
The lesson we were given. Will you not

"Sit by and listen, dearest one, while I
Repeat the piece?" And happy to comply

Was she, as he expected. A mistake
With that same purpose would he slyly make

109

Upon his slate, and timidly request
Leili to find it out and do her best

To put him right. It filled him nigh with glee
When his pretended lapse of memory

A smile brought to her lips, and she would cry,
"An error, Geis, and here's another. . . . Fie!

"Do you not know your grammar, love?. . ." To hear
Her playful reprimand, the sweet and clear

Tones of her voice was all that Geis did seek.
He wished for naught except that she might speak

To him at moments, whether in reproof
Or praise, no matter, for to hold aloof

From her he could not. For Leili and Geis
Who parting feared more than they feared disgrace

To chide each other e'en at lesson-time
Was to partake of happiness, to climb

To heights of joy. The lesson over, they
Went on dissembling. . . . Geis might put away

A book of his, and then call for Leili
And tell her that the book had stupidly

That morning been mislaid. . . . If but she could
Help in the search. . . . "Oh, love, thou'rt wondrous good!"

Because they stood for her beloved name,
The letters "l" and "i", his soul aflame,

Whole hours on end in writing out he spent. . . .
To him they were as light by Heaven sent.

Translated by Irina Zheleznova

Leili Imparts Her Secret to a Butterfly and Lays Bare Her Heart

"O winged, fragile thing fore'er in flight
That hearest lovers whispering at night,
To live and die for love thou art content,
Thou art love's symbol, its embodiment.
Thou givest all for one sweet moment's bliss;
For thee, the sages say, to perish is
To know fulfilment and felicity.
Throughout the ages all have honoured thee
For that thou art to sacrifice resigned
Both worlds for love. . . . And yet I am inclined
To think my torments greater than thy own,
For in my chamber, numbed by grief, alone
I sit and pine, and watch thee, dazed but free,
Spin round and round in drunken ecstasy.
Thy pain is brief, and mine can never end,
For I would live and to the depths descend
Of anguish and despair. . . . O butterfly,
To have a thousand souls is all that I
Deep in my aching heart am praying for,
In order that a thousand times and more
My agony and pain be multiplied. . . .
And thou, a pain dost thou discreetly hide
Within thy breast? . . . I doubt it sorely. . . . Nay,
For were it so, thou'd weep, not dance and play.
Where are thy chilly tears at morning's rise?
Where findest thou the patience to devise
A means of masking suffering, a way
Of bearing torture such as might betray
The stoutest heart? . . ." Leili, in speaking thus,
Sought no relief, no help: the frivolous
And lovely butterfly knew of no balm
To soothe her spirit and to bring it calm.
It was to Heaven that the maid addressed
Her plea. . . . With clouded eye and heaving breast,
When out her den the furtive moon did creep
And float above the sands, and buried deep
In slumber was the household, she would sigh
And pray for strength. Alone the moon and sky
Her secret heard. For she, so full of pride,
In none but them dared openly confide.

Translated by *Irina Zheleznova*

111

In vain did Geis try subterfuge, in vain
Did he from speaking openly refrain
To his Leili. . . . Rewarded were the two
By suffering. For love, if it be true,
Can hardly find a fitting partner in
Hypocrisy. Such wedlock is akin
To mating good with evil. So it was
That gossip took the legend up, alas,
Of this young love, and spun a pretty tale
Around it shamelessly. No tongue did fail
To say that Geis had fallen captive to
The charms of her who only sought to woo
A youth's attentions. Soon the rumour reached
Leili's own mother who, in tears, beseeched
Her daughter not to bring disgrace upon
Them all. Cried she, "O child, thou'lt be undone
If aught of this be true. Pray, speak, how came
These rumours to be set afloat? Thy name
Is sullied. O, bethink thyself, my good,
My lovely daughter! Why dost thou give food
To tongues of venom?. . . Thou'rt a budding flower
Not yet in bloom, but 'tis within their power
To put a blemish on thy purity.
Persist not in this folly, guided be
By modesty and reason, and beware
Lest thou who art a precious thing and rare
Be grasped by idle hands. A vagrant stream
May stray at random, but a maid, so deem
The worldly wise, may not. Remember: wine
That gives such pleasure, is, without design,
But evil does because 'twill often flow too free,
By many treated lightly, carelessly.
Do not be like a broken looking-glass
Distorting all it mirrors, and, my lass,
Dance not as if thou wert a candle flame,
For candles gasp and flicker, and a tame
Wind snuffs them out at will. Show not thy face
But hide it from all men; know that thy place
Is in the home, and there perforce remain,
Nor ever in the street appear. Restrain
Thy youthful fancies, pray, and do not wear
Apparel that attracts the eye; take care
That none suspect they conduct. Be discreet,

Her Mother Appeals to Leili, and the Springtime of Youthful Love Is Turned into an Autumn of Falling Leaves

112

Efface thyself. Believe me, it is meet
For maidens to be shy. Be as a song
That carries not abroad for fear the throng
Make sport of it. Keep always in the shade,
But be a shadow not that doth invade
A spot where 'tis perceived. Keep thou apart
From this vain youth who thinks to steal thy heart.
What's love, what's passion?—Nothing that a chaste,
Well brought-up maid will dwell upon or waste
Her time on even. Let me tell thee plain:
If thou obeyest not, thou'lt put a stain
Upon our honour. We whom all, 'twould seem,
Regard as worthy, and in high esteem
Have ever held, will be abused and scorned. . . .
By these my words, dear child, I beg, be warned.
Thou'rt silent. Dost thou think that no great hurt
Thou'rt threatened by?. . . O dear one, to avert
Thy father's wrath I strive; if he should hear
Of thee and Geis, thou'lt fare not well, I fear.
I think it best for thee not to attend
Thy lessons more. Thou mayest with profit spend
Thy time on toys and needle-work. Away
With pencils, books and such!. . . Thou'lt have to stay
Indoors and take up household tasks that none
Dare to reproach thee or to look upon
Thy person with contempt. A maid may not
Be seen in public; such is e'er the lot
Of her who would command respect. Be meek,
To hide from strangers' eyes, obedient, seek."

Translated by *Irina Zheleznova*

A mountain suddenly before him rose.
It was majestic in its calm repose
And awe-inspiring, for above it soared
Swift-winged falcons, and within were stored,
Deep in its bowels, such precious stones and
                                          rare
As can but be imagined. 'Twas not bare
Of greenery, far from it; full 'twas grown
With trees and luscious grasses, while its cone
Like brightest silver gleamed. The fowls it fed,
And nurtured many springs, and oft the dead
And barren desert stretching nigh, a plea
Might send to it and humbly, wordlessly
Ask to be given life, for was it not
Life's very source and had it not begot
By Heaven been and granted strength and might
And rich and gorgeous beauty to delight
All who approached it? . . . In the Holy Book
'Twas named the Chosen Mountain. Medjnun's
                                          look

Medjnun Converses with a Mountain and Compares Its Fate with His Own

Held sadness in't as he came near; a sigh
Escaped his lips. Distracted, in reply
He heard the mountain echo it. "Thou art
My friend!" he cried in joy. "For in thy heart
I find at last the sympathy that I
Have sought but never found. O mountain, my
Torn heart cries out to thine. . . . An anchorite
Art thou that knows the pangs of love. Thy
                                          plight
Is to mine own akin, thy suffering,
I feel it, equals mine. Did love not fling
A stone at thee that pierced thy stony breast? . . .
Hills are like lovers—nay, I do not jest,
For tears pour from thine eyes. O speak to me,
Confide thy sorrows, mountain. Willingly
I'll hear them out. Why is't that blood doth
                                          flow
From out thy side? Thou'rt wounded? Ah, if so,
Who is the one that raised the bow and let
The fatal arrow fly? . . . Forget, forget
That thou'rt a hill and I a man, that we
Together may our lot bewail and be
Joined in our grief! . . ." And to the firmament

114

Their plaints, their moans, their anguished cries
                                          they sent. . . .
After a time, Medjnun calmed down at last
And turned his steps, his face still overcast,
To where the house of his beloved stood.

Translated by *Irina Zheleznova*

O thou whose eyes are closed and heart is worn,
Whose feet are bound, whose spirit is forlorn,
Let us together sigh, together weep;
Disclose to me the secret that so deep
Within thy heart thou keepest hid from all.
Why moanest thou, why dost thou softly call
As if thou wert a wounded nightingale?
Why is thy flame screened by a smoky veil?
Why burnest thou with such intensity?
What spark hath set thee blazing?—Answer me!
What maketh thee one moment flush and glow,
And then, the next, be drowned in tears? What
                                        blow
Hath fortune dealt thee? Why dost thou
                                        intone

Leili Speaks with a Lamp but Hesitates to Impart to It All of Her Sad History

An invocation? Come, thou'rt not alone
In thy adversity.... For stricken by
A grief as great am I or greater. My
Defiant heart is heavy, weighted down
With anguish such as thou hast never known.
Thou burnest only in the dead of night
While I burn night and day. O lamp, my
                                        plight
Is not to be compared with thine—it is
By far the more lamentable; of this
Rest thou assured. Thou art in pain, and yet
Thy misery thou dost at times forget
Or freely speak it. This I may not do
But must refrain from even breathing to
The world that my poor heart is rent in
                                        twain....
But, O, for ever loyal 'twill remain
To him I love.... O lamp, they'll never
                                        wrest
My secret from me. Always in my breast
I'll keep it locked.... Until the day I die
Their threats and their abuse will I defy!
And e'en to thee my tale I'll not impart
Lest that it break thy simple, aching heart.
Nor would my own the telling of it bear,
Succumbing, well I know it, to despair.
With one dear friend my grief I shared, and so
Perturbed was she and dazed and full of woe

116

That she did fly from me. To tell the whole
Of my sad tale to one without a soul
Is all that's left to me, a candle, say,
Or else a butterfly that fast away
Will fly, unscathed, and carefree as the wind. . . .

Translated by *Irina Zheleznova*

By fate's unfairness am I sorely stung,
And my distress has slowed my ready tongue.
From offering me wine, I pray, forbear,
For I am drunk with grief and crushed with care.
In happy unconcern my life I passed,
But how 'twill end I know not. Overcast
And shadowed is the path that lies ahead;
My strength has ebbed, and all of hope has fled.
Whate'er was done by me was done in vain,
Naught but despair is left to me, and pain.
'Twas tyranny that, ruthless, sealed my doom
And plunged me deep in everlasting gloom.
Said I to Fortune, "O tormentor mine,
Your turning wheel has brought the bard no sign
Of joy to come. . . . Instead, enchained am I
By sorrow's fetters, for, I know not why,
You injure those who of the best deserve.
Had my Medjnun been witless you would serve
Him well, not ill, and his commands obey,
And give him strength and wisdom, and essay
To make of him all that in fact he is.
But since you knew him to be good and wise
And brave, you humbled him and made him bite
The dust, and scurvily did taunt and slight
The youth, and punished her he loved and who
Was no unblushing hussy but a true,
Sweet-hearted maid and faithful to Medjnun,
Unlike yourself that wishes him undone
And uses him thus cruelly, hurtling him,
A youth of parts and with a genuine
Passion for learning, into an abyss
Of madness, of a frenzied bitterness,
A sorrow nigh insane. . . . Had I been born
A hypocrite, you'd not have thought to scorn
My most unworthy self. . . . O Fortune, know
That I mistrust you, that within me grow
A doubt and scepticism. But being proud
And mutinous by nature, I am cowed
Not easily, and outwardly retain,
Though seething with resentment and disdain
And tortured by your cold malevolence,
A kind of calm. . . ." And Fortune answered,
                                        "Whence

118

Come sentiments like these, o ignorant
And foolish mortal?... I am adamant
In all I do, for mine to carry out
Is Heaven's own command which thus to doubt
Means to run counter to the way of things.
You sin.... Your sinful speech, though loud
                                    it rings,
Is empty sound.... A bard you chose to be,
One versed in lies, in cant, in trumpery.
This learned youth whom you Medjnun did name,
Medjnun or one possessed, was not his fame
Spread wide by you whose very thoughts he voiced?...
You gave them birth and like a fiend rejoiced
In having ruined him.... I sought to shield
The beauteous Leili—why did you wield
Your vicious pen and thus disgrace the maid?
Ah, there were many, bard, that you betrayed
In this same thoughtless way: Nofel, for one,
And Ibn Salaam[1]—what was this tale you spun
Around him coolly, injuring thereby
A good, a blameless man?... Can you deny
That you made use of him and others too
To speak your heresy?... The foul brew
That you did cook gives off an evil smell.
You slandered, you blasphemed, and victim fell
At last to these concoctions of your brain....
You suffer, aye, but have yourself to blame."

Translated by *Irina Zheleznova*

[1] Ibn Salaam—historic Islamic religious leader.

Quatrains

(From LEILI AND MEDJNUN)

You whose hands shape the glorious sculptures of love,
You whose hands build the noble foundations of love,
You whose hands plait the sweet-scented tresses of love,
You whose hands bound Medjnun with the fetters of love!

If a pathway to truth I am fated to hew,
If the tale here unfolded is found to be true,
If in praising Leili fortune's favour I woo,
In the words of Medjnun I will say unto you,

Give me hope, give me faith, give me happiness, pray,
Let my future be paved with your charity, pray,
Let the name of Leili kindle sympathy, pray,
Let Medjnun's woeful tale haunt the memory, pray.

Translated by *Irina Zheleznova*

Rubaiyat

* * *

If 'tis food that you worship and sweet, heavy drink,
If from prayer you recoil and from fasting you shrink,
If you turn in disgust from the true Word and Faith,
If 'tis only of pleasing your palate you think;

If the kitchen you stupidly choose for your shrine,
If to banquets and revels your dreams you confine,
Let me ask—was it this God created you for?
Were you born, foolish mortal, to thwart His design?

Translated by *Irina Zheleznova*

The Shah makes uncommonly free, with his moneys and
              land
When preparing for conquest the host that is his to
            command.

'Tis through cunning and craft that in taming his foes he
             succeeds,
But rebellion breaks out in the countries he plunders and
              bleeds.

After that it is war till he dies by a treacherous hand,
Death and ruin is all that he brings to his host and his
              land.

Though a sultan am I, yet no conquering sword do I wield;
With my conquering pen do I force all and sundry to
             yield.

Every word that I write serves, relentless, the truth to
            advance;
'Tis a weapon, I swear it, as mighty and sharp as a lance.

Of its subjects no tax it exacts, not a tribute or loan,
And no harm will it bring to the land it will choose for
             its own.

Those that seek to destroy it, 'twill boldly and freely defy;
Evil winds and adversities pass without harming it by.

Though the princes begrudge me their purses, they do so
            in vain;
Rare and wonderful treasures lie hid in my heart and my
             brain.

Free from all of the petty concerns and the strivings am I
That belong to the mortals who know they are fated to die.

      Translated by *Irina Zheleznova.*

122

* * *

O thou, vizier, limb of the country's law,
The sultan chose thee 'mongst his subjects all
To be his proxy; in thy hands he placed
The fates of men, this being Fortune's will.

Beware lest that the robes of office change
Thy very nature.... For 'tis oft the case
That power corrupts, and just and worthy men
Too soon become impious cavillers.

A lack of faith in thee the people brings
Despair and grief.... Avoid the influence
Of dissolute retainers and their praise,
For such as they, I swear, are Satan's spawn.

Translated by *Irina Zheleznova*

* * *

My love is a greater love than that which possessed
Medjnun;
Through love did I lose my heart, through love did he earn
his name.

If only my eyes could gaze without sleep on your lovely
face—
What joy would be theirs and mine, how hot would my
passion flame!

Leili had her poor Medjnun, Shirin had her brave Farhad,
While you, o my love, have me, whose life you can freely
claim.

Compare me not, my blushing rose, to a nightingale, I beg,
For he utters a thousand moans while in silence I bear my
pain.

Only he who has suffered much, finds relief in the woeful
sight
Of an anguish as fierce as mine, of a spirit by love made
tame.

Do not soar, o my winged heart, to the menacing skies of
love,
Lest by arrows with poisoned tips you be wounded and
cruelly slain.

Scorn the fleshless, unearthly love that your mentors
preach, Fisuli,
Born of reason, 'tis cold and starved, and is not of true
love's domain.

Translated by Irina Zheleznova

✳ ✳ ✳

Know this, o thou who is of wit possessed:
Two men may do thee harm nor let thee rest.

The first is one who is to thee no friend,
And, meeting thee, his way elsewhere will wend.

The second is thyself who, loathing thee,
Is yet obliged to keep thee company.

Translated by Irina Zheleznova

✳ ✳ ✳

My life's beginning passed, of grave reflection free,
In ignorance, in mirth, in feasts and revelry.

Then later was I plunged in bitter pain and woe,
For years did I no joy, no sweet contentment know.

And when my dreary life was drawing to its end,
In fast and pious prayer my leisure did I spend.

Why did I starve my heart and all it craved deny?
Why did I foolishly let rapture pass me by?...

Translated by Irina Zheleznova

124

Take not the beads into your hands; kneel not upon the rug
                                             of prayer;
Believe not those who promise bliss and in their raptures
                                             do not share.

When in obeisance to your God, you bow, from fervent
                                             bows refrain;
Whilst being cleansed of sin, stay calm, lose not your
                                             precious sleep in
                                             vain.

Beware of entering a mosque, and if it happen that you do,
Then linger not within its walls, for to yourself must you
                                             stay true.

Heed not the call to prayer that comes, insistent, from the
                                             minaret;
Do not approach the doors of Hell, the preacher's nagging
                                             voice forget.

A crowded mosque too oft becomes a scene of seething,
                                             scalding hate;
Amid disorder stay serene, no brawls, no quarrels instigate.

Think not that priests are men of God, their words mistrust
                                             and judgement too.
Apostles err; do not allow the faith they preach to burden
                                             you.

O Fisuli, remember this: false, spurious prayer avails
                                             naught.
Pray from the heart, be pure of heart, as by the wise you
                                             have been taught.

Translated by *Irina Zheleznova*

*   *   *

If 'tis love you would have, then your soul must you lose;
If your soul you would keep, then surrender your love.
One the other excludes, 'twixt the two must you choose,
For to cherish your soul is your love to abuse.

Do not fear erudition and knowledge but prize
Their achievements, and shrink from obtaining them not;
Scorn not books; they are there to direct and advise;
Shrink from being a dunce midst the lettered and wise.

To be filled with aversion for drink is a sin;
Well I know it, o hermit, put faith in my word.
If I visit the mosques in a spirit benign,
'Tis because I am filled to repletion with wine.

Translated by *Irina Zheleznova*

126

* * *

My pain and sorrow none, I fear me, can dispel;
That you have cast me off I know, my love, too well.

And yet I am, in truth, reluctant to complain,
For though you flee from me, you flee, my love, in vain.

I feel that you are near no matter where you are;
Your lovely image sears my spirit from afar.

And should I early die of love, of love and grief,
At least, sweet love, my life would have been full if brief.

That 'tis for love alone, as I have wished, I live,
My warm and humble thanks to Heaven do I give.

My love for you is fierce, it turns my heart to flame;
I fear lest all of me the fires of passion claim.

One wish was ever mine—to love you unto death;
If this be not the truth, embrace my soul, o death!

The heart of Fisuli would long have burnt away
Had not the tears he shed kept love's hot flames at bay.

Translated by Irina Zheleznova

127

I bow to all idols wherever I see them, for such is my way.
Apostates to me are no worse than the pious, for such is
my way.

Speak not of the slender and red-cheeked nasturtium,
o gardener, pray.
'Tis changeful and fickle, while I ... I am constant,
for such is my way.

With tear-blinded eyes that were once bright as embers
I gaze on the world.
Through torrents of tears do I gaze on it sadly, for such
is my way.

I weep day and night, but it brings me no solace, I weep
day and night;
In tears do I foolishly seek consolation, for such is my way.

I longed for my tears to be dried by your kisses—no dreams
were so sweet....
With words that were bitter you poisoned their sweetness
and went on your way.

Not even Medjnun knew an anguish so bruising, not even
Medjnun,
And yet I endured it in stoical silence, for such is my way.

I know, Fisuli, that the thoughtless despise you, but loud
will I speak,
I'll speak, and their scorn will be changed to compassion,
for such is my way.

Translated by *Irina Zheleznova*

With delight in my heart on your dark, curling tresses
I gaze;
Numb of tongue, on your lips that are sweeter than roses
I gaze.

When I see you before me the tears cloud my eyes, and
I weep;
When your face haunts my dreams, sorrow gnaws at my
heart, and I weep.

With a great secret joy do I think of your beauty and grace;
Free of shame, full of rapture, I gaze on your beauty and
grace.

When they see me in anguish, the heart-broken victim of
love,
Many passionate lovers refuse to pay homage to love.

To be parted from you is to burn in the fires of Hell;
Tested thus, e'en giaours would no more scoff at Heaven or
Hell.

To a rose-bud his love's tender lips will a lover compare;
To a ruby your lips e'en a stranger, enthralled, will
compare.

If I humbly forbear of the torments I suffer to speak,
They who see me in pain of my love with compassion will
speak.

Like the plaint of a flute sounds the sorrowful voice of my
love;
Flay the skin from my back, yet would I, weeping, call for
my love.

She whose captive I am spurns my love, and I yield to
despair;
Help me, fate, kindly fate, lest, forsaken, I yield to
despair.

Love's unquenchable flames burn, untamed, in my pain-
weary heart,

129

And its wounds never heal, leaving permanent scars on my
heart.

At the sight of my tears she I worship will suddenly
smile,
And I find wondrous bliss in this fleeting but radiant
smile.

E'en if Fortune to keep us apart should revengefully
seek,
Yet for you would I long and for you would I stubbornly
seek.

Who is right—he who, offered a cupful, partakes of the
wine,
Or the one who declines it, unwilling to drink of the
wine?

Not a dervish is there but despises a tyrant, in truth;
Fisuli who is meek is regarded with favour, in truth.

For your slender and beauteous form, filled with longing,
I sigh:
For your lips that to me are like delicate blossoms I sigh.

Like a madman I rave when I think of your musk-scented
plaits;
I am driven insane by the sight of my love's raven plaits.

Drink with love, sick with longing am I for the gem that
is you;
All the blood of my heart would I give for the gem that is
you.

On the day when we met like a candle my spirit was
lit;
On the day when we part I will put out the light that was
lit.

Like a chain is my love, from its burden my heart I would
free;
O, to look at you, love, and my heart would refuse to be
free!

130

Long did I pay you court but you carelessly played with
my heart;
Though 'twere but for a whim, take my life as you've taken
my heart.

At your feet Fisuli bends his knee in obeisance to you;
Praises offered to God are the praises I offer to you!

Translated by *Irina Zheleznova*

Gobsi Tabrizi

GOBSI TABRIZI was a 17th-century lyric poet. We have little factual data about his life, and the information supplied by the ancients who compiled his poetic collections is contradictory. Scholars voice the suggestion that there were three poets writing under this name: father, son and grandson. Two volumes of Gobsi Tabrizi's poems have been preserved: one of them is in the British Museum, and the other—in the Georgian State Museum. His poetry, written by a skilled master, carries a protest against feudalism, against oppression and slavery, and champions freedom of human feelings.

*   *   *

At ev'ry corner lovers stand in woeful plight;
Light of my eyes, tell me, who is the lucky wight?

And should sorrow slay me, I happiness will feel,
Should I but learn that for me you some compassion feel.

And will she e'er remember, she, my candle bright,
That I have singed my wings, attracted to her light.

Then burn ye too—like all who hopes upon you place;
Cries in air are lost, but of you remains a trace.

Heartless beauty, all who see you once or twice,
Will say a thousand times or more that you have fearsome
eyes.

Like a captive moth, you attract me to your flame;
In triumph down you look, as I cry out my shame.

When you are near her, Gobsi, a thousand times you die;
Indeed a torch of sorrow, of mis'ry am I.

Translated by Arthur Shkarovsky

133

Let Them Say

I would not wish my mistress sweet my sighs to hear,
I would not want a word of woe to reach her ear.

Why, for black-tressed Leili lovely, I would gladly die;
May all those, who do not care, a madman say am I.

Flies the moth to candle bright and burns up in the flame.
Proud am I and would not care of moth to bear the name.

Still, would I like all, who hear the cry of pain that
                                    rends my heart
To whisper in my rosebud's ear a word on my behalf.

Will I bird and bee beseech, as flit they through the trees:
Carry word of my condition to my loved one, please!

Translated by *Arthur Shkarovsky*

What Have I Done?

O, cupbearer of my day and age, what have I done?
Flames of parting have consumed me, what have I done?

Your starry eyes have made me falter; I am undone.
O, oracle, whom Moslems worship, what have I done?

Desire has made me weary, my goal I have not won.
O, my love whose slave I wish to be, what have I done?

But yesterday had wings I, that glistened in the Sun,
Now, heartless one, you've burned them, O, what have
                                                    I done?

I dared question her but once; yet answer gave she none.
What did I say, Almighty God, O, what have I done?

Adoring, worshipped I the ground she trod; now I'm numb,
Knowing not, poor miserable I, what have I done?

Reflected in my heart your face a glorious Sun!
Gobsi, how fell you from her grace? What have I done?

Translated by *Arthur Shkarovsky*

No close friend have I to tell about my
                                    love;
Only my faithful flute—but have I words
                                    enough?

The word of truth is strong, all will be impressed,
Whether to crazed lover or sane mind addressed.

Do not drop pearls precious where they are not
                                    prized.
Spare your breath, say no word, be by me advised.

Empty words—empty sounds goes a maxim wise;
Words may soothe, may say naught, may to action
                                    rise.

Words

Hypnotised forever by her brilliant eyes;
Is there any sign of hope, or naught but lies?

Words that fail to carry are like eyes that cannot
                                    see.
Only words of price to hearts present the key.

Care I naught for sloth who fritters time
                                    away;
For the busy brain is meant all I say.

He that's tasted bitter what sweet is knows
                                    well.
Lips that utter sweet words—let them their story
                                    tell.

Diff'rent is the meaning ev'ry glance implies,
The ill and the tormented voice their sorrow with their
                                    eyes.

Candle flame will never chase the moth
                                    away,
Nor will flaming words ever make me fey.

That I stand here tongue-tied is to my
                                    disgrace;
Others words can find to turn a pretty
                                    phrase.

Coruscating gems ne'er store in jar of clay.
Words galore in Gobsi that he burns to say.

Ev'ry sentence weigh, from Fisuli try learn;
Then for pithy speech reputation will you earn.

Translated by *Arthur Shkarovsky*

Sahib Tabrizi

SAHIB TABRIZI (late 17th-early 18th centuries) was one of the more gifted continuers of Fisuli's tradition. He wrote practically in all the genres of Oriental poetry, and left us an enormous legacy of ghazals extolling wisdom, the beauty of life, and love. He spoke up against religious fanaticism and asceticism, and in some of his poems there is a feeling of general discontent. "What good is your song when there are none left to appreciate it?" he asks in one of his bitter ghazals.

Ghazals

My Queen, how much longer must I stay
Outside your door, when you hold full sway
O'er my heart. Mis'ry is all I feel;
I suffer anguish when you're away
And every night I toss and turn.
Your heartless wiles will kill me one day.
This parting is appalling torment;
To salvation can I see no way.
Your orbs, like two giaours on Moslem
Fall and kill with their glitt'ring ray.

Translated by *Arthur Shkarovsky*

* * *

O, give me wine, for faint I feel today.
My heart is wounded; bleeding, woebegone.
Bereft of wings, no longer soar can I;
So quench with wine the flame alight in me
A consolation pure for weary soul.
From woe and sadness heal my empty heart,
Grief has made the blood curdle in my veins,
So give me wine to fortify my soul.
When the moon is eclipsed then cymbals clash—
A tradition this with my folk of old,
Perchance a drop of wine will courage lend.
In sea of sorrow flounder I, Sahib,
And naught but wine will bring back life again.

Translated by *Arthur Shkarovsky*

Mollah-Panakh Vagif

MOLLAH-PANAKH VAGIF, the dean of realistic Azerbaijanian poetry, was born in 1717 in Salakhly, a village in the Kazakh district of Azerbaijan. He left us many love poems glorifying earthly joys and the beauty of real, flesh-and-blood women, written in an idiom closely approaching popular speech.

Vagif was a highly educated man for his day. He was a gifted statesman, and as the chief vizier of the Karabakh khan conducted all the diplomatic negotiations with the khanate's neighbours, in particular with Catherine the Second of Russia, whose help was sought in the struggle against the aggressive policy of Aga-Muhammed-Shah Kajar, the ruler of Iran, who had already made two attempts to seize Karabakh. In 1796, Kajar finally succeeded in seizing Shusha, the capital of the khanate. Vagif was put in prison and sentenced to death. Kajar was assassinated on the night before Vagif's execution, but the former ruler of Karabakh, Ibrahim-khan, who had fled from Shusha was away and the reins of power were taken up by his nephew. He slaughtered his uncle's supporters and brutally murdered Vagif by having him and his son thrown down a precipice. This happened in 1797.

Recently Vagif's 250th birth anniversary was marked by Soviet literary circles and the general reading public.

Having given all, I begged and prayed to find
A present for my love. I found you, shamama[1]!
Pomegranate-coloured, fresh from off the vine,
You are like her breast, sweet-scented shamama.

How delicate your flesh, as subtle as the rose,
As fragrant as the air when springtide lilac blows,
And yet your hue, like mine, a saffron tint now shows
Do torments rack your heart, poor little shamama?

So shapely and so tender—those graces both you claim,
But since my love has beauty far beyond acclaim
I fear that you would know the taste of bitter shame
If placed beside her breast, smooth, rounded, shamama.

My loved one's shamama is more than honey-sweet,
And if the angels saw, they'd kiss her very feet.
Fine marble is her breast—no whiter could one meet.
With sighs our hearts it wounds, o sweetest shamama.

I falter when I see my love beside her door.
My mind is overcast and I know nothing more.
Why should she make Vagif with childish tears implore
That comfort she should give with her sweet shamama?

Translated by *Tom Botting*

* * *

For long, how long my love and I were parted!
We met again. As strangers we departed.
Although we two did not exchange a word,
The memories shared had left us heavy hearted.

Our faces gave no sign. Our glance was cool.
Each stood and stared like some benighted fool.
I was no moth that winds a burning spool
Of love around a lamp. . . And we departed.

[1] Shamamá—a small deliciously flavoured melon.

We stood together less than half an hour.
We were not singed. The flame had lost its power.
We felt no warmth. Our love could not reflower.
She went her way. Unreconciled we parted.

Once we admitted neither of us cared,
We suffered much as through this life we fared.
The birds that in our souls once sang were scared—
Like us they fled and wander heavy hearted.

Vagif once loved, but she deserves disdain.
Yes, false she was—he suffered all in vain.
We never spoke or thought of love again. . .
Without embracing, strangers we departed.

Translated by Tom Botting

*   *   *

No dark-haired beauties grace Kura's long banks
With drake's-head sheen and captivating faces.
My soul has fled to far-off mountain peaks.
It cannot rest in such low places.

*

No silk or linen natural grace enhances.
No wilful woman preens with tempting glances,
My heart forgets those tender darts-love's lances.
A merchant would be lost in such strange places!

*

No maiden paints her face to seem more fair.
No golden gauze upon their heads they wear.
No scented breast is draped with silken hair,
Enhancing creamy skin with dark silk tresses.

*

In dreams I see the one I love today.
In foreign parts I'll wake to my dismay

142

And find my heart's delight is far away.
I feel that I must die in these far places.

*

You see Vagif is pale, his heart oppressed,
For he was torn away when he caressed
The luscious swelling mounds of your sweet breast,
So grief has marred his cheek with saffron traces.

Translated by *Tom Botting*

* * *

Now weep, my eyes. From love we have been parted!
Shed tears and let the people hear you cry:
"Oh, visit her abode—behold such beauty
As you may never see before you die!"

*

You are all, my love, my heart's delight.
Your lips are sweet, your mouth is rose-bud bright.
Without you I am dumb. My sorry plight
Reduces all my world to one great sigh.

*

Vagif, the fluttering nightingale grows weak.
In your love's lips the cure to ills it seeks,
On snow-white breasts and blushing apple-cheek,
From which may God avert the evil eye.

Translated by *Tom Botting*

The fragrance spread by your hair enhances every sense
For my soul is bound by love and held in beauty's sway.
A letter could not describe the depths of my great pain.
So I give the morning breeze a message to relay.

You sit—your beauty enchants, you rise and hold in thrall
My two eyes that see your figure, lissome, slim and tall.
Your ways are graceful and kind. You win the hearts of all.
My ideal the Lord has made you—lovely, charming, gay!

Ah! Amber brought from the Yemen—your lips, so pure
                                            and fair!
When I picture them in my mind my heart writhes in
                                            despair.
Your beauty glows in a frame of jet-black waving hair,
Iridescence in it gleams—the drake's most vain display.

My love embellishes thoughts that heart-strings weave
                                            about you.
Most delightful words I hear when I can talk about you.
My love, my heart, o my soul! My life would end without
                                            you.
May the Lord protect my love from evil eyes I pray.

Vagif must languish in pain, if love he cannot win,
In the house of sorrow held—bitter, wan and thin.
Vagif suffers torments of hell—yet love is not a sin.
Oh, show mercy to Vagif, with love his pain allay.

Translated by *Tom Botting*

*   *   *

Her face and features, rose and tulip tinted,
Were framed in sable locks. She gathered violets.
How well the colours blend with eagle features,
When on her creamy breast there nestle violets!

Her body carved from marble, locks of black
And silky waves, can steal your heart, alack!
And like Medjnun, you shall not get it back,
She'll pin it to her breast mid purple violets.

At eighteen summers she has just begun
To count the many hearts that she has won.
O'er hills she walks in beauty shared by none,
Mid rustling leaves and fragrant whispering violets.

Display your limbs and body, warm and nude,
But never let my rival's glance intrude,
Nor tolerate his touches harsh and crude. . . .
Unworthy hands should never pluck sweet violets.

When one beholds her scintillating grace
The blood like wine makes heart-beats throb apace,
And when Vagif composes verses to her face
The first and final words should be sweet violets.

Translated by *Tom Botting*

* * *

From birth a lovely woman crowns the world's creation.
Through middle age and on, her charm shall still exist—
A jewel that time in passing can never touch or ravage—
A hundred winters' storms her splendour shall resist.

A woman of true beauty shall never cease to please,
Delightful, slim and supple as swaying cypress-trees,
Her winsome, sweet enchantment always shall increase. . .
Our love for her, our trust, forever shall persist.

Let her hundreds birthday come!—Still upon that day,
Though her hand be weak and tremble, although her head
                                                    be grey,
With a quick glance of her eye she can steal our hearts
                                                    away,
We fall beneath her spell and do whate'er she list.

145

Her dignity increases beyond that of her youth.
Her eyes are clear, serene, as limpid as the truth.
Against her sharp-tipped lashes no man's heart is proof.
The arrows from her bow their aim have never missed.

Vagif, to know delights of loving at its best
Choose one whose proven heart will stand life's sternest
test,
And not some wilful girl who gives the soul no rest,
Or night and day you'll swear from loving to desist.

Translated by *Tom Botting*

*   *   *

If a beautiful girl walks with coverless hair
Her person the following points should unite—
Like a mirror her body should always be fair,
Her locks should be ebon and set off her height.

Her cheeks should recall springtide tulips a-blowing.
Her lips should be red and like cut amber glowing,
Her body, a jewel no fault ever showing,
From her head to her toes should be pure pearly white.

Her dress should be neat and impeccably clean.
Her manner must never be mincing or mean.
Her breath should be sweet and her glances serene,
Her hair with cool violets' scent should delight.

Both her arms and her legs should be graceful and slim,
Her buttocks well rounded, not fat, or too thin,
On her ankles two dimples and one on her chin,
Her face should be round and her bones should be slight.

At the door of maturity—fifteen, not more,
With no band on her brow that might cover some flaw,
She must not be precocious, or push to the fore,
Yet charming to guests that her lord may invite.

146

Let her beauty each morning attention excite—
A fine preening pheasant, delighting the sight.
She should not talk too much, but be gay and forthright.
Attentive she must be, and always polite.

Her allure should grow greater as time passes by.
Reserved she should be, retiring and shy,
Giving jaded men strength with a sweet-scented sigh.
Her words should be honeyed, her smile should be
                                                bright.

She must always be honest in deed and in word.
Intrigues by her prattle should never be stirred.
She should stand like a pine-tree and utter no word
Though fearing her head from her neck you may smite.

O Vagif, to the soul a sweet girl should appeal. . .
Our Khan needs a beauty, why waste so much zeal
Describing what powers-that-be ought to feel?
Let her heed our great Khan and bow to his might.

Translated by *Tom Botting*

* * *

I went out to talk to a girl with dark eyes.
She said, "You must go, I cannot let you stay!
Many people can see us. With signs we can't speak—
It's no time to bring winking eyes into play!"

Your coquettish warm languor is my deadly foe.
The breezes are brushing your curls to and fro.
It's time we should kiss. I beg you, don't go,
But come, let us love, there is no more to say!

Vagif says, be bold! Such a chance never miss.
Stroke the nape of her neck as you beg for a kiss.
Wasting time in discourses would be quite amiss. . .
Now my breath comes in gasps—do not tease me I pray.

Translated by *Tom Botting*

147

The tips of silk tresses that outline your face
Make an ebony frame to set off your skin.
Each lock has a sister and the two interlace,
With serpentine grace encircling your chin.

Your two flashing eyes are a soul-stirring sight
And each has ten thousand great elephants' might.
There's a rosy-hued bud on each breast round and white,
Glimpsed through a fabric transparently thin.

Your features the Goddess of Fortune amaze,
White houris and angels at such beauty gaze.
Golden bracelets with amber and diamonds ablaze
Clasp your delicate wrists with their velvety skin.

My heart she has hidden, where, nobody knows.
But my mind and my faith go wherever she goes.
Her cheek is of ivory, tinted with rose,
Couched in soft hair and each curl has a twin.

My name is Vagif, to my dear one I say,
I keep watch on the road through the night and the day!
Oh, queen of all beauties, will you not come my way?
You are breaking my heart—and that is a sin. . . .

Translated by *Tom Botting*

* * *

My Kaaba, Karbala, my Mecca, Medina, my own!
The earth that you tread is a sanctuary, love's sacred place.
I worship, adore you. I call you my holy Black Stone.
When I bow down before you, towards you I first turn my
face.

Do not take to heart any maladroit words I may say.
My mind is confusion, inebriate, fuddled and fey.

148

If you are not near, if you bear your slim body away,
It seems that the world is confounded in time and in space.

My faith, my beliefs, my whole life to your braids I have
bound.
No love like my love for your curls in the world could be
found.
Departing I wreathe in your hair my emotions profound,
So keep them secure as a pledge till my path I retrace.

O my sky, O my sun, O you full moon of mine!
You're my treasure, my glory, my soul's light divine!
Your great beauty my heart shall forever enshrine.
Every word about you leaves a honey-sweet taste.

The drake's iridescence is dulled when you come.
The cockatoo hearing your voice is struck dumb.
Vagif has been wounded, his heart is now numb.
He claims that his pain has been caused by your grace.

Translated by *Tom Botting*

* * *

Although Bairam, the feast, is on its way I sigh.
At home there's not a sack that holds a thing to eat.
The jars that held the oil are empty and quite dry
There's not a whiff of cheese and not a shred of meat.

We put no faith in God, who pity never shows—
If country bumpkins knew they'd drive us off with blows!
In every village house the honey overflows.
It's only in our own there's nothing sour or sweet.

In this wide world of ours we've not a groat to show,
And ne'er a pretty lass to set the heart aglow.
Vagif, don't ever boast about the things you know.[1]
God knows our store of wisdom's poor and incomplete!

Translated by *Tom Botting*

[1] Vagif means knowledgeable.

149

Kura's sweet banks abound with lovely places.
How sad that other beauties should be missed!
Those silken tresses, captivating faces—
Alas! It seems that here they don't exist.

Our wintering-place is in Giragbasan—
The lowest plain that lies beneath the sun.
A lodge we dwell in, but there's only one.
Alack! No villages near here exist!

Yet there are girls of beauty living here,
With tulip lips and eyes both proud and
                              clear;
But no sweet-tongued and playful little dear
To warm the heart and give its strings a
                              twist.

Though balmy air is wine throughout the
                              night,
No lips with languorous moan exhale delight.
Although the girls are such a lovely sight,
Among them well-groomed beauties don't exist.

A mass of glory flows from every head. . .
By jet-black hair a glow of light is spread.
Their dress is silver-trimmed. Their kerchief
                              red,
Without a trace of tule like morning mist.

With golden thread their bodices are sewn.
On milky skins dark beauty-spots are shown.
Their hair hangs free and loose by breezes blown.
It seems that well-trained curls do not exist.

Like crested kestrels each one sports a crown.
Uncovered are their lips and eyes. They frown
Like headsmen when the axe comes flashing down.
If looks could kill I swear I'd not resist.

In far-off parts my heart is dull and sick.
I know girls' winning ways and every trick.

Slim arms are decked with bracelets wide and thick.
There's not one amber bead on any wrist.

They'll primp before a mirror, using paint
To stress a dimpled curve that seems too faint,
To eyes applying shadows with restrain,
But your slim hennaed fingers I have missed.

Vagif has hopes that God may help him yet.
If I stay here the graveyard cough I'll get,
For our sweet nymphs my heart cannot forget.
And yet it's here I still must long exist.

Translated by Tom Botting

*　*　*

I beg you, look among the wedding guests.
If one most lovely girl is present by some chance,
—I shall not tell her name, but most of you can guess—
Sweet daughter of our friend, beguile us with a dance!

Impatiently we wait to see her whirl and swing,
And trust that anguish from our soul's she'll fling.
With bracelets on your wrists and on each hand a ring,
We beg you show your grace. Beguile us with a dance!

Her figure's newly formed, supple, slim, divine.
She holds my heart in thrall. For her true love I pine.
Now to her loving friend, oh, let her give a sign,
And at this marriage feast beguile us with a dance!

Mollá Vagif shall call for help with bitter cries.
Not tears, but blood shall spurt from his lamenting eyes
Unless that lovely girl to show her grace will rise.
Although it breaks my heart, beguile us with a dance!

Translated by Tom Botting

151

Her brows like quivering bowstrings set me yearning.
I'd sacrifice my life for what I see.
I touch one lock and round my head starts turning. . .
Like some bright lamp she sears the heart in me.

*

How well I know youth's beauty in full spate—
That glowing hair and skin, the supple gait!
My eyes caress that figure slim and straight.
Its grace outdoes the swaying cypress-tree.

*

Amid the mountain rocks I spend my night
Consumed by dreams to which her face lends light.
If beauty steals my health, as if for spite,
From that sweet sickness never set me free!

*

I dedicate my trust, my faith and fame
To lovely women. Theirs is my good name.
If their bright eyes condemn me, then, for shame,
From death I shall not flinch with mercy's plea.

*

Oh, Lord above, I beg you, help Vagif
And grant the solace of a sweet relief.
Let her appear, although her stay be brief,
And as my guest spend just one night with me.

Translated by *Tom Botting*

* * *

I suffer hell's fierce torments, ghastly flames now sear
My soul, forever seeking you, my love divine.
This separation dulls my spirit. Death is near,
But then forever yours shall be this heart of mine.

The softness of your chin on softer tresses lies.
My soul they try to steel, those scintillating eyes.
He who seeks to flee from love, from life itself then flies!
That is what the people say—I seek you, love of mine.

I swear by Kadija, by Sakina I swear,
I swear by Heiranisa, by Amina I swear,
By Kaaba, Mecca and Medina I declare
That sorrow grips Vagif's hot heart, beloved mine.

No pine or cypress-tree more graceful have I seen,
For figures such as yours are few and far between.
I'm half the man you knew, I now am sick and lean,
I shall get worse unless I see your face divine.

Translated by Tom Botting

* * *

Don't seek a cause to part. I hoard each word you say.
So do not cut the bonds that our two hearts still tie.
I would no other man should ever come your way,
For fear lest with strange love my love might have to vie.

I long to drink my fill from those eyes deep and dark
And to your gentle words forever I would hark,
So, darling, be my sun when death is looming dark,
Then from my soul's warm nest my dream shall never fly.

Vagif's true heart can never from your love be free.
Forever I'll adore you. Can you not love me?
Oh, why when I approach you, darling, do you flee?
My kiss would draw no blood. No cannibal am I!

Translated by Tom Botting

* * *

You have plagued me for years, you have wounded and
stung me, my beard!
May Allah visit His wrath upon you, and promptly, my
beard!
Such disaster no hurricane brings, nor a sand-storm, my
beard!

153

Ah, if only a foe's yatagan smote and trimmed you, my
beard!
By a spiteful shaitan and a mad were you fashioned, my
beard!

As a rosy-cheeked youth I was beardless but gay and
content,
For I kissed many lips, and my days were agreeably spent,
And not once did the fairest of maids my attentions resent.
But 'tis all in the past, and today they deride and torment
Him who, thinking to please them, did thoughtlessly sprout
you, my beard!

Not for naught so despondent am I, not for naught do I
brood:
You embarrass and shame me, disgrace me and leave me
subdued;
You are matted, ill-smelling and greasy with remnants of
food,
And, disgusted, the damsels away from you turn, in no
mood
To accept my advances and treat me with kindness, o
beard!

Were each hair that you boast strung with diamonds and
pearls, even so
I would wish to be rid of you, beard, for to you do I owe
The disdain that the fair ones for me unmistakably show.
Less than grass are you worth, yet like grass you continue
to grow.
If I had but my way, for a mat I would use you, my beard!

Sad and grieved is Vagif, for the thought fills his heart
with dismay

That his dark, shining beard will too soon turn a lusterless
grey,
That a mangy white dog he will come to resemble one day,
That alone at a feast where the young wax lighthearted
and gay
He will, shivering, sit in a corner, unwanted, my beard!

Translated by *Irina Zheleznova*

* * *

In this world there is nothing in which to believe.
All things are distorted I clearly perceive,
And friends' declarations are meant to deceive.
Fulfilment of promises I can't perceive,
While for falseness in love my whole being must
                                        grieve.

A servant, a hermit and even the Khan
Submit to great torments to gain what they
                                        can
And chase after riches with grisly elan.
We've watched and we've listened to many a man,
But found only nets of deceit that men weave.

The world rings with voices that howl and incite.
Men outwit each other, they struggle and fight
For gold all around us—a miserable sight!
Subordinates *should* know their leaders are
                                        right,
But gold for subordinates leaders don't leave. . .

Mankind always follows a rule that seems mad—
Give help to a man when he's down, make him glad,
He'll do you bad turns till you're sorry and sad!
Whatever is good incites all that is bad.
Close friends become foes, they quarrel and
                                        leave. . .

No savant, no student, or fool can be free.
They are slaves of the Shah and the powers-that-be.
The truth is distorted—this great sin I see.
The sheiks, rogues and preachers oppress you and me,
They're not worth our prayers—to faith they don't
                                        cleave.

Each man has a passion for one thing alone—
Some pine for a woman, some lust for a throne,
While shahs dream of grasping the land others own.
Distraught with desire, they must languish and groan,
But peace in this world no one tries to achieve.

155

I studied and mastered the alchemist's art
And turned simple dust into gold for a start.
Black stones became rubies as red as the heart.
From beads I produced the best pearls on the mart.
Not thanks, only curses were what I received!

Who Jamshid's fine palace brought down to the ground
Destroyed other halls where great feasts would resound.
A man without grief in this world can't be found.
For me Goddess Fortune her wheel oft span round,
But only misfortune from her I've received.

You may help a man who seems bright as the sun,
But he never will thank you for what you have done.
Don't seek self-respect, or restraint—there is none,
Nor truth. Since they said that men's trust may be won
I worked to that end but could nothing achieve.

Turn away from this world which is wicked and cold.
What is good and what's bad is not what you're told.
When rulers doubt friends trusted roughs are made bold.
The rich have no heart and the good have no gold.
Men act against teachings that all should believe.

What goes with great wealth in this world I have seen,
But greatness and pomp brought to nothing I've seen,
And ugliness, too, that once beauty had been.
An impotent end to sweet loving I've seen.
Fair bodies are doomed. Beauty knows no retrieve.

O Great God above, you rule over all!
The true faith is dead. None pay heed to your call.
Do not let our world into Satan's trap fall.
Oh, show us your face. Tear away this foul pall.
Light up the sad world and the true faith retrieve.

My life becomes harsher. My hair has turned grey.
Great misery entered my life on that day
A self-centered beauty my heart took in sway.
My Maker, O Lord, my great sorrow allay
For no mercy from men shall I ever receive.

Translated by *Tom Botting*

How fickle fate and fortune are, now see, my Vidadi!
And how the tide has changed today, O Vidadi, now see!
One moment sealed a tyrant's doom and now he is no more.
Now to the letter see fulfilled Almighty God's decree.
'Tis dawn, and lo! the light which people worshipped, now
is dead.
Last night—Commander of the Faith; at morning—dust
is he.
No longer does the haughty monarch wear his golden
crown—
For now his head lies at his feet—O what a sight to see!
At his command, unhappy I unto the block was led.
Now look on him who from a tyrant's clutches rescued me,
Who rescued me, a wretched blacksmith, from a shameful
death.
Now in this monarch's coffin lid, that blacksmith's nails
you'll see.
Remember, O unhappy mortal, Khan Aga-mamed.
The end of that bloodthirsty Khan let not forgotten be.
So you just shun the multitude and walk not in their way;
Nor daughter, son nor sweetheart trust—nor friend,
whoe'er he be.
So close your eyes, Vagif—the ugly shun, eschew the fair,
And you'll be wise if you Mohammed's favourites will flee.

Translated by *Louis Zellikoff*

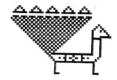

Mollah-Beli Vidadi

MOLLAH-BELI VIDADI (1709-1809) was a contemporary and friend of Vagif. Vidadi's lyric poetry is often melancholy in mood: he speaks of homesickness, of disillusion, of violence and social injustice. In style his poems are akin to folk poetry. For a certain period of his life Vidadi was the court poet of the Georgian Prince Irakly the Second. His correspondence in verse with Vagif is very popular in Azerbaijan.

* * *

Day and night I am burning, devoured by fire
Because of a beauty with raven-black hair.
My tongue cannot tell, nor my pen describe
All the sufferings she has made me bear.

Bitter grief overwhelms me, wave after wave,
Such as neither Varga nor Medjnun, love's slave,
Ever knew. With bitter sorrow I rave
Flooding the world with my tears of despair.

Yet how wonderful is this state caused by love.
Like a moth on a candle, I burn in my love.
It suffices me but to remember my love
For my blood to boil—Ah, those moments rare!

Poor heart, how you grieve when anything hinders
Love's progress! Like glass, you break into splinters,
Like a tree struck by lightning, you burn into cinders
On the day when you part with your mistress fair.

In this mortal, this wretched world of ours
All my dreams have been crushed by Fate's dread powers.
O poor, ill Vidadi, love your heart devours;
Life holds nothing for you but black despair.

Translated by *Dorian Rottenberg*

❧ ❧ ❧

O you with the sugar-sweet mouth and cup-like lips,
To my eyes your delicate face seems a mirror
Into which my loving heart looked and was stunned—
How I wish I could own that magic mirror.

Love, I look upon you and myself as one.
Do not leave me, I pray, o my moon, my sun!
Since the day we parted my troubles began.
I keep counting the days and the hours, my mirror.

Summers and winters drag slowly without you.
I've wept oceans of tears; if I only knew
Where you are! Do not veil your face from view,
So the sun and the moon may deliver my love to my mirror.

Show your beautiful face, lighten up the skies,
Let the soberest men lose their heads from surprise!
Tears of blood pour forth from my eyes.
Rise again like a new moon, my mirror!

I've been ill since the day my first look I took
Of your face. Burn my soul with your dazzling look.
Who, unable to read beauty's book,
Can understand the Koran, my mirror?

Translated by *Dorian Rottenberg*

* * *

The soul cannot bear too long
The absence of the one it desires.
Love survives where lovers stay true.
Without constancy love expires.

*

Be faithful to those who stay true,
The faithless make haste to eschew.
Your virtues reveal not to view
Where no one virtue admires.

*

O my friend, again and again
I repeat: where there is no shame,
No honour, there's nothing to gain,
There's nothing your soul to inspire.

*

God shield the abandoned and lone,
The souls that in solitude groan.
Sad and lone as a rolling stone
Is he who no friendship acquires.

*

Acknowledge the truth, o my heart,
Or conscience will make you smart.
How can men from the truth depart
When nothing such baseness requires?

*

To you, o my bosom friend,
This admonition I send.
But answer me—in the final end,
Can there be a rose without briars?

*

The heart loves as long as it lives,
Love no rest to the spirit gives.
How can I live—Allah forgive—
If gone is the one whom my heart desires?

Translated by *Dorian Rottenberg*

161

Crazy heart, there's no joy in a foreign land.
The day will come, you will think of home and weep.
Amid strangers life runs out like a handful of sand.
The day will come, you will think of home and weep.

When fortune smiles, you have so many friends.
But when it frowns, all friendship ends.
A stranger whom everyone hurts and offends,
The day will come, you will think of home and weep.

I've drained my full cup of sorrow there,
I suffered more pain than man can bear.
A stranger forever with no one to care.
The day will come, you will think of home and weep.

In your ghazals you will weep and complain
Of your heart's unrelieved, unabating pain;
Remembering the past you can never regain,
The day will come, you will think of home and weep.

You will recall the orchards and gardens,
The snow-capped summits of your native mountains,
Your youth when your energy surged up in fountains;
The day will come, you will think of home and weep.

You will remember every hour of the past.
Regret will torture you until the last.
All countrymen for news of home you will ask.
The day will come, you will think of home and weep.

Every cemetery, every grave you find
Your parents' graves will bring back to mind.
You'll pine for all that you left behind.
The day will come, you will think of home and weep.

Translated by *Dorian Rottenberg*

Care not for the fleeting world, things cannot stay as they
are.
Weep blood; even weeping eyes cannot stay as they are.
The rose's time will elapse—flowers cannot stay as they
are.
Souls that rejoice at all hours, cannot stay as they are.
O cup-bearer, bring me the cup, things cannot stay as
they are.
In time, dust will cover us up, things cannot stay as
they are.
Just as all other beauty, beauties must turn into dust.
Their waists, so slender and pretty, must turn into dust.
Their flowing locks, their ravishing bodies must turn
into dust.
All that Nature creates is futile, must turn into dust.
O cup-bearer, bring me the cup, things cannot stay as
they are.
In time, dust will cover us up, things cannot stay as
they are.
Since the world's richest, too, must retire to eternal rest,
Believe not in earthly grandeur, 'tis mortal both east
and west.
Even Suleiman's throne is shortlived, although thrice-
blessed,
So if you are wise, do not trust fortune's turns and twists.
O cup-bearer, bring me the cup, things cannot stay as
they are.
In time, dust will cover us up, things cannot stay as they
are.
A hundred springs will come when tongues by wine are
made loose,
A hundred fair tulips bloom when men drink the
grapevine's juice.
All the world's gardens revive, the rose's bloom renews.
Yet my soul will rejoice no more, whatever knots are
made loose.
O cup-bearer, bring me the cup, things cannot stay as
they are.
In time, dust will cover us up, things cannot stay as
they are.
I am tortured by pain and grief, parting burns me like fire.

163

I am drunk, I've drained the cup of sorrow, torment
and desire.
It were well if she were near, the one that I most admire.
While there's a chance, hold on to love, till the last
of hope expire.
O cup-bearer, bring me the cup, things cannot stay as
they are.
In time, dust will cover us up, things cannot stay as
they are.

O my sick Vidadi, this world is an empty shell,
Monotonous is this world as the groan of a bell.
For in this fickle world all is vanity, all is hell.
Life passes—so take your chance, seize it and hold it well.
O cup-bearer, bring me the cup, things cannot stay
as they are.
In time, dust will cover us up, things cannot stay as
they are.

Translated by *Dorian Rottenberg*

Beware, o my friend, you will drown in my blood:
'Tis best not to trouble my wounded heart,
Forced to part with my people, my native land,
With the dearest, most cherished friends to part.

I gave my faith to a perfidious crowd;
Life has passed in vain, now I know beyond doubt.
Traitress fortune has brought my spirit to rout,
And my sorrowful heart has been torn apart.

My tears mixed with blood daily flow faster.
My soul is drowned in a flood of disaster;
Of my fortunes I am no longer master;
No one can know how my wounds smart.

If my tears will flow faster day after day,
If I drown in blood, don't rebuke me, pray.
Were a thousand new suns to arise one day,
They could never bring light to my grief-darkened heart.

I, the sick Vidadi, from my household and land
And from all whom I loved and cherished was banned.
No physicians, no doctors can understand
My disease, much less cure it, for all their art.

Translated by *Dorian Rottenberg*

* * *

For months I dreamed of our rendezvous;
Thank Allah, the day came and I was with you.
How I longed for you! I would give all my life
For your locks, for your smile like the sun, my love.

With your coquetry, darling, my heart you stole.
Play, my love, your coy tricks to bewitch my soul.
Chain my thoughts to yourself, to take my all.
Say sweet words, if only for fun, my love.

165

You are brilliant, darling, lively and gay;
The moon loves you at night, and the sun by day.
You are heaven itself, though with hearts you play.
Who can count your charms' full sum, my love?

I'm falling in love with you more and more.
It's happiness someone like you to adore.
Even flowers admire your beauty with awe,
By their envy of you overcome, my love.

You are a heavenly gift to me from fate.
No evil from you can I ever await.
Shoot me—your arrow brings love, not hate.
The contest of hearts you have won, my love.

Translated by *Dorian Rottenberg*

Cranes

Following closely one after another
Why do you soar through the sky, o cranes?
Like mournful, unwanted strangers you move.
To what land through the sky do you fly, o cranes?

One after another like rosary beads
You follow after the bird that leads.
But when each on his own looks for grain and seeds,
You stray farther apart than in the sky, o cranes!

Yet I know why you keep so close in flight:
With assassins and murderers you must fight,
Hawks and eagles are watching for you in the night,
In unequal battle you die, o cranes.

Baghdad and Basrah were the place of your birth.
For the beks your feathers were gifts of great worth.
When I hear you hooting as I stand on earth
For your plight my heart breaks well nigh, o cranes.

Come down, pay a visit to poor Vidadi,
Hear him sing his complaints to a sad melody.
Bring the men of Baghdad the tidings that he,
The sick Vidadi, will soon die, o cranes!

Translated by *Dorian Rottenberg*

Kassum-Bek Zakir

KASSUM-BEK ZAKIR was born at the end of the 18th century into the family of a bek in Shusha. In his satirical poetry and fables Zakir lashed out at the vices then rampant in society, at the hypocrisy and bigotry of the clergy, at the venality of the officials, the greed of the merchants, and the cruelty of the landowners. He was persecuted by the authorities on the instigation of the mullahs and beks, and was finally deported to Baku and put behind bars. His son and nephew were deported with him. Thanks to the intervention of relatives and friends, among them the prominent Azerbaijanian writer Mirza Akhundov, the poet was released from prison and allowed to return home. Zakir died in 1857. Besides satirical poetry he is also the author of some morality stories in verse.

A dervish there was, an unscrupulous knave,
With a heart full of lust, to his passions a slave.
Though outwardly pious, his thoughts were unclean.
He chanced on a maiden whose like he'd not seen,
As slender as cypress, a grace all her own,
Pure rapture to look on—and she all alone.
The place was deserted, towards her he went
As she carried water to her winter tent.
Sweet creature, I'm dying of thirst—was his plea.
I'd be glad of a drink. Give some water to me.
As she filled up his cup, the old reprobate caught
The hem of her garment, and held her arm taut,
Until the young maiden fell into a rage
And boiled with a fury that nothing could gauge.

Till now not one stranger had fingered her dress,
None so low as to look on her nakedness.
Her lovely young body not one thing had touched
But her shift.... Now insulted, her anger was such
That she screamed, broke away, and started to run
In search of her brothers to tell what was done—
And ask them to punish or kill this cool knave.
The dervish, he sensed things had turned rather grave,
And started to plead in an excess of fear:
For the sake of Allah, have some mercy, my dear...
You're angry, of course, and I must pay the price.
But first I would give you some moral advice.
Should it not please, should my words you disdain—
Just the same, come and take up your pitcher again.
If my words do not move you, then do what you will.
The maiden, surprised as a fawn, then stood still
To hear what the dissolute dervish would say.
Modest maiden, he said, shy and honest as day...
O thrice cursed be Satan who evil inspires!
And his allies Lust, Passion, and Carnal Desires,
Who often rule man and his reason unthrone:
Mind is helpless before them and quite overthrown.
Passion and Lust pull us ever which way,
We are blockheads, and stupid, the easiest prey...
Those like me, slaves of passion, however devout,
Will burn in the fires of hell, there's no doubt.
I wouldn't for anything spoil your good name,
But remember till death—this moral on Shame:
Should you argue with someone disgracefully loud,

169

In protest, abuse him and gather a crowd,
Bad women will always think you are like them,
And all of your noise just a stratagem.
So is it worth while for a true modest maid
To give food for gossip, be thought a mere jade?
Oh, pardon my blunder, please do, for God's sake!
Shame and scorn upon me! 'Twas an evil mistake.
But... "She and the dervish," ill tongues will suggest.
Why, if to a breeze you your secret confessed—
Five days are enough for bad talk to go round.
And if to be clothed had no meaning, no grounds—
The Creator would not have said: Cover your sin...
"To shut people's mouths," they say, "you can't begin—
By letting the cat from the bag." Well, that is life!
After thinking it over, with some inner strife,
The maid took her pitcher, and went on her way.
The most valiant of women are those who display
An uncovered face with no feeling of shame:
Even so, stupid women and men will make game
And say she is one who gives in to temptation...
But don't you believe it—evil thoughts, allegations,
Sink their tentacles deep in the pure human soul—
Yet rumours contain little truth, on the whole.
Of chastity, bad women always did prate—
But give one the eye... and you won't have to wait.

Translated by *Gladys Evans*

A pity, a thousand pities—again no averting the fray:
Again our mullahs disgraced themselves with an ugly
display.

*

Once more on Shusha Mountain,[1] Evil Fate hailed stones
of torment—
And Islam's stronghold broke: Glass Mountain was broken
today.

*

People honoured the Madrasah: but gave their respect
in vain.
For again the quarrels broke out there; none could the
ranting stay.

*

The Shusha Mullahs

All peace is rent in the Madrasah, though not much time
has passed—
Our holy mullahs cursed and swore, and each had a
score to pay.

*

Still yesterday they were at peace and spoke on friendly
terms—
But now they call down the wrath of Allah, and each
other flay.

*

The gossip and the whispering had long faded out of
mind,
The town bazaars once more all buzzed with voices loud
and gay.

*

While mullahs rule, we cannot enjoy the holy Bairam fête,
The doors of all the mosques were shut on Greater
Bairam Day.

*

By light of early morning we walked gaily towards the
mosque:
In downcast mood, funereally, we dragged our homeward
way.

[1] Glass Mountain; Shusha—glass.

171

The mullah's unity cracked deep, split like the nib of
a pen—
Again each other they reviled: it was close to an affray.

*

What kind of agreement was it, when from pulpits
thundered down
Again amendments to holy writ, and each put a different
way?

*

Two days had hardly passed before commotion had passed
all bounds—
And defamation, discord, everywhere was in full sway.

*

We suffer enough at the mullahs' hands, without all this
as well:
Yet follow them once more, but what fools we—not to
break away.

*

And if among the mullahs all, a deserving one is found:
His holy brothers say he's crazed, and peck at him
night and day.

*

Our only hope is the Shah of Shahs—to end all their
disputes:
So the people finally get a rest from mullahs such as they.

Translated by *Gladys Evans*

* * *

Why has she such a heart of stone
That she ignores my heartsick cries?
Why won't she see the tears of blood
All crimson streaming from my eyes?

Uncurling eyelid buds, she peers;
Then is transformed to only ears,
The nightingale is all she hears—
Sees not this fading rose who dies.

But Shirin, Leili, where are they?
Their loves they never would betray,
Their cries rock Heaven in dismay:
Such love, why cannot she apprise?

Oh, when I glimpse your tender eyes,
Almost my soul from body flies;
To see you but intensifies
My wish—oh, bend on me your eyes!

Passing my rival, she always turns
And smiles at him; yet me she spurns.
But is it fair her unconcern?
Zakir the more deserves her sighs.

Translated by *Gladys Evans*

The petalled rose, O maid, confess that it is so...
Her fragrance and her tenderness has learned from thee?
But she: With petalled rose I've never been so close:
'Tis hearsay that her tenderness she learned from me.

*

To ruin and to desecrate love's holy fane,
Your hunter's dwelling devastate with mild disdain,
To glide and then to hesitate, and look again—
The delicate gazelle but lately learned from thee.

*

With airy grace to pierce the heart and not repent,
To spill the blood and rend apart the innocent,
With hunting eyes to speed the dart that brings lament—
The bow its perfect skill and art but learned from thee.

*

Since Sun and Moon became the prey of your sweet face,
Of you alone the talk held sway in vaulted space,
Sad Jupiter and Venus can't extol your grace—
Through other planets' lipped relay, they learned of thee.

*

But when Zakir she has to pass, she drops her veil;
Cruel, she won't let him tell his passion's tale:
I think at times the moth, alas, its wings so frail
To burn within the candle's flame—has learned from me!

Translated by *Gladys Evans*

I'll be here next Bairam, so my beloved said.
I'd wait a lifetime, not a year, I swear—
To take and twine the ringlets round her head,
To smooth the spicy softness of her hair.

My love prefers a kerchief black as night,
Her black braids kiss the earth like pilgrims might;
Her kerchief suits her well. Oh lovely sight!
How sweet of her, a single pearl to wear.

My being drowns in seas of bitter tears:
I'm twisted inside out, I know no cheer
Since I was parted from my love. . . my dear.
God sees I'm caught by torrents of despair!

My heart is like a child who desires the moon:
He wants it now—each one he'll importune.
But to his pleas, my love, you're quite immune. . .
To live alone, a lunatic could not bear!

Zakir, to trust this world is quite absurd:
Evil or good, never believe its word.
Best lean upon your loved one's arm so fair
And quiet and dignified, mount Heaven's Stair.

Translated by *Gladys Evans*

I know not why I do not die,
I'm like the dead, with you not here.
That I still live surprises me—
God knows it does!—with you not here.

Wave after wave, love's rough despair
Destroys my heart beyond repair.
May blindness strike, if my eye dare
Look elsewhere, love—with you not here.

First to my left, then to my right,
I seek someone to tell my plight.
Such grief, deep sense of loss—a night
That swallows me, with you not here.

But come... you'll know without dispute—
Of all my strength I'm destitute,
So absolutely lost, I'm mute
And drained of speech—with you not here.

I, Zakir, go weeping everywhere,
Like a nightingale whose nest is bare.
I walk, my crossed arms hug despair—
How long, how far, before you're here?

Translated by *Gladys Evans*

Since your departure—O Inconstant One—
I wait beside the road, my spirits low.
I asked a breeze what I should do, it said:
Pay her obeisance, if her curls you'd know.

Heaven hears my cries: deaf-eared, you let me rave—
Why won't you pity your unhappy slave?
Your love brought many lovers to the grave:
Can twigs be saved where tumbling torrents go?

Your charms long since my heart made desolate...
She has not come, still by the road I wait...
They say where curls veil cheeks that captivate
With every smile her dancing dimples show.

A Christian's ringlets made cruel war on me—
Despoiled me, heart and being, utterly.
And none should judge or even censure me—
That I, before Love's forces, meekly bow.

Now parted from your native climes, Zakir,
The steppelands roam, the mountains climb, Zakir;
From shock of this despairing time—Zakir
Lies helpless as absinth when gale winds blow.

Translated by *Gladys Evans*

The Lion, the Wolf, and the Jackal

I remember a fable a book once told
Of a wolf and a jackal, in times of old.
* * *

Who were friends with a lion, the King of Beasts,
And they shared meat and drink, for a time at least.
* * *

It so happened that all of three days and nights,
Every hunt was in vain—they had not a bite.
* * *

Towards dawn they were lucky—in one small glen,
Caught a ram and a lamb and a nice fat hen.
* * *

Now the lion's big appetite knew no bounds—
To the wolf he said: "You do the sharing round!
* * *

"Let us eat or our dinner will start to cool!"
But the wolf did not catch, like an utter fool.
* * *

"O our Sovereign Lord," he rose to the bait,
'Twas decided in Heaven by Allah the Great—
* * *

"It's His hand. For you ram, for me lamb, and then
For the jackal Allah sent the big fat hen."
* * *

This is sheer impudence, thought the lion, put out;
Why this insolent wolf needs a good hard clout—
* * *

And his powerful paw struck the wolf on the head
So his eyes both fell out and he lay half dead.
* * *

But the lion still had the poor jackal in view—
And he said: "The decision now rests with you.
* * *

"Go ahead, show how clever you are, be bold!
For at this you're a master, so I've been told!"
* * *

Now the jackal had seen how the wolf fell flat;
In the lion's manoeuvre, he smelt a rat:
* * *

"It has been in our blood since the world was made—
Yet, my Lord, you first turned to a Fool for aid.
* * *

178

"I shall share out the trophies with such skill and art—
That till Judgement day comes, you will say 'How smart!'
*

"On the ram, Forest King, you will break your fast,
For your supper the lamb will be kept—and last,
*

"There's the hen, Mighty Lion, and in my view
It will make just a nice morning snack for you."
*

Said the Lion: "I'm speechless, you are really smart.
But who taught you to do it, and with such art?"
*

And the jackal: "In this art I was not refined—
But I learned quick enough from my brother, now blind!"
*

If a senior to you says the day is night,
You must say: "Yes, the stars in the sky are bright!"
*

If he figures the night to be day, just agree;
You may tell him: "The sun is too hot for me!"
*

Master Gadjigul, that was not this way—
When the Khan's garden ripened, he took survey...
*

Sent the better fruits home, this fine paragon,
And delivered the Khan inferior ones.
*

Blames the people, brings them to the judgement stand—
And himself, he lives off the fat of the land.
*

What a blot upon trade, upon commerce throughout,
What a swindle, and it is called being "devout".
*

And these pharisees—oft with purses that fat—
Stoop so low: even children could never do that!
*

Sold their conscience for gain, these false devotees—
Allah save us from hypocrites such as these.

Translated by *Gladys Evans*

Kheiran-Khanum

KHEIRAN-KHANUM was a 19th-century Azerbaijanian poetess whose love and philosophical ghazals and rubaiyat have come down to us, but practically no biographical data.

Cup-bearer, I'm by grief beset—the flowing cup for me!
And let me drink upon this earth and in the world to be.
However much I groan, no one a helping hand will lend,
So you, O Lord, with me must bear and hearken unto me!
O Morning! all about my grief a letter you must write,
And pass it on to god Novshad, wherever he may be,
With your four tresses trap the songbird of my heart,
And with your glance deliver it to the hunter that you see.
And if the hunter pity takes and does not shed its blood,
Deliver it to him whose whims torment me endlessly.
Since pangs of parting have enclosed my heart in dungeon
dark,
Oh spare me, death, do not delay, but hasten unto me.
Within the school of love, Kheiran, each soul a line has
writ,
Now take your line to him who can assess its quality.

Translated by *Eugene Felgenhauer*

My soul's bird hovers where your tresses flow,
It seems to hang 'twixt heaven and hell below.
See how confused it is, completely lost
Amongst your charms and knows not where to go!
My grief and sorrow to a peak have soared,
I'm like a vessel lost, when tempests blow.
My heart rejoiced in your delightful face,
'Twixt woe and hope I wander to and fro.
Behold the wonder—where a desert was
There now is life and luscious grasses grow!
My love has turned from me, where is the friend,
Who'll help distraught Kheiran recover from her woe?

Translated by *Eugene Felgenhauer*

O rose, can anyone not worship at your shrine,
O angel, who can not adore your grace sublime?
And where that sage who with your beauty is in love
But does not dedicate his life and does not pine?
To see your face, O moon, I can no longer bear,
And so I grieve and suffer torments all the time.
I fear that should I see you, I at once would die,
My life will be a hell, if you will not be mine.
There's nought that I can give to you except my soul,
But fear it prove unworthy of a rose so fine.
Kheiran, you hope he will be yours sometime?
You needn't hope for he will not until you die.

Translated by *Eugene Felgenhauer*

Mirza-Shafi Vazekh

MIRZA-SHAFI VAZEKH, the "sage from Ganja", was one of the best-known Azerbaijanian poets translated into nearly all the European languages. Vazekh was born at the end of the 18th century in Ganja into the family of a prominent architect, Kerbelai Sadykh. He was educated at a madrasah, where he made a brilliant success of his studies of Arabic and Persian, and where also he earned fame for his daring verses against the ignorance and fanaticism of the mullahs and the landowners. The persecutions he was subjected to compelled him to leave his country and settle in Tiflis where, with the help of friends, he secured the post of junior master at a boys' school. It was in Tiflis that Vazekh met Friedrich Bodenstedt, a German poet and traveller, who took down his poetry, translated it into German and published it. The book created a stir: it was re-published again and again, and translated into other European languages. In his poetry, Vazekh glorifies the joys of life, and the wisdom and goodness of Man. He died in Tiflis in 1852.

* * *

My head and my heart work in opposite ways,
But both will succeed in making me perish.
"Keep away from love," so one of them says.
The other is all for the woman I cherish.

Daily and nightly my reason revolts
At my heart's excess of passionate fire.
But what heart can restrain the flame that it holds?
So mine, too, always burns with love and desire.

Translated by *Dorian Rottenberg*

* * *

If I don't come to you and steal a kiss,
This paltry world will offer me no bliss.
There is no other joy that it can give.
Your love alone can make me glad I live.

Your glances flood the world with light sublime
So that all secrets it contains I may divine.
I owe my noblest feelings to that light,
Imbuing all my life with pure delight.
My loving dreams soar higher than the skies.
My guiding stars are your beloved eyes.

Translated by *Dorian Rottenberg*

* * *

At the hour when breath joins breath, when flower joins
flower,
At the hour when loving hearts join into one,
And lips from lips drink madness—at that hour
The mind gives way and sanity is gone.
So do not justify a transient feeling,
And shun the common animal delight.
Love is a force that elevates our being
Only when it emits a spiritual light.

Translated by *Dorian Rottenberg*

185

Ghazal
As numerous as the stars in the moonlit sky
Are the wounds in my breast from the knives of your eyes.
Not a star in the sky, no celestial body are you,
Yet you always attracted my eyes—my love I cannot
disguise.

My life has become a burden, one gloomy, eternal night.
Such a sweet tormentor's victim, can I refrain from sighs?
I live, but my life has been poisoned by hopeless love
for you.

My eyes have become like a fountain that never dries.
This woeful ghazal has been written by lovesick Vazekh.
Behold how, smitten with jealousy, slowly he dies!

Translated by *Dorian Rottenberg*

* * *

Accompanied by wine, attended by a rose
With pretty lips that hardly ever close
Except to favour me with a delicious kiss,
Let Satan have my soul—I'll have my bliss.

Translated by *Dorian Rottenberg*

* * *

The winds bring windmills into motion,
Steam engines are propelled by steam.
A storm of turbulent emotion
Moves us to struggle for our dream.

But stronger far than steam or storm,
More powerful than even death
Is something mild, humane and warm:
Your charm, my love, your gentle breath.

Translated by *Dorian Rottenberg*

186

When one fine day the golden gates of heaven
Fly open for believers' motley crowds,
The sinner and the sinless both together
Will probably stand waiting, torn with doubts.
Among the sinners only I will be as calm
And fearless as I always was since birth.
Why should I vex myself when you, my life's sweet balm,
Already opened heaven's gates for me on earth?

Translated by *Dorian Rottenberg*

* * *

Look at the stars revolving in the heavens.
As far as ever from this world of ours they seem.
It looks as if this beautiful umbrella
Above our heads is woven of our dreams.

The stars stand far apart from one another,
They shine or hide in fair or cloudy weather.
Do they feel sad to be so distant from their lovers
And do they long, like you and I, to come together?

Translated by *Dorian Rottenberg*

* * *

Let my life drag on as slowly as time,
Let old Fortune's wings droop as low as mine;
Dearly we pay for remembered bliss,
But that also has its reward, which is this:
Although, my sweet love, you're no longer near,
Your face I still see, your voice I still hear.

Translated by *Dorian Rottenberg*

187

Though every time you utter words both true and wise
A thousand storms break out and countless dangers rise,
Pay little heed to that, whatever may befall.
Mirza-Shafi Vazekh, prize honour above all.
For truth and beauty are so closely bound
That either one without the other can't be found.
Mirza-Shafi, try persecution to elude,
Be prudent as you can, be cautious and be shrewd.
Do veil your words, a little, sound more sooth,
In any case, take care to sweeten bitter truth.

Translated by *Dorian Rottenberg*

* * *

What shall I do—shall I laugh or complain:
Half the world lacks the implement known as the brain.
Unrepenting and shameless, tranquil and cool,
They repeat all my words—the words of a fool.

And yet, O Creator, accept my praise
For the plentiful fools that we have these days.
If the fools weren't so many, then I fear
True wisdom would never be held so dear.

Translated by *Dorian Rottenberg*

* * *

O you who help to save men's souls from hell and dirt,
You, greatest gift of God, beloved work,
Your loyal servitors you comfort and console,
The first desire, first dream, first need of the wise soul.

Only the knave from hard to easier work will fly.
Were I not bound to you by countless ties, I'd die.
O greatest gift of God, believe my word,
I will stay true to you till I'm interred.

Translated by *Dorian Rottenberg*

188

At every moment a grain of our life is spent.
However you call, it will not come back, all that went.
From the very outset a noble aim you must choose,
Determine what you are out to gain and what you can lose.
It's not our fault we are born into this world,
If you live an empty life, your groans will never reach God.

Translated by *Dorian Rottenberg*

* * *

The swifter to rise in the eyes of those you serve,
There are two conditions you must by all means observe:
Wherever you ought to be outspoken—be quiet,
Wherever you ought to be silent—speak outright.

Translated by *Dorian Rottenberg*

* * *

If you hear bad words about somebody else
Do not pass them on, do not ring all the bells.
It is easy to ruin another's home,
But it's harder by far to build stone upon stone.

Translated by *Dorian Rottenberg*

* * *

Ignoring all, I've given in to madness,
And troubles in my heart no longer throng.
Youth has returned and I am full of gladness
All thanks to wine and love and you, my song.
Drink wine, Mirza-Shafi, and waste no time.
Intoxicate yourself with women, wine and song.
Only when drunk, you come in streams, my rhyme,
And so, my songs, be drunken, come along.

Translated by *Dorian Rottenberg*

189

Old Love

There was once a time when with arms young and strong
I would hold you close in my tight embrace.
And still today, when I'm no longer young,
With the same old passion my blood will race.

In the ring of my life, you are the gem,
How beautiful with you it appears!
All my songs—for you I have written them.
Look into my heart, love, and never mind years.

Translated by *Dorian Rottenberg*

*   *   *

If a sharp sabre falls on a bed
The silk coverlet shields the sleeper's head.
Cruelty often proves helpless when faced
By kindliness, gentleness, spiritual grace.

Translated by *Dorian Rottenberg*

*   *   *

Let the wind as much as it likes raise dust,
The dust will be nothing but dust—just dust,
While amber, though hid in the dust of the valley,
Will never lose its lustre or value.

Translated by *Dorian Rottenberg*

*   *   *

A scholarly man addressed me one day,
"What do you think of the Shah, please say?
Is his mind as broad as his brow appears?
Is his heart big? How does he hear with his ears?"

"He is a man just like all the rest,
Like us in a gown and turban dressed,
But he knows that people are cowards and fools
And that is the secret whereby he rules."

Translated by *Dorian Rottenberg*

190

With his own hand the Shah once signed a manifesto;
O people of Iran, how greatly it impressed you!
"How wise he is, our Shah, to say the very least!"
Then all began to celebrate and feast.
"O one and only Shah, salam to you!
What other shah could do the wondrous deeds you do!"
Mirza-Shafi looked on in meditation;
He felt astonished at the people's exultation.
What quaint opinions have the people of Iran
Of high-placed persons like a shah or khan!
If one of them should happen to do good,
They seem astonished that he ever could.

Translated by *Dorian Rottenberg*

* * *

Can a man fall in love with a woman? He can:
None will accuse him—he won't have to quarrel.

If a woman, though, falls in love with a man
The world is against her and calls her immoral.

Translated by *Dorian Rottenberg*

Mirza-Fatali Akhundov

MIRZA-FATALI AKHUNDOU (1812-1878)—the great Azerbaijanian prose writer, dramatist, poet, materialist philosopher, enlightener, and the initiator of the realist trend in Azerbaijanian literature, was one of the best-educated men of his day. His first published work was the Oriental Poem *(1837) written on the death of Alexander Pushkin. He laid the foundations of realistic prose with his story* Cheated Stars *(1857), and with his five plays—comedies and dramas— written in the early 1850s, established realism as the leading trend in Azerbaijanian literature. He gave a powerful impetus to the development of prose and dramaturgy written for and about the people. In his philosophical treatises, publicistic writings and literary criticisms, Akhundov condemned tyranny and oppression, and championed education of the masses in the spirit of the time's advanced materialistic ideas.*

Akhundov launched realistic dramaturgy in the Middle East, and theoretically substantiated the principles of realism in Oriental literature, particularly in poetry, which he wrote both in Azerbaijani and in Persian. He was born in Nukha, and died in Tiflis where he had made his home for many years.

In 1962, by the decision of the World Peace Council, the 150th anniversary of Mirza Akhundov's birth was broadly celebrated.

I spoke at night, my eyes not tasting sleep:
O Heart, you treasure pearls of mysteries
deep!

Why has your nightingale now ceased to sing?
Why does your voice of eloquence silence keep?

What bars the flight of your poetic word?
Why halts your day-dream on the pathway
steep?

Behold the spring: like maidens' beauteous
charm—
We sing the praise of nature's verdant sweep.

On the Death of A. S. Pushkin
(An Oriental Poem)

By meadow streams the violets, clustering,
blow,
And flaming buds from rose-trees bravely peep;

The vale is decorated like a bride,
The flowers on the hills their jewels
heap.

A tree all crowned with blossoms like a king,
Stands in the garden with majestic air,

The lily and the lilac drink its health
In dewy wine from cups of tulips fair.

Narcissus' eyes from ecstasy grown dim,
The lilac's brilliant radiance cannot bear.

The Nightingale extends to passers by
The petal of a rose, with friendly care.

The clouds will sprinkle dew on flower-beds,
A breeze takes back on high a fragrance rare.

The morning songsters sing their roundelays:
—O verdure, pierce the pall of bleak decay!—

All have their gift who tread upon the earth,
And talent has its market-price, I say.

193

Some sing their love with captivating charm,
Others lament it in a mournful way.

Yet all have bid farewell to grief and pain
Delighting in a life of pleasures gay.

All, all around, yet you alone are mute,
Not joining in the rapture, you, my Heart!

You relish not the dreams of poesy,
And from the joys of glory you depart.

Aren't you the heart that in a sea of
                                    thoughts
As bright as pearls, would try the poet's
                                        art—

And with those pearls the brow of speech
                                        adorn
That to young maidens beauty do impart?

Now I know not from whence your sorrow
                                        comes,
Why you despair, and play a mourner's part?

My heart replied: Friend of my solitude,
Depart, I beg you leave me all alone.

Had I not known that in the wake of spring
The stormy autumn winds ascend their throne—

Then for the glorious fight a sword of
                                    words
For Poesy I'd forge, in whirlwind's moan.

But I have learnt the treachery of fate,
My end foredoomed by her, perfidious
                                        grown.

The bird that sees the net is surely mad
To seek the grain mid dangers, fully
                                    known.

194

The cries of glory loud now echo faint
'Neath turning sky, in yawning distance
                                thrown.

Speak not of day-dreams, for I know the
                                prize
That fate will give the dreamer for his
                                own.

O have you not then, ignorant of the world,
Of Pushkin—greatest of the poets,
                                heard?

Of that same Pushkin who was glorified
Throughout the world for wondrous verse and
                                word?

Whose pen in touching paper, a desire
To lose its whiteness in that paper stirred?

Bright as the movements of a peacock fine
His Muse a thousand vivid flowers girt.

Great Lomonosov decked the muses' fane,
But Pushkin's vision made it his domain.

Derzhavin won the literary realm,
But Pushkin was appointed there to
                                reign.

By Karamzin the cup was filled with
                                lore,
Yet Pushkin was the one that cup to
                                drain.

The glory of his genius ruled the West
As kingly power reigns o'er land and main.

His wisdom clear shone brightly in the North
As shines the eastern moon, with stars in
                                train.

The seven heavens and the elements four
To bear a son so fine would try in vain.

Now listen with amazement to the way
These parents dealt their son a deadly
blow:

They sped a fatal arrow at the bard,
And cruelly stopped his life's poetic flow.

One hail-stone smashed the fruit on his life's
tree,
And this was done by order of his foe.

The cruel wind of death put out his lamp,
And plunged his body in the dark of woe.

With ruthless knife the gardener pruned his
shoots
As of a tree not destined more to grow.

His head that held the treasures of the mind
Became a nest of thorns with snakes below.

The heart where nightingales his genius
sang
Is covered now with naught but thorny
sloe.

His soul has left his body like a bird,
To sorrow binding both the young and old.

The Russian land in grief and sorrow cries:
—Now death has caught its victim stark and
cold!—

O bard, your talisman could save you not,
The witch's grip has not relaxed its
hold.

You leave the earth, but may your Maker's
love
Your soul in mercy heavenly enfold!

Bakhchisarai sends you the fragrance sweet
Of your two roses, wondrous to behold.

The age-old Caucasus answers now your songs
With lays of Sabukhee, in anguish told.

Translated by *Olga Moisseyenko*

Khurshid-Banu Natavan

KHURSHID-BANU NATAVAN (1830-1897) was the Orient's first poetess to have a monument erected to her by her countrymen (in Baku). Natavan was born in Shusha, into the family of a khan. In 1872 she founded a literary circle in Shusha which united all the progressive poets of the time. Natavan's graceful, subtle verses speak of love and the beauties of Nature. But many of her poems are permeated with a tragic sense of loss caused by the death of her young son from tuberculosis.

Parted with you, I burn night and day,
Like a thoughtless moth in a candleflame.

Like a rose you were destined to fade and die;
Like a nightingale mourning its rose sing I.

My heart aches with longing to see you, my star,
I roam like Medjnun in search of Leili.

I whisper your name, for your presence I sigh,
Like a grief-stricken dove on a bough sing I.

Like Farhad from the source of my happiness banned,
At the foot of the mountain of parting I stand.

To My Son
Abbas

Your name all these days I have chanted and sung
Like a parrot with sugar under its tongue.

Haunted with sorrow, all day I wander;
Burning with grief like a Salamander.

My heart, that once soared in a heaven of love,
Broke its wings and was dashed to the earth from above.

Blind to the light of the sun and the moon,
Like a moon eclipsed, I am shrouded in gloom.

Through my tears your image I always see,
You dried up so soon, o my cypress-tree!

Oh, would I were blind not to see you dead.
The sun now scorches the earth, your last bed.

My hopes were frustrated; you left me and died,
I did not live to see you join your bride.

Your brown eyes expectantly looked at me;
Was it only that mine your shrine should be?

I weep tears of blood, to sunlight I'm blind,
As a lost soul I wander, Abbas, my child.

The anguish of losing you gnaws at my breast,
Tears flow from my eyes without respite or rest.

Translated by *Dorian Rottenberg*

Lilac

O flowering lilac, whose was the skilful hand that drew
you?
O Radiant-Featured, was it a loving slave that drew you?

Chancing to penetrate into your palace, garden,
O poppy-cheeked, was it a skilful gardener drew you?

In this flowerbed world there were all too many plain
faces;
Was that the reason why the almighty keeper drew you?

The flowers take their colours and fragrance from you,
As a flower the hand of the world's creator drew you.

What a wealth of gentleness shows in your beauty!
With her gift of fancy bestowed by God, perhaps it was
Natavan that drew you?

Translated by *Dorian Rottenberg*

* * *

Time has plunged me into an ocean of pain and woe,
Parted me with my sun-faced; all is dark wherever
I go.

My patience has reached its limit, O God almighty on high!
Either allow me to join him, or have mercy and let me die.

In vain I implored and begged you, you left and never
returned.
Now come and look at me, sun-faced, see into what I have
turned.

How long must I pine in longing—my life is all misery.
Have pity, at least for a moment; beloved, remember me.

What terrible tortures I suffer! Our parting I cannot bear.
Am I worthy of nothing better than eternal grief and
despair?

Our parting has stolen my reason, my soul has forgotten
repose.
Behold how merciless fortune has doomed me to endless
woes.

I wonder why my cruel lover will not have pity on me.
I burn in the flame of parting—the one who lit it was he!

How beautiful were those days when I was together with
you.
Now I am broken-hearted, sadly my fate I rue.

For a while I was reunited with my lover, that pitiless man,
But now I am once again lonely—I have become Natavan.[1]

Translated by *Dorian Rottenberg*

* * *

Beloved, how could you break the oath to me you swore?
Beloved, am I today not the same as I was before?

You seek new company, love, with other women you meet,
Have you forgotten me, the one that you once called sweet?

Yes, you have found another before whom you bare your
soul;
She is receiving the joy which from my life you stole.

My life is now a nightmare of infinite, black despair.
People talk of my madness always and everywhere.

Your heartlessness, o beloved, is driving me insane.
Have pity on me, have mercy, come back to me again.

[1] Natavan—miserable.

201

O Destiny, how cruel, how ruthless you are to me!
Who does he give his love? Who can the lucky one be?

Life overflows with anguish, with tears overflow my eyes;
But he, my fickle lover, turns a deaf ear to my sighs.

Why, have you been avoiding me all this time,
Me, the unlucky slave of a lord so truly sublime?

Love, you have driven your slave to the limit of
                                    desperation,
Gossips are calling me now the victim of sinful temptation.

Have pity on me, your slave, o my lord, my Padishah!
My lamentations echo throughout the world, near and far.

You and your love make merry, carousing day and night,
And I, your unlucky victim, have forgotten what is delight.

There was a time when you wanted nobody else but me.
Now you have changed, and your old love you even refuse
                                    to see.

What was the cause, my monarch, explain to your subject,
                                    pray?

What have I done that you leave me like a flower plucked
                                    and thrown away?

What shall I do, distraught and unhappy as I am now?
How could I ever have given my heart to you, oh how?

Make merry, my love, with my rival, feast and have a
                                    good time,
While I must weep tears of anguish because you're no
                                    longer mine.

Chirp with your newly-found mate like two nightingales
                                    on a bough;
And I—remember what I was like, and what have I turned
                                    into now?

202

Kill me, let Allah give strength to your ruthless hand!
What have I done to you that such torture I have to stand?

I sigh and I weep in sorrow, pain is tearing my heart.
Poor Natavan, your lot was unfortunate from the start.

Translated by *Dorian Rottenberg*

Said-Azim Shirvani

SAID-AZIM SHIRVANI (1835-1888) was the author of love ghazals, instructive poems and satirical verses. He was born in Shemakha, but went to school in Syria and Iraq where he received a higher ecclesiastical education. On return home, he renounced his cloth, and took up the pen to fight against the hypocrisy of the clergy. He made a lot of enemies among the fanatics, but undaunted by threats and persecutions, founded a secular school. Shirvani's trenchant satire which hit the oppressors between the eyes and at the same time called for brotherhood and honesty between men, was mainly printed in Ekinchi *(Ploughman), a progressive Azerbaijanian newspaper.*

A Word of Advice

My son! The unschooled man is an arrant ass!
For purest truth this saying will always pass!
It is, too, a truth of undoubted import
That beside the scholar, the rustic is naught.
The gift of tongues, it has been truly said
Is the greatest blessing bestowed by God.
He who adds one language to his store
Will be possessed of one blessing more.
Lay hold, then, on knowledge, my son, with both hands.
Seek always to learn, and seek to understand.
My son, learn as many languages as you may
But special attention to Russian pay.
We need to communicate with our brother
And must learn the language of one another.
In the Sharyat, my son, it was never written
That Arabic is the language of heaven.
God is no Arab, Greek or Abyssinian,
Nor yet a Frenchman, a Negro or Russian.
The words "God" and "Allah," "Khuda" and "Jehovah"
Are charged with the selfsame content. Moreover
No words should be subjected to abuses
By fools; but should serve those who know their uses.
And then no language will be accounted more
Or less worthy by God. Indeed, we have four
Books, each one written in a different tongue,
First, the Old Testament, in which God is sung
According to Moses in words of Hebrew.
Then the Gospels in Greek, in Persian—the Zabur.
Mohammed was born in Arabia, son,
And in Arabic we received the Koran.
However, had the Prophet from Turkey sprung,
It would surely have been in the Turkish tongue.
In a word, all who follow the twelve Imams,
Whether they dwell in Baghdad or Sham,
Are united to a man in the belief
That the Prophet can speak any tongue he lief.
We know the infallible Imam uses
Both French and Russian, even as he chooses.
If the Imam strove to learn new tongues,
Why should you not follow his lead, my son?

Translated by *Avril Pyman*

The Ploughman and the Khan

A ploughman walked cheerfully homeward one day
And met an illustrious Khan on his way.
On seeing the Khan he stopped and bowed low
To which the grand noble responded so:
"Get out of my way, you hound," he cried,
"Don't stand like a swine, or I'll rip off your hide!"
The ploughman, being accosted so
Came home in a flurry, all aglow.
His wife, observing his exultant mood
Said: "O my master, my radiant moon!
O Milky Way shining in my skies,
O sower of light, o light of my eyes,
O luminous star that guides me through life,
Explain your exultant state to your wife."
She begged and implored until her man
Said: "Know then, today an illustrious khan
Was haughtily coming along the road.
I stopped and, facing him, humbly bowed,
And the Khan condescended to speak to me."
"I'll never believe such a thing could be.
Who heard of a khan ever speaking to you?
Oh, tell me about it, husband, do!"
Beaming with joy, the peasant began:
"These were the words of the glorious khan:
'Get out of my way, you dog,' he cried,
'Don't stand like a swine, or I'll rip off your hide!'
Now, wasn't it gracious of the great khan
To deign to speak to a humble man?
Don't you see what a joy it is
To have lived to witness such heavenly bliss?
It will be the pride of our family;
Let it live till we die in our memory,
To be passed along to our children's sons,
That I spoke to a khan and met such response."

Translated by Dorian Rottenberg

In Support of the Newspaper
EKINCHI[1]

Salam to you, respected countrymen,
Whom cruel misfortune's chosen for its prey.
Salam to you, bent under ignorance's yoke,
My ignorant, illiterate native folk!
Already years ago poor Hassan Bek
Whose works like gems our Nation's history
                                    bedeck,
Arrived at the conclusion that we should
Publish a newspaper that would employ the good
Old language of our grandfathers and sires.
The authorities complied with his desires,
A proper cause for public jubilation.
He will gain nothing from its publication,
Yet what it means for the ordinary man
I will explain to you as best I can.
First, he will print the news of the whole
                                    world
Which earlier we never could have heard.
That in itself is much, you must agree.
Another benefit not lower in degree
Is that we'll gain new wisdom and new culture,
Learn news about the handicrafts and agriculture.
The seeds of knowledge will Hassan Bek's paper
                                    sow.
All about art and industry we'll know.
It will describe the modern ways of farming,
Our peasants with progressive knowledge arming,
Which is of course a veritable boon,
Because our people will be able soon
To reach the level of the most advanced
And cultured nations. Life will be enhanced.
In other languages we print a lot of papers
And yet their contents totally escape us,
Because we don't know either French or Russian.
We know a little bit of Turkic and of Persian
And that refers to a minority, alas!
Our people are illiterate in the mass.
Most suitable for us is *Ekinchi*,
Accessible to all and costing cheap.
I'm sure that *Ekinchi* will be our pride,
Our well-informed, superbly written guide.

[1] *Ekinchi*—Azerbaijanian for "ploughman".

So, men of wisdom, men of learning high,
Come, do not let our newborn paper die.
For if our paper ceases its existence,
Jesus himself won't render us assistance.
So, in the name of newborn *Ekinchi*,
Do not abandon it, whate'er may be.

Translated by *Dorian Rottenberg*

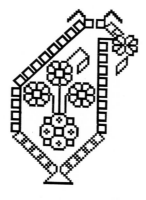

Modern Poetry

**Mirza-Alekper
Sabir**

(To Moslem and
Armenian Brothers)

The spirit of the times demands that we unite, my friends.
Peace is the aim for which we all have pledged to fight,
my friends.
In our beliefs there is no contradiction, am I right, my
friends?
Then why do bitter controversies us divide, my friends?

Movjuz Mirza-Ali Shabustari

(A Living Corpse)

No wonder at Ramadan trouble and quarrels reign.
If a poor man dares to complain, he is always found in
the wrong.
But if a rich man, for example, knocks out a poor man's
brains,
The officials will punish the one who dares to go and
complain.

Hussein Javid
(Yesterday and Today)

Today is not concerned with Yesterday.
New knowledge lights each minute of each day.
In every Darkness throbs at least one Gleam.
Each Truth—a womb that bears at least one Dream.

Samed Vurgun
(Azerbaijan)

Men know that you are mine by birth:
My nest, my refuge, and my hearth,
My mother, native land, dear earth!
Sever soul and body?? Death but can.
O Azerbaijan, my Azerbaijan!

Mirza-Alekper Sabir (Tair-Zade)

MIRZA-ALEKPER SABIR (TAIR-ZADE) (1862-1911) was a major folk poet, the initiator of revolutionary satire in Azerbaijanian literature, and an active contributor to the revolutionary-democratic journal Mollah Nasreddin. *Sabir was born in Shemakha, and he lived there all his life. The Revolution of 1905 had a powerful effect on Sabir's writing, infusing it with a revolutionary spirit and filling it with a social content. His pen did not miss a single political event, a single problem typical for the feudal Moslem world, and he embodied his ideas in stirring, thought-provoking images. He wrote about the arbitrariness of the tsarist officials, landowners and beks, about the duplicity and avarice of the mullahs, about the predatory policy of the imperialists, about the downtrodden status of women, and the position of workers and peasants. Sabir was an innovator in poetry, he experimented with form and style, extending the range of subject matter to reflect the social reality as fully as possible, and polished his verse to perfection, until it rang as clear, resilient and melodious as a taut string. Often he used a form which, without exaggeration or hyperbole, made the negative character expose and castigate himself. Sabir was very poor, he boiled soap for a living and was often ill. The last year of his life he taught Persian and Azerbaijani in a working-class suburb of Baku.*
The centenary of Sabir's birth in 1962 was celebrated as a national holiday in Moscow and Baku, where a monument to the poet was unveiled.

Thanksgiving

Dear colleagues, thank the stars above for the luck
we've had today!
The missionaries are our friends; now aren't we
glad today!
By every means we tried to close all schools until this
day,
But lacked the power to gain our goal, poor fools, until
this day.
Though we ordained that schools be closed, they scorned
us till this day.
We lost authority and weight, my friends, day after day,
But now our lucky star again ascends day after day.
Things have improved and our position's not so
bad today.
For the missionaries are our friends, so aren't we
glad today!
The missionaries have ideas—they're intellectual giants.
In Petersburg they've signed with us a business-like
alliance.
Why have, they say, so many schools to serve our Moslem
clients?
Can't they get on just as they are? What use have they
for science?
They'll get acquainted with philosophy and history and
so on;
Well, well, they say, we can't permit this sort of thing
to go on.
So let us see that schools enroll no girl or lad
today,
For the missionaries are our friends, and aren't we
glad today!
And since the missionaries had performed such noble
deeds,
How could we sit with folded hands and not take part,
indeed.
In short, we Moslem clergymen, with our business to
proceed,
A ban on certain sciences henceforward have decreed.
For children to be taught at school there surely is no need.
Of independent thought and arrogance we must stamp
out the seed,
While there is still the slightest chance, let's act, by
god, today.

219

For the missionaries are our friends, so aren't we
glad today!
You curbed the Moslems, missionaries, Allah bless your
souls!
And bring you to the true faith, missionaries. Allah
bless your souls!
Let Allah put the schools in ruins, missionaries. Bless
your souls!
Let Allah's holy will be done, O missionaries! Bless
your souls!
Let all of those who ever tried to open up new schools
Cry, rave, go mad, go wild with fury, idiots, poor fools!
Let teachers be thrown out of work throughout the
land today,
The missionaries are our friends, and aren't we
glad today!

Translated by *Dorian Rottenberg*

Ploughman

Don't wail, don't cry, don't pretend you're
                    unhappy, ploughman!
You old, sly fox, you won't catch us napping,
                    ploughman!
Under some pretext or other, daily you stand at my door;
Don't beg, don't ask me, don't stretch out your hand at
                    my door!
I'm sick of seeing the whole of your clan at my door!
Don't get ideas, don't wear out my patience,
                    ploughman!
Be dumb and obey me while I am gracious,
                    ploughman!
If the year brought you peasants no gain, what do I care?
If there was no rain and no crop of grain, what do I care?
If drought spoiled the rice and barley again, what do I care?
If last year your debt with your blanket you paid, what
                    do I care?

Now carry your rug to the market to sell,
                    ploughman!
Be dumb and obey, for assistance don't yell,
                    ploughman!
Don't try to explain that from hunger you're dying, wretch!
You'll never persuade me, so no use trying, wretch!
Pay what you're due—don't tell me you can't—lying
                    wretch!
Bring me barley and wheat, and rice, ploughman,
Or I'll take off your skin in a trice, ploughman!
Swear as much as you like that you can't—I'll have it!
By Allah almighty, I'll get what I'm due—I'll have it!
You'll be whipped and flogged black and blue—I'll
                    have it!

Don't forget yourself, pay your arrears, ploughman,
Don't overreach yourself, don't spill vain tears,
                    ploughman!
Your job is to plough; eat millet yourself; give me wheat,
                    ploughman!
As long as it's softer than stone—any stuff you can eat,
                    ploughman.
If you don't have water, their's plenty of snow to heat,
                    ploughman!

You have never seen butter or cream or meat,
                    ploughman,

You're used to a simple life, like a beast,
ploughman!
Haven't I always declared that I want good relations?
All an aristocrat wants is leisure and relaxation,
Idling, gambling, drinking and eating without cessation.
Such is a gentleman's life by tradition, ploughman;
It was Allah appointed to us such an earthly
mission, ploughman!

Translated by *Dorian Rottenberg*

To the Workers of Baku

The wheel of fortune's turning in a new way
nowadays:
The working men begin to think they're human
nowadays.
They poke their noses everywhere and always nowadays.
What are we coming to when working men breathe freer
nowadays?
They fight for rights and disobey the *overseer* nowadays!
The wheel of fortune's turning in a new way
nowadays;
The working men begin to think they're human
nowadays.
Now tell me, why do you demand respect, a simple
worker?
Why raise your voice, and what can you expect, a simple
worker?
All you should do is serve the rich, though they neglect
a simple worker.
Well-paid or not, you must be gratefully subdued, you
simple worker.
But the wheel of fortune's turning in a new way
nowadays;
The working men begin to think they're human
nowadays.
Don't plunge yourself into distress, take care, beware,
rich man;
If any worker speaks the truth, don't give him ear, rich
man!

222

Don't let the poor breathe freely—don't you dare, rich
man!
Don't yield, don't budge an inch, don't give in anywhere,
rich man!
For the wheel of fortune's turning in a new way
nowadays;
The working men begin to think they're human
nowadays!
Don't pay attention, even though they may complain, the
poor.
They've no expensive clothes nor homes—they've got no
brain, the poor.
No property, no riches do they ever gain, the poor.
All they possess are ragged coats, shoes torn, clothes
plain, the poor.
But the wheel of fortune's turning in a new way
nowadays;
The working men begin to think they're human
nowadays.
If you intend to be both free and merry in this world,
Just think about yourself, don't have a worry in this
world.
If you would have no load of woe to carry in this world,
Forget that other people's lots are sorry in this world!
Yet the wheel of fortune's turning in a new way
nowadays;
The working men begin to think they're human
nowadays.
To think about the plight of your poor nation? By no
means!
To sooth poor orphans and to stop their lamentation? By
no means!
To help the poor, to give them consolation? By no means!
Yet fortune's wheel is turning in a new way
nowadays;
The working men begin to think they're human
nowadays!

Translated by *Dorian Rottenberg*

To Moslem and Armenian Brothers

The spirit of the times demands that we unite, my friends.
Peace is the aim for which we all have pledged to fight,
my friends.
In our beliefs there is no contradiction, am I right, my
friends?
Then why do bitter controversies us divide, my friends?
To rash hostilities our enemies incite my friends.
Ah, is there nobody to show the way to light, my friends?
Speak up, authoritative, reasonable men,
And let us call for peace and friendship among men.
Two nations, two good neighbours lived and thrived in
one fair land,
For centuries they lived in peace and friendship in their
land,
But then the devil interfered, for quarrels tear their land.
And plunderers and robbers now run riot in their land.
Just look what ignorance has done to us, God give us
patience!
God help us bring to reason our two warring nations.
Speak up, authoritative, reasonable men,
And let us call for peace and friendship among men.
Who stands to gain from it, who's the inciter of the feud?
What inhumanity! What, in the first place, caused the
feud?
Did Moslems or Armenians first spill their brothers' blood?
Sheer ignorance or someone's secret hand must have set
off the feud.
Our tragic strife we surely have the right to blame
On those who vilely instigated it and fanned the feud
to flame.
Speak up, authoritative, reasonable men,
And let us call for peace and friendship among men.

Translated by *Dorian Rottenberg*

"My friend, in what state is your glorious city today?"
"God be blessed, it's the same as it was in Noah's day."
"Have you new schools for the young of your country to
learn in?"
"No, we've only Madrassahs, which stand since the year
Adam was born in."
"Do the citizens in your land read newspapers every day?"
"Some literate madmen do, but I don't, I must say."
"Now tell me, my friend, are there libraries in your town?"
"Young people opened a few, but we turned them upside-
down."
"Are the hungry helped in your country by other men?"
"God sees their sufferings himself—why should we help
them, then?"
"Do you take care of widows and women that are in
need?"
"To the devil with them—can't they marry again,
indeed?"
"Is the need for unity talked about in your land?"
"Yes, it is, but for eloquence's sake, you must understand."
"Is the nation split into shiites and sunnites still?"
"What do you mean? For such words, young man, you
ought to be killed."
"Well, there is nothing else I can say to you, so good-bye."
"Good riddance! I wish you to fall in a pit and die!"
"Just look at him! Look at his face—what a loathsome
sight!
"The way he talks! Why, he can't even put his cap on
right!"

Translated by *Dorian Rottenberg*

The Odd Sneeze[1]

As soon as we start to realise things
It sounds among wise men—that mighty odd sneeze.
When we say we have got to normalise things,
    It sounds among nobles, that mighty odd sneeze.

Or else we decide on some fine enterprise
For years keep discussing it, buzzing like bees.
It's time to get money and start, say the wise,
    But then all through the country it sounds, that odd
                                                sneeze.

This misfortune happens not only with us—
It sweeps all the Caucasus like a foul breeze.
If Kakhi, Kazakh or Sheki start to fuss—
    In Shusha and Shirvan it sounds, that odd
                                                sneeze.

It never stays in one place, but goes on,
It changes its residence with the utmost ease.
They say it was heard in Gyanj, but it's gone
    Away to Salyani, that mighty odd sneeze.

That unlucky odd sneeze—be it ever accursed—
It won't let us speak, it resounds without cease,
As if thunder has sounded and lightning must burst,
    All over our squares sounds that mighty odd sneeze.

It won't think of decency—never a bit;
At meetings, assemblies—wherever you please,
There's nothing like shame or fear for it:
    In mosque cells, in shops sounds that mighty odd
                                                sneeze.

Translated by *Dorian Rottenberg*

[1] According to Oriental superstition, when anybody sneezes once or any odd number of times, all undertakings decided on at that moment are doomed to fail. A double sneeze is a good omen.

When the people of Iran heard the news that their country was to have a constitution, one old man fell on his knees in the fields and exclaimed:

> Great Allah be praised; over Iran, our prison,
> The dawn of the Constitution has at long last arisen.
> The very foundations of evil have suffered a blow;
> No more will the village elder plunge us in woe.
> The foul flame of tyranny has been put out.
> Iran will again be a paradise, no one can doubt.
> The wanton authorities have been bridled at last,
> And the peasants' sufferings are a thing of the past.
> The ploughman will never be beaten again any more,
> He will not be insulted, maltreated again any more.
> The landlord won't squeeze us out any more,
> No, from now on he will never curse and shout
> any more!

A Short
Sketch

No sooner had he finished, than a farrash (official) sent by the authorities appeared on the scene and, in full sight of his family, tied the old man's hands and bade him go to the landlord on foot, while the official himself rode after the peasant on horseback.

The landlord came out with a whip in his hand and thus addressed the peasant:

> Yeah... a whole month has gone by since the day
> When the wheat was threshed and stored away,
> And where have you been, you worthless old lout?
> You took all the crop for yourself, no doubt!
> And what did you bring your landlord, eh?
> All the fruit from your garden you hid away.
> Neither barley nor wheat have you given your lord,
> Neither peas nor beans have you given your lord.
> You ought to be pinched a little, peasant,
> To teach the rest of your people a lesson.

The unfortunate peasant, with downcast head, shivering and shaking, replied to the landlord:

> I am a beggar, I swear by our Maker!
> I own no land—not even an acre.
> All I have is a family to clothe and feed;
> We are always hungry, neck-deep in need.
> All this, my lord, is well known to you.

227

This year brought a drought—which you also knew.
We lost all we saved, it was hot and dry;
Our wailing and moaning shook the sky.
We ourselves, I swear, have no clothing or bed;
At home there isn't a dry crust of bread.

On hearing this, the landlord flew into a rage and shouted: "Make a good fire, my lads, fetch the canes, heat the skewers!" Four hefty servants bound the man hand and foot and began beating him without mercy.

LANDLORD
Beat him, beat him, he didn't bring grain.

PLOUGHMAN
Can anyone human stand such pain?

LANDLORD
Whip him, beat him, I am drunk with rage!

PLOUGHMAN
I can bear it no more; pray, pity my age!

LANDLORD
Beat him—he didn't bring butter and cream!

PLOUGHMAN
Spare me! My cows have died—you have seen!

LANDLORD
Go on; the Mejlis[1] has driven him mad.

PLOUGHMAN
Spare me; the government took all I had.

[1] Iranian parliament.

228

LANDLORD

He's been utterly spoiled by that cursed constitution.
I'll teach him to dream about revolution!

PLOUGHMAN

The tails of your whips are like hornet stings!

LANDLORD

The coming of freedom has given him wings!

PLOUGHMAN

God help me, this torture is too much to bear;
Accursed be oppressors, everywhere!

Translated by *Dorian Rottenberg*

For Sale

People won't be silent, uncle, when they hear the tale;
Bah! It doesn't matter, does it, what sneers it may
entail.
Write it down on paper on a wall to nail:
I've opened here in Reh[1] a new tremendous sale!
    Dirt cheap, the wares my shop displays for sale;
    Come buy! The whole of Reh today's for sale!
And what is more, I do not sell that article alone,
But with the Jami-Jam, Reh's subjects, Kubbad's
throne,

Although I'm somewhat hindered, I must own,
By certain Young Iranians[2] well-known.
    But never mind them—wholesale and retail,
    Come, buy, the whole of Reh today's for sale!
What shall I do with all that bric-a-brac?
So many cares it brings, it sure will break my back.
That "Salty Water"[3]—not much use, alack!
I'll better sell it all before the sky looks black!
    The palace of Shiraz, the heritage of Reh today's
for sale!
    Come, buy! The whole of Reh today's for sale!
I hate the light—I offer gloom for sale,
I love to see Iran under its veil.
I want to leave the city—deserts, hail!
I'd be a khan—being a shah seems stale.
    Sabsivarah and Meyameh's for sale!
    Come, buy! The whole of Reh today's for
sale!
My will is mine, my words, my home as well,
My honour, self-respect, the shame into which I fell.
My wealth—who else but me its fate may spell?

My Kajar[4] crown and state today I sell.
    Whose business what goods I display for sale?
    Come, buy, the whole of Reh today's for sale!

[1] Reh—former name of Teheran and Iran as a whole.
[2] Political group opposing the Shah.
[3] Caspian Sea.
[4] Dynasty rulers in Iran before enthronement of Pehlevi.

Instead of being constitutional shah,
A publicly elected guiding star,
The army's puppet—not a sovereign by far,
Instead of always saying Oh! and Ah!
    I'd drink wine as a khan—my crown today's for sale!
    Come, buy, today the whole of Reh's for sale!

Translated by *Dorian Rottenberg*

Abbas Sikhat (Mekhti-Zade)

ABBAS SIKHAT (MEKHTI-ZADE) (1874-1918)—was one of the first Azerbaijanian poets to write for children. Abbas was educated at the Teheran University, in the department of medicine, and had, besides his native Azerbaijani, a perfect knowledge of Arabic, Persian, Russian and French. His home was in Shemakha, and he lived there all his life. He made a name in literature as a romantic poet, talented and progressive educator who compiled the first textbook in Azerbaijani, as the author of poetry about Nature which children gladly memorise, and as a translator of Krylov, Pushkin, Lermontov and Nekrasov into Azerbaijani.

It is a beautiful evening in May, soon after sunset. The silver crescent of the moon rises and moves through the soft blue skies, gliding among the fragrant trees, pouring its light on the fields and the calm, smooth surface of a river. A poet sits alone on the riverbank, gazing at the beautiful moonlit landscape. Suddenly he stands up and begins speaking:

The Poet, the Muse and the Citizen

For months, for years I have gone without
occupation;
This idle life has already exhausted my patience.
I know not why I am wasting my time and health.
Such a state is a burden, God knows, to myself.
Instead of sitting and gazing at a beautiful view
And wandering lonely all day, brushing off the dew,
Were it not better to find a means of mending my
plight,
To forestall future troubles, to put my affairs to
right?

He rises, intending to go away. But at that moment there is a crash like a peal of thunder. Everything around is thrown into confusion. On the top of a tall hill he sees a radiant apparition—a young maiden with a musical instrument called the *santura* in her hands. She addresses the poet with these words:

My poet, look around at Nature's wealth and
wonder;
Behold my beauty: is it not a theme for a ghazal?
The apparition approaches the poet, holds the instrument
out to him and says:

Take this *santura*, poet, play, for spring is yonder.
The time has come for songs and love, and all is
well.
Caress me, come, kiss my sweet lips and brows,
My golden curls, my lovely, daffodil eyes,
And let my love an ecstasy in you arouse;
Come, sing a song and let it fly into the skies.

POET

Sweet maiden, I have long grown weary both of
passion and of love.
Life's cruelty has put a curb on my imagination.

No more thirst I for lips soft as the feathers of a dove;
Now all I think of is my family situation.
One asks for bread, another cries for shoes and clothing;
An angry creditor reminds me of my debts.
In this mood all I feel for rhyme is loathing.
Go, find a freer heart and mine do not upset.
I have renounced all love, all passion and all beauty,
Forsaken you, my muse, my poems and my pen.

MUSE

O thankless man, to have forgotten inspiration's light!

POET

You think that I am full of gratitude to you
For that fine gift of yours, for urging me to write,
For winning me with beauty? It was you who made me
                                                    rue.
Had I not met you, foes would never mock me now.
Had you not thrilled me, I would never earn men's hate.
I'd be a merchant hoarding money, rich and proud.
People would honour me! They'd come and celebrate
A gorgeous funeral after my death; "What a good man
Was that Hodjah!" Or I'd be a mollah and tear
The hides off people while explaining the Koran
Just as I wished. Both child and adult then would bare
Their heads before me, calling me defender
Of shariat and fearless champion of Islam.
But ever since I was enslaved by you, your lips so tender,
Behold, in what a sorry, awful plight I am!
No longer do I yearn to sing and to write verse.
They will not mend my terrible condition.
My love for you has only been a curse.
See—everybody shames me. Is it not sufficient?

MUSE

Ungrateful man, in this fast-fleeting world what lot
Can be more splendid than the lot I granted you?
The dazzling heights gained by your spirit—are they not
The best reward? I have inspired you, and made you live
                                                    anew,
Saved you from mental torture, opened up your eyes.
I let you feel the truly heavenly bliss
That human spirits feel when they attain the skies.

234

I let you contemplate both hell and heaven, and for this
You tell me that I only made you feel unhappy!
I, best of all your friends; how did it happen?

POET

My muse, you are the cause of my disastrous plight.
Now, thanks to you, I have no hope, no money, no delight.
When, as an unexperienced boy, I went to school,
You first appeared to me and gave me inspiration.
At first arithmetic seemed easy with its rules,
Mere childsplay—then I shunned division and multipli-
                                                cation.
Day after day you gradually drove me mad,
And made me hate my school and wander idly.
So I gave up my studies for my verse, however bad,
Began to write sheer nonsense and behave quite wildly.
My childhood ended soon, and yet my muse was not
                                                forgot.
In step with public taste, I chanted songs and wrote ghazals.
Whatever trade I took up to improve my lot
I would forsake: you came and said, write verse and
                                          nothing else.
You put into my heart my people's aspirations,
You filled me with compassion for the burden that they
                                                    bore.
All for my love of you, I followed you with patience,
Spoke out against the rulers for injustice that I saw.
Soon my melodious words aroused the hate of evil men,
The crowd of my ill-wishers grew throughout the land.
At one time people, angry at my caustic pen,
Would beat me up, but still my foes I'd brand.
Then, losing hope of changing my behaviour, at long last
My family became my enemies too—you know it.
Now I have understood my fault; my craze has passed.
Farewell, my muse. And know that I denounce the calling
                                                of a poet.

MUSE

My poet, don't regret; this is a transient world.
Only the spiritual world will last, believe my word.
Now go, in service to mankind seek your reward.
Only in truth can lasting joy be found, so let your word
By all the world, by all humanity be heard,

235

And may the force of evil not destroy your thirst for good.
Come, rise into the realm of pure delights,
Upon the evils of this world do not forever brood.
Do not forget in your frustration poetry's pure heights,
Do not succumb to baseness; fly like birds on high!
Shun slavishness if you are longing to be free,
And be prepared to sacrifice yourself for truth, even
to die.
Give up your comfort, leave vain hopes, for only he
Who loyally serves truth deserves a poet's name.
A poet's thoughts must be forever free and pure.
Come with me, I will lead you on to fame.
Yes, come with me, and you will taste real bliss,
be sure.
I will acquaint you with a world of unknown joys.

POET

O my beloved, joy of melancholy hearts,
With boundless gratitude I take your offer. This day starts
A new life for me. Where you say I'll go.
No other guide but inspiration will I know,
Only to free myself from insults and from lies,
From bleak despair, from thoughts that torture night and
day.
Let me look down with pity on this world from the pure
skies.
Come bear me on your wings, my muse, let's fly away!
Let me compose new songs that will relieve men's woes.
And let my word make hearts rejoice where'er it goes.

The poet utters these words in mounting ecstasy. Then
he falls into a swoon and lies motionless upon the ground.
The heavenly apparition disappears from sight. The poet
is lost in wonder and confusion. An unknown citizen
appears before him. He approaches, looks at the poet
attentively and with a bitter smile, says to himself:

CITIZEN

Now look upon this fellow here, how peacefully he sleeps,
Does nothing, does not write, just idles time away.
But wait! Perhaps he's ill? How motionless he keeps.

236

Is he alive or dead? I cannot really say.
The poet hears the citizen's words, opens his eyes, sits
up and says:

POET

Dear man, you also ought to say, to add to your description,
That I am like Medjnun, intoxicated with my woe.

CITIZEN

Yes, truly a fine picture! Now explain me your
affliction.
What is this apathy? Are you alive or dead? Why so?

POET

I am tired out. What can I do? Man, what would you
advise?

CITIZEN

Listen to me. Just be a man. Get up, open your eyes.
Indeed, this is a picture fit to make one sick.

POET

Well, have you said all that you wanted? Go now, quick!

CITIZEN

Why, are you not ashamed, young man? What a dis-
graceful state!
Think what you're doing, man, before it is too late.
In times as grave as ours a person with your powers
Should not stay basking in the sun, idling away the hours.
At times like these all men who heart and conscience do
not trade,
Who aren't indifferent to the fate of their own nation
Must feel obliged to rally to its aid.
Indeed, its awful plight should rouse their indignation.
With all the fame, all the authority that your poetic gift
has won,
It's a disgrace that you sit idle when so much has to be
done.

POET

Well, even if I do have talent and poetic power,
How could I be of help to my compatriots at this hour?

CITIZEN

What nonsense! Listen, you're a poet—am I wrong or
right?
Well, does your pen no more obey you? Man, can't you
write?
God sent you to this earth to offer people aid,
Their hopes, their joys, their sorrows to express—for that
you're made.
Arise, be bolder! Speak, rouse hearts to action, go
And help your nation cast into the depths of woe.
Do you not see how much we suffer, your own folk?
Your brothers, sisters, all your land is in distress.
Do you not notice how they pine under their yoke?
And all you do is roam, make love, play cards and chess.
You spend your time on boulevards at night, in clubs by
day.
How can you squander time like this in various sorts of
games.
When you should help your countrymen in every possible
way,
When your long-suffering land your swift assistance claims.
Say, must a son not think about a mother in distress?
Say, can a son not feel deep anguish for his mother's plight?
A man should sacrifice his all at such a time, unless
He's sacrificed his conscience in pursuit of vain delight.

POET

Stop, man, your aim's quite clear to me, don't lecture
here in vain.
Only the really talented are fit to do such deeds.
And I am weak, a coward, idle and inane.
To win men's favour, I make up ghazals and songs indeed,
Yet most of what I write is void of content, life and
motion,
Just baubles, jingles, jokes and senseless puns.
Where shall I take the talent, tell me, and the high emotion

To be a nation's hero and a leader all at once?
You think a poet ought to be immortalised in song?
Believe me, all your notions on the subject are quite
wrong.

CITIZEN

You needn't be a genius that lays new roadways for
mankind
Or write great poems with ideas we never heard before.
I do not say that talents such as yours we seldom find,
But since you have the gift, come to the fore!
Write, but not empty songs and meaningless ghazals.
Express your thoughts about your land, be heard, speak
out,
Set free the noble soul that in your bosom dwells!
For you must be a patriot at heart, I do not doubt.
Today all citizens must rally without fail.
Come, be a man and join your people, aid your brothers,
speak!
Or sit at home like an old woman, wrapped up in a veil.
Yet whether man or woman, young or aged, strong or
weak,
Ruler or subject, never mind, all to a man
Must do their duty to their motherland as best they can.
Just as on winter nights the light of tiny stars
Illumines the expanse of all that pitch-black vault,
Just so must you, with your unpolished, modest verse
Stir men with great ideas, compelling like a thunder bolt.
Come, poet, raise a tempest in men's hearts and minds.
Put all your misery and grief into resounding lines.

POET

You speak the truth, I see that there are things you
understand,
And yet you have no knowledge of the motives guiding me.
Don't think I have no feeling for my nation or my land.
It is impossible to write with a pen that isn't free.
I swear by all that's true, by my own honour, by my pen,
By sky and earth, by heaven and hell and by the midnight
star,

239

My conscience prompted me to write again and yet again—
To write the truth, the truth alone, and yet I can't, so
there you are.
Just try and start to write of the divinity of truth,
And they will stop your mouth for you. Do you need any
proof?
A fist will always hang above you as a ruthless token.
They stop your mouth—all words stick to its roof,
And then you bitterly repent that you had spoken.
And so I'm forced to write ghazals and songs that idlers
sing.
I overstrained myself—the road's too heavy, all uphill.
How can a bird soar skyward when a trapper ties its wings?
And so I pine and lose my strength and weaker grows my
will.
Helpless am I. Though a grown man, I can't hold back
my tears.
My heart is tired and can no longer bear the weight of woe.
I beg you, give me patience, God, a spirit proof to fears;
That is my final, only plea to you before I go.

Translated by *Dorian Rottenberg*

Progress and the Law of Nature

One summer evening I walked for an hour
On the hill of the ancient Virgin's Tower.
I surveyed the old battlements one by one,
The tower and the walls in the setting sun,
And unusual thoughts arose in my head.
The world is like us, to myself I said.
It is born, it lives, develops, grows old,
Then dies, leaving ruins lifeless and cold
Where owls make their dwellings, inspiring awe;
At the root of all life lies a single law:
All is born, develops and then decays—
It is the principle on which all Nature is based.
Change underlies progress; if there were none
Life would not develop, would not have begun.
This law is of infinite scope and range:
Evolution continues only through change.
Men, too, are born to bear offspring and go.
Nature teaches a lesson that all should know:
Renewal prolongs the life of a nation;
This was true from the earliest days of creation.
All passes on from one state to another.
Where is ancient Greece—art and culture's mother?
Where's the progress of old and old renewals?
How many towers like this lie in ruins,
Replaced by new towers with new sculptures and pictures!
Where are the Assyrians, Romans, Egyptians?
Babylonians, Persians, Parthians, Midians?
Time has destroyed them by millions and millions,
Leaving nothing behind but a meagre trace;
And it happened because they were out of pace,
Because they did not improve, but stagnated;
Deterred on their course by beliefs outdated,
They all disappeared as if never begot.
Now tell me, what does not alter, what?
In plants and animals changes are wrought;
Then why should there be no change in our thought?
By Nature's law, all must change and move,
'Tis a fact that History, too, can prove.
It's to change that all nations owe their birth;
Stagnant nations are swept from the face of the earth.

Translated by *Dorian Rottenberg*

241

Movjuz Mirza-Ali Shabustari

MOVJUZ MIRZA-ALI SHABUSTARI (1873-1934) was a revolutionary satirist, prominent in southern, Iranian part of Azerbaijan. He was born in the village of Shabustar (hence the pen-name) into a merchant-class family. He lived for many years in Turkey, returning home just before the first Russian revolution of 1905, where his satirical verses aimed against the rich who exploited and oppressed the people made him subject to ruthless persecution. Movjuz also wrote a large number of poems about the revolutionary awakening of the people. He wrote about Lenin and the Soviet Union with admiration. His poetry enjoyed great popularity, and people learnt it by heart in those days when writing in Azerbaijani was prohibited by law in Iran. Movjuz died in Iran of tuberculosis.

Only sultans and generals taste peshmak and nogul,[1]
Chicken and Sadri rice are for those whose pockets are full,
When he's got tasty plov, kebab and meat in the larder,
"Potato soup's good after breakfast," says nobody's fool.
Sugar is sweet and clean, it needn't be peeled,
Though imported from Lakhistan,[2] it does fine for a meal,
Poor man, don't narrow your eyes, don't look with suspi-
cion at sugar,
For plov, orange-juice and syrups are for the rich man's
meal.
Horse-radish, beetroot, salt peas, bread and cheese are
the poor man's lot.
Oranges, tangerines, lemons and cream are only for
Khans, by God.

For Sultans Only

Those underpants swathing your legs and your belly in
blue
Come to us from the Sudan—Iranian cotton? It's not!
Bright samovars, teaspoons and tablespoons, glasses and
saucers,
Teacups and teapots, they all come from foreign sources.
Mirrors and doublewick lamps, chandeliers, braziers and
wall jugs
Are German in make—a fact unknown only to horses.
But, friends, why worry your heads when earthenware
pestles and pitchers
Are genuine Iranian products, though certainly not of
the richest.
Telegraph, telephone, motorcar—all these gewgaws are
foreign.
Yet the horse, camel, donkey and mule are truly Iranian
creatures.
Anasha,[3] too, comes from Iran, and opium's Iranian too.
Drink and smoke! But don't use vodka—it's the devil's
own brew!
These lamps that hang on their posts and illumine our
streets at night
Are made by giaours, unbelievers—who'll venture to say
I'm not right?

[1] Oriental sweetmeats.
[2] Poland.
[3] Alcoholic drink.

243

Gaji-Rassul[2] matresses weighing a full three batmans[1]
each
Are fit but for fatnecked bullies with fists of enormous
might.
Ladders, four-legged stools, rolling pins, window-frames,
doors,
Rattles, walking-sticks, logs all have Weigan[2] as their
source.
But—the phonograph costing you 55 tumans
Which you daily enjoy, comes from the U.S. of course.
Prostitutes, whores and fast women—all those who cater
for Man,
Travelling brothels and public houses—all come from
Khorasan.
Witchdoctors and fortune-tellers are certainly foreign
produce,
Just as bowls on which fortunes are told come from Zanjan
and Kashan.[2]
Crows are the national airplanes, sparrows—our air-
balloons—
A brittle category of goods; rough handling gives them
wounds.
A team of seventeen preachers has taken hold of our
mosques,
Yet people think these "commodities" belong to Allah—
what fools!
Dissension, conflicts and sects are alien to Islamic religion.
They say such things are imported from Loristan and such
regions.
O my people, Movjuz is in a sarcastic mood,
But the things he chastises really deserve derision!

Translated by *Dorian Rottenberg*

[1] Batman—measure of weight.
[2] Towns in Iran

Unlucky Ghuneian[1]

Have you heard the news, disappointed, unlucky
                                        Ghuneian,
That a new official has been appointed, unlucky Ghuneian?
The government wants two thousand workers, Ghuneian,
Their provender to be supplied by you too, unlucky
                                        Ghuneian.
They must go to Tauriz, rocks to hack, unlucky Ghuneian,
And build there a brand-new horse track, unlucky
                                        Ghuneian.
Those spendthrifts spend money on vases, gold and silk
                                        blankets,
Slaves of the golden calf, money in heaps they stack,
                                        Ghuneian.
The Shah's henchmen tie your people to trees to flog them,
                                        Ghuneian.
In the words of Kulsum Khala, they plunder and rob them,
                                        Ghuneian.
They levied six hundred tumans for winter fuel, Ghuneian,
Allegedly for the troops in Sharafhana,[2] Allah curse them,
                                        Ghuneian.
The rich, the Mollah and the scribes are exempt from
                                        taxation, Ghuneian.
All the burden falls on the poor, all the grief and
                                        vexation, Ghuneian.
Let them shoulder the other end of the log, Ghuneian—
Those gentlemen, should not they pay like the rest of the
                                        nation, Ghuneian?
And as if that were not enough—grief comes not alone,
                                        Ghuneian,
Though Lenin's cause is alive, he himself is dead; what a
                                        blow, Ghuneian!
The tears don't have time to dry in Ghuneian eyes;
It weighs us down, the unbearable burden of woe,
                                        Ghuneian!
The roads to Tiflis[3] and Stambul are all blocked, Ghuneian,
And the starving people sit home as if locked, Ghuneian.
Learn Russian, learn to weave wool—that's the only way
                                        out.

---

[1] Ghunei—small town in Southern Azerbaijan.
[2] Sharafhana—village near the city of Urmia, now Rezaiah.
[3] Tiflis—old name of Tbilisi, capital of Georgia.

245

But heavenly voices forbid us—bad luck, Ghuneian!
The mollah curses those who learn to control machines,
                                                 Ghuneian,
To be able to weave woollen fabric—do you see what it
                                          means, Ghuneian?
The mollahs teach you grammar at school, nothing else;
They forbid geography-teaching—quite funny it seems,
                                                 Ghuneian;
Is anything said about aircraft-building in the Koran,
                                                 Ghuneian?
Read its thirtieth chapter, please, if you only can,
                                                 Ghuneian.
It speaks about loving your land, but I doubt whether you
                                               understand,
Though you shout about it both day and night, you're
                              an ignorant man, Ghuneian!

Translated by *Dorian Rottenberg*

Nakhichevan Has Turned Soviet

Allah be praised, at last our nation is glad:
Nakhichevan in a crimson gown is clad.
Just Soviet power has been established,
The exploited masses are ruling the land.
The Shah is mated, his viziers dismounted,
The elephant[1] tramples on the khans uncounted.
Buds are unfolding, the season of flower has come,
The nightingale's singing his song of love.
The people everywhere feast and rejoice.
Other regions envy Nakhichevan for its choice;
Tauriz, Khamina, Shahbustar[2] show their envy
Together with Azerbaijan[3] in one voice.
Not in vain is our envy, its cause is clear:
While they're having a wedding, we're mourning here.
And yet, Movjuz, do not weep bitter tears:
The day of delivery for us, too, is near.

Translated by *Dorian Rottenberg*

[1] Shah—Persian for king; *elephant* is the Persian equivalent for *castle* (pun on chess terms).
[2] Towns in Iran.
[3] Movjuz comes from Southern Azerbaijan, implied here.

247

A Living Corpse

Plunging me into cares, it has come, the month of the Fast.
How I wish it would give us miss and would hurry past!
Cup-bearer, if by chance you encounter that holy month,
Give it a few good kicks, take it, I beg you, to task!
Say to it: "O month of the Fast, O Ramadan, cruel knave,
Don't torture us, wretched people, don't come on like a
tidal wave.
Go wherever you like, but do not come to Tauriz,
We have got to save our bodies, before we can save our
souls".
A poor man has anyway nothing to eat from dawn to dusk.
Allah should never allow poor men to face such a task.
O you who have juicy *shashlyk* for supper every day,
Rich people, come and observe how we save on every rusk.
When night falls, my poor Khanum fills with water a
jug to the brim—
And cooks in it a morsel of meat, my poor Khanum.
Now look at the harm all this fasting does to us, poor
people.
It weakens a poor man's heart and makes his reason
grow dim.
I begin to thrash the children, and Khanum acts like a
mad dog:
Khanum starts scolding me; her, too, I kick and flog.
No wonder at Ramadan trouble and quarrels reign.
If a poor man dares to complain, he is always found in
the wrong.
But if a rich man, for example, knocks out a poor man's
brains,
The officials will punish the one who dares to go and
complain.
Oh, these awful days of spring, what a commotion they
bring!
Lay your head on a pillow, lie until night as if slain!
O infidel, don't let your eyes to the clock in the corner
stray!
Should a Mollah command, "Lie down, we'll cut off your
head"—I'd obey.
But I can't bear serving God with such terrible tortures
as fasting.
By my soul, by my heart, I swear I prefer any other way.
If I don't drink tea at dawn, I go around as if lost;
If I am cursed for not fasting, I'm ready to pay the cost.

The Mollah, he plunders the poor, and I am an honest
man—
He has more sins than I—let him pray to God and fast.
O miserable Mollah, you'd declare Ali[1] a giaour,
Like a wretched Yesid you'd usurp, if you could, all
power.
You and your clownish like have quite a definite aim
Which is clear to anyone who has brains in his head and
not flour.
Honour is all that remains in your poor flock's lockers,
While the golden tumans have leaked away into the
moneybags' pockets.
You embezzle 10,000 tumans collected for the needy and
poor,
Then pretend you are poor yourself, spreading mats on
the floor for carpets.
Cup-bearer, today I chanced to travel through Beraber.[2]
My eyes were drawn of their own accord to a woman
lonely and old.
Sitting there in the street, tormented by hunger and cold.
She had nobody in the world—an outcast without any
rights,
All she lived on was alms, torn by want and despair.
The sight of that living corpse wrung my heart with pain.
As I looked at the woman, I tried to hold back my tears,
but in vain.
The wretched woman resembled a time-ridden plank of
wood
As she sat begging alms on the ground in the darkening
lane,
Her black hair round her yellow face like a funeral frame
of crepe.
She laid her head on a stone, seemingly half-asleep.
There was something in her that showed she had once
seen pleasure, too,
But then had suffered defeat, drunk the cup of grief in
full measure.
Whoever looked at her face could tell that she was quite
weak;

[1] Ali—cousin of Mohammed, dethroned by Yesids, a tribe of
flame-worshippers.
[2] Persian town.

249

And when I saw her I thought: this is the end, I'll
                                                    wager!
But she opened her eyes with fright as if at a distant
                                                    crash.
And when they opened I caught a black, all-expressive
                                                    flash.
But soon they had closed again and her head fell back
                                                    on the stone,
And she sat there again as before, forsaken, defeated,
                                                    alone.
The rich hurried on to the mosque to perform their
                                                    daytime prayer,
And your poet drew a deep sigh, a searing sigh of despair.
God, is there any way of saving this wretched nation
From its burden of want, and starvation, sorrow and care?

Translated by *Dorian Rottenberg*

My nation, may I implore your forgiveness;
I called a prayerhouse a tavern—my mistake.
Someone knocked his head on the wall and broke
it:
I called the wise man a fool—my mistake.

How could I know the crow has a pretty voice?
I call an owl an owl—too much risk I take.
Also, I was a little upset at one time
And called a rascal an owl—my mistake.

I dreamed one fine night that a certain young
man
Lay in bed with a beauty—both wide awake.
It seems I was drunk with the juice of the
grape—
So the dream was just rubbish—my mistake.

My Mistake

Stop your eternal abuse of moustachios,
Wearers of gold teeth to task do not take,
Live in accord with the spirit of the times
And learn from your children, said I—my mistake.

The dread foe of Islam hovers over your heads.
Wake up, or your temple he surely will break;
Be silent, think about saving your soul—
I said to readers of the Koran—my mistake.

On seeing the newspaper held by Jafar
The Mollah, with fury, began to shake.
Like a bomb he exploded when I compared
His fat features with bellows—my mistake.

Said I, Meshadi, give your cash to the poor,
And all your sins on my head I will take;
Help the needy, naked and helpless—no need
To go praying to Khorasan—my mistake.

Dear brother Haji, do not worry in vain,
Give your wealth to your nation, deprived by fate;
If the giaour grants our nation his credits
He will pocket Iran, I said—my mistake.

251

My brethren are sleeping as if they were dead,
Day and night they sleep on and never awake.
I thought they were silent, just keeping a secret,
So I said to my faithful kalyan[1]—my mistake.

They got up and in fury seized their daggers
And beat me—I thought my bones they would break.
And I had expected the Moslems to praise me
For waking them up from their sleep—my mistake.

Any friend must tell a friend all he thinks,
To set him right for his own dear sake.
I thought religion was my nation's enemy,
But they called me an infidel—my mistake.

Translated by Dorian Rottenberg

[1] Oriental smoking implement.

Lenin

We will always rely on Lenin, following in his wake;
You must always give Lenin his due, O Movjuz,
In these difficult times he overcame all for our sake,
Bringing poor people happiness, justice and peace.

Translated by *Dorian Rottenberg*

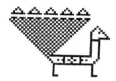

Gadjikerim Sanyly

GADJIKERIM SANYLY (1878-1937) wrote mainly about the life of Azerbaijanian peasants. In 1937, he was slandered and arrested on false charges, but his good name has since been cleared. He published several volumes of verse in which he described the hard lot of the peasants in tsarist times and the changes wrought in the peasants' lot by the Revolution.

Our Mountains

Land of freshness are our mountains,
Ravine-pitted are our mountains,
Lovely, queenly are our mountains—
Without them will I pine away.

Pierce the white clouds do our mountains,
Friends with stars bright are our mountains,
Snows in winter on our mountains,
Flowers in summer blossom gay.

Spring's a fine time in our mountains,
Grasses green adorn our mountains,
Grand and glorious are our mountains—
Indeed a paradise are they.

Translated by *Arthur Shkarovsky*

Hussein Javid

HUSSEIN JAVID (1882-1944) was an outstanding representative of Azerbaijanian romanticism, poet and dramatist, the author of tragedies in verse. His popularity has spread well outside the country. Javid was born in Nakhichevan and educated at the University in Istanbul. He taught Azerbaijani and literature in Nakhichevan, Tiflis and Ganja, and then, in 1919, settled permanently in Baku. Despondency and disillusionment are characteristic moods for his poetry of the pre-Soviet period: he complains against the injustices of the world, calls for protest, and dreams of better times, of freedom. It was then that he wrote his historical drama Sheikh Sanan, *which is still popular with Azerbaijanian audiences, telling about the love of a Moslem for a Christian girl, and the triumph of love and humanism over religious bigotry. In the subsequent period Javid wrote historical tragedies and romantic dramas preaching humaneness, and also poems and verses about the new Soviet reality, about working people and their lofty ideals. In 1937, Javid was slandered and arrested on false charges, but his name has now been cleared and his rich legacy restored to its rightful place in literature.*

It was a fashionable salon, and how the laughter rang;
The glasses clinked with mellow sound and only half-
tones sang.
The gilded chandeliers like diamonds shone with facets
seven,
And dripped with crystal star-drops bright as any stars
in heaven,
As they caught the maze of lights, reflection-wise.
O many were intoxicated, with bright and swimming eyes;
And languidly they kissed, or in a frenzy and with thirst,
Through the laughter and the noise reciting lyric verse.
As if on a stroke of the clock, the mood changed all around,
The tints and the tones of rapture faded, the cries died
down.

Prisoners of "Freedom"

And the rhythm of dance music throbbed, and the dancing
began—
Each invited his lady-muse, and in whispers the song-
motif ran
Through the dancers who swayed on their toes,
Clinging, enraptured, and dancing with eyes half-closed.
The music fell down to a whisper remote, and the lights
went down—
A crimson spotlight beamed, and the room into darkness
drowns
Lit only by falling leaves, leaves of a sharp September
That flutter down like sparks in embers.
The merry eyes seem dulled in a drowsy dream,
And from some far horizon appears a rosy gleam
That glimmers and melts, as lips to lips are pressed,
Like a friend concealing secrets in its breast.
The quiet of the steppes recalling Spring from a far
recess—
And the flowers nod and speak with tongues of sweetest
tenderness;
The fountains wreathe in a murmuring movement of
spray...
Of a sudden, this beautiful panorama dwindles away,
And the music fades and passes.
Through the reigning silence again rings the tinkle of
glasses.
In the semi-darkness, twilight-soft, like a muffled guitar,
On the stage appears the chanteuse, a famous star.
First in a throaty whisper her voice pulls at your heart,

257

Then rises with warmth as quick as birds' wings dart,
And falls again to a doleful sound
As the singer breathes of her love profound:
O God! Around me a net it wove—
Love, love, and forever love.

*   *   *

Wild flowers knelt before me,
After me the turtle-dove cries,
Dawn spreads its light within me:
They found passion in my eyes.

When the Shepherd's Star upon me smiled,
I was sure that I was Heaven's child;
I never knew Life's bitter sting,
Till a golden cage confined my wings.

*   *   *

The curtain fell, and the ovation broke the trance...
And the music called for another dance.
Again the languorous eyes light up with passion's bliss,
Again the desire rose in each to embrace and kiss,
Again the goblets are filled with rosy wine;
To get their breath back, the dancers take their seats and
                                        half recline.
The stage lights up, and then appears
The answer for all hearts, despite their years:
Living statues, nude, but a rhapsody
In flesh, their lissome bodies all one ecstasy.
And one young goddess, surely of Music's fane,
Stands on the stage like a thoughtful, sad refrain.
"Oh, what art, what loveliness and charm!"
The public cry, as the curtain closes like fronds of a palm.
Now several people leave, but the rest stay on.
Lovestruck fanatics, wanting to postpone dawn.

*   *   *

Eyes flash with passion, hearts seek the bud-like Spring
                                        to claim,
And every hunter closes on his game.
But rich Americans come in, say five of them or ten—
And the ring of gold comes ringing then.

258

The naked girls, as if from an old, exotic fable,
Take heart, spread wings, and join them at the table.
The target's reached by every glass of wine,
Anything goes, and nobody draws the line.
Passion throbs in the temples, intoxication drowns the
                                                    mind:
Into one curtained loge, a couple stagger as if blind.
And laughter bursts till the curtain shakes with the gust,
And then all hell breaks loose in unbridled lust.
The proud American stags don't spare their gold
To kiss the European girls, such lovely things to hold.
Watching this Bacchanal orgy, Azer holds his head,
Swept by nausea, wishing he were dead.
Not far away, three women sit alone:
Faded and old, and talking in low tones.

FIRST WOMAN:

"My poor daughter's still quite young. But we've little
                                                    means.
Our lives were wretched. Troubles strike unforeseen.
And even this stinking place seemed to us paradise.
But she's going crazy—from drink, and all this signifies."

SECOND WOMAN:

"In the war, my husband and my brother died.
Left me poverty and two girls—none wanted them as
                                                    brides.
(points at one curtain)
There's only lust and passion in this den,
Given full reign by wild and aging men."

THIRD WOMAN:

"Behind that curtained silk, it's strangely silent, I fear.
But my daughter said: 'Mother, wait for me here.'
So I wait. I have to: there's no other way.
Whatever she gets, small or big the pay,
We live on it, though little enough it buys."

And she could not hold back the tears that filled her eyes.
From all this, Azer's heart within him bled.
He thought for a moment, and suddenly said:
"Once upon a time, perhaps, in the Asia of yesterday,

In the Caucasus, as in Africa, it was the way
To sell and buy a girl by force, for gold.
Yet Europeans called it vile, I'm told.
They called us depraved, and made believe they were
shocked. . .
Made drawings and took photos—all our ways they
mocked. . .
But what do you call this? The soft-natured eyes
Of these same Europeans avoid and quite despise
A young maid's tenderness and love when for sale?
Are these the so-called 'normal situations' that prevail?
Aren't they ashamed, this dreadful business to uphold,
Where a loving daughter must sell herself for gold
And her mother sits and trembles, waiting for the pence.
O hateful, wild society whose culture is all pretence.
It looks like a thriving business: poetical, but for their
wages,
The doves themselves fly into all these golden cages
In hope of getting enough to last life through.
Any cage is good, if there's plenty of money, too!
They fly after money. . .
and settle like flies on honey. . ."

⁜ ⁜ ⁜

"Let go of me. I'm choking. I'm dying. . . Ooh!"
"Whose voice was that? Who called? Oh no!"
And the mother guessed; no sound, and all was still.
She screamed—her voice was loud and shrill,
"O God!" she sobbed, and fell half in a faint.
Her voice, "O God, they've killed her!" cracked all
restraint.
So the curtain was pulled back, but it was too late.
Such a crime, only wild passion could generate.
In the fashionable salon, now a terrible silence fell. . .
And the silence smiled on a flower dead, but the smile
was out of hell.

Translated by *Gladys Evans*

Masud and Shafiga are talking on their way to the oilfields beside a settlement near Baku called Balakhany. Shafiga draws Masud's attention to the oil derricks some distance away.

A Talk Between Masud and Shafiga

SHAFIGA:

Look! As far as eye can see—a forest of enchantment!
Like a panorama viewed from a magic casement!
Do you see it as I do? All that you said is untrue...
You told me—remember?—if one searched the whole
town through
One could not find a single park; there'd be not one in
sight.
But aren't those trees, after all, now dry, don't they prove
you were right!
How's this for a view? How really marvellous it seems!
You look, and the joy of Spring enters your heart. It's a
dream.
Who could help being happy, walking through such a
wood?
Why, heavens above, Masud! Doesn't it do your heart
good?
(her face darkens)
That's a sarcastic laugh you have... your look's simply
frustrating!
What's on your mind, then? Talk, don't keep me waiting.

MASUD:

Well, what can I say? It's a very pretty picture you drew—
Everything's beautiful... love on earth: but too good to
be true...
Not an everyday sight. The place makes a marvellous
impact—
But your fantasy's a dream. It doesn't agree with the
facts.
People are always looking for happiness in day-dreams.
But Truth—is more tears than smiles, strange as it
seems.
Take that cypress there, for instance, it certainly draws
the eye:
But better take a good look at those towers like cypresses
high.

261

They're not green, are they? But black as the soot from
a stove.
A forest of dirty oil-derricks—grove after grove.
They are dark ranks of tombstones, alive with awful
sound:
And what a foul, repulsive smell they spread here, all
around.
This is no forest cool, with flowers and grass—all is bare
and harsh.
If you go closer, you will see there's only an evil marsh.
You won't find even water fit to drink. It's pure hell.
Black, ugly pools all over from these ever-spouting wells.
And what you call a forest... stinks to heaven! Nothing
grows.
It kills a man, chokes him to death: and no one cares, or
knows.
Those working here lose all their strength and forfeit all
their health:
And from the workers' sweat and toil—why, others grow
in wealth,
And fatten on the poor fools' patience, utter lack of rights.
On the workers' faces you may read their fate, their plight
Among the boring-wells, smoke-blackened.... There's your
lovely view!
Yet they keep hoping sometime things will change, a new
Life will dawn, and fortune's smile at long last on them
will beam...
Oh, what dreams they have! What sorry, ridiculous
dreams!
And what they don't endure for all those dreams. If you
but knew
Just what their life is like. I wish you'd look, and look
anew!
What you would see you could not bear, from tears your
eyes would grow red—
And that is how these human souls must earn their daily
bread.

SHAFIGA:

No, oh no! I do not want to look. Come, let's go away.

MASUD:

But why? Won't you tell me why, my darling? Why not
stay?

262

SHAFIGA:

Need you ask, why? Bend down and listen how my heart
beats:
You'll know then how I feel. I did not know all this deceit.
Look at me! Now I see here only cruel catacombs.
How can I bear to look, unmoved? While it's light, let's
go home.
Now I shall think only of the needy, the strangers and
the sick—
Who come to work here for a crust of bread ... and are
foully tricked.
Why, our parts give only bitter fruit to these unfortunates.
I'm sorry for them. Such cruel labour brings no benefits.
If you think of the kind of labour, the pay is very slight:
On their bent backs the sun burns down as if in spite.
They are black with oil. They keep on coming... here
awaits
Them only a hard life. Even death may be their fate.
They all have mothers, wives, and children, a home
abode—
These wait for their return, with eyes turned ever on
the road.
Sad and lonely, hungry families in some far off land
Expect them back ... today, tomorrow ... just as planned:
In vain. The workers' eyes will close upon the world. They
won't survive.
And could you call this life, even if some do stay alive?
They live as if in mourning—live on hope, on hope alone.
They all have sunken chests; half-naked, skin and bone.
So they live today; and so tomorrow, if at all—
Backs bent, up to their knees in mud, until their final fall.
The slimy holes and oil-filled pools will form their graves:
Fate itself prepared such bogs for all these sorry slaves.
Such is life, hard life; and somehow people drag it out.
I wonder how many souls have died on these derrick
torture-racks?
Some with smashed ribs, or hands, or broken backs....
No matter where they come from, here they are all equal:
One end is sure—a bitter cruel death will be the sequel.
No, no, I won't go closer. My pity knows no bounds—
I feel that trouble haunts each derrick, waits all round.
The workers have tormented faces: there's no joy here,
or peace...

263

Only a torrent of black oil, and faces dark with grease.
Yes, they are ranks of tombstones and not cypress trees:
A forest, but a dead one, no grass, no green—I weep
That some such torment sow and others suffering reap.

MASUD:

Upon this question, angel mine, you've made a slight
mistake.
You have the right idea, love, but I wouldn't have you
make
It out that all the world is pain and grief; with no delight.
Homes now have light and warmth; and all our world's
more bright.
The black oil gushing from these wells is a real force:
For people's happiness it has become a living source.
This is gold, real treasure, flowing from these fields.
Just think what these wells mean, and what they yield:
They are man's new idol, and the road to riches pave—
The country without them practically faces the grave.
The cities grow in splendour, and in social eminence—
A wider, happier life will come from this magnificence.
The fine statues, the beauty, improvements that come on
the scene,
In town all you've felt or heard about or ever seen
Is the proud product of these wells—so evil-looking here...
Now do you understand? You know what it means, my
dear?

SHAFIGA:

Better than you, perhaps. It is clear, some will have
splendour,
Live the rich life of the well-to-do big spender—
And never know grief or sorrow, or deepest poverty.
Well, let them have it, their full life. But here is misery.
All these needy creatures slaving among the oil wells—
Let them swallow and choke on this gas straight out of
hell?
Let them fade from day to day until at last they die?
The question is: Why? Why must they live like pigs in
asty,
In damp sod dug-outs, through the hottest sun or pouring
rain?

264

Then where is justice, and where is truth? You think
it is humane?

MASUD:

It's a complex question, and one difficult to solve;
I haven't the strength to do it. Yet we should involve
Ourselves. To find the answers in our day
Is almost beyond us. But these questions will not stay
Unanswered, as sure as there's a sun up in the sky—
To all the questions in our hearts, the Future alone can
reply.

Translated by *Gladys Evans*

Yesterday and Today

Happy the shining eyes—but yesterday:
Here grief and mourning lies—but come
                                    today.
Brave words so full of cheer—but yesterday:
Full of despair and tears—but come
                                    today.
Gay heart of yesterday—it aches
                                    today.
Dead dreams of yesterday—revive today.
Old Fortune is a jade—without a heart:
Always with man has played—and torn
                                    apart.
With her it's all in play —to smile,
                                    betray.
He, sentenced yesterday—is judge today.
Unlucky, yesterday—in luck today.
Those happy yesterday—are sad
                                    today.
A different world today—new laws, in
                                    fine;
The cups of yesterday—held blood, not
                                    wine.
The king of yesterday—a slave today.
The slave of yesterday—a king today.
The pledge of yesterday—washed out
                                    today.
The long-time enemy—a friend today.
And Nature's not able on land or sea
To stay quite stable, eternally.
Without exception, changes all creation.
The law of life is "perpetual alteration".
What does not change? It's inconceivable.
Could there be such a law—inflexible?
Just as firm steel is gnawed away by
                                    rust
At ever step the Great turns into
                                    Dust.
Today is not concerned with Yesterday.

266

New knowledge lights each minute of each
                                                    day.
In every Darkness throbs at least one Gleam.
Each Truth—a womb that bears at least one Dream.

Translated by *Gladys Evans*

Abdulla Shaik

ABDULLA SHAIK (1881-1959) was a well-known poet, playwright, prose writer, teacher and enlightener, who did a great deal to elaborate the principles and methods of teaching Azerbaijani in the primary school. He was the first writer to depict in prose the plight of oil workers under the conditions of predatory capitalist exploitation at the beginning of this century. His popular verses for children and his educative stories in verse laid the basis for modern Azerbaijanian children's literature. Abdulla Shaik is the author of Araz, a novel dedicated to revolutionary youth, several plays, short stories and memoirs.

The Promised Bride

In the dark of night she sits alone—
Tomorrow's bride—and bitterly bemoans
Her hopeless lot, nor have her hot tears quenched
The ardent protest in her heart entrenched.
She sits, hands clasped about her knees, despairing,
And with just revulsion dully staring
Upon her jasper ring. And her wild curse
Should sear with burning shame the universe.
So speaks she: "With this ring I am mated.
This ring, this heart! Each, alas, ill-fated!
Oh spirits, say, how have I roused your ire?
That Div and Peri to my fall conspire?
Like a beast, for gain I have been traded.
Like a felon, sentenced and degraded.
Oh fate, why should you mock at me and scoff
Tending a gold spittoon when blood I cough?
There is no help for me. I am alone.
My cry would sure get pity from a stone.
My father slammed the shutters on my Dawn.
The unopened bud is paired with the gnarled thorn."

Translated by *Avril Pyman*

To the Revolutionaries of Our Time

Where are you, helmsmen of our native land?
Your ships are tossed on the waves of the ocean.
Is it silenced, your voice full of fire and emotion?
O my people's glorious heralds, respond!

Has the courage that once filled your bosoms failed?
Have the storms and tempests barred your way?
Have your arms lost their strength and vigour, say?
No, you're strong and brave as when you first sailed.

Strive forward to reach your great destination,
Arise and struggle, alert and brave.
Fight with the tempest and storm the wave,
Forward, my heroes, with determination!

At dawn, when the sun in the sky ascends,
You will cast your anchors safely near shore.
The gloomy mists will detain you no more,
And your native land will welcome you, friends!

Translated by *Dorian Rottenberg*

Look Forward

Don't think of the past, my lamb, let it sleep, let it lie.
Don't raise the curtain hiding it from your eye.
It conceals a thousand steps leading down into a dark
abyss,
And on every step dragons and snakes twist and hiss.
Try no more to unveil it, let memory spare your heart,
Don't play on the saz of the past, or your wounds will
begin to smart.
Do not touch it, let it forever stay in its tomb;
Don't allow your life, o my flower, to be drowned in
eternal gloom.
Go forward, never turn back if there is no need.
Think of days to come, to the future alone pay heed.
Remember, those starry eyes, the ornaments of your head
Are given to you to see only that which lies ahead.
Let your eyes watch the radiant road that leads you
onward to light.
Always strive forward, my love, do not stop, keep your
aim in sight.
On the dark, tempestuous past let the veil of oblivion drop.
March forward with steady steps, march forward and
never stop.
For in front, believe me, there lies, a beautiful, radiant
world
Where the banner of happiness will be forever unfurled.

Translated by *Dorian Rottenberg*

All of Us Are Born of the Sun

Used to oppressing and being oppressed,
Is there no feeling, no fear in your breast?
O man drinking blood and vomitting blood,
Has your conscience been nipped in the bud?
Are you pleased with the bloody life you lead?
Men's kinship has been forgotten indeed,
Yet all of us come from a single nest,
All were born of the sun and fed at its breast.
No difference of language should tear us apart,
No distance should sever heart from heart.
Neither Gospels should part us nor the Koran,
Nor the boundaries set by shah or khan,
Neither rivers, nor lakes, nor seas, nor oceans,
Neither mountains, nor deserts, nor storms ferocious,
Neither North, nor South, nor East, nor West;
Let us tear hostility out of our breast:
This foul-smelling butchery—let it cease.
Let us give to each other the hand of peace.
Let us tear out the roots of oppression and strife,
Let fraternity lead us towards a new life!

Translated by *Dorian Rottenberg*

The cocks begin their crowing before the dawn.
Before the mists from vales and mountains are torn,
The chabans drive out their flocks to meet the morn,
Surveying with pride this land where they were
                                    born;
    All these mountains own the shepherds' sway
    For here the chaban is both khan and bey.

Beautiful is the morning in these places,
To me it is inestimably precious,
Birds sing and shy flowers deploy their graces,
Lovelier than tongue can tell are these great
                                    spaces.
    All these mountains own the shepherds' sway,
    For here the chaban is both khan and bey.

Master of the Mountains

The sun has risen and climbs above the heights,
Touching the clouds and flowers with colours
                                    bright,
Putting the scurrying mountain mists to flight.
The towering peaks with beauty are bedight.
    All these mountains own the shepherds' sway
    For here the chaban is both khan and bey.

Friendly are these vales to those who look for rest;
A myriad flowers on the meadow's breast
Bloom, making the earth itself a land most blest,
Clear as a crane's eye, springs well from depths
                                    unguessed.
    All these mountains own the shepherds' sway
    For here the chaban is both khan and bey.

When the sheep and goats return at evening
Ewes maa, lambs baa, the hills themselves are bleating,
And dogs are barking an exuberant greeting
To set the echoes ringing at their meeting...
    All these mountains own the shepherds' sway
    For here the chaban is both khan and bey.

On mountain, meadow, steppe, where'r you look,
Behold! The chaban stands, resting on his crook,
He keeps his sheep beside him and will not brook
Their straying! Master and servant of his flock.
    All these mountains own the shepherds' sway
    For here the chaban is both khan and bey.

With his staff the shepherd strolls mountains, valleys.
A truss of firewood is all he carries
Except his flute: sheep are his only worries
And wisdom gleams in all his saws and sallies.
     All these mountains own the shepherds' sway
     For here the chaban is both khan and bey.

At pure, ice-cold springs his honest thirst he slakes,
For meat the fattest, tenderest lambs he takes,
On flowerstrewn valleys he walks, and sleeps, and wakes,
And drives his flocks away before the first snow-flakes.
     All these mountains own the shepherds' sway
     For here the chaban is both khan and bey.

All his property: rags for his booted feet,
A rope for firewood, a wool chukhá to beat
All weathers; a treasure, which his day dreams sweet
And cheerful bayat most richly do complete.
     All these mountains own the shepherds' sway
     For here the chaban is both khan and bey.

Translated by *Avril Pyman*

Aliaga Vakhid

ALIAGA VAKHID was born in 1895 into the family of a carpenter in Baku, lived there all his life, and died there in 1965, a few months short of his 70th birthday. His satirical verses and ghazals began to be published in 1914. Later, he mainly wrote ghazals on traditional themes of love, loyalty and the pain of separation, which gained wide popularity and were usually performed to the tune of classical folk melodies. During the Great Patriotic War (1941-45) Vakhid was a frequent guest at army units and field hospitals where he recited his love poems and satirical verses. For this he was awarded the medal "For Valiant Endeavour in the Great Patriotic War", and also the title of Merited Art Worker of Azerbaijan.

* * *

My heart, beware of maidens fair with tresses black and
smart,
Their wiles will drive you to despair and make your wits
depart.
How can a man so madly love and die not in the flame,
Just think of what the moths must bear that round a
candle dart.
For you have not been yet ensnared within the net of love,
Do not be tempted, like Medjnun, by tresses loose, o heart!
If Rose were faithful, she would not be friendly with the
thorn,
And Nightingale in garden fair would not despair and
smart.
To be a friend of charmers is a woeful thing, indeed,
There'll come a day, they'll turn away, from you they
will depart.
If new Zuleika were your love, and you a Yusif were,
Aspersions soon would hasten you into the grave, o heart!
Among prim beauties did Vakhid spend all his adult days,
Think not this truthful word absurd, I beg of you, o heart!

Translated by *Eugene Felgenhauer*

* * *

She has turned her back upon you—very well and good.
But you pine and languish for her—tell me why you
should?
I have told you not to suffer and your longing quell,
But in yearning you've persisted—very well and good.
She, the one you loved so dearly, loves another now,
You can break your heart with sighing—very well and
good.
I have told you: shun black tresses, tell me, was I right?
Now you've really lost your senses, and I said you would.
Why did you allow a stranger to approach your love?
Satan hasn't gone from heaven, though he really should.
Oh, Vakhid, we've reached a juncture in this world of
ours,
When the people all run equal risks, now is that really
good?

Translated by *Eugene Felgenhauer*

This beauty has poetic, charming eyes,
Bewitching eyes that daze and paralyse.
Of all the earthly beauties she is queen—
There is no other with such charming eyes.
This lovely beauty that can soothe the soul
Has rarest eyes that draw and hypnotise.
Take care, my heart, when you that beauty see—
Her eyes intoxicate and tantalise.
A lover that she meets is soon ensnared—
Her eyes can all attract and paralyse.
No other beauty has as much been praised,
For she has tender, charming, crafty eyes.

Translated by *Eugene Felgenhauer*

Mikail Mushfik

MIKAIL MUSHFIK (1908-1939) was a poet-innovator who left an indelible trace in Azerbaijanian literature. During his short life he produced an enormous number of poems and verses which give a panoramic view of life in Soviet Azerbaijan. In his lyric poetry and large poetic canvases carrying a compelling civic message, he extolled the new man, and the new world where emancipated labour and creativity have triumphed. Mushfik used a colourful idiom, almost colloquial, and his verses are songful and sincere. He seemed to have a premonition of his early tragic end, because he called himself, or rather his poetry "a crescent that will never become a full moon".

Sing, Tara[1]

Sing, Tara, sing, Tara, sing!
Verses of beauty go dancing around,
Sing, Tara, sing, Tara, sing!
Dew on my soul is each sweet ringing sound.
Sing, Tara, sing, Tara, sing!
Who can forget you who once heard you sing?
Grief of the people, the tears of their
       heart—
This is their music, their fiery art.

Buildings that face the kiblah heard your
       scales,
Everything heard you, the sky and the ground,
Fathers in fur caps and mothers in veils,
Sighed as they listened to each singing
       sound.
Now it was gladness, now sadness again,
Gaily but warily glided the strain.

Full of deep sorrow you sing your lay,
Making all travellers go the wrong way,
Mountains and gorges re-echo your tunes,
Waves give an answer and echo the dunes.
Sing, Tara, sing, that in reverie I'd hear
Vernal ghazals of Seid, ringing far,
Sing, Tara, sing to enliven and cheer
That town of Shirvan—the entrancing Ganja.

Those who feel ill, find no pleasure in food,
Those who have heart-ache, a sorrowful mood,
Those who don't welcome the merry Spring-tide,
Mounting no more the inviting hill-side,
Those who are racked by pain in the breast,
Luckless and loveless, whose souls find no rest,
Found consolation and comfort once more,
Relish of life, peace of mind at your door.
Tara, your high notes and low notes are heard
Piercing the air like the song of a bird,
Yet by a different emotion you're stirred,
Charmed is your heart, sweet your melody rare—
See the sad maiden with long, wavy hair;

1 Oriental musical instrument.

279

Grief in your chords, Tara, painfully throbs,
That is the reason your melody sobs,
Numbers of people all heard how you groaned,
Palaces heard you of Shahs and of Khans,
Hearing you wailing, in unison moaned
Times immemorial and century spans. . . .
Sometimes your strings pacify and console,
     Tara, the love of my soul!. . .
Carpets with patterns so colourful, fine,
Tints from the labouring hands, showing blood,
There on the carpets, in leizure, recline
Women with lips like a flowery bud.
Cup-bearer, help me, your wine has grown cold,
Come, do not harass the girls, you're too bold!
Eloquent poets with hungering heart,
Poets inspired to work with their art,—
Bards like Vagif and Nadim, men of lore,
Fathomed of beauty the charm to the core,
Listening, they heard how you murmured and sighed,

Heard how you sang, how your chords rang and cried.
Now for us, Tara, come, tune up and sing!
Who can forget your heart's wonderful ring?
Tara, no mosque did your song ever serve,
Always you struggled for life's happy verve.
Some disregarded your wonderful song,
Had no compunction in doing you wrong.
Who were the foolish who caused you to smart?!
Brainlessly, wickedly breaking your heart,
Dashing above you—a black, cruel wind,
Hurting your strings, causing pain of all kind.
People who loved you—to grief were assigned!
Kindly you said to the people: "Be gay,
Laugh! do not sorrow, let grief fly away!"
Still the deep funeral melody swelled,
Tears through the melodies gathered and welled.
Sorrow remained and we saw no one smile,
People were sad and they wept all the while.
All of us wept, shedding hot, bitter tears,
Torn by predicaments, tortured with fears.

Tara, sing now, times have changed it appears.
Over the radio sounds your dear voice,

Over the wide world for folks to rejoice.
Tara, sing louder and gladden my heart,
Sing to my ear your melodious part.
Bard, take your saz, sing of freedom at last,
Turbans and robes are now things of the past.
Tara, tune up, sing; your fiery lay
Called forth the blushes of many a fay—
Blushes of maidens so lovely and gay.
Strings of the tara are golden and bright,
Songs of the tara—a source of delight.
Sing, Tara, sing, let your strings evoke
Happiness in the hearts of my folk.
Tara, in hearing your beautiful strain—
Happiness, peace I am sure to attain.
You are a weapon today in my hands,
I can make use of your tunes hot as brands,
Using you, Tara, quite freely at last,
One of your songs is enough to cast—
From every soul all the ghosts of the past.
                    Sing, Tara, sing!
People are standing about you, a throng,
Waiting to hear the delight of your song:
Workers of factories, women and maids,
Men on the tractors, and hands of all trades!
Sing, there is no one your song to restrain!
Bitterness, sweetness are part of your strain:
This is the fiery beauty in you—
Art of my native, industrious Baku,
Cotton-fields vast of Ganja—poets' town,
Silk of Sheki,[1] its silk-worms of renown.
          Sing, Tara, sing, Tara, sing!
Songs of great beauty go dancing around,
          Sing, Tara, let your chords ring!
Dew on the flame of my soul is each sound.
          Sing, Tara, sing, Tara, sing!
Who can forget you who once heard you sing?!
Life of the people, the joy of their heart,
Here is their wonderful, fiery art!

Translated by *Olga Moisseyenko*

[1] Azerbaijanian town.

What My Heartbeats Said

My heartbeats said:
"There's luck ahead. . . .
Great, glorious days
That brace and daze
    Are yet to come!"

There's more ahead. . .
My heartbeats said:
"Noble work, no fret,
Toil's pearly sweat—
    Are yet to come!"

My sires define:
"Past times were fine". . .
These words I hate,
My heart says: "Wait!
The sun's hot rays,
Cool springs, bright days
    Are yet to come!"

Translated by *Olga Moisseyenko*

Love of Life

O how to part with this great world around,
That grows more beautiful as time goes by?
O how to part with friends, forever bound
To struggle with the earth and with the sky?

Do not become the dew at break of day,
Shine like the sun, o heart, on mornings
                    new!. . .
How from this world to tear myself away
That revels at the hem of skies deep blue?
Look over there—the sky seems growing light,
And friends have met beneath the morning star. . . .
O how to part with dawns that shimmer bright
Like nuggets of pure silver, shining far?
How rich is Nature, how mysterious too,
When you disclose her secrets, engineer!
How to discard the sense, the feeling new
Attached to stones in quarries, rising sheer?

282

Here hawks soar high where lofty mountains loom,
There pheasants breed, and springs like mirrors gleam...
The nightingales, the gardens fair, in bloom,
O how to leave this sight, this lovely dream?

With life that is an endless, lasting fight,
With kindling flames that rage in blood and heart,
With sun and moon, with morning and with night,
And with the sky's vast cupola, how to part?

Before my eyes the iron breakers fume,
The sea is grim, the storm winds keen and tart,
Like lacy flowers sweeps the snow-white spume....
With poetry, with day-dreams how to part?

O stars—the candles of each cherished thought,
O clouds—dream caravans that stir my heart,
Celestial sphere—my feelings' airy port,
With these vast azure heavens, how to part?

My cherished love appears before my eyes,
I feel the flame of my poetic art,
My burning breast must ease itself with sighs:
With her sweet raven tresses how to part?

The nightingale is sorrowing near the rose,
Though autumn comes—he lingers to depart,
Life, life! this cry of longing ever grows:
With love, with burning passion how to part?

With feelings new you string your singing lute
My youthful pen, now just about to start!
O friends, give answer to my pain acute:
With this great seething fire-flame how to part?

Translated by *Olga Moisseyenko*

Samed Vurgun (Vekilov)

SAMED VURGUN (VEKILOV) (1906-1956)—poet, playwright and academician, a writer who truly belonged to the people, marked a new stage in the history of Azerbaijanian poetry. Using a great wealth of expressive means he depicted the life of his people at the turning points in its history. He sang a hymn to the women of new Azerbaijan, to revolutionaries, to working men and to our heroic ancestors who fought for the independence of Azerbaijan. He expressed the image of Azerbaijan, "whose son I shall forever be". Vurgun's best-known works are his heroic dramas Vagif, Farkhad and Shirin, Khanlar, the poems "Basti", "Komsomol" and "Mugan". He translated Pushkin's Eugene Onegin into Azerbaijani, for which he was awarded the "Big Pushkin Medal". Vurgun's death from lung cancer was mourned by the whole nation. A monument has been erected to him in the square in front of the railway station in Baku.

I've walked these mountains again and again,
Passed by the springs bright-eyed as cranes,
And caught the distant plashing strain
Where quiet Araks' waters moved:
Here love and friends I've truly proved.

Men know that you are mine by birth:
My nest, my refuge, and my hearth,
My mother, native land, dear earth!
Sever soul and body?? Death but can.
O Azerbaijan, my Azerbaijan!

Azerbaijan

As mother to me, as child to you—
Such is the bond we ever knew:
I'd come back wherever I flew,
For you are my people, you—my nest,
My native birthplace ever blest.

When I'm away, your face unseen,
When times and forces intervene,
My hair is touched with silver sheen—
For months and years press age on me:
My land, don't blame your absentee.

Your mountain crests are topped with snow,
And cloud—a shawl of fleecy flow,
Your past is greater than we know.
Your age from everyone obscured,
And none may guess what you've endured.

Evil tongues spread defamation—
You lived through years of dark privation.
Still, generation to generation
Your fame lives on: a benison
To happy daughter, happy son.

Across your valleys long I stare,
On clear days full of lucent air;
My spirit broods on faces fair,
Thirsting for poetic tongue—
Creating verses makes me young.

Khazar the sea you border on
Where floats the legendary swan...
My day-dreams sweep me swiftly on
To Mugan Lowland, on to Miell:
A long life road—half-done, I feel.

The mountain ranges, valley sweep,
Gladden the heart till it could weep...
Glimpse of startled fawn and chamois leap—
How much beauty on which to gaze!—
Pastures cool and steppes ablaze.

Cross the mountains, over steppe-land,
Or through Astar, Lenkoran—
From African and Indian strand
Birds fly to visit, with us pause,
Freed from oppressive grasping claws.

It's here the yellow lemons grow,
The heavy branches weighting low.
Up in the mountains, white the snow
And deep from winter's opulence:
Since Creation—a true defense.

Lenkoran is a dazzle of flowers,
Refreshed by the springtime showers,
Clustering on beds and bowers,
My motherland's delightful daughter,
Bordered on by Khazar's water.

The golden wheat we grow—our bread,
Our cotton—wealth of snowy heads;
Squeeze the juice from grapes wine-red—
Before you breakfast, drain a cup
And feel your spirit surging up.

In Khazakh[1] mount, and give free rein,
Lean well over the horse's mane,
A sweating gallop then maintain:
On reaching mountain pastures high,
Look down on Gyok-Gyoll—mirrored sky.

[1] Small mountain town.

A day that's free, a man that's free,
A spring like this invites a spree!
Seek out the shade of a plane tree
To spread a rug that's rainbow-spun—
And hail the country of the Sun!

Through Karabakh my spirit fares,
Wings over mountain here, now there;
From far away down the twilit air
Drifts the song of Khan of Shusha[1]—
Famed through all Caucasus and Russia.

Beautiful birthland! Your meaning deep,
Cradle of Beauty that never sleeps,
Where songs of bard, inspired, sweep.
The sun's embrace—your counterpart,
O land of poetry and art.

Spirit immortal, works immortal;
Nizami, Fisuli—are immortal!
On pen and paper, open the portals
Of your soul, record the flow:
The word once writ—through time will go.

Look at the sea near our Baku:
Its shore a bright-lit avenue,
The derricks roaring right in view;
They thunder where the steppe-land swales—
To light the mountains and the vales.

The cool wind is a merry tease,
We bare our chests to the off-shore breeze.
Our heart, Baku on Caspian seas.
Its light—our very strength adorning:
Our Morning Star—clear eye of morning.

Beautiful birthland! I was born
Together with freedom's dawn
Which crimson banners did adorn—
Life seemed one endless, joyous feast;
Gay songs and laughter never ceased.
Dear country—gate of the Ancient East.

Translated by *Gladys Evans*

[1] Well-known folksinger.

287

Moscow

Your spirit permeates me, flesh and bone,
And sets my life in orbit round your own,
O ancient city! Phoenix—scorning time.
What magic miracles your heart-beats prime?
The bitterest storms that rage, you meet
With a staunch heart that keeps a steady beat
Eternal as arrows from the Archer's bow. . .
And proving ancient adages that go:
> Though Darkness have a moment's rule in space,
> Its curtained reach falls short of the sun's face.
> No lasso may running waters hold.
> No art of execution Truth withhold.
> The mind enwrapped in love for man—thereby
> Draws close in spirit to both earth and sky.

O City Beautiful! Dome up on dome of gold!
You light the nations, brotherhood uphold.
Your loving arms so like a mother's arms
Beckon to hearths of welcome and hearts' balm:
When bread-and-salt we shared, my heart was won—
I owned you mother and you owned me son.
Moscow! Spelling kinship close and dear:
Your kinsfolk close their ranks in times severe.
Moscow! You crush your foes as a ship cuts waves.
A living monument—no man here is a slave.
The land of Lenin, motherland we love,
Enriched by Pushkin's timeless treasure-trove,
Powered by Moscow's heart—that constant fount
Whose pulse beats stronger as her trials mount;
Whose hand the Torch of Freedom lifts on high—
The ages through that torch will never die:
Unquenchable come thunder or come storm. . .
Moscow! Spellbinding. . . brotherly and warm,
O City Beautiful! Dome up on dome of gold!
You light the nations, brotherhood uphold.
Your arteries bear life to member-lands,
So we must guard the heart from hostile hands.
The very earth, the stones, protesting rise
When you are threatened—and our hearts likewise,
Each daughter, son, a solid phalanx-wave
Against the horde that for your riches crave. . .
Attacking you, the enemy digs his grave.

Translated by *Gladys Evans*

288

Highgate Cemetery—the tomb of Karl Marx—
Here I feel the earth's patience is too much to bear,
No memorial or stela that simple grave marks,
Though the genius of centuries lies at rest there.[1]

At the head of the grave is a half-sunken stone
With a patchwork of patterns the running drops trace.
Karl Marx, as I saw, does not lie here alone,
Beside him the daughter he loved has a place.

A pond shines nearby, to the left, on a rise—
Filled with icy-cold water from a source underground.
It reflects the tall trees that soothed the tired eyes
Of a man deep in thought as he strolled by the mound.

At the Grave
of Karl Marx

By that still little pond he would stroll with his daughter,
Hand in hand through the park, stopping to gaze
At the sunset reflected in cool tranquil water,
Global thoughts half subdued by the English skies' blaze.

Nature, say friends, would fill Marx with delight.
For hours he could gaze at a fast-flowing stream.
With spring in the air, verdant and bright,
His heart would rejoice at its beauty supreme.

It seemed he embraced both the meadows and heath,
Bared his soul to each flower and bud in the park,
After lightning at night hid its sword in its sheath,
His thoughts illumined the night's deep dark.

Only grew weeping skies overhead can be seen.
How sadly the raindrops from drooping boughs drip!
The trees, standing gaunt, show no traces of green...
The earth is still held in winter's chill grip.

Our hearts, all the world, all the people around
Are stilled by respect. Not a whisper is heard.

[1] This poem was written in 1950, before the memorial bust of
Karl Marx was put up in Highgate Cemetery.

Nature breathes quiet, making no sound.
To converse with infinity souls need no word.

In silence we halted to muse and commune
Without words about life and approaching spring days.
In my mind I could see Marx abandon the tomb.
I saw his sad smile and his clear friendly gaze.

With the might of a mountain, majestic he stands,
His hair like Olympian snow gleaming white,
His face reflects joy as he holds out his hands—
He has seen both his dreams and ideas blossom bright.

Yes, Marx is alive! The truth cannot perish!
He approaches, and nature itself seems to pause,
"For what I once fought," said he, "you men still cherish.
You have crowned with your triumph our noble cause.

"My theories in practice you proved to be true.
Like a missile each word of my teaching you hurled
Against the exploiters, the avid few.
In your hands you now hold all the hopes of the world.

"I know that my voice—the call to be free—
Is heartening millions of men in their fight
For justice and peace. The workers can see
That the way Lenin chose to the future was right."

We stand with heads bared, contemplating the grave,
Though the drizzle continues and black branches drip.
Not a leaf, not a bud could such weather brave—
The earth is still held in winter's chill grip.

But cold days are waning and soon must depart.
Young springtide shall find in old Europe its home.
The noblest of urges that lie in men's heart
Shall sprout like new shoots out of warm, fertile loam.

That is not just a wish—the old system is dying
Like a wick that is quenched by the fat it consumed.
In the skies above Europe like a great eagle flying
Looms an oracle telling a class it is doomed...

290

The image of Marx makes us confident, brave.
To the workers new hope for the future he gave—
The Communist epic was traced by his pen—
His genius dug King Capital's grave!

Translated by Tom Botting

The Old Lady of London

For eons and ages our world has existed,
Yet no one has ever seen babies born old.
Age comes with time and can not be resisted
By man or by woman, no matter how bold.

The Old Lady of London, no different from others,
Was once just a tiny thing, pretty and droll.
Like all little girls, and before them their mothers,
She loved to play games and to dress up her doll.

The lass burgeoned and blossomed and thought about marriage,
When much to her sorrow both parents expired.
So the heiress was left with a fortune to manage,
But knew what to do with the wealth thus acquired.

To New York and Paris she flew for a start,
Where she sipped every luxury riches could give her,
But hated the thought that with money she'd part—
To the Land of Hereafter she'd fain take it with her!

She flirted with suitors, but chances pass by. . . .
"A home and a family, all that sort of stuff,
Such pleasures," she said, "let the working class try!
As for me—why I find being rich is enough!"

In London society dandies adored her.
They thought she was lovely, though somewhat too tart.
But passion she found was most irksome and bored her...
She never let sentiment soften her heart.

She was Queen of the Ball when she whirled in a waltz.
Though her partners would gather like bees around honey,

291

She was sure their attentions were feigning and false—
And saw only cynics out after her money.

Thus the years fled away, and so did her youth.
At fifty she wasn't so spright any more. . .
The looking-glass told her the terrible truth.
She thought that was why no one knocked at her door. . .

She became more eccentric through long lonely years,
As avarice seeped through her mind like a fog.
She lived without people, a prey to her fears,
Her faithful companion—one very old dog.

Only petting the creature could still give her pleasure.
She fed it with titbits, dainty and sweet.
She decided the dog should inherit her treasure,
Though millions of children have nothing to eat.

At three-score-and-ten she could still get around,
A slatternly miser, all bony and bent—
One dog-in-the-manger and one poor old hound.
Not gold, but her life in vain she had spent!

One day the old lady remained in her bed.
Disease had attacked her without any warning. . .
Ah, soon the Old Lady of London was dead—
And only a dog met her passing with mourning.

They read out the will the beldame left behind:
"One half of my money my old doggie gets—
And mark you I'm perfectly sound in my mind—
All the rest I bequeath to a kennel for pets!"

The late London papers came out with a gush
About sweet Old Women and Dogs that they Cherish.
Society columns proclaimed with a hush:
"The Old Lady of London!
                    May Her Name Never Perish!"

                    Translated by *Tom Botting*

The officer points, "That's the Reichstag up there!"
Nothing but walls remain—wall after wall.
Deprived of its dome, the structure stripped bare,
Its shrapnel-scarred body stands pockmarked and tall.

Those gaunt sooty walls of explosives still reek.
Dark wall after wall their black secrets still hide.
So many a time did our heavy guns speak
To batter those walls. Now recall it with pride!

The building that sheltered brown killers and spies,
In its precincts they plotted and challenged the
world,
Now stands like the grave-stone of those we despise,
Proclaiming oppressors to death shall be hurled.

This building heard Hitler the great boaster hail
Berlin as the force that the earth would enslave.
In spite of his menace the world did not quail,
But shared our belief that mankind would be saved.

Our soldiers were led by a lofty ideal,
It guided our aircraft to where Berlin burned,
Till the world saw the beast in its fetid lair reel,
And soldiers with victory to Moscow returned.

From the shadows of death we helped Europe arise.
Then our friends knew the world had been saved on
that day.
In the land of their birth a great song never dies
Composed by the soldiers who died on the way.

Brave sons of my nation, you died not in vain,
You helped write an epic with blood that you shed.
When bright springtime days warm the world once again
The sun rises to greet them, then bows to the dead.

The Reichstag stands stark in the cold sunset's glare.
Nothing but walls remain—wall after wall.

he Reichstag

293

Deprived of its dome, the structure stripped bare,
With the howl of the wind in its vast ruined hall.
Great snowflakes like ghosts round the dead Reichstag fly.
The wasted cadaver with shrouds they enfold.
"Thus the aggressors forever shall die!"
—That is the tale which the dreary sight told.

Translated by *Tom Botting*

On the rostrum he leant—in silence he paused,
Immersed in deep thought, a frown on his brow...
... When proud, muted courage has unsheathed its sword
In deference deep all the world bow. . . .

The hall was astounded. There wasn't a sound
While thousands of eyes probed the man with their gaze.
The Negro's sad face told of suffering profound,
His whole life a saga of long lonely days.

His heart had been bruised from the time of his birth.
Indifference to joy—that's what silent lips tell.
No songs shall they sing, they are strangers to mirth.
His soul's like a town razed by missile and shell.

he Negro

(xcerpt from a poem)

As though in the cabin the day he was born
His mother was keening as if for the dead.
Yet the heart of a mother can not always mourn,
Though her lullabies echo entreaties for bread.

His eyes are dark clouds from which forked lightning
                                          clashes.
His great knotted hands hold the strength of a giant.
Over tense rows of people his sombre glance flashes—
His heart is tormented—his spirit defiant.

Tall thunderheads burst, as they must, releasing
Their torrents, for such is Nature's law—
The Negro's lips parted, emotions unleashing,

"A Negro am I, and a painter, what's more!
My mother gave birth to an artist and man.
It's full thirty years since my life's work began.
The New World, America, that is my home,
My ancestors' bones have enriched its dark loam.
My birthright's the heavens, the land and the sea.
My dreams have built nests in the fork of each tree.
Revering this land, held under its sway,
My soul is enamoured of its night and its day.
Its sun sets and rises in works I create.
—But, gentlemen, stay! I shall not make you wait. . . .

Just answer me this—with what painting can give,
Inspired though it be, do you think I can live?
If a man must tramp on until he feels faint—
And must sleep in a hedge, do you think he can paint?"
          His eyes are dark skies where the thunderbolts dart,
Ideas and intelligence sparkle and glisten,
His surging red blood seems to pulse in my heart,
While nature itself, it would seem, stops to listen;
          "I start on a journey and suffer from thirst,
Some white men pass by, I ask of the first,
'Say, where can a man get some food and a drink?'
'There ain't no such place, for a nigger, I think,
White folk can get food any place in the town,
But they can't abide a strange darkie around. . . .'
          He is white, I am black. We need say no more—
So I aged in my youth where Jim Crow is the law. . . .
An alien am I in the land of my birth.
Can you gentlemen tell me what such a life's worth?"
          I sense how the hall by emotions is riven.
Compassion in many kind faces I see.
In waves ever-rising blank wonder is driven
As high, banked-up storm clouds before the wind flee.
The Negro breathes harshly, his heart racked with pain.
He frowns and his muscles show taut as a cord.
Enigmatic his thoughts. . . Will the man speak again?
. . . When proud, muted courage has unsheathed its
                                             sword. . . .
          "Oh yes, my America, you are my love,
With long prairie rivers, the spring moon above,
In the heat of the summer, or snow-bound and cold,
The black soil of my birth, rich in silver and gold.
Yet within my own homeland I'm under a ban. . .
Can a man with no homeland still live like a man?"
          A white man is sitting tense on my right.
As he wipes his damp glasses he keeps his gaze level.
Such passion must surely not leave him unmoved. . .
He's grinding his teeth—partly man, mostly devil.
He's intent on the Negro—he can hardly sit
With chagrin those wolf-fangs and yellow teeth grit.
He is grey, then he flushes, with chill he is shaking.
His pale eyes are hooded, his face sandy-white.
He writhes as black fingers his conscience are raking.
He coils and recoils—Ah! the serpent would bite!

Evil incarnate, quintessence of cunning!
Who's this man? It is Taylor in terror and fear.
"Our Yankee oppressors!" Like blood words are running
Till they throb in my temples, my bosom they sear.
I recall how the British shot our men from Baku—
Those twenty-six commissars, brave men and true....
The Negro's great hands shall burst chains in his ire.
He's a gun that is aimed and ready to fire,
Or an island resisting the rage of the sea....
He stands with clenched fists. In our ears his words ring
Having gnawed through its tethers and bonds to be free
With dark heaving flanks the panther shall spring...

Translated by *Tom Botting*

A Mother's Send-Off

The hero donned his uniform, his rifle he slung with zeal,
His heart swelled so there was no room in his chest of
muscled steel.
"Oh wait!" they told him, and all came up and kissed
him one by one—
That morning clear with a mountain breeze that eased
the summer sun.
"I'm going, mother, take care of yourself," he said, and
kissed farewell.
His mother hugged her son so brave and her tears began
to well.
She kissed his cheeks and his eyes, and then she tightly
held his hand—
Her valiant and manly boy, true son of his native land.
Her words rang clear: "My son, my dearest, apple of
my eye!
Just see how grey my hair is, from the ordeals of times
gone by.
I know you'll be a hero, and I have raised you not in vain.
Remember my words! We'll get by without you, come
shine or rain.
I wish you all the best of luck. May your arm have the
strength of three,
Whenever you raise your sabre high against the enemy.
But in his sight be proud and brave though his fire seems
from hell.
Keep your rifle clean, and love your horse—be sure to
groom him well.
A jigit keeps his weapon ready, and never puts it by:
News of his latest victory each day to us must fly.
My brave good son! Though I'm the mother that bore you,
understand. . .
You grew up here and ate our bread—and your mother
is this land.
Our home lies in a Land of Heroes,—Chapayev[1] and
Köroglu[2]:
Strong as hundreds each—no weapons made could break
their spirit true.
Well, so you're off; a lucky trip. . . if your way through
Moscow lies,

[1] Hero of the Civil War (1918-1921).
[2] Legendary Azerbaijanian hero.

Salute our leaders—a mother's heart would bless their
enterprise.
With autumn, when the quince in the garden ripens till
it's browned,
When peaches, gold and juicy, weigh the branches down
to the ground,
I'll send a parcel packed with fruit that eye and palate
please.
And your strong arm and daring deeds will increase our
victories.
Now go! Be proud and brave before the foe, though his
fire seems from hell,
Keep your rifle clean, and love your horse—be sure to
groom him well!"
The soldier started on his way—the mountains watched
him, old and wise—
The sun withdrew its radiant light from the hero's native
skies.
The mother watched her vanishing son, threw water for
luck on his trail.
And from the scene, one poet's heart was moved to
great travail—
"Hail to the hero!" said his heart. "Hail to you, Motherland!"
And the poet's lips bent down to kiss his mother-earth's
brown hand.

Translated by *Gladys Evans*

Osman Sarybelli

OSMAN SARYBELLI (b. 1905) was born into the family of a poor peasant in Shikhla, a village in the Kazakh district of Azerbaijan. He was educated at Moscow University. During the Second World War he was a political officer at the Sevastopol and Kuban fronts. In his early poetry, he made wide use of folk forms. The natural, simple flow of his melodious verses has endeared them to the popular masses. Osman Sarybelli describes the miserable existence of the common people in pre-socialist times, which is embodied for him in the image of his shepherd father, and shows how greatly life has changed under Soviet power.

The sea is like a lamb,
                the night is calm and clear,
And from the deck we see
                the distant flaming space.
And on the rippling waves
                ahead our boat we steer,
It leaves upon the surf
                a deep and lasting trace.

Our homes have twinkling lights
                that golden radiance pour;
They seem so very near,
                and each of home life speaks,
The blue transparent lights
                upon the Caspian shore
Have pierced the Apsheron
                with patterns of golden streaks.

The monument that looms
                above the hill—we know,
We know the heart of bronze,
                the mighty hand of steel,
The hand that reaches high
                into the sky's bright glow,
The hand of faithfulness,
                of brotherhood and weal.

This is real light, real light!
                I'm plunged in reverie deep:
Who will not sacrifice
                his life to serve his land?!
To labour in this town,
                its beauty safe to keep—
For those who love their Land—
                it is an honour grand.

I still recall the time
                of living in the dark,
And, thinking of the past,
                I pity those far days.
The sun lit up the world,
                but now we steer our bark

Into a sea of lights,
                  like million stars ablaze.

The village I recall
                  where I had lived of old,
A sooty hut, a lamp
                  with tiny flickering flame,
And now this town of lights,
                  a sea of molten gold.
Just living here today—
                  this happiness I claim.

I want this town beloved
                  against my heart to press,
But though of age, alas,
                  too small in height, I can't,
Instead, Baku has stretched
                  its arms in warm caress,
And, with a mother's love
                  has pressed me to its heart.

Baku with million lights,
                  and hearts—an endless tide,
My land beloved, my town,
                  my country dear and free!
The reason why my heart
                  beats full of joy and pride—
Is that among these lights
                  one light belongs to me!

Translated by *Olga Moisseyenko*

Spring Flowers

The Spring has come, the earth is wrapped in haze,
And in the woods the birds sing doleful songs,
One way alone I turn my troubled gaze,
And grievous thoughts assail my mind, in throngs.

I long to know: where is my dearest love?
What are her thoughts of me, what is her fate?
And does my star resplendent from above,
Pour down on me its radiance, as of late?

There is a custom—on a festive day
We send our friends a gift, from anywhere,
And I am not of stone in any way,
I think each minute of my peri fair.

But here machine-guns pound, and heavy tanks,
And shells and missiles whistle without end,
From here where march the valiant soldier ranks—
Say, my beloved, what present could I send?

Before my trench I see a wondrous sight:
Spring flowers have opened wide their petals frail,
But as the war went on with thundering might
They changed their hues from colourful to pale.

My beauteous one, let not my gift offend,
I've nothing more to offer at your shrine,
The flowers that to you from here I send
Smell more of smoke than of their perfume fine.

Although not worthy of your beauty bright,
My life, my sweetheart, this is no affront!
I here enclose them in the note I write,
Receive my humble present from the front!

My native Land is flecked with red today,
Blue lights along the coast-line shine with glee,
Young girls and women, decked in fine array,
Watch as they stroll by the Caspian Sea.

Their hearts are happy, faces smiling gay,
Upon the bright-lit shore where waters heave,
Put on your best, your brightest silk array,
Join others on the shore this festive eve.

Just three short months and there will be no
                                        Spring,
And you so far, yet in my thoughts so near;
Look, these fair flowers to life so weakly cling,
They will be faded when they reach you, dear.

But if as heralds they should reach your nest
To say that we shall meet with no delay!

303

I beg you, dearest, pin them to your breast,
And think of me upon that festive day.

If someone says: "Your flowers are flowers no more!"
Be not confused, but answer him with pride:
"Though faded, they are presents from the war,
My soldier-bridegroom sent them to his bride!"

Translated by *Olga Moisseyenko*

Before her eyes silk, woollen gowns were spread,
"Which shall I wear, the black one or the red?"
She studied them with an uncertain frown,
Then made her choice, and donned the scarlet
gown.

That evening guests appeared, a very crowd,
Familiar voices echoed, gay and loud,
To each his place was specially assigned,
The rooms were bright with flowers of every
kind.

And in the midst I saw one vacant chair.
The question troubled me: all guests were
there,
Whose place was it? Through merry voices' hum
I felt one guest alone had not yet come.

This Is His Place

Why was his food untouched, and cold the
course?
Perhaps the mountains were too high to cross?
Or he was absent, in a most sad plight?...
Why were her eyes like stars that shed no
light?

And at his portrait glancing, wrapped in gloom,
She wiped her eyes as with a sense of doom.
Then seemed to whisper: "None shall settle
there,
It is his place, his own dear place, his chair";

A message mentally to him I tried to send:
"Your absence is a void, I feel it, brother-
friend."
We waited for the new to supersede the past:
The clock struck merrily, New Year had come at
last.

The master then proposed a toast in accents clear:
"Raise high your glasses, friends, to welcome young
New Year!"
We all stood up and raised our glasses in a toast,
And drank to him who stood a soldier at his post.

305

And at his portrait glancing, wrapped in gloom,
She wiped her eyes as with a sense of doom.
Not to offend tonight a single guest,
She, lost in thought, approached to join the rest,
With trembling lips, not uttering word or moan,
She clinked her glass with his, that stood alone. . . .

Translated by *Olga Moisseyenko*

The Girl in the White Overall

Far from the window the distance I sight,
All is enveloped and picked out in white,
Mountain slopes gleam, swept with silvery thread,
Snowy-white gauze decks my hospital bed.
White is the yard, and the house is grey pearl,
White is the overall sheathing my girl!
Daily the wound in my arm she would tend,
Healing it thus with the love of a friend.
Yet I've a wound that is painfully felt,
Here in the hospital cruelly dealt.
Shells fell like hail from the brown-coated pest—
Wounded my arm but avoided my breast.
Yet she in white shot one single swift dart,
Finding the way to my heart, to my heart!
Though I concealed my great love for that girl,
Love like a moth sped around, in a whirl.
Gently she bandaged my wound sore and deep,
When I looked grim, she would silently weep.
When I felt weary—she felt so likewise,
When I smiled—bright stars shone in her eyes.
Once she brought milk, but the glass I put down,
Grimly my eyebrows were knit in a frown,
Making a compress, she tended my ache,
Ready to lay down her life for my sake. . . .
"Is your pain relieved?"
                              "No, the pain is still there,
Now I am dying with no one to care."
Sharp as a dagger her dark eyebrows meet,
Her cheeks aglow with blushes sweet,
"Call in a doctor?"
                         "He's wanted elsewhere,
No one can fathom the pain that I bear.". . .
Dark as a cloud was the face I love well,
Smiling, I said to my lovely gazelle:
"Wounds will be healed if you do what is best:
Put your dear hand on my quivering breast!". . .

Translated by *Olga Moisseyenko*

Suleiman Rustam

SULEIMAN RUSTAM, who is one of the initiators of Azerbaijanian proletarian poetry, was born into the family of a blacksmith in Baku in 1906. In the 1920s he played a prominent part in organising and guiding the Krasnoye Pero (Red Pen) literary society which rallied the young proletarian writers together. Rustam is best known for his clear-cut, fiery poetry glorifying the revolution. He is also a playwright and translator of repute. For his contribution to Soviet poetry, dozens of books of verse, Suleiman Rustam has been awarded the title of People's Poet of Azerbaijan. He uses the old poetic forms—ghazals mainly—with skill and virtuosity, and fills them with a new content. Very popular with readers is Rustam's poetry about the hard lot of their brothers in southern, Iranian Azerbaijan.

The Earth   How I cherish in my heart my native ground,
Every bit was by my fathers handed down.
The earth is part of me, and all I have on earth
Was bequeathed me by the land that gave me birth.
Millions who once lived and loved, alas, are dead,
Over their love and tenderness, now we tread!
Only history can say what things were done,
Earth and many tender smiles are now as one.
I think oft of those who now beneath us lay,
Knowing well that I shall also lie one day.
I believe the stars we see above today
Are immortal words of great men passed away.
And the stars that wander nightly o'er the skies
Are of those who sleep below the glowing eyes.

Translated by *Eugene Felgenhauer*

'Twas   'Twas autumn, the Apsheron tempests were raging,
The plum-tree I planted when my first son was born
Autumn   Was bent to the ground by the wind and tormented,
The leaves one by one from its branches were torn.
I wondered, if it could withstand the wild onslaught,
The wind then died down, but no solace it brought me.
The tree called to mind my first son now departed:
With every leaf gone, it looked dead as could be.

Translated by *Eugene Felgenhauer*

309

I walked the streets, the moon shone bright,
My steps resounded in the night.
Such vigil I quite often keep,
When it is far too hot to sleep.

I pace among the windows blind,
The thoughts are racing in my mind.
And in my head songs form anew
From sleeping leaves bedecked with dew.

And something in my mind does spark,
As I stare hard into the dark.
And like a flame within my heart
A poem of itself may start.
The night demands: "The password, pray."
The password "Lenin" I then say.
With which our country meets the day.
At night my thoughts like breakers rush,
The dawn at last is seen to blush.
I breathe the flying drops of light.
"Awake, awake, unheard-of might!
Ring out, resound, courageous tread!"
The stars are circling overhead.

From house to house my shadows dart:
My land is young within my heart,
Upon this strength-endowing night,
This night that's borne on wings so
                                light!
O'er gates those are not lamps that
                                shine:
It's verse that's born in heart of mine.
With lamp in hand by window shade
My loved one looks—the heavens fade.

This night my love went not to bed;
"Where have you been?" to me she said.
No stars or moon for her did shine,
She thought of me, for me did pine.

And in his dimly lighted flat
My poet-friend o'er poem sat.
He said: "O heart! Please find me words
That would as winged be as birds."

Nocturnal Romance

310

With Lenin's book that night in hand
Sat black-eyed maiden of the land.
Awake an engineer did stay,
While books and charts about him lay.

Oil derricks will soon arise
And gush black oil to the skies.
What fiery glances probe the dark,
What verses sing within my heart!
My country's heart will always beat!
What sights unfold before my feet,
Upon this strength-endowing night,
This night that's borne on wings so light!
I watch the dome of heaven pale,
The restless waves the seashore flail,
Inhale the breathing of the sea,
Waves waiting for the dawn with me.
The waves their darkness slowly shed,
The moon is fading overhead,
And I unto the darkness say:
"It's time that you had gone away,
For very soon it will be day,
The sun will shine, the morning play!"

Translated by *Eugene Felgenhauer*

The Quill of the Cranes

Again I sailed upon the broad Khazar,
The billows sighed to me that spring was near.
My town is one within a land of peace
And it has learned to laugh with child-like cheer.
My poet's soul sent greetings to the spring,
And I was hailed by oil-derricks at sea.
No charm is there like that of early morn,
The water's cold, the heart is full of glee.
I raised my eyes to heaven, and I saw
That cranes were flying in the azure sky.
How gracefully and swift they winged along,
It seemed that they past Lenkoran would fly.
It seemed to me that I had known them long,
Just watching them to me brought peace and rest.
The voices of the cranes rang in my ears
And brought to life new songs within my breast.
　　Blue water to the right and to the left,
　　A blue and boundless road in front of me.
　　From joy it seemed my head was in the sky,
　　How good it was that I had put to sea.
There was the sea that woke my sleeping muse,
But I'd no sheet of paper nor a pen.
The things I'd seen, how could I write them down?
It seemed the cranes had overheard me then,
From azure sky was wafted down a quill.
Another moment and my work could start.
With all the pride and fervour of my muse,
The words that were imprinted in my heart,
On blue and living note-book stretching far,
Upon the flowing breast of my Khazar,
I wrote them with the quill the cranes had sent,
The song was finished—I could rest content.

Translated by *Eugene Felgenhauer*

Give Your Eyes to Me

My own Party, I your faithful warrior be,
Give the hills I've crossed and fertile plains to me.
So I wouldn't stumble on the road of life,
Give your gait unbending, give your strength to me.
You, whose breast bears a million burning words,
Words that penetrate the spirit, give to me.
So that I could tell our enemies from friends,
Give your eyes to me.

Translated by *Eugene Felgenhauer*

I'll Give My Heart to You

(to my brother)

If the winds your garden scathe, flowers I shall give
to you,
If your table victuals lacks, bread I'll give to you.
So your blow would carry weight to the tyrant's head,
All the power of my fist I will lend to you.
If the foes pollute the air, so you cannot breathe,
Then my breath that's like the North wind, I will give
to you.
If a mighty tempest rage, bringing mountains down,
To uphold you, my own back I will lend to you.
If your heart fails in the fight, mine I'll give to you.

Translated by *Eugene Felgenhauer*

What Is Khazar Like?

If you asked me in the morn:
> "What is Khazar like?"
I would say it's like the sky, and the sky like it,
It is like a velvet cloth by a gold light lit.
Every hill is strewn with grapes, fruit-trees all around,
And the mighty dashing waves crash against the ground.
Little children on all fours crawl among the grass,
They are very much like songs sung by lad and lass.
I have lost all track of time in the sunny lull,
Khazar's like a giant book read by a flying gull.
Every cliff for ages has Khazar's onslaught bore,
Every cliff is like a guard standing on the shore,
Like one of bold Babeck's[1] men, ominous and black
And as furry as the cloak he wore upon his back.

Translated by *Eugene Felgenhauer*

---

[1] Revolutionary leader.

the Heart of ə Highlands

I said I'd return, wherever I'd roam—
The tall Talysh Highlands I've always called
                                    home.
I never liked those, who promise in vain,
And so I am back in Lerik again.
The day is breaking, the new sun I see,
From distant horizon it's winking to me.
White clouds far away the heaven's dome ring,
And quail in the meadow so merrily sing,
And though it is said nightingale songs are
                                    best,
Their simple refrain wakens peace in my breast.
In forests the pheasants are cackling today,
The trees sooth the soul, as they peacefully
                                    sway.
The sun far away is still rubbing its eyes,
But be not in haste it will very soon rise.
The cocks in the yard raise their clamour
                                    on high:
They're straining to reach with their song to
                                    the sky.
And there is no reason why I should deny
The pleasure I get from the cocks' homey cry.
My friend, ere from here you on wanderings jog,
Please stop for a while ere you pass Khan Bulag.
Maids going to work in the morn gaily sing
And braid their black locks by the mirror-like
                                    spring.
For here in the hills for each maid there's a place,
And when they're at work, then their hands simply
                                    race.
In Lerik betrothals and weddings oft ring,
We want no dour fortress of baron or king,
We happiness, brotherhood, freedom support,
Each man is a tower, each tree is a fort!
Though everyone knows from Baku I have hied,
Yet half of my heart does in Lerik reside,
When sunrise I see, then my heart fills with bliss,
The bees gather honey from flowers they kiss.
The mountains look friendly upon every hand,
Much taller than New York's skyscrapers they
                                    stand.
Here spring on the spirit has a firm hold,

315

Here men of a hundred are never called old.
The hills will not laugh, if men stop to sing,
In Lerik the crop is ensured from spring.
The iron trees sing, as if clear mountain rills,
As they stand on guard over old Talysh hills.

Translated by *Eugene Felgenhauer*

At the Forge Where I Make My Iron Verse

Once again I see a dream, that I'm a youth once more,
I wear a skull-cap on my head, and an apron on my knee,
And again I'm at the forge, bellows pumping as before,
Bellows pulled by knotted rope, that's as frayed as it can be.
Heaps of iron by my side, which my hammer will yet know.
Many patches in my clothes, in the bellows many too;
But I hold my hammer firm, and I hear the anvil's tone.
Rusty iron seems to beg me to give it life anew,
So that it could live again 'neath my hammer, in my tongs,
So that men would once again take the iron in their hands,
And that people would recall and extoll it in their songs,
So like travellers of old it could visit other lands. . . .
Black fumes heaving like a sigh, mingle in the chimney
                                                    smoke;
If your hands are full of skill, sparing of them you must be.
Over there the smithy doors dust-beladen cobwebs cloak,
Carried off by youthful dreams in those webs a sign I see.
In that mirror sooty black I can see my day arrive:
'Tis my dream the highest skill would be vested in my hand,
To be master of my trade is the thing to which I strive.
But I never loved nor love to obey or to command.
In the language of the smith to the iron bars I speak.
Many sparks about me fly, falling down on me like rain,
Which for me is like applause that all master craftsmen
                                                    seek,
So my heavy sledge I ply, reviving iron once again.
From the springtime of my youth hasten I to future day. . .
But then I waken from my dream, in the present world
                                                    immerse,
Yet the dream still follows me, coming back to life today:
Once again I'm at the forge where I make my iron verse.

                    Translated by *Eugene Felgenhauer*

Mamed Rahim

MAMED RAHIM (b. 1907), People's Poet of Azerbaijan, and Merited Art worker. Mamed Rahim was born in Baku and has lived there all his life. He began to write in 1925, and since then has published dozens of poetic volumes which present a comprehensive, panoramic chronicle of Azerbaijan's past and life there today. In his poem "Sayat-Nova" he speaks of the friendship of nations; in "Over Leningrad"— for which he won the State Prize—he extolls the heroism of the people in the Great Patriotic War, and in "On Apsheron Soil" he describes the labour feats of Azerbaijan's working class. Many of his verses have been set to music and have gained nation-wide popularity. Mamed Rahim is also known for his translations of European poets into Azerbaijani.

Most keys can close and open a lock,
Yet there are keys that hearts can unlock.
Keys there are, too, that sometimes we use
Locking together hearts that should fuse.

Tongues always have one secret key
Fitting a lock that no one can see.
Just look around you—keys you will find
Made to fit locks of every kind.

Keys we possess that often reveal
Secrets that nature longs to conceal.
Deep inner meaning we can discern
If we can find the right key to turn.

Keys

Since the closed reign of locks first began
Mankind, it seems, has lost faith in man.
Just as if hearts no longer could know
How to feel trust, its warmth and its glow.

So now, my lovely, let us be free,
Let's cast aside each lock and its key.
Out in the darkness let them be cast,
Or in a museum exhibit their rust.

Fuss about locks and keys ought to cease.
Let them begone and leave us in peace!
But, my own darling, please keep one key—
That of your heart—and give it to me.

Translated by *Tom Botting*

The Dearest Thing

Men say that like some tranquil river gently sped their life
Until one day the Kabardinian spoke thus to his wife:
"I wish to wed a girl," he said, "A lovelier wife she'll be,
Yet you, my dear, have always been a loyal wife to me,
So take whatever you desire, the dearest thing, and leave."
The wife kept calm and told herself this was no time to
grieve.
So Salimat got down to work and soon at her behest
The house was ringing with the sound of laughter, song
and jest.
The wife kept full the husband's glass and she made sure
he drank.
It was not long before her man in tipsy slumber sank.
Then in a flash the woman ran to hitch the bullock team.
The laughing neighbours asked the wife what such a scene
could mean,
Yet on the cart, at her request, they helped to load the man.
Then Salimat addressed her guests and thus her discourse
ran:
"My dearest friends, I wish you joy and health with all my
heart.
...Heigh ho! You bullocks, lift these hooves. It's time for
us to start!"
The cart rolled on. The drunken husband never felt it sway
Until the night-time chill crept in and woke him on the way.
"Good Lord!" said he, "Where can I be? Does anybody
know?"
Then Salimat made her reply, "You said that I must go
Away from home, yet bade me take the very dearest thing,
Of gold or silver, silk or wool, or pearls thread on a string.
You said, 'Take what your heart desires, then come back
home no more.'
I pondered on the dearest thing and found my choice was
sure.
More precious than to live at ease—for what yearned I
knew—
With none to be compared, most dear, and that, my dear, is
you!
The fondest memories of life hid deep within my heart
Commanded that I take my love with me upon this cart.
Yes, since our life is breaking up, divorcing us, my spouse.
You are the one I chose to take to my old father's house."

Translated by *Tom Botting*

The Stairway

Unhurried, step by step, I climb the flight of stairs,
The setting sun of life grows weak and palely glares.
My step is grave and slow, when in a sudden flash
I see a youngster dart, and down the staircase dash.

For him I am a shadow, just a silhouette.
He hums, but I must gasp, not half way up as yet.
I stop to catch my breath and then turn back to glance,

With antelope-like grace I see him leap and dance.
He's going down so fast while I creep up the stair,
And as that lad descends, he hums his happy air.
As I ascend my heart is burdened down by woe.
                    Those steps,
                    Those cold stone steps,
                    Up one by one,
                    So slow. . .!
But on the stairs of life that's all reversed, I know—
For there I must descend,
                              while watching youth ascend
Like some untrammelled arrow, shooting up Life's stair.

A girl climbs with the boy. For no one else they care
But who that lad might be I really cannot say—
Perhaps it is my youth that fled so fast away.
I watch the lad's career and heave a bitter sigh,
For he is climbing up, while down those steps go I.

                    Translated by *Tom Botting*

Bridges

A bridge may be of wood, and some of stone are made.
Steel, too, is used to build a bridge, the toughest finest
grade.
Long arcs of welded metal make the strongest bridge of all.
A bridge may be a monument, majestic, proud and tall.
Some bridges straddle rivers, others cross the waves of blue.
With wishes, too, some folk build bridges, hoping dreams
come true.
With all my heart I love those bridges that are dreams'
ideal.
Men cross them boldly knowing life new prospects will
reveal.
Another bridge you may not notice even when it's near,
And yet that bridge is made for you, so cross it without
fear.
That bridge is built on purest love which wells up from
the heart.
Through raging storms it stands quite firm and can't be
torn apart.
The harshest trials it will resist, though years of winter
frown,
And evil slander hurled against it cannot bring it down.
The bridge of goodness rest upon foundation stones of love.
Of truth its columns down below—respect for man above.
And everyone who crosses over happiness shall know,
New prospects will be opened up while bright new vistas
glow.
Such bridges, bringing closer friendship, all mankind finds
dear,
So more such bridges mankind builds with every passing
year.
If love of life can make you raise a structure of that kind
Be sure among your fellow men your rightful place you'll
find.

Translated by *Tom Botting*

Stars

At night as a boy I would gaze at each star
And walk through the world of my dreams there on far.
My grandmother told me the tale of the skies
In silvery light when we watched the Moon rise.
"That mist," she would say, "is the Good Pilgrims' Way.
Those seven are brothers—the brightest are they.
And many a star," she said, "bears someone's name.
In each of them burns a man's fate like a flame.
The Shah's star hangs there, like a sun burning bright,
Majestically lighting the world through the night."
She drew my attention to a star clear and cold,
"The man who owns that must have great stores of gold.
By that waning star, far away, all alone,
The fate of a solitary, poor man is known. . ."
And as she would speak at the stars we would gaze
And sometimes a shooting star fell with a blaze.
Then frowning she said, "Some poor soul has been hurled
To life after death, far away from this world."
She put me to bed, but before I could sleep
To stars up in heaven my mind seemed to sweep.
The angels with golden wings took me away—
New roads they unfolded and destinies fay.
Like caravans passing the years soon were gone—
The star of my grandmother no longer shone.
That kind-hearted woman lies under a mound.
So life like an autumn leaf falls to the ground.
Though grandmother left I recall what she said
And think of the star of my fate overhead.
One night my star, also, will flash through the sky
And maybe some grandmother, gazing on high,
Will sorrow and so to her grandson, will say,
"I see that another good soul passed away. . ."
Unhappy is he when his star has declined
Who made nothing noble to be left behind.

Translated by *Tom Botting*

The Fisherman

There's a tumble-down shanty on the dunes by the shore.
The family it shelters is bitterly poor,
And a boat rides the waves as it rocks to and fro,
The boat and those waves became friends long ago.
In that cockle-shell skiff a man sails all his days
As he sets out to sea for good fortune he prays.
He fishes alone, as men did long ago,
But for all of his labours there's not much to show.
Many times out at sea the fierce wind swept down,
And battered his boat till it seemed he must drown.
Many times man and dory, the tempest defying,
Sailed out of Death's jaws, over white-horses flying.
That slave of hard labour
Once flung his nets wide.
His haul was one fish, golden scales back and side.
As he felt its firm weight his heart surged with delight:
"The kiddies shall have a fine supper tonight!"
Elated the fisherman strode up the shore,
But before he could open the old shanty door
The head of the village with a threatening stance
Stood measuring the man and his fish with a glance.
Now with that sort the fisherman wanted no truck,
But the headman said, "Fisherman, don't curse your bad
                                                    luck—

Why, just look at your haul! A fish fit for a king!!
If I could dine daily on such a fine thing,
Like you I'd forget both the headman and king!
Neither taxes nor fish for a year have you paid!"
The fisherman faltered, but said, unafraid,
"From my fish in the past you have taken a share,
And I've worked with no pay at your house over there."
"That was then! But today?
Come fisherman stay!
You'll account for your taxes, right here! Straight away!
With that fat golden fish you can just pay your way."
The fisherman pleaded, but pleaded in vain—
His children tonight would go hungry again. . . .!
The head of the villagers laughed to himself,
"With this fish I am sure I can add to my wealth,
To the Vizier I'll render it, shimmering gold.
He is sure to repay such a gift I am told.
My lord will applaud when he sees how I serve,
And heap me with favours I richly deserve. . . ."

324

As he mounted his horse his heart seemed to sing.
His steed raced to town like a bird on the wing.
On approaching the palace he shortened the rein,
At the doorstep his voice sounded haughty and vain.
"Noble lord, take my present. . ." he uttered aloud,
So a serving wench took it and turned the man out.
As she slit the firm flesh of the fish could she guess
How the fisherman's heart beat and bled in distress?
No, she never could know his deep chagrin, his pain,
On seeing his children go hungry again.
At the palace the Vizier invited to dine
A highly placed guest who was partial to wine.
From the States he had come and today he would find
That his host was attentive, courteous and kind,
For the functionary hoped that after the meal
With the Yankee he'd manage to push through a deal.
On a platter of silver, 'mid crystalware bright
The fish, steaming gold, was a fabulous sight.
The aroma of spices and herbs rose as sweet
As the scents of the garden where they sat down to eat.
The guest from abroad, when he savoured the dish
Made short work of the golden delectable fish.
The pile of sharp bones on the plate grew and grew,
He was truly delighted, but never knew
What hot blinding rage seared the fisherman's breast
Or the sight might have warned him perhaps it was best
Not to swallow a morsel lest people might wish
He would choke on the bones of that fine golden fish.

Translated by *Tom Botting*

There's Nothing New in the Lebanon

There's nothing new in the Lebanon—that is what they say.
All is well in the Eastern port and the hours slip away.
While some folk find that life is bright, others find it black,
And one of those is a stevedore, toting bales upon his back.
The docker bears his own heavy thoughts—a load beyond
belief.
Besides toting bales he has to lift the burden of his grief.
Though he labours long he has no hope. In Beirut there's
many like him.
Back at home his wife is ill, so his thoughts are bitter and
grim.
The props of his life are shattered, he cannot find support.
Perhaps that's why he had today a lightning flash of
thought—
How many bales can there be like the ones I sling and shift?
Is there nothing left in the world for me but bales that I
must lift?
And those tall ships anchored out in the road,
Whose ships are those and the cargoes we load?
Who will buy and who will sell?
They buy and sell, but never will tell
How much a bale do the purchasers give?
And where in the world do the ship-owners live?
Strange signs on each bale
Tell the ships where to sail
Till the world to the docker seems one mighty bale. . . .
With relief he remembered this was the day
When the men at the docks would line up for pay.
Now the first thing to do is to buy for the wife
Medicines to soothe her and lighten her life.
But nothing turned out the way he had planned.
In events of that day Fate had a hand.
As he walked up the plank by his luck he was dogged.
As he climbed to the ship his mind was befogged. .
The load was heavy, the day was hot and misfortune at
his heel.
The farther he walked the worse he felt, till his head began
to reel.
His ears seemed to ring with his little ones' cries,
And he sensed that forever his wife closed her eyes.
The thought that the woman had been taken by death
Came like a blow and halted his breath.
The bulk on his back started to slip—

326

It hurtled right down by the side of the ship. . .
There's nothing new in the Lebanon—that is, not today—
All is well in the Eastern port and the hours pass away.
To the warehouse office pretty soon he was called,
"You're just a trouble-maker!" The docker was told,
"You'd better knuckle under, for it's high time you knew
We can knock some common sense into sore-heads like you."
They reckoned up the cost
Of the goods that were lost
And they held the money back.
The bosses were tough
And their manner was rough,
So the docker got the sack. . . .
There's nothing new in the Lebanon—nothing new today!
For all is well in the Eastern port and the hours slip away.
So the man couldn't buy what he'd planned for the wife
And he took nothing home—a hell of a life!
He'd load no more dates, no bananas or chrome,
So there'd be no more wages for him to take home. . .
Bareheaded he walked, disheartened and pale,
And misery hung on his back like a bale.
A deep-ladenship on its charted course lay,
Sailing for harbours far, far away.
Ah! He himself was a rudderless ship and sorrow the
                                    bitterest sea.
As he walked with a cold and deep-laden heart not a
                            glimmer of hope could he see.
There's nothing new in the Lebanon—so it seems today. . . .
What the future holds for the docker is more than I can say.
But I know for sure he never will lack
A bale of sorrow clamped fast on his back.
When the accident happened the docker was poor,
But now starvation stands at the door.
With a heavy heart and a slow sad step to his home he
                                    made his way
There's nothing new in the Lebanon—that is, not today. . . .

Translated by *Tom Botting*

The Power of Beauty

At home I have a statuette—a thing of pure delight—
A tender nympth of rarest beauty, half-unrobed, is mounted
Upon a lion, unafraid. It's such a lovely sight!
Enchanted guests perceive a charm that cannot be
                                              recounted.

They sense some mystery, inner meaning, more than meets
                                              the eye—
How can a nympth subdue the lion, a beast untamed and
                                              pearless?
The King of Beasts could lift a paw, and loveliness would
                                              die!
They feel disturbed at beauty riding unconcerned and
                                              fearless.

To dissipate that mystery, friends, in verses is my aim.
The jungle lord became a lamb and could show no
                                              resistance
Because the power beauty wields the fiercest beast can tame.
A woman's beauty wields such force—the greatest in
                                              existence.

Translated by *Tom Botting*

I Dreamt...

I dreamt last night that we had parted.
We strolled no longer through the lane.
No nightingale its trilling started
In gardens sear—all life was pain.

My misery like a cloud above me
Deprived my soul of laughter's lilt.
I asked, "Why does my love not love me?
In what, o love, consists my guilt?"

My tortured thoughts were turbid, sickly.
To questions there was no reply.
How could her fancy change so quickly?
How could such love abate and die?

I woke to memories reassuring,
For yesterday, to my great pride,
I heard sweet words of love, ensuring
That you will never leave my side.

To die a little, parting seems,
So let us only part in dreams.

Translated by *Tom Botting*

Mekhti Seidzade

MEKHTI SEIDZADE (b. 1907) was born in Ashkhabad into a working-class family. After the death of his father in 1915, the family went to live in Baku where Mekhti was educated at the teachers' college. He is known for his children's verses, his magnificent ghazals which have made the text of popular songs, and last but not least for his translations of Omar Khayyam into Azerbaijani.

In summer once through mountains green
A youthful stag was seen to pass;
He roamed the meadowland serene
Where flowers bloomed among the grass.

He fell within a hunter's sight
Who trailed him artfully and slow,
And waited for the moment right
To speed the arrow from his bow.

Upon a hill the stag stood clear,
The hunter let his bowstring twang.
And when the arrow struck the deer,
His heart leaped from the sudden pang.

**Legend
of the
Stag**

The poor stag into gallop burst
And ran for life across the plain.
The day's heat tortured him with thirst,
His breast-wound burned with growing pain.

O'er vale and hill his feet took wing,
Until high pastures he traversed
And stopped beside a mountain spring,
Bending his head to quench his thirst.

And while with sobbing breath he drank,
His sad eyes brimmed with many a tear.
A frog hopped out upon the bank
And spoke to him: "O Brother Deer!

"Please tell me why your noble heart
Is cramped with sorrow, heavy woe?"
The stag said: "I'll my grief impart,
This morn on meadows far below

"An arrow caught me by surprise.
O hard indeed the hunter's heart!
The sun grew dark before my eyes,
So near my heart . . . had struck his dart."

The frog with pride began to swell.
"My God," he cried so boastfully,

"What do these hunters want, do tell,
From you, O Deer, and such as ME?"

On hearing this cheap braggart's cries,
The stag's heart blazed with sudden ire.
The lightning flashed from out his eyes.
Through every noble vein swept fire.

And swinging on the frog, he spoke:
"Your words, I'd have you understand,
A deeper wound in me provoke
Than arrows loosed by a cruel hand."

Translated by *Gladys Evans*

In the Thick of Storms

When in the sea of life the waves are at war to the death,
Children ashore, who think it play, delighted, hold their
breath.
All who are young are ignorant of tempests that await:
Think that the sea of life is fun that never will abate.
Deeper will grow the sea of life as year after year proceed,
Battling the bitter waves will go those who are capable
of the deed.
People there are who, aimless, selfishly live out their lives,
Only to drop like stones to depths, not even a chip survives.
But others fight in the thick of storms where the black
waters swirl,
Those are the ones who draw from the sea its hidden
treasure of pearl.

Translated by *Gladys Evans*

Love of Life

Each human born has heart-ties unto earth.
But into life's deep secrets none may peer.
The babe begins by crying, right from birth.
Why not by laughing, what's the secret here?

However, life is sweet; none like to go.
They want to live who are at brink of death.
No matter how much grief is here below,
Still, life seems good till our very last breath.

Such is the law of life, a thing eternal.
Though death reduces men to grains of dust
Not differing from Nature's end autumnal—
The love of life makes life for us a must.

Translated by *Gladys Evans*

In Buchenwald up to our times
The taint of blood pollutes the air,
Within this fascist lair of crimes
So looms the image of despair

That over us the very skies
Hang heavily, as if of lead.
Here's proof—for every nation's eyes—
Of crimes against the tortured dead.

Cremating ovens, blackened, still
Exude an acrid burning smell,
Where thousands suffered, then lay
still
Here in this corner sliced from Hell.

Buchenwald
Death Camp

Like graves, to keep our memory green,
The death cells stay just as they were—
And parchment faces, sensed, not seen,
Mid rusting chains make hollow stir.

The chains that once on human hands
Rang tonelessly as if to pray—
If you but listen to the winds
Their echo you can hear today.

Like leeches, fascists drew the blood
From children innocent of harm—
Upon you like a surging flood
Beat cries of mothers in alarm.

You feel the depths of grief within
Each cranny of this hell of tears.
Inhumanly, from human skin,
The fascists made their souvenirs.

A human heart—see, here it lies—
Preserved, the bullet left its mark.
And so to be some brute's dread prize—
Expired a living human spark.

What hopes and dreams it must have held—
Someone's daughter, someone's son,

Died with every hope dispelled,
Exiled under an alien sun.

A heart that held a sweetheart's love,
Alive with youth's impassioned flame;
A patriot's heart that fed and throve
Upon his motherland's dear name.

In Buchenwald ruled Death alone,
Menacing, giant Juggernaut.
On every wall, on every stone
Blood spilled and left a crimson spot.

Prisoners that were here installed
From Europe came on every hand—
The tragedy of Buchenwald
Cuts sharper than the heart can stand.

What did mankind here not endure!
Where now the dread memorial stands
Thousands found a sepulchre
Driven from many Soviet lands.

And so this monument arose
For Buchenwald, for all the dead...
To comfort the bereaved, for those
Who go today, by sorrow sped.

Dead souls of Buchenwald still vernal—
This monument retains your worth.
Its message clear remains eternal—
Reminder, warning, for all Earth!

Translated by *Gladys Evans*

Rasul Rza

RASUL RZA (b. 1910), People's Poet of Azerbaijan, an innovator in poetry aiming to free Azerbaijanian poetic diction from the burden of old imagery, obsolete expressive media, and empty versification. Rasul Rza's completely uninhibited poetry is packed with meaning, and has a fresh, original sound. He was born in Geokchai, but practically all his life he has lived in Baku where, besides writing, he engages in important state and public activities. At one time he was the Secretary of the Union of Azerbaijanian Writers, then the Minister of Cinematography, and is now the chief editor of the first Azerbaijani translation of the Big Soviet Encyclopedia to be published in Baku.

The entire world with all its contradictions, conflicts and contrasts is reflected in his poetry. He is concerned about the future of our planet, but believes that peace on earth will be safeguarded by people of good will. Among Rasul Rza's best-known works, mention must be made of his large narrative poem Lenin *for which he was awarded the State Prize, his poem* Mushfik, *the cycles of poems about Africa, and* Colours *where the poet's notions of the world, of emotions, of people and events are expressed through the medium of associative colours.*

Thus spoke the sea—
"I am squeezed in my coastlines,
Suffering, constrained
By bonds of endless rock.
The dance of my waves should never deceive you,
Nor the scattering of dawn on my waves.
Skylines of thunder that fade on my breast—
Don't let them deceive you. . .
Vast is the bitterness lodged in my depths!
Ah, torment!—Hooped in by the ring of the shores!"
I went on my way
Lost in deep thought,
Not looking out to the sea—
I walked on and whistled,
Leaving a track through the sand.
I quickened my pace, hastened away
To find some respite from that voice
Imploring response.
I moved and the sea moved in behind me.
It moved, never ceasing its clamour,
Beseeching—"Oh—scoop up in your hand some water of
mine,
To carry away,
Withdrawing, perhaps, one drop of this grief
That poisons my depths.
The winds slap my face, belabour my breast,"
Grumbled the sea,
"Tall cliffs lash at me, cleaving my waves.
. . .Do you hear me, my friend?"
I slowed down my pace and shouted aloud,
"What cause have you, sea, to moan?
Have you never seen fishermen frozen in woe?
Their great hearts contain
As much as your heart,
Whole worlds they encompass—
As great as the heart of Nasimi[1]—

Those hearts, too, are held,
Constrained in the cage of the breast,

**A Song
of the Sea**

[1] Azerbaijanian classic poet.

337

Yet a northerly wind leaves the fishermen silent—
While a wind from the north sets you roaring."

II

In my eyes is the sea
With its changing colours
No man has ever yet named.
In my ears is the sea,
Its waves steady beating,
Its tranquility, too.
In my heart is the sea
With its sadness
And solitude,
Eternity, too.
I walk to the shore,
Aware of the whims of the
                    sea.
I regard it in silence.
The sea roars and howls
While the waves charge each
                    other,
Foaming and seething
Like a hoary-haired ancient
Driving a long raft of blue.
Calm yourself, sea!
You are no child. . .
Some evil may seize you. . .
Your vast breast is heaving
From skyline to skyline.
You are bound by the shore not as your
                    doom,
Or some dire obligation.
You are the sea.
What would remain of the land
If you were to thrust over it?
Calm down, I say!
Come, let me kiss your salt lips.
Not restraining my tears I shall weep
                    with you,
If you will but weep with me.

III

If for one day I don't see the sea
It is as though I were starved.
I may gaze at the sea every day,
Yet I yearn for the sea.
Forever I long for the sea.

IV

When the extent of the sea has no wave
I pity the sea—
Some offence it has suffered,
Or waits tense and expectant.
Only lakes should be tranquil,
And puddles lie still,
But the sea is the sea
Because it is turbulent.

V

In the night with no moon
I cannot distinguish the sea.
Closing my eyes I listen intently—
The sea then recounts
In sibilant whispers
All that occurs in the darkness.

VI

The sea is miraculous
When the sun rises over it—
Gold sifts from the net of its hair,
Yellow fish
Leap and skip
From the crests down the waves,
While distances seem to retreat
And colours play hide-and-seek
Whether the sea is calm or rough.
Before the sun rises
I will climb up the rocks of Buzovny[1]
And shout from the heights,
"Do get up all you people!

[1] A township near Baku.

Snap the blinds from your windows
And gaze at the sea!
How can a man sleep
When the sea is awaking at dawn?"

VII

Tonight I kissed the sea
Departing from the shore.
Its lips were wet
And salt as tears.
I asked myself, why kiss the sea?
A wasted kiss, I know. . .
But I am glad I also know
The sea is not salt tears.

VIII

O, sea of mine!
Throughout the night you did not sleep
And would not let me rest;
But unlike you I need to sleep,
For you are the restless sea,
And I—I am a man.
You do not care if you never sleep,
For what are you
But brine?
While if I were to heed you all day and all night
Who then would describe
Sleepless watches at night
In verses to make the rounds?

IX

As the night speeds on into the early hours
I open my window onto the sea.
The moon guards the gates
Of the night-time horizon.
Yet the sea does not slumber,
Never closing its eyes.
What is there for the waters to lave?
Now the beaches are empty,
Although the sea is full.

The waves are swimming over the sea,
Plunging and rising, dipping, then climbing,
The better to scan the horizon.
It seems the waves, too,
Are longing for dawn.

X

Men have made derricks pace far out to sea.
In clusters they gather,
Or stand quite alone.
Posts of steel skirt the sea.
Iron trestles puncture the sea.
The sea is still calm.
Do not trust its docility.
It is awaiting the wind.
The sea is lurking in ambush.
If I were myself in the place of the sea
I would not fret nor seek for a quarrel.
I would merely repeat, Khazar was my name,
Khazar I remain.
I would shed my vast solitude,
Were I the sea,
My breast would surge with pride
As I gazed at the shadows of the derricks,
Listening night and day
To continuous voices,
Voices of men,
The voice of Man. . . .
What is the sea without Man?
A giant trough
Overflowing with brine.

XI

The sea. . .
Fishermen's boats,
And in the boats—men.
Beside them lies
Bread
With jars of fresh water. . .
In their hearts lie
The cares of a lifetime—

Fear of the storm . . . storm-dread is theirs.
Soon red will infuse the heavens at dawn.
And morning approach.
Early hours augur good hauls for the men—
The last fateful trip through sea-lanes for fish.
The sea is wheeling,
Indifferent
Both to the morning
And the trip.

* * *

Of a sudden the sea awakes—
Over its face run wrinkles of rage.
It rises in tumult ever more furious,
Each wave now a ravening lion.
It seems the sea sweeping from stem to the stern.
Must sweep the cabin away from the hull
As a man brushes sweat from his face.

* * *

For three days and nights men fought with the sea,
Struggling,
Men fought on,
Exhausted.
Now dugouts of blue
Where battles once raged
Are sweeping deserted and silent.
The lips of the boats cling to those of the sea,
Boats and sea have at last made their peace.
With slow, swaying gait
Fishermen walk up the beach.
The nets that they carry are tattered and rent.
The jars for their water are empty.
In their hands they still carry bundles of
                                    bread.
And in their hearts they still carry
Premonitions of storms.
The sea is enchanted and sweeps after men
Far up the sloping beach
Singing a saga that all should hear.
Over the masts of vessels
Like gulls fly weary songs.

342

XII

Nights out at sea
Are unlike nights on shore.
On shore streets and houses
Are blazing with light
And cigarettes glow.
At sea all is darkness and night.
Out in the shadowy deeps
Armies of fish
Move towards dungeon-like nets.
Nights out at sea can be utterly lonely—
The fish make no sound.
The harsh rocks are silent.
Nothing but a roll of distant thunder,
A glimpse of a cloud—
A ghostly face with the slash of a scar.
The night at sea is in no way like
Night on shore.
The shores are crowded with sun-flooded words.
In verses and lines they form
                           into songs.

XIII

On the earth
Before Man
There also was water.
Was it too much,
Or maybe too little?
In places the water was deep,
In others stagnated in shallows.
Perhaps the Khazar then did not live alone
And its arms were linked up
With other seas, its brothers.
It could still sense the breath
Of its grandsire, the Ocean
In the wind.
The land was once covered by water,
The months and the long years rolled by.
Man gave his own names to the stretches of water—
"This," said he, "a lake shall be called.

343

That, I proclaim, is an ocean!"
Since then the sea became the sea.
Alas! I do not know the day
The sea became the sea. . . .
So each day I visit the shore
For the birthday of the sea.

XIV

For many days now
The sea has been in my every thought.
In my eyes—the sea.
In my ears and heart—
The sea, the sea, the sea. . . .
I have not yet discovered the sea,
Though I know it is near.
It is here in my dreams day and night.
But I have not discovered the sea.
Elusive, the sea!
I would write of the sea
So that people might sense it
Surging before their eyes.
My sea should smack even more of the sea,
And be even slightly more real,
So that people might hear the sound of its surf
Just as it is. . . .
But the voice they hear should be more than the seas,
More than ever the voice of the sea.
For many long days
With the sea on my mind I have slept and awakened.
The sea laves my eyes,
It caresses my ears
While the waves sweep through my heart.
My eyes behold the sea. . .
My ears can hear the sea. . .
My heart is full of the sea,
My lips sing songs to the sea,
But I cannot find the sea. . . .
Oh, I do not mean the way it is,
For that would be easy to do!
It ought to be as the wide sea should be,
As we really could see it one day,

344

So I might prove to all men
When the sea is not there
Still in my eyes is the sea.

XV

What colour is the sea?
Maybe it's blue?
Is it?
Yet I have seen it green.
Is it?
Yet I have seen it black.
Can the sea be black?
Can it?
But I have seen it white.
I've seen the sea when it shuddered with
cold.
I've seen the sea perspiring.
I have seen it both angry
And laughing.
What colour then is the sea?

XVI

An old sailor told me
That the sea is sometimes pensive.
And cunning at times, so he told me.
Mysterious, too, it can be.
The sea, too, can be foul, he declared.
The old man added,
"Just like a man!"
Then he mused for a while,
"Just like our fate. . ."
So ended our talk.
I said not a word.
He did not speak.
The sea—like a man!
The sea—like our fate!
That is quite clear.
So why waste words in explaining?

345

XVII

Our wake. . .
Like a twisting canal that seemed to hang
From some star still unseen.
We set out to sea before the sun rose,
Now it will soon be setting.
How many slopes and crests are there
Still to be crossed?
Above the steep wall of rocks cleaved by lightning
The sunset is caught and held.
On every small sea-shell
A spark hangs relucent—
The sunset has lit it
And lights all my dreams.
The blue of the sea
Has passed through my eyes
And then through this heart of mine.
I saw etched on the rocks
The signs of the waves
That the sea had now left behind.

Translated by *Tom Botting*

The Third Eye

Every man has his two eyes,
If one of them has not been gouged out
By a man, by a stone, or a bullet.
Every man has his two eyes.
But this man had three.
Two in his head,
Like you
And like me—
And one in his soul.
With two he gazed at the world.
With one he laughed and he wept.
Such was the friend that I had.
I see it is clear
That every one needs
A third eye!

Translated by *Tom Botting*

Man

With cries and with tears he arrives in this world,
Not knowing yet of its days of harsh strife.
With cries and with tears he takes leave of this world,
Not having had his fill of this life.

Translated by *Tom Botting*

347

Time

For the first time he saw her. . .
Ah, what hair!
Ah, what eyes!
Ah, what lips!
Burning womanly passion
In the guise of a human being!
Dante's Beatrice!
The Venus of Titian!
Leili of Fisuli!

. . .They met again.
He gazed at her hair,
At her eyes,
At her lips.
Ah!
Where is the force,
Oh, where,
That could bring back to life
Beatrice,
Venus,
Leili. . . .

Translated by *Tom Botting*

The Working Day

Although the rain may be falling,
Though the day may be stifling hot,
In spite of the hardest frost,
Today is a working day.
And so will tomorrow be too.
Men can shorten the working day,
Men can make it longer.
But Mankind's working day can never have an end.
In orbit beyond orbit Mankind will fly,
Way out to the cradle of stars.
One day we shall paint all the deserts with spring
And in sunshine shall bathe our own nest!
Let our life not be darkened
For one moment or day
While the stars still are shining above,
While fertile seed swells, embraced by the earth.
Our sphere as the seasons pass by
Is changed and always renewed.
The working day of the universe can never end...
Yesterday, too, was just such a day...
Today, too, is one of them,
And so will tomorrow—
Working days of our life.
Away with the idly waiting,
Those who mark time till the holidays
Printed in red on the calendar squares.
For life itself is one long working day
And let it ever be free!

Translated by *Tom Botting*

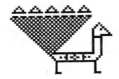

Mirvarid Dilbazi

MIRVARID DILBAZI (b. 1912) is a poetess whose lyricism, subtlety and novelty of perception commanded immediate attention. She was born in Musakala, a village in the Kazakh district of Azerbaijan, and was educated at a teachers' college. She began writing poetry when she was sixteen years old, and has since published a large number of books of poetry devoted mainly to Man and Nature depicted with a depth of philosophical penetration.

The Forest and I

Tonight I lay without sleep, while the forest,
The forest was full of holiday joy,
And I lay brooding....
The forest had only to wish for love
And there were the stars, tender and coy.
Then it began a romance with the moon.
Till dawn the sweet whispering never ceased.
The forest, lucky one, knew
That at daybreak the sun would be rising too,
While I have only one lover
And that one far away.
So I lay
In my lonely room,
With only my heart to talk to.

Translated by *Dorian Rottenberg*

Songs

The voices of many nations
Through the loudspeaker reach my ear.
Converging from all directions
They sound in my room, loud and clear.
Some of them sad,
Some of them glad,
Fragrant, fresh as opening flowers,
Sweeter than any flowers I have had
Are those songs that come at all hours.
Let the universe every day
Meet its radiant dawn with songs.
May they never die away,
Songs ringing joyful and strong!

Translated by *Dorian Rottenberg*

Azerbaijanian Landscapes

Winter has just sprinkled her first snows over the ground
But still the crimson rose-buds glow among the leafy green,
Still the bobbing red apples among the boughs abound.
See, what a land is ours, how blessed our native scene!

Uniting all the four seasons of the year
Fragrance of flowers on snow, and snow on flowers lies....
Rare, bright, autumn flowers, bedizening here and there
The tracery of dry leaves through which the sweet Spring
pries.

The verdant carpets of the fields are striped with snow.
Refreshed each time they are newly washed by snow or
rain,
The fields tell the sun their memories of long ago,
Tell him how rich their hidden hoards of golden grain,

And how the ripening ears rise from the earth's dark womb
Swelling in the caressing wind, drinking in the sun.
Oh, land of golden apples, orchards and fragrant blooms,
You grant us the delights of all four seasons in one.

Golden and yellow leaves carpeting the roads which run
Between rows of chinar trees to the very feet of the hills
As though on each tree's breast were cradled a sleeping
sun....
One after the next, landscape on landscape follows still:

The golden fall, grottoed gardens in sweet perfumes deep,
Mountains and mist, torrents leaping in noisy fountains
To languorous silence like some beauty half-asleep,
And precipitous cliffs, bastions of the high mountains.

Here, curly clouds are tangled in some intricate game...
And, as upon the eagle-pinioned steep I stand,
Looking out from the mountain summit, my heart aflame,
I rejoice in the green gardens, in all this my land.

As the sun sets and silence comes with the night hours,
Lost in the lowland fields I yield to its still power
And I note in the hush, while my heart rejoices:
At home the wind and the rain have different voices,
And different, too, is the fragrance of the flowers.

Translated by *Avril Pyman*

It Smells of Violets, This Earth

It smells of violets, this earth,
In the early days of spring.
It smells of leaves just come to birth,
Of woods where birdsongs ring.
In May it smells of roses,
In summer—of ripe wheat;
In autumn pomegranates
Half-sour and half-sweet.
Winter smells of logs ablaze
Of fresh, delightful snow.
All its charms the world displays
As the seasons come and go.
Warmed with sunshine, washed with showers,
This blessed earth of ours
Breathes the smell of meadow flowers
And vines entwining garden bowers.
Sweet in December as in May,
Earth—breathing of the land and sea,
Though I must part with you one day,
My heart at rest will be.
So generous and tender,
A mother to us all
Your sons will always love and tend you;
The children of your womb,
I know they will defend you
Against the atom bomb.
O bearer of our bread and oil,
Our redolent, free-hearted soil!

Translated by *Dorian Rottenberg*

Beautiful Azeri

Washed with streams that hurry by
From mountains reaching to the sky,
Singing the fields a lullaby,
I watch her with enchanted eye:
A maid of eighteen years I espy
With chestnut tresses soft and light,
Which mountain breezes take delight
In combing down on shoulders white.
Like stars through mists, her eyes shine bright;
In water to her naked knees
White as the foam on stormy seas,
With cheeks like petals of the poppy
Upon the white snow softly dropping.
Her lashes are like splashes spilled
From cups with molten amber filled.
Red rubies glitter in her ear,
Her silken frock is poppy-red,
Her virgin dreams are pure and clear,
Pure are the thoughts in her sweet head,
Clear as the morning sky in spring,
And in them not an evil thing.
Her words are sensible and modest;
She keeps her head when things are hardest.
Though storms may rage within her breast,
Her lucid eyes remain at rest.
So with my mental eye I see
My native land, my Azeri,
With springs that babble out aloud,
Framed in mountains tall and proud.

Translated by *Dorian Rottenberg*

355

Catching fire up in the sky
The plane dipped and shuddered
Like a wounded hawk on high.

The pilot, hands and arms
                    burning,
Stuck to the controls bravely
Out over the wide sea turning.

He leapt with his parachute
When the shore was out of
                          sight
And opened his rubber boat.

A Lad from Baku

Water and sea surround him
He fights against storm and
                          wave,
But she will not confound him,

The sea, she will not betray
This lad who by her still shore
First saw the light of the day.

Lashed by the streaming foam,
The manes of the white
                    horses
Unleashed by the fierce storm,

Riding the crests of the waves,
For three days and three long
                          nights,
The maimed lad struggled to save

Himself and to reach the shore.
And high courage conquered
                          death
As so many times before.

Now the brown face is scarred
And when I meet him, I see
How frightfully war has marred

This lad from Baku, I see...
And I think how good it were
If such storms should cease to be

And if, in this world we love,
No brave young man should be cursed
With a wooden hand in a glove.

Translated by *Avril Pyman*

City of Flowers

Here in the flower market,
Flowers on every hand
Spilling from jar and basket,
There's not even room to stand.

My heart is a burning flame
Fired by these red carnations.
From hot Apsheron they came,
Home of sweet, spicy fragrance.
An armful of blooms is pressed
In a bright bunch to my breast...

I bury my face in flowers
And their scent envelopes me...
The scent of the morning hours
Beside the Caspian Sea.
Their petals are redolent
Of saffron fields by the foam.
Their perfume—an eloquent
Evocation of my home.
In newly laid-out gardens
Samur's waters they drank,
Beneath translucent heavens
Light and delight they drank.

A bunch of red carnations
From Shuvelyani—a dower
Fair beyond estimation
Fit for a Queen of Flowers.
The home of this crimson rose
Is fragrant Mardakyani
And this white lily grows
In luscious, green Tyurkyani.
She has taken her fresh white
From the white crests of the waves;
These blue flowers, dark as night
From the blue Caspian caves;
These sky-blue ones from the sea
In her warm tranquility.
On the breast of the Apsheron
By true lovers of flowers
These blooms have been nurtured, grown
To glow like lamps embowered

358

In the dark leaves of our Land
But you who have not been, you
Who have not seen! Understand
And hear now that our Baku
Is no mere city of oil
Through which the dry wind scours.
No, Baku springs from the soil
Which bore these vivid flowers.

Translated by *Avril Pyman*

Creator

The day approaches its decline;
There, on the couch, you sit
                    again.
I try to look into your mind
And watch your thoughts arise and
                    wane.

You seem relaxed, you sit far back;
You close your eyes, yet do not
                    sleep.
Between your eyebrows, thick and
                    black,
Again those two deep wrinkles creep.
Grey smoke curls from the cigarette
Held limply in your fingers,
It smoulders with a feeble red;
On its tip the ash still lingers.
But a brighter flame burns in your
                    breast

Intensely and incessantly.
It might appear you simply rest,
Sitting there so silently.
That far-off look upon your face,
It might be taken for fatigue;
But no—upon your brow I
                    trace
The working of a force unique.
Your face grows brighter for a
                    space,
Then darkens like the cloud-veiled
                    moon.
What are you moulding in your mind
From light of joy and sorrow's
                    gloom?
What heart's unopened book are you
Perusing as you sit so still,
Oblivious to everything
But visions that your fancy fill?
Maybe you are soaring high
Near the summits of the mind?
Night comes on. The hours go by.
Peaceful sleep enfolds mankind.
Only you, with burning heart
Do not seek repose and rest,

Roaming in a world apart
By your fantasies possessed.
You are here and yet not here,
Talking with an inner voice
Which no one but you can hear
In a language of your choice.

Translated by *Dorian Rottenberg*

Jamil Ahmed

JAMIL AHMED (b. 1913) was born into the family of a craftsman in Yerevan, and educated at the teachers' college in Baku. Although some of his works had been published in the pre-war times, it was during the Great Patriotic War (1941-45) that his talent developed to the full and brought him renown. The themes of his short verses are either patriotic or lyrical.

It's good I am no God but mortal man
Whose heart contains both happiness and
                                    grief,
Coevals two, and that my daily bread
From sea and soil I reap... Within the brief

Span of my life I travelled much and saw
The globe entire... Were I indeed a God,
I'd have been crushed by all I gazed upon,
The brutal carnage and the streaming blood.

Were I a God, I'd not have made the world
Just to amuse my fellows and inflict
Upon the being fashioned by myself
Such bitter suffering... I would elect

t's Good
Am No God!

To wield great rods of lightning and destroy
The treachery I witnessed, for the weight
Of crime and misery would otherwise
Have been too much for me... I'm glad that
                                    fate

Refused to make me cast the son of man
Into the flames, that I was not the one
To force him to his knees with cunning
                                    words,
With promises of paradise to come.

I could not be a non-existent shade
And blight existence with my godliness.
I could not be a hypocrite and bask
In never-ending, in celestial bliss!

Were I a God, not even then could I
The anguish bear of unrequited love.
What answer could I make the dying
                                    stars,
Their tortured doubts how silence or
                                    disprove?

It's good to think that, waking in the night,
My mother used to hold me to her breast....

363

No! No! To wound her now, to make her
                                    dread
The days ahead, I could not, I protest!

It's good I am no God, and that my heart
Is flesh, not stone, that sorrow it contains
And joy as well, that from the sea and earth
My sustenance I gratefully obtain!

Translated by *Irina Zheleznova*

Song of a Pine

I was a pine whose green and juicy branches,
Unsinged by flame, were dried by angry winds,
A pine by rude and thankless folk deserted
Who in my shade sought refuge in the spring.

I was cut down and cleared of bark and fashioned
Into a boat and tossed about by waves.
A tempest crushed me and the sea engulfed me,
But, rescued from a dark and watery grave

By roaring breakers and reduced to fragments
Upon a rocky shore, by gales was I
Into a fire swept at last, becoming
A dancing flame that burns but will not die!

Translated by *Irina Zheleznova*

I read all of your letters, Grimau,
And it was as if I had read
The whole of your heart,
A heart that laughed at defeat,
Line by line,
Beat by beat.
Your letters were the song you had
                                    sung

A year, a month, an hour
          Before you were put to death,
And I was stung
By the thought that our

Parting had preceded our meeting,
That I was hearing your songs
All too late,
That it wasn't fair of fate.

Julian Grimau

1963, Saturday, 20 April,
They led you away to die. . . .
Now where was *I*
On that day?
Can't remember, hard as I try.
Not that it matters. . .
All I know is that you were
                              there,
In that dank prison cell,
And I, I wasn't. . .
That is something I know very
                              well!

All your letters began with the words
"Angelita, dear love. . ."
And I knew it then as I know it now
That you never died, Julian Grimau!
When the native soil hugs her heroes close
To her motherly breast,
They turn into banners and songs,
With the living, with life they belong!

Full of hope was your heart,
                         full of dreams;
To make them come true you sought.

366

Where the battle raged fiercest, there
You, intrepid, fought.

You were never a sputtering light
That burns out and dies,
For your spirit blazed bright
As flame. . .
It cannot be that your eyes
Will not gaze on a happier Spain!

Before the shots rang out
In the prison cell where you had been flung,
Like a mother's heart
Was the heart of Spain
By a terrible anguish wrung.

Poor, long-suffering Spain!
Her sons age behind prison bars,
Poverty stalks the land, and mars
The lives of her daughters. . .
I will not say more,
Though there's much I would like to impart.
I will not say more
Lest I touch the strings
Deep down in your tortured heart.

I was in Moscow this spring,
                    and I saw
A street that seemed part of spring.
It flaunted its beauty,
It laughed, played,
Almost it seemed to sing!
High on its houses
Your name was inscribed,
And seeing it there
I knew it to be
That spring's and that song's
Refrain!

Translated by *Irina Zheleznova*

Snow, falling snow, and darkness all around. . .
Ahead of us—the foe, and just behind—
                                        the sea.
Guns spitting fire, a cold and lonely trench
Where, leaning on my rifle, silently
Dawn's slow and painful coming I await.
The sky, unlit by stars, is without light,
A moonless canopy. . . .
At break of day
We are to go into attack and fight,
Our bayonets in deadly combat crossed.
Come, morning, come,
Come, morning, to your post!
The flares of rockets pierce the dark. . .
                                        A brief

Come, Morning, Rise!

Exchange of fire. . . The blizzard takes command,
And wildly flings the snow about. . .
                                        My dreams
Draw near to me and firmly clasp my hand
And lead me far away. . .
And like a child,
I break into a run, afraid that they
Might plunge ahead and leave me. . .
                                        I am wrong,
For they are not mere empty dreams. . .
                                        Some day
Time will pronounce its verdict, and the world
Will put an end to suffering at last.
No longer will the skies be overcast
And dark. . . And like a sea, the fields of
                                        wheat
Will golden, spread across the giant plain.
The children of those days will, jubilant,
Recall our deeds and triumphs, and our fame
Sing joyfully. . . . And in my trenchcoat, I
Will with them be
And with them celebrate
The victory my generation won. . .
Surrounded by the young, if so wills fate,
I see myself, my hair to silver turned
And leaning on a crutch, replying to
Their eager questions, and with secret pride
The story of the days of war, a true,

368

Grim and heroic tale unfolding, with
The blood-red, sacred banner of my land
Clutched tightly in my one remaining hand...
No! That is not a dream. Come, morning, rise,
And let our bayonets pierce through the fronts,
And let our armies go into attack,
And let no more my country sorrow know,
Let victory's bright flags above it glow!

Translated by *Irina Zheleznova*

We Came into the World in Time!

We came into the world in time!
We came
Just when it needed us and, restless, ached
To be rebuilt, when seas of molten flame
Awaited dawn's embrace and yearned for peace.

Fate summoned us to train the battle-guns
Of the "Aurora" on the Winter Palace;
The people called to us, and we arrived
To wake the planet from its torpid sleep.

It was the will of this our age that we
Lift high and set alight the mighty torch
Of justice, that with calloused hands and strong
We build a new and better world for all.

Such precious gifts as land and fruit and joy
And also sunshine did we bring to men,
And, Lenin's glowing banner bearing proudly,
Marched, confident, along achievements' path.

We called for peace, with rays of hope we lit
The world entire, to future generations
Sent out a bold and daring challenge, blasting
Across the skies a pathway to the stars.

We taught mankind a great and wondrous truth
Whose name is communism. The glory of

369

Those days must be inscribed in flaming letters
Upon the walls of grey eternity.
We came into the world in time!
                                    We came
Just when it needed us and, restless, ached
To be rebuilt, when seas of molten flame
Awaited dawn's embrace and yearned for peace.

Translated by *Irina Zheleznova*

Bakhtiar   My heavy head encircling with my arms,
For long, long hours at a time I dream. . . .
A frenzied wind knocks wildly at my window,
The snow keeps falling, falling,
                                and I seem
To see you wading through it, tall and proud,
A mighty figure shouldering a gun;
I see you smile, I hear you sing, "A sword
Was I that did not fit its scabbard. . ."
                                Numb
I stand while you stride towards me, and
Stretch out your hand to me. . . . "It's wrong
                                to dwell
To long upon the past," you say, and add,
"I know you think of me, I know it well,
But sorrow is a crushing burden. . . Come,
Let's hear some verse. . ." And your tobacco-
                                pouch
To me you offer, and we roll ourselves
Two cigarettes, and smoke, and talk of such
Small things and big as matter most to us.
Then, with your eyes upon me, you repeat,
"Let's hear some verse. . ."
                        I take my note-book out
And read. . . . Along the dusty roads of war
It travelled with me always, and as I
Begin to read, the guns of battle roar,
And every line becomes a snow-bound road,
And every word, a bitter blast of wind. . .

370

A heavy fog descends, and in a mood
Of grieved unease I watch a loaded cart
Move towards me from afar. . . The horses drag
Despondently along, and in my heart
Their mournful tread is echoed. . .
       By the road
Twelve blood-bespattered, awful corpses lie,
Their sightless eyes turned to the leaden sky. . . .
Stretched out among them is the body of
My friend, a man who single-handed felled
Eleven wolves, and then himself succumbed
To death. . . . This is Bakhtiar, and stamped upon
His brow is all my people's pride. . .
        Alone
Am I today. . . Bakhtiar is not with me.
I lift my head. . . The darkness noiselessly
Descends upon the house. . . . The wind and snow
Rap at my window, and I hear a low
Voice say to me, while, deep in thought immersed,
I, silent, sit, "Come, friend, let's hear some verse."

Translated by *Irina Zheleznova*

Nigyar Rafibeili

NIGYAR RAFIBEILI (b. 1913), the daughter of a doctor, was born in Ganja (now Kirovabad) and educated at the Moscow teachers' college, the department of literature, which she graduated in 1936. Nigyar Rafibeili began writing poetry at the age of 17, and was one of the first Azerbaijanian poets to be translated into Russian and published in Moscow. She speaks on behalf of the mother, the loving wife, and the citizen of her country, rendering their emotions in evocative images. She is not a prolific writer, but then her every work bears the stamp of genuine talent. Her "Kitchen Lines" are a recent success. Nigyar Rafibeili is the wife of the poet Rasul Rza, and the mother of Anar, a gifted Azerbaijanian prose writer.

Crane

I, as spring advances, take another form.
    In the night time
I become a crane and, spreading my wings,
    soar away from the earth
To join the ranks of cranes
Thronging the wide spaces of the sky—
We fly and fly and fly
To the limits of the horizon. . .
We fly—and in our hearts
Are the most sweet,
Most tender,
Most joyful thoughts
Which we have received of the earth.
We fly and fly and fly. . .
We fling feathers
To humans who look after us with longing.
We fly to the high mountain peaks
And pause for rest, lingering guests.
We carry the fragrance of the earth
Up into the world of stars. . .
We carry the cry of life
Into the heart of loneliness,
    the cold breast of the moon
      alone in the sky. . .
In the morning,
    the glow of sunrise wakes me. . .
I awake joyfully,
Rise from my bed;
And then, all through the day,
I neither wish
Nor have the time
To spread my wings,
To soar from the earth,
    To become
      a crane. . .

Translated by *Avril Pyman*

The Artificial Heart

They are saying that doctors
Will soon be able to give
New hearts for old, out-worn ones. . .
Artificial hearts, substituted
With daring and precision.
Men shall rejoice and shall live
In joy and comfort, on and on
Until they are quite sated
With life and satisfaction.
But as for me, I beg now,
    Before, oh great physician,
You attain perfection in your art,
That, should paralysis strike
Disabling arm or leg now,
You should make me an artificial
Limb; if memory should fail,
Prescribe a medicine like
To ease headaches and tired brain.
Only, wise physician, refrain
From meddling with my sick, suffering heart. . .
Hearts that are artificial
Do not know heartache or pain,
Sweet dreams, golden memories
As unknown to such hearts as these
As joy and sorrow must remain.
And so, even should the tale
Of my life break off half-told—
Leave me my heart. For I hold
Most dear the wounds of my heart!

Translated by *Avril* **Pyman**

Kitchen Lines

I

If I were not a woman
I'd have no dealings
With saucepans,
Crockery,
Ladles. . .

I would meet the dawn on the seashore,

among the rocks,
And inhale the sea air
by the lungful.
I would stay for hours
in the untold bliss of the beach,
Baring my breast
to the wind of the plains,
Leisurely composing
Quiet,
Languorous songs
To the Apsheron gardens.
I feel so heartsore
in this kitchen world;
After all,
There is something of a poet in me.

II

There are poems devoted to sweethearts,
To the flowers of spring,
To the falling leaves of Autumn.
Poems are dedicated to the pain of separation,
To the joy of reunion,
To a woman's sweet face.
Then why are there none devoted to steam rising from a
saucepan,
To a humming samovar?
Why shouldn't there be
Poems about clean dishes
Washed in transparent water?
Some like their food well-salted,
others don't.
Some like jam,
others—raw tomatoes.
One can not tolerate meat,
Another likes his dinner without onions or garlic.
So I must stand there all day,
wiping, frying, cooking.
Some are destined to occupy high posts,
Others to wash up dishes in the kitchen.
Ah well,
sometimes an ordinary kitchen

May be cleaner
                and purer
Than it is in certain high quarters.
If I don't watch out
                while onions fry on the gas-stove,
They'll turn into ashes
And dinner will be ruined.
But who's there to see
That the cook burning by the stove
Doesn't turn into cinders?
Who cares for the cook
Whose heart isn't quite tranquil?
Don't grumble, cook,
        Watch out,
                don't dare burn the onions
                        that give taste and flavour to the
                                                dinner!

III

If a flowergarden can inspire a poem,
                Why can't a kitchen?
Just the same as a flower,
        A stove,
                And a grimy saucepan, too,
May ascend to the throne of art.
Poetic themes are countless,
As long as you see the world
        With the eyes of a poet.

IV

From the tiny window of my kitchen
I watch the four seasons of the year:
Summer, Winter,
                Spring, Autumn—
                        I see their real faces.

In Spring
        A tall poplar
        Next to my window
Is gradually covered with buds,
                Then leaves appear
And it puts on green apparel.

A light breeze blows,
    The branches whisper.
In Spring the tree stands swaying in all its grandeur.
In Autumn the wind buffets its breast
And with grief it turns yellow.
Then Winter comes
                and the tree strips bare.
No more greenery to inspire me.
Naked
        the tree,
Alone with its grief,
Baring its breast to the frost and the cold,
Hoping against hope to survive
Till spring.

V

With a generous heart,
                with a mind that sounds the depths
                            of existence,
Your dreams will not die,
                your thoughts will not fade.
If there is a divine light in your soul,
                hold it up as a torch
And from your tiny kitchen
                you will be able to see the great world.

Translated by *Dorian Rottenberg*

A Flower Blooming Amongst the Ruins

A flower blooming amongst the ruins set me wondering
Why do men say that in such desolation no flower can
                                                grow?
The walls of the little house were broken, the roof had
                                            tumbled in.
It had become the dwelling place of fierce winds and
                                        winter snow.
The untame winds had laid waste the dear comforts of this
                                    once-loved home
And had pierced the passer-by with melancholy pity.
The curtains, by gentle women's hands so lovingly stitched
                                    and sewn,
Hung ragged like shell-torn banners over a desolate city.

377

Amidst the heaps of stone and rubble bloomed the
                                                beautiful flower,
And that flower filled all my thoughts with one all-
                                                important question.
I asked: what gardener planted and nurtured you here,
                                                frail flower?
Tell me your story, the *dastan*[1] of your life, and I shall
                                                listen.
Perhaps although this place is no more vibrant with nigh-
                                                tingale's song
Abandoned by birds, yet you were called to being by
                                                Spring's first breath?
"I am the voice of the Earth," the flower answered with
                                                human tongue.
"I am that Greater Life which must for ever triumph over
                                                Death."

Translated by *Avril Pyman*

I Love You, Man!

I do not know where you come from,
Who summoned you to the aid
Of the mother sitting at the bedside
Of a sick child burning with fever,
Who called you,
Opened the door,
Let you in—
But I know:
The compassion that lives in your bosom,
The generosity that shows in your eyes
Opened the padlocked door.
You are neither brother nor sister to me,
And yet, though a stranger, I know who you are.
It was you who made well that baby,
Brought relief to the mother's despairing soul.
I do not know where you come from,
But I love you, **Man!**
The train, out of breath, came to a halt
Near a lilac-flooded township
In Northern Caucasus.

[1] Epic.

378

It looked like a flock of cranes, the township,
Alighting upon green grass,
Among white houses
And clustering lilac.
Girls and lads strolled along the platform
With lilac-sprays in their hands.
One of the girls held out
A bunch of lilac to me through the window.
Our eyes met, smiling,
And I said "Thank you!" to her.
And she said in reply: "Happy journey!"
The train set off on its way,
Surrounded by silence and clear, warm air.
I looked at my watch.
Our acquaintance had lasted one minute,
But the girl with the spring of lilac
Still lives in my memory.
In my memory I still gaze
At the golden-haired girls,
At the lilac-flooded township.
How I love you, Man!
My water, my salt, my bread,
My feelings, my aspirations, my dreams,
I share with him
Who breathes the same air as I do.
In our bosoms we carry love
For the same native country.
He regards my joy as his own,
My distress as his.
When I laugh, he laughs as well.
When I weep, he wipes his tears.
My comrade,
                    my countryman,
                                        my brother,
We feel and think as one.
With all my heart I love you,
I love you, Man!

Translated by *Dorian Rottenberg*

Zeinal Khalil

ZEINAL KHALIL (b. 1914) is the author of both short lyrical miniatures about love and the beauties of Nature, and large poetic canvases (Tatyana and Stars), as well as some dramas in verse. Zeinal Khalil was born in Ganja (now Kirovabad), and was educated at the Baku teachers' college, department of literature. He inclines to philosophical interpretation of life's phenomena. His poems are reflections about the times and people.

Through angry skies the jagged lightning flashed
As if a storm through mountain gorges dashed.
A moment passed—on mountains fell a hush
And they forgot that brawling, stormy rush.

* * *

The heart is like the sky, because in love
The thunder roars and winds rush high above.
Men are the heart's best friends right from the start.
Each heart-felt word must nest in someone's heart.

* * *

Miniatures

If you would fell a tree whose fruit you ate
To be a barren tree may be your fate.

* * *

My neighbour's brow is wet—
                    He broke a wall today.
Into his room he let
          The sun's first tiny ray!

* * *

My neighbour would not help himself,
Not even for his mean soul's sake.
He'd throw no light upon his pelf—
A window he would never make!

Translated by *Tom Botting*

381

O Give Me Not

Your nightingale
　　In a golden cage—O give me not!
White roses in
　　a flower pot—O give me not!
Your city doves,
Your circus lions
　　That cannot rage—O give me not!
Your fishes in aquariums,
On movie screens—your rains
　　And hurricanes—O give me not!
Friends who behind my back are foes,
Who change their guise each day—
　　O give me not!
Associates who are unloyal,
Respect, which seeks but to betray—
O give me not!
The praises sung by servile knaves
And doomed before their time to fade—
O give me not!
All that which earth and heaven hate,
Which neither heart nor mind can take,
　　O give me not!
That gain which is my neighbour's loss,
And riches won dishonestly—
　　O give me not!
O give me not!
O give me not!

Translated by *Louis Zellikoff*

* * *

One man said, "You're tired and weak!
 You should walk along the beach
 To see the moon and star-lit sky,
 Where the noisy crowd can't reach—
 Sea and heavens sooth the eye. . ."
One man said, "You're tired and weak!
 Once again the spring is here,
 Ride your horse and climb the hills.
 Life in town, I greatly fear,
 Makes men suffer many ills. . . ."
One man said, "You're tired and weak!
 You study hard and want to know
 What passed one hundred years ago,
 And what will be—you rack your brain—
 When just as many pass again?
 Such loads! You bear them all,
 The heavy and the light!
 At every battle-call
 Why dash off to the fight?"
One man said, "You're tired and weak. . ."
 "Just a minute there," I said,
 "Don't you feel that such words reek
 Of falsehood and things long dead?
 If I did not dream at night,
 If I did not think all day,
 If no news of our great fight
 Came from places far away
 If I did not add my word
 When the workers' shout is heard,
 If in pulsing city streets
 There were not my own heart-beats,
 If my strength I did not lend
 To great Africa our friend,
 If my help I never gave
 To bring freedom to the slave,
 If I did not stand and fight
 For what we believe is right,
 If I did not feel the heat
 Of my words and deep belief,
 And ignored the bitter-sweet
 Of a joy that's shared with grief,

If I let my footsteps lag
On the march with our great flag,
Then my verses none would read,
My native land would not pay heed!
If I must die then let it be
When Mankind's battles rage round me. . .
Then let me see the eyes of Man,
Let my hand grasp the hand of Man!

Translated by *Tom Botting*

Talking of Poetry

"O what a shame I wasn't born a poet!"
"What would you do if you were born a poet?"
"Give my heart away to her I love,
    "Compare her to the moon and stars above."
"No more?"
                "Everyone would read my poetry,
    "And everyone would point and stare at me."
"And then?"
                "They'd say—'what poems he can write!'
"And I would make a fortune overnight,
"And I'd become a famous man, you know,
"And to all great events I'd be asked to go."
"Dear friend! O what a blessing for the nation
You've neither talent, time or inspiration!"

Translated by *Louis Zellikoff*

* * *

Darling, I am weary,
    Very weary, dear;
I want no doctors near me,
    Dear, when you are near.

Darling, draw your chair up closer—talk to me—
    I want to hear your voice
    And see your face once more.
Bend your slender waist, my darling, over me
    And with your fingers cool
    My health restore.
Darling, I'm weary,
    Very weary, dear.
I want no doctors near me,
    Dear, when you are near.
The warmth of your dear hand,
    Your human love—
    For me are quite enough.

Translated by *Louis Zellikoff*

Enver Alibeili

ENVER ALIBEILI (1916-1968) was a famous writer of songs, and the author of a large number of verses, mainly, about Baku and the Bakunians, friendship and true love. Enver Alibeili fought all through the war, and often sent back poetry to Baku which was printed in the newspapers there. These last few years he has been chairman of Azerbaijan's Radio and Television Committee, doing a great deal to promote the development of these mass media.

Wishes

I'd like to be the moon up in the sky,
But not to wane,
I'd be a mountain path and run up high,
But never down again.
I'd be a flash of lightning far away,
But not to fade.
I'd like to turn into the light of day,
But not night's shade.
I'd like to pull the nose
Of death itself,
And die—when my eyes close—
A deathless death.

Translated by *Dorian Rottenberg*

Never Alone

A man who is needed by fellow-men
Will never remain alone.
I hope I will never have to spend
Even a day alone.
I want to live
Not as long as decreed me,
But as long and as much
As people need me.

Translated by *Dorian Rottenberg*

Stokers

A cold and wintery evening. It snows.
Out in the streets—not a soul.
But the people asleep in their warm, snug homes
Know nothing about the cold.
Although the wind may knock at the window,
The children aren't scared by the guest from the North.
Like borderguards, on nights cold and windy,
Stokers stand guarding their health and their warmth.
Until the frost and the snowstorms go
Chimneys will smoke like the heaviest smokers,
And warmth will come to every home
From furnaces fed by stokers.

Translated by Dorian Rottenberg

A Question

The oil extracted from the soil
Is often called black gold.
And surely, friends, the sight of oil
Is joyful to behold.
But if black oil is really gold
Then how, my friends, should he
Who draws it from the earth be called?
Suggest some name to me.

Translated by Dorian Rottenberg

388

On the Beach

Plenty of water, plenty of light,
Plenty of laughter and every delight,
Plenty of white-winged, blue-eyed waves
And the fiery, eternal breath of the sun
Turning white bodies into dark bronze.
The song of the waves
Blends with young laughter.
With millions of stars
The sun dots the water.
Even the bee, why even the bee
Forgets about honey and flowers
And tickles the girls that lie by the sea
Half-naked, for hours and hours.

Translated by *Dorian Rottenberg*

You Went Through the Garden

Early at dawn this morning
You went through the garden to breathe the sweet air.
How I can tell, you wonder?
The flowers bear the smell of your hair,
In the coy looks of daffodils
I see the light of your eyes,
In the nightingale's tender trills
The notes of your voice arise.
In the plane-tree's slender waist
There are traces of your own grace;
With the first rays of the sun
Comes the warmth of your tender heart,
In the petals of the poppy
I can see your sweet lips part.
All of it seems to say:
You went through the garden today.

Translated by *Dorian Rottenberg*

The Proverb

"This world that didn't become Suleiman's
Will never be yours, either."
So says the proverb
Passed on from mouth to mouth. . . .
    It is true,
    We will go,
    But the world
    And everything in it
    Will be left for the people.

Translated by Dorian Rottenberg

Truth

Truth is a thing
No one can hide.
Like a mountain spring,
Clear, undefiled.
Whenever you try
To block its source
It finds a new outlet,
Resumes its course.

Translated by Dorian Rottenberg

The "Happy" Fish

A fish got caught upon a hook,
So to get free again,
It turned and twisted, leapt and shook,
But all—alas!—in vain.
Another fish came swimming by
And saw the sorry sight.
"O me, o my!" that fish did cry,
"She's dancing with delight!"

Translated by *Dorian Rottenberg*

Waves
(Song)

Waves, o waves, are you birds on the wing?
Where do you fly from, what do you sing,
Waves, o waves?

You look at me with your eyes of blue,
Bright and clear, a heavenly hue,
Waves, o waves!

You shine in my heart long after we part;
You yourselves are a beating heart,
Waves, o waves!

All day long as you roll along
You compose new tunes to your own sweet song,
Waves, o waves!

You boil and break into shining spray—
What do you whisper, what do you say,
Waves, o waves?

Each wave resounds like a zither string,
May be it is of love you sing,
Waves, o waves?
    Waves, o waves!

Translated by *Dorian Rottenberg*

Talet Eyubov

TALET EYUBOV—poet, librettist and translator—was born in the town of Kazakh in 1920, and educated at the Azerbaijanian teachers' college, department of literature. His principal heroes are oil workers. He is the author of the libretto for the popular opera Sevil *based on the drama of the same title by Jabarly, a classic of Azerbaijanian literature. Talet Eyubov has translated several of Shakespeare's tragedies into Azerbaijani, and also the poetry of Pushkin, Nekrasov, Simonov, Antokolsky, and other classic and modern Russian poets.*

The scalding tea you served me spilled upon your
                                                    hand,
And instantly the world went dark before my eyes;
I thought till then you did not understand...
You did not look at me and to my great surprise
Said softly: "I know," and to me turning:
"Some burn their hands, and others' hearts are
                                                    burning."

When I heard you speaking about my desire,
Round and round all the world began to go.
How did you know that my heart was on fire,
Tell me, lovely one, tell me, how did you
                                                    know?

Tell Me, How Did You Know?

You never suspected until that day
That my soul pursues you wherever you go,
For I wouldn't tell you on that spring day
Of the winter burying my heart in snow.
Now I stood before you as if in a trance.
How, lovely one, did you disclose my desire?
From what chance movement, from what secret
                                                    glance
Did you know that my heart was indeed on fire?
As soon as I see you or hear your steps
Flocks of birds take wing in my lovesick breast.
I am no Medjnun to go out in the steppes,
That birds should alight on my head to nest,
That my troubles should forever be retold and recounted,
That I should make my home in the desert bare.
I am not Farhad to go splitting the mountains,
The sound of my pick being heard everywhere,
As the lips of Shirin stood in my eyes,
As Mount Bisutun trembled before me.
Nor am I Romeo to wait till the moon should rise
And do wonders, walls and balconies storming,
Or take up my faithful sword in my hand
And challenge my rival to a bloody fight,
Or under your window like him to stand
And sing serenades to you all through the night.
It would be ridiculous—like a bad jest;
In this age of the atom I leave it to others.
Then tell me, how did you know that my breast
Held all the love that tortured those lovers?

393

Tell me, lovely one, tell me, how did you know
That my heart had been burning since long ago?
Tell me, lovely one, tell me, how did you know
That my soul pursues you wherever you go?

Translated by *Dorian Rottenberg*

On the Banks
of the Volga

On the bank of the Volga, so proud and steep,
Stands a house near which bombs once raised black
                                                    fountains.
When the city stood flooded in blood knee-deep
It remained indomitable as the mountains.
Under shells that came pouring down in a shower
It became a fortress for many a day;
Sergeant Pavlov's men showed the foes their power—
It was here they started their westward way.
It means much, the name of that simple lad.
Any person with whom you may have to do
In the wonderful city of Volgograd
Will be able to show Pavlov's house to you.
What, indeed, does it mean to each of us,
That house once torn to its very foundations?
Every stone, every plank, every brick in that house
Is a monument to the friendship of nations.
On that fire-scorched wall, upon snow-white marble
Are written the names which explain its meaning.
In that fortress together with Sergeant Pavlov
Stood Russian, Georgian, Kazakh, Armenian.
True to his friends to the very last breath,
Stood the son of Azerbaijan as well.
In the terrible whirlwind of fire and death
With his comrades-in-arms, he fought and fell.
As one man they stood for the whole world to see,
Sons of their Motherland, true and courageous.
And for that on the day of our Victory,
Their names were inscribed on History's pages.
The house stands today as it stood before.
Symbolic of valour, supreme dedication,
A Monument, tested and tried in the war,
To the glory and comradeship of our nations.

Translated by *Dorian Rottenberg*

The Helm of My Heart

The Black Sea lies calm and clear,
Calm as a lamb just born,
The hills like the horns of a deer
Curve in the light of the dawn.
Our boat sails over the sea,
Gentle and mild as a dove,
And within our hearts you and me
Silently talk of our love.
Nothing on earth but the deep
Blue sea and we in our yacht.
Do tell me, why do you keep
In chains this heart that you caught?
You have no fear of the sea,
For the sea lies still and calm,
No danger for you and me,
No tempest to do us harm.
But oh, if you only knew
What tempests rage in my heart!
No, they are unknown to you.
But what if a real storm should start
On the sea and do us harm,
And we get drowned in the waves?
No—as to that, you are calm.
You know I am strong and brave
And storms cannot frighten me.
But with you in front of my eyes
I am helpless before the sea;
It can take me by surprise.
Do you know, at least in part,
My thoughts? Do you understand:
Today the helm of my heart
You, my love, hold in your hand!

Translated by *Dorian Rottenberg*

The brass-band is playing, the floodlights pour
                       light,
Then stormy applause dies down to silence,
And everyone catches his breath in delight
As a hush falls and in come the lions.

With a whip in her hand a frail-looking girl
Enters the cage where the lions are crowded,
And on seeing the girl, they begin to whirl
Around her, growling and roaring loudly.

But the girl just looks at the lions, smiling,
And suddenly they turn timid and meek.
At her very first word, black-maned lion
Comes forward and kisses his mistress'
                       cheek.

Before the Looking-Glass

At a word from her, to tempestuous applause,
The lord of the jungle lies down on the floor.
She takes in her hands his dagger-like claws
And dances around. Now the audience roars.

Applause bursts like thunder two minutes,
                       three...
Then the girl waves her whip and at her desire
The beasts form a circle obediently
Their hides aglow like a leonine fire.

Mighty lions who make the mountains shake
And the jungle resound with their terrible roar,
At a word from her without a mistake
Dance around and do tricks on the circus floor.

Applause bursts out, then the lights start fading.
As she leaves with her beasts, the girl waves her
                       hand.
The people go home, with impressions laden.
But why are the eyes of the girl so sad?

Why does she suddenly feel so unhappy
As she slowly walks to her room in a trance?
What's worrying her? What has happened?
By the side of her mirror a picture stands—

It's the man she loves, the man of her dreams,
With whom, lion-tamer, she's like a dove.
How many months more can he be so mean
And show no response to the poor girl's love?

Before the mirror in sorrowful silence
She sits and weeps, her grief unconcealed.
This girl who lords over tigers and lions
Can't bring the man of her choice to heel!

Translated by *Dorian Rottenberg*

Ibrahim Kebirli

IBRAHIM KEBIRLI was born in 1920 into a peasant family in the village of Kebirli. Upon graduation from the agricultural technical school in Akdam he worked as an agronomist at a machine-and-tractor station. He fought in the war (1941-45) and was decorated with several orders and medals. It was at the front that he first began writing poetry. This was in 1944. After the war, he studied at the Gorky Literary Institute in Moscow, graduating in 1954. He has published a number of poems depicting life in Azerbaijan today, and short philosophical and lyrical verses on lofty moral themes.

A Good Friend

When scandal's barbed and poisoned
                                    dart
Is hurled against your inner soul,
And when you find a cutting word
Is deeply thrust to wound the heart
A trusted voice can sooth like balm
And kindly words you need to hear—
Oh, then to have a good friend near!

Though eyes and lashes be jet
                                    black
And flash with fire, they seek the
                                    light.
If you are strong, then bitter words
Will shatter on your breast and back,
But if you have no strong defence
To meet those words, or make them
                                    veer—
Oh, then to have a good friend near!

A good friend's eyes their light won't
                                    hide,
But share it when the world seems dark.
A good friend's words a man can
                                    trust.
New hope they broadcast far and wide.
The road through life is hard and
                                    harsh,
When evil forces domineer—
Oh, then to have a good friend near!

Let no man yearn for praise unearned—
Each has one heart and lives but once.
A man is strong, but often weak.
And sometimes lets his head be turned.
When troubles seem to block your way
And evil counsel seeks your ear—
Oh, then to have a good friend
                                    near!

A man who's trusty, good and wise
Renews the senses, gives new strength.
And not to recognise that man

Would be a sin for any eyes.
When evil hands have gripped your heart
And darkened days when life seemed
                              clear—
Oh, then to have a good friend near!

Seek out a friend. Do not be weak
And do not let your spirits flag.
If you are poor, among good men,
You should not be ashamed or meek.
A man foresworn and gone astray,
Be he the richest profiteer,
Will weep to have a good friend
                              near.

Go seek a friend throughout the world,
Although the search be long and hard.
Though hatred's nets your feet enmesh
And highest hopes are downward hurled,
Thrust hate aside and clear your road,
March on because your goal is near,
You soon shall meet that friend most
                              dear.

So tread your own path till the end—
If you forget where true friends live
And their good name with mud besmear,
Do not lament that none is near.

                    Translated by *Tom Botting*

Freckles   My window shone. The glass was crystal clear.
The morning rays aroused me from my sleep.
When I walked out I saw that far and near
A mirror seemed to stretch along the street.

You surely know how Moscow winters glaze
The earth and sky a frosty white that makes

The breath float like a cloud of steamy haze,
While Jack Frost's flowers fall in little
flakes.

The morning walked to college at my side
Past Pushkin's statue where the snow-drifts
swirl.
When near the school I faltered in my stride—
Approaching me quite fast I saw a girl...

A dozen pretty girls will meet the eye
In busy streets on passing near that place,
But this one's eyes were bluer than the sky,
With scattered golden grains upon her face.

In fact she was as freckled as could be.
She hurried on as I stood thinking there:
For five years I've been here, but did not
see
In all of Moscow such a girl, I swear!

We used to meet each other every day.
It must have lasted some two months,
or so.
At first our glances met. We looked away,
Until we came to nod and say hallo.

No nearer did we come for quite a while.
Our glance grew softer, that I'll not
deny,
Until at last we couldn't help but smile
And then we'd stop and chat, not just pass by.

So time had done its work and each day flew.
Acquaintance ripened. Soon I got to know
That certain things in common linked us two
We both were students—that made friendship
grow.

But one fine day she did not come along
The pavement at the time she always did.
For three whole weeks I wondered what was wrong.
I smiled—I tried to keep my sorrow hid.

Her absence grieved me, hurt me to the
                                          quick.
A thousand "ifs" and "ands" beset my brain. . .
Perhaps she's caught a cold and lying sick!
Oh, ghastly thought—we may not meet
                                          again!

She would have told me where she lived,
                                          I know.
I did not ask. How impolite, unkind!
This town is huge. I could search high and
                                          low
Without a hope that that one girl I'd find.

At night my flagging spirits sometimes
                                          rose.
They fell each day. She never came in sight.
The bitter thoughts a lonely person knows
Gave me no peace throughout the day and
                                          night.

So time dragged on. Each day was dull and
                                          slow.
My life went on, but, ah, how bleak and
                                          hard!
But then one day, as I trudged through the
                                          snow,
We met again on Tverskoi Boulevard.

I saw the girl approach and gave a start,
She seemed so changed I had to stop and
                                          stare.
The most fantastic feelings stirred my
                                          heart—
Her springtime beauty seemed beyond
                                          compare.

Her eyes were azure blue, so clear and
                                          bright!
She walked across the ice. It seemed to
                                          thaw.
I gazed—that girl was such a lovely
                                          sight,

She could not be the one I knew
                              before.
I felt my heart renew its throbbing beat.
An inner voice was urging—"Don't be shy!
She is the very girl you used to meet,
But this time you make sure she won't pass by. . ."

Translated by *Tom Botting*

Zeinal Jabbarzade

ZEINAL JABBARZADE (b. 1920) was born into the family of a seaman in Baku. He graduated from a teachers' college just before the outbreak of the Great Patriotic War (1941-45) and served in the Navy all through its duration. His pen is mainly devoted to writing lyrics and verses for children. For a number of years he has been editing the magazine Young Pioneer *which is very popular with Azerbaijanian schoolchildren and which plays an important role in the development of literature for young readers. The work is after Jabbarzade's own heart in view of his training.*

If   Ah, if the skies above
Were always clear and cloudless,
So would our hearts be too!
Then our dreams,
      Our dreams would be beautiful, many-hued
                                      flowers;
Our faces and souls
Would be as pure as the snow
      Falling in blossom-like
                flakes.
The spring song of birds
Would be the melody
Heard all over the world.
Honey just taken out of the
                combs
Would be the bitterest word.
What use then would doctors and medicines be?
We would live to a thousand years!

                Translated by *Dorian Rottenberg*

A Conversation   One night, with my watch still on,
I got into bed,
Listened to the watch:
Tick-tock, tick-tock, tick-tock!
Then to my heart:
Thump-thump, thump-thump.
The watch said to the heart,
"Rest!
Have a bit of sleep.
You're tired!
How long is it since you were wound up?
You've a sort of hollow sound
                sometimes."
The heart began beating
Ever so fast.
It said: "What do you mean,
'Wound up'?

I've been hurt,
I've been angered,
I've been broken,
I've been hit,
But never wound up.
Whether I beat quietly,
Loudly
Or unsteadily,
I'm a heart
And I don't need winding.
If I could be wound up,
They'd call me like you—a watch.
And then I'd sit calmly
        Wherever they put me—
        In pockets, or on wrists.
As it is, I just go on beating,
Unwound,
        Untouched,
And I'm proud of it!"

Translated by *Dorian Rottenberg*

This World

This world of ours,
Is like a fine lad,
A fine young girl;
Don't spoil it!
It's like
        an enormous melon
Always
        ever so round,
        ever so cool,
        ever so sweet.
Everyone with a raper's hand
Sticks a knife into its side;
And look what they've done!
"I'll tell you a few things with rifle
                        and cannon," they say,
"Eat you whole in a single day," they say.
There were many who died of greed

Among those
Who divide it by force.
But nobody has eaten it
And never will!
The Earth rotates,
Spins on
Cheerfully.
All knives will be taken out of its sides!

Translated by Dorian Rottenberg

A Question

Once I was asked
"If
You were born once again,
What would you wish?"
If,
I replied,
I was born once more,
All alone,
A stranger among men,
My heart wouldn't bear it.
Yet if we could come to birth
All together—
You, he, and I,
I'd live this life
All over again!

Translated by Dorian Rottenberg

Balash Azeroglu

BALASH AZEROGLU was born in 1921 in Baku. His father was a worker. He spent his youth in southern, Iranian Azerbaijan, until about twenty years ago, when he returned to Baku for good. In 1952 he graduated from the department of philology of the Azerbaijanian University. Azeroglu's poetry is civic in content. His principal theme is the life of his brother Azerbaijanians beyond the Araks which makes the boundary line between Soviet and Iranian Azerbaijan. His trenchantly publicistic, emotional poem "The Motherland Demands Just Such a Son" is particularly popular.

*To the friends in penmanship
and struggle—Ali Tude and
Gamza Fatkhi*

The night was deep, the midnight hour had passed,
And still we talked, disputing without end,
I sat with the philosopher my friend
Both smoking packets, that till dawn would hardly
                                                    last,
And drinking tea, a samovar at least.
We talked.
Our voices rose and fell and never ceased,
Our words with fiery pathos would ascend,
But, like the Chinese Wall, there was no end
To words, opinions, running in one trend.
No matter whether long or short
This autumn night,—
But like a conquered warrior in his flight,
It cast its wasted weapons
One by one,
Before the advent of the rising sun.
The night, the stars, were melting in the
                                            sky,
And, like a sword besheathed, the moon did
                                            wane;
My friend breathed on his glasses,
Wiped them dry,
Methodically, put them on again,
Then looked at me above their rim
And said:
"Although you are a poet, you've a head
That can extract the root of the unknown.
And in society it is the same:
Society has laws and customs of its own,
You must not be regardless of its claim,
Or else no freedom can you give your folk,
And you'll not find the root of the unknown. . ."
I listened.
Of the laws alone he spoke,
And patience has a limit of its own,
And, candidly, I felt a little bad.
I longed to say a word to damp the fad
Of this life formula,

The
Motherland
Demands Just
Such a Son

409

And yet, controlling myself, heard him teach,
And cursed him, mutely, for his speech!
"My brother, stop your lecture, if you please!
You'll treat to this your students, at your ease.
Now listen well to what I have to say:
When banishment became Faruk's sad lot,
And when Feyssal[1]—the enemy, was shot,
The tyrant was dethroned and sent his way,—
Just tell me—was the formula transgressed,
Or was it not? or did it pass the test?
The twentieth century—a grey, old man
Of sixty, undertook
Its twenty-five campaigns
In Africa;[2] according to this plan
How many peoples triumphed for their pains?
How many lands got independent rights?
I'd like to know—the root of the unknown
Was found, or not? or it remained unknown?
And in Algiers how long went on the fights
With French authorities
Called civilised,
The wailings of the people for their rights,
And trampled down for what they yearned and prized.
And I should like to know
With whose just law
Does all this tally? Tell me this, and more:
Iran—a land with endless counsellors, just see?
You first take counsel with them, then you speak....
That's how things are!
The Land of Firdousi
Must counsel take with strangers—
What a freak!
The times are such—
No barrier can withstand
The ocean waves,
The masters understand,
And vote for the colonial downfall, too.
The white and black
Awake to freedom new.

[1] Last king and crown prince of Egypt.
[2] Allusion to the liberation of 25 African States which took place
in the year 1960, the year when the poem was published.

But here Azerbaijan
Has kept its feudal state:
You think. . . .
Your thoughts are red-hot, of a power great,
They burn your brain;
They burn your very hands.
You try to word them—
Breath and tongue
Are brands!
Since the 20th century marched across the land:
Three times Iran has grappled with its King,
Three times a progressive government was formed,
By the people who arose in mortal struggle.
But never once retreating in the fight,
Each, in the name of freedom, did his best,
Yet finally were crushed by the lords' might,
The nobles triumphed, fattened like a pest;
No schools to teach the language of Azerbaijan,
No alphabet to learn the ABC,
This is the vengeance of great Teheran,
'We are a mighty nation,' says Iran.
Encouraging, they pat our shoulder blade,
Yet use of our own language they forbade. . .
Who will repay for this atrocious
Crime!
While the orientals rise in force sublime,
While the oppressed their rulers overthrow,
Our tongue's forbidden!! This is mean and low,
So cheeky are the despots, as you know!
The tongue in which the Shahs wrote out their laws—
Prohibited! And one man is the cause.
You watch:
His human speech is full of flaws!
And then
Not worth a button
Is his hide. . .
Today they call our language purely local,
Upon which subject they're extremely vocal.
The folk whose Nizami
Is vaster than the world's great wide,
Is crammed into this same 'locality'!
Here is the tyrant's cheek:
And this is what

411

The grandson of the great Sardar[1] has got
Whose forebear gave Iran its freedom code!
This is
The greatest tragedy bestowed
On us by our 20th century. My friend,
My friend philosopher,
Please tell me now,
What law
Condemns us to such suffering without end?
O no, my friend,
O no!
There's no such law,—
It's just a legend old
That very soon should wholly cease to be:
The power of brandished swords,
And volleys free—
That is the Truth. . . .
My friend philosopher,
Our land today
Calls for a son, a hero in the fray,
Who would
With words of flame attack the foe.
Who Mount Savalan would then ascend,
And of an ailing nation's heartwrung woe
To all the East a thundering message send.
Let ancient Orient hear
The voice of those
Whose tongues are tied,
Whose blood stream ever flows
From shackled hands and deeply wounded breast,
So that the masters know and all the rest—
Those, playing with Azerbaijan's sad fate:
The ashes smoulder,
Flames, though low, yet burn!
Who plays with fire
Risks hand
Or beard to burn.
The Motherland for such a son would crave
Who'd have the heart of Sattarkhan the brave,
The breath of Khyabani,

---

[1] Ruler.

The ideals of Movjuz,
That from his flaming sword,
His fierce abuse,
And from his strong-spelled word of poet of **renown**,
The foe should take to flight, abandoning town **by town**.
My friend philosopher,
The Homeland wants today
A son who, in the tongue of the poetic lay
Of Fisuli,
Would deal a fatal blow
And with the mighty sword of Hatai[1]
Would break the heavy cannons of the foe;
Who, with ten heroes
In a little band,
Could thousands of the enemy withstand,
The sorrows of the 'small ones'
Are unending great.
Each man who has the force,
Whose word has weight—
Must be aggressive and protest,
If not—
He may be bullied easily, and shot.
There was a time
The Ruler of the seas,
The 'Master' of the negroes,
Forced his way
Into the East and said that 'these
Were not yet ripe', and then, without delay,
Proclaimed himself the 'guardian'
Of many a land.
Then the Lord Chancellor took the upper hand,
He shoved the laws into a safe of steel
Alongside peoples' independent weal,
As if they were a bank-note to conceal.
The ones who dared to speak
Were ordered to shut up:
'Your independence is in danger,' they were told.
'And if you speak—the devils will eat you up.'
Dear friend philosopher!
We have a proverb old:
'If you rely upon your neighbour's hand or head,

---

[1] Sattarkhan, Hatai—poets and national heroes.

413

Without your supper you will go to bed.'
If of your own complaints you take no care,
And do not see to forging your own rights—
No man will be concerned with your affair,
You are the one who for his own luck fights. . .
Who hears the wailing of the ocean fish
When sharks in hunger make of them a dish?
The hour has struck when for the people's lives
To fight, a son is summoned by our Land,
A son who with his teeth would break the gyves,
And, facing bayonets, would bravely stand
With fearless breast, and strong, undaunted air,
Whose breath would melt the heavy-armoured **tanks,**
And, further than a shot his voice would fare—
Shouting of justice to the people's ranks.
That Isfahan he'd reach with one strong hand,
And with the other Mahabad,
So to unite
Beneath one banner hearts of many a land.
A nation that would march for Freedom's **cause to fight.**
So let Iran then mount again its steed
Of revolution, and in one whole unite
The sword, the word, the pen's poetic might.
Let people march, let thirst for freedom—lead!
Who can refuse to die in trenches deep?
Is it not worse in wretched life to weep?!
My friend philosopher!
Who can refuse?
If one point of the law we violate—
Believe me,
There's no reason for abuse,
Our planet will not change, at any rate,
Believe me,
Neither will the 'unknown' suffer pain,
Then will the people's rights and power reign.
I know that then
You'll also find the way
How the root from the 'unknown' to extract.
The people's power must make
Existence bright and gay,
And use its sacred rights
With honesty and tact.
To make the law a noose—

That makes it hell;
Though a philosopher,
You ought to know this well:
The masses' greatest law is freedom,
That is so,
The other laws are wrong,
They bring us woe!
My friend-philosopher!
It seems that you agree?
There is no other way
To make all mankind free.
The nation may be weak,
Yet she must have her say,
The radical from her
You cannot take away!"

Translated by *Olga Moisseyenko*

Islam Safarli

ISLAM SAFARLI, poet and dramatist, was born in 1923 in Shekerabad, a village near Nakhichevan, which means "sweet town". During the Great Patriotic War he served in the army in the field and has been decorated with orders and medals for gallantry in action. Upon demobilisation in 1945, he enrolled at the Oriental Department of the Azerbaijanian University. His contemporaries, their joys, sorrows, loves and thoughts, constitute the content of his poetry. Islam Safarli's plays are noted for the sharpness of the issues he raises in them, and the lofty moral qualities of his heroes.

Far away from your dear homestead, from your native
                                                town,
Ever share a hostel room—a students' residence?
Live for years with college mates, sharing ups and downs,
Live a spartan student life of mixed experience?

Did you stay up late to study, nose inside a book?
Fall asleep beside it without switching off the light?
Sit in fear and trembling then at each exam you took,
Even though you'd crammed for weeks on end both day
                                                and night?

Cooked your dinner on a primus, thinking it a spree—
Scrounging matches from a coed in the dorm below?
Brewed within that silver teapot brought from home, your
                                                tea—
Strong tea, Lenkoran tea, that you never could forgo.

Students' Hostel

On a chilly autumn night, ever have an argument
Hot enough to keep you and the fellows up to three?
When at last you went to bed, you slept in deep content
Like a brave, all-conquering hero fresh from victory?

Hey there, fellow, did you get the very most you could
From those student days you spent in our beloved Baku?
Did you have a rare old time? It's never been so good?
Sometimes weren't you homesick? Yes, and thought of
                                                Mother, too!

I was there four years myself in our old 'Varsity,
Climbed like you the seemingly interminable stair.
Took my pen in hand and sought the muse of poetry,
Wrote my rosy dreams of youth and castles in the air.

Times there were when all were fast asleep in our hostel,
Far past midnight mine the only room that showed a light.
Many heroes—in my work I've come to know them well—
Seemed to stand before me in those lonely hours at night.

Mothers, too, encourage, help us through our college years!
Students don't forget it, though perhaps no word is said.
Tell me, hostel mine, of those who started their careers
Here before my time. Who was it slept in my old bed?

417

Maybe a geologist, now on a mountain trek?
Maybe just a teacher working in a country school?
Maybe, like Michurin, he is working out on spec
New arboreal theories that may challenge Nature's Rule?

Maybe, now his scientific thesis has been wrought,
In philosophy he is determined to expand?
Maybe he's a poet plunged into creative thought:
Word-paints into verse the wonders of our native land.

Students' hostel, months go by, and years go sliding past—
Hopes you planted in my heart still flower on renewed.
Nor will I forget you, my whole life to the last...
Of your kind maternal warmth, I write in gratitude.

Translated by *Gladys Evans*

Girl Engaged

In and out, the house is clean and neat,
Mother's baking scones on the griddle-sheet,
All the rooms are filled with fragrant spice—
Saffron-flavoured pilaff, lamb and rice.

Bustling nervously, the girl betrothed,
Glances out the window at the road.
This, the greatest day in all the year—
The groom-to-be must come, her cavalier.
Rose-water scent upon her hair, the lass—
Witching charmer—
        Lifts the looking-glass:
Slender crescent eyebrows, each an arc
Over almond eyes of umber dark.

Moon-breasts tremulous as gentle seas...
Gleaming braids that fall below her knees.
Yes, today's the greatest in the year—
The groom-to-be must come, her cavalier.

Mother gazes, words come tumbling fast:
"So it's done, and you're engaged at last..."

(Fights her inward sorrow—tears no more.
No man's strength and warmth, not since the war,

To her home has lent security...)
"Mum, don't think of how it used to be,"
Says the lass, with blended smile and tear—
The groom-to-be must come, her cavalier.

Translated by *Gladys Evans*

White-Caps

Wind upon you beating fretful,
Swift as flying stormy petrel:
Soar like cranes on wings of surf-swell,
Hoot with strident laughter, White-caps,
Crest in seething foam, O White-caps.

You are dancing-hot rapscallions,
Ardent, brightly silvered stallions,
You—white wings of my song-galleons,
Out from happy shores, O White-caps,
Kissing crest to crest, O White-caps.

Arched the moon in bending crescent,
Shooting stars rain phosphorescent,
Skyline lit by dawn quiescent—
Sleep a little, rest, my White-caps,
Pearl-white, milky flowing White-caps.

Gone to sea—my Love Abading,
White his sail out yonder gliding,
Swept by waters into hiding—
Run, you rainbow-arrowed White-caps,
Keep him safe for me, O White-caps!

Leap from depths and grasp the blighting
Jagged arm of forking lightning.
On his raven hair cast brightening
Briny kisses, frosty White-caps,
Turtle-doving, blue-eyed White-caps.

419

Let my loved one know the Ocean
In my breast of love's emotion:
In my breast, in boundless motion.
Beat within my breast, O White-caps,
Sigh and surge within, O White-caps.

Translated by *Gladys Evans*

One Glance

One glance—a look of withering fire
That burns away your heart entire.

One glance such measured cold employs,
No spark of life disturbs its poise.

One languid glance takes witching toll—
Beguiles away your very soul.

One glance breaks into radiant rays,
Turns arctic nights to tropic days.

One arid glance your love denies—
Compels such grief the spirit dies.

One glance, one look, all hearts subdue—
In love with it is all Baku.

This winning look such charm proclaims,
My heart is startled into flames.

You—a world beyond surmise—
O glances! Glancing eyes!

Translated by *Gladys Evans*

Silent Moments

Hooded Kalagai[1] a nimbus white
On moon-head sailing through a sea of cloud.
Should my love not meet me as she vowed,
Then what misery will drown the night...

...Feathered touch of hand upon my shoulder;
Turn and see, dark eyes with amber glaze.
Eyes that shine with such a lucid gaze—
Are they from the very moonlight spun?

Hushed and still the sea-cloud moves no more,
Hardly heard, the sea laps on the shore.

She is silent, mute and silent I—
Swift our sail moves toward the line of sky.

By Allah, they are worth the whole world wide!
Priceless silent moments, side by side.

Translated by *Gladys Evans*

---

[1] Eastern figured white silk shawl with striped border, worn as woman's head-covering.

Kasum Kasumzade

KASUM KASUMZADE, a poet and scholar, was born in 1923 into the family of a forester. His native village is Khodjamsakhli in the Kubatly district of Azerbaijan, a land of snowcapped mountains, alpine meadows, brilliant sunshine and impetuous rivers. And all his life, Kasum Kasumzade has been striving to express in his poetry the wonder and beauty of his native landscape. He has many poems about the forest and its mysterious world. He is very keen-sighted for the colours and details of the surrounding world. His verses are imbued with affection for the workers of the soil—wine-growers, cotton-growers and ploughmen. Lately, Kasum Kasumzade has devoted much time to literary studies.

He gripped the phone, then felt a tinge of fear.
He spun the dial, but found his hand was shaking.
The mother's voice he hoped he would not hear...
That voice rang out and he retreated quaking,
For yesterday's encounter rankled yet,
"Please be so good to call her..." he began,
"I mean, please call your daughter Malahét..."
"And who are you to call her up, young man?"
"I'm someone whom I fear you never knew."
"In that case I can only say goodbye!"
"Oh dear...!"
          "My daughter shall not speak to you!"
"Oh please...!"
          He said no more. His lips were dry.
He sensed the fire in every searing word.

The Telephone Call

She frowned to see the girl stood near the phone.
Incensed she thundered when his sigh she heard,
"Now call no more! You leave my girl alone!!"
Don't call! And yet his finger turns the dial.
He tells himself, although he's very shy,
"She'll get to know me in a little while.
I'll make her like me. Anyway I'll try!
For after all, that's what she ought to say.
Her stand was right. She could not take another.
That girl will guard her daughter, too, one day
As she is sheltered now by her own mother."

Translated by *Tom Botting*

The Shore Lay Still

The shore lay still. The people went their way.
Impassioned waves adorned the cliff with spray.
I said, "Let's take a boat, we'll rock and sway."
You frowned and shook your head,
"We can't, we can't!" you said.

The midnight moon hung, lighting troubled seas.
Your dress was thin and fluttered in the breeze.
"Oh come," I said, "draw closer lest you freeze."
Your cheeks with angry shame grew red,
"I can't, I can't!" you said.

Now scarlet dawns aurora starts to grow,
While gleaming dew-drops set the grass aglow,
I say, "We two our separate ways must go."
You hold my hand, your glance grows fey,
"We can't, we can't!" you say.

Translated by *Tom Botting*

Immortality

If those who sprang from one man's loins
Could leave their graves and form on
                                   earth
Just one long line that links and joins
There'd be a million, old and young,
Of every hue and every tongue—
So many hearts of sterling worth.

And in that line that still must grow
Should stand the ones to follow me,
For in their veins my blood must flow
The blood of our own ancient line,
Of honoured ancestors of mine,
True men of honour, bold and free.

That line's a chain that stretches back.
It has no end, no final stage.
And not a link that line can lack,
For if just one were torn away
I would not see the light of day,
Nor know the wonders of our age.

Perhaps the final link am I
In what I thought an endless chain. . .
To plumb profundities I try.
My hair I see is iron-grey.
My heart is sad and held in sway
By bitter thoughts and gripped by pain.

A thousand lights made thoughts shine
                                 clear. . .
Anxious for those to follow me,
For those I feel so close and dear;
Yet in my heart I envy youth—
I wrote this poem filled with truth
With thoughts about the days to be.

My happiness at least unfurled.
Now in our home my children sing.
I sense the joy of our fine world
And know with all my heart and brain
In that unbroken, vital chain
I am no final, unlinked ring.

425

How many branches has a tree?
How many grains one cob of corn?
So death, don't pride yourself on me.
This blood that pulses through each vein
A million times shall live again
In generations yet unborn!

I'll see the future with the eyes
Of millions stretching out on far
To time's horizons in the skies.
For generations yet to be
This world of ours have yet to see,
The sun, the moon and each bright star.

Translated by *Tom Botting*

Blessed

This morning going down the stairs I mumble,
"Such muggy weather,
Anyone would grumble!
            A silly winter—
                    There's no ice or snow."
For years it's been that way. I even know
Some kiddies who are five but have not seen
The snowflakes whirling when the wind is keen.
How fine to walk when snow lies all about,
To raise one's voice and with the snows-storm shout!
My neighbour's daughter hurries up the stair.
Although it's winter spring is in her hair,
For she is wearing flowers white and gay.
I sense her cheeks aglow from far away.
A bride she seems, with orange-blossom wreath
As fragrant as that charming face beneath.
I stop and take her hand and then I know.
Her hair is white with freshly fallen snow.
But also let it be as first I guessed—
Let snow and orange blossoms both be blessed.

                    Translated by *Tom Botting*

Nabi Khazri

NABI KHAZRI was born in 1924 in Khurdalan, a village near Baku, into a poor peasant family. He studied at the Gorky Literary Institute in Moscow, from which he graduated in 1952. His works have been translated in Moscow by such well-known Russian poets as Vladimir Lugovskoi, Yevgeny Yevtushenko, Yevgeny Vinokurov, Vladimir Soloukhin and others. Translations of his poetry in the languages of other Soviet republics have also been published. His poems are philosophical meditations about the world, Nature and Man. His lyrical hero is tender and sensitive, strong and wise. Of especial popularity in Azerbaijan are Khazri's poems "Sumgait Pages" about the young workers of Sumgait, a new industrial town, and "The Sister of the Sun" whose heroine is a girl tractor-driver. For the last few years Nabi Khazri has been head of the Republic's Television Board.

The evening cloud has formed above the deep ravine.
In silence stand the woods below the mountain peak.
Ah, how I long to know what tranquil moments mean!
For silence has a tongue—tranquility can speak...

Oh, listen to the spring where forest waters well,
Or near a mossy pool where moisture slowly drips.
Those waters sing the tales the mountain ranges tell,
Forever through the ages grand sagas pass those lips.

The wind can sing a song. Perhaps its words would
say
It really is the breath of mountain woods on far.
Perhaps the crystal dew on which the moonbeams play
Would claim deep in the night to be another star.

The Voice of Nature

Let nature's sounds go sweeping over hill and dale
And see how mountain torrents foaming water hurl.
So when you quench your thirst the water without fail
Will tell how through the eons rivers leap and swirl.

Let rivers thrust on down and press upon the sea,
While this old world exists the sea will hardly
change.
The waterfall shall leap, forever breaking free,
It is the dearest child of this great mountain range.

May poplars' skilful singing fall upon your ear
Their songs are hymns when trees are bursting into
leaf.
But later if you listen yellow leaves you'll hear
Intoning with the twigs a dismal dirge of grief.

If nature's heady speech throughout your soul can rise
Within your heart you'll know the greatest joy of all.
Perhaps there's fixed upon you, like a deer's dark eyes,
The wonders of all nature, since you heed their call.

O learn to sleep and rest—in fragrant meadows lie,
Where scarlet poppies blow and little insects hum.
If you keep still all Nature moves before your eye
And with her breathless beauty will seem to strike you
dumb.

Oh, see the branches wave to that lass on the shore.
Beside the mountain lake the countryside is wild.
The woods and peaks have beauty, yet the girl has more.
Without us Mother Nature is like an orphan child.

Let nighttime thunder roll and let the lightning blaze,
At dawn the face of Nature soon will shine anew.
Let Mother Nature lave your soul with soothing rays
And like a cleansing flood let light go sweeping through.

The countryside you'll find has springs on every hand,
To hear the earth and sky your travels you should start,
And inch by inch explore your lovely nature land,
Its throbbing heart you'll sense deep down in your own
heart.

Translated by *Tom Botting*

I feel here live great legends all around.
With deep respect here come sons of our land
To where great men are resting in the ground—
Balzac is sleeping somewhere near at hand.

In one most honoured spot here stands a wall
Where deadly bullets left their searing mark.
The stones can speak and you may hear them call,
They sing a thousand sagas if you hark.

That wall has now been standing many years
And many times the dawn has stained it red,
As when the killers shot to calm their fears
And Paris wept for Communards now dead.

A Minute of Silence

(In the Père Lachaise[1] Cemetery)

We feel the surge of men's most noble dreams
As we stand near that wall with lowered head.
A thousand hymns of praise must sound, it seems,
To break that minute's silence for the dead.

The silence reigns. Through clouds appears the sun.
A hundred vivid scenes flash to my eyes.
The silence breaks before a roaring gun—
The blood of Communards to heaven cries...

The silence fled. Great storms surge round the
                                                    wall.
I hear defiant songs those heroes sing.
"Long live our great Commune!" I hear them call,
And in their voices tones of triumph ring.

The deadly bullets sing their whining songs.
To curse this scene Marat shall yet come back,
When France's heroes suffer such great wrongs,
A shudder shakes the tomb of great Balzac.

The years flash by in one unending race.
Those men are now their country's great ideal.
Those jagged holes where bullets left their trace
Are wounds the nation bears and cannot heal.

[1] Père Lachaise, the cemetery in Paris where many Communards
were shot after the fall of the Paris Commune of 1871.

431

Some wounds we can't forget, nor yet forgive.
A thousand hearts forever bear their pain.
And so the heroes evermore shall live.
Ideals for which they died now rise again.

The rolling earth and sky like thunder boom
And tell me that my heart is wounded, too.
On desert sands of far-off Ak-Djar-Kum[1]
The killers' bullets pierced me through and through.

The minutes pass. The wind has stirred the sand.
The heroes final song sounds far and wide,
Like one great voice. Unflinching there they stand.
"Long live our great Commune!" they shout with pride.

When news of our great spring I first received
From battles I had come, and then returned...
I saw our heroes' bloody shirts and grieved.
I held them to my breast and hot they burned.

The cause of heroes cannot ever die.
Their love for man is deep as any sea.
They take men's dreams and raise them up on
high.
So people's hope alive shall always be.

Our red-starred spring has shared with all its
light.
"We found the truth!" in silence we declare.
"We who salute you won the people's fight—
Our land is free!" in silence we declare.

To each of us that silent minute gave
A flood of feelings none of us could hide.
It seemed to me Balzac had left his grave.
And stood in pensive silence by our side.

My heart, don't grieve, though sorrow be profound,
For your great love is our new age today.
In one short minute's silence I have found
Far more than words in many years could say.

[1] Site of massacre of 26 Commissars of Baku.

The minute passed and every heart then bloomed
With hope new born, with one most cherished thought.
Beside the wall that stands amid the tombs
We heaped the blossoms each of us had brought.

So many heartfelt words whirl in my head,
A minute's silence cannot tell them all!
If any wish of mine remains unsaid,
Let flowers speak to you beside this wall.

Translated by Tom Botting

To our Venerated
Poet Samed Vurgun

The Stag

Through dense protective thickets you appear,
With timid eyes around the forest glade you peer.
Perhaps you would have crossed it, but now veer...
Is that because you set your eyes on me, O stag?
Now tell me, why you bend that graceful neck, O stag?

How large and soft are those black velvet eyes,
How many hearts bear wounds dealt by your eyes?
Oh tell me where you turn those lovely eyes?
And why should they hold sadness, noble stag?
Your glances wound my heart, majestic stag.

Through what sweet valleys do you proudly pace?
In what retreat have you your drinking place?
Through your domain what pathways do you trace?
I long to tread your forest paths, O stag!
And drink, like you, from Sylvan springs,
                                                    O stag!

Oh, leave the thicket. Do not stand at bay!
My head is reeling—do not run away...
For just a little while, I beg you, stay!
Oh, let my eyes behold your beauty, stag!
Oh, do not hurry off, you regal stag!

I long to come to you, sweet creature, stay
And let me stroke your silky flanks, I pray.
The tears you shed, my hand shall brush away.
Your eyes reflect your doubt, majestic stag,
But I am not a hunter, noble stag!

Translated by *Tom Botting*

434

Kiapaz

At times the clouds above you softly stray,
At others storms with lightning flashes play.
I feel the warmth of valleys giving way
To chilly winds upon your flanks, Kiapaz!
See people come to speak with you, Kiapaz.

Do you take pride in crags that touch the skies?
Has not all history passed before your eyes?
Does not the snow that round your summit lies
Date back to times of Nizami, Kiapaz?
Must you be silent? Won't you speak, Kiapaz?

May flowers always deck your slopes, I say.
And may you sleep embraced by stars, I say.
The father of our earth are you, I say.
Gyok-Gyol, your tender daughter, waits, Kiapaz,
So warm your daughter on your breast, Kiapaz.

How could the streams that from your ledges leap!
Ravines that gash your sides are green and deep.
No man can scale your summit tall and steep.
How dear and close to me you are, Kiapaz.
Approach, I would embrace you, my Kiapaz.

Forever I would watch you, face to face.
Let all your winding trails my footsteps trace.
We must draw closer yet in our embrace.
You hold my very soul in sway, Kiapaz.
My heart is always yours, O great Kiapaz!

Translated by *Tom Botting*

Hussein Husseinzade | *HUSSEIN HUSSEINZADE, a popular writer of lyrics, was born in 1924 in the village of Eni-Gyun, which means "new day", in Akstafa district. He comes of peasant stock. Hussein Husseinzade fought in the Great Patriotic War and after that studied in the Oriental department of the Azerbaijanian University. His style is terse, in the tradition of folk poetry, and aphoristic. It is melodious, songful and clear cut. Husseinzade seems to know all the folk poetry by heart and can recite the verses of ashugs and the quatrains of nameless authors for hours. His perception of the world is cheerful and optimistic. Besides songs, Hussein Husseinzade is also famous for his long poem about Samed Vurgun entitled "On the Road".*

Curtains

There are curtains hiding evil,
Hiding lies of seasons gone.
There are curtains like a barrier,
So you know not what goes on.

There are curtains hide the heavens,
That the stars to shine forbid.
There are curtains hiding secrets
That for months and years are hid.

There are curtains of all colours,
Made of silk and made of lace,
Made of clouds and made of fire,
Even of a smiling face.

Let us live without these curtains,
Leaving only one, although.
That's the curtain of politeness
We to older people owe.

Translated by *Eugene Felgenhauer*

Care

I was leaping 'midst the boulders,
Never stumbled anywhere.
Neither did I lose my footing,
When I scaled the mountains bare.
On ascents I didn't stumble,
On descents I didn't stumble,
For I picked my way with care.
    On the ice I kept my footing,
    Then on level ground, howe'er,
    I fell down, though dry the pathway
    And no obstacle was there.
For no more as in the mountains
Did I move about with care.

Translated by *Eugene Felgenhauer*

In the Zoo

The zoo... Oh, what a crowd today,
The people's merry voices flow.
My son and I walk hand in hand,
The cages stand all in a row.

I see a deer, its eyes are moist,
An eagle broods, as if in pain.
A lion sleeps against the bars,
A tiger languor seems to feign.

And when we'll both come home again,
My son will tell all what he's seen.
It's true, my son, your eyes are keen,
You saw the cages with your eyes,
But, son, what did you realise?

Translated by *Eugene Felgenhauer*

Wind

Pass across the meadow, wind,
Flower fragrance spread apace.
Pass across the grain-field, wind,
Spread its scent to every place.
You may sweep the whole world's girth,
All the plains and mountains, wind,
Only spread not o'er the earth
Acrid smell of war, oh wind!

Translated by *Eugene Felgenhauer*

Springs

A spring's as clear as limpid eye,
As pure as rarest medicine.
Fast springs to distant oceans hie,
And it is just because of springs
That streams grow big and turn to seas.
Within the body of a sea
A thousand springs have gone to sleep,
And all the rushing mountain springs
The sea inside itself can keep!

Translated by *Eugene Felgenhauer*

Narcissus stopped me on the bank,
Said, "Linger yet in this fair land."
And grasses said to me, "Recall
The friend you walked with hand in hand."

* * *

Remember

The pinks looked straight into my eyes,
Said, "Linger here and try to think."
A clover showed its drop of dew:
"Who my sweet balsam would not drink?"

* * *

You need not talk to Spring—just laugh,
Just gather flowers in the dell.
You need not know the tongue of flowers,
Remember but their fragrant smell.

Translated by *Eugene Felgenhauer*

My Saz Speaks

I am thinking in my room,
    As I listen to my saz,
To its lilting melody.
And my saz, it speaks to me,
    Calmly, softly,
    And I list
    To the strains of "Keremi".[1]
And I listen as it sings
    Of the ages sad gone by,
    Of the lovely maid Asli,
    Of her lover poor Kerem!
Strings of saz, they say to me
    In a language all men know
That if human life doth end,
    Human love will still go on,
Human dreams and human deeds
    Will live on—
                are not in vain.
Thus my saz, it speaks to me
    In the quiet of my room:
Though Kerem will pass away,
    "Keremi" will still remain.

Translated by *Eugene Felgenhauer*

O My Songs

O my songs,
If after I am gone,
To someone you bring joy,
To someone prove a balm,
From sickness someone cure,
    Then well you may live on.
If not, depart with me,
When I have travelled on.
And do not waste the space
Of progeny to come.
    For there are many such,
    Who to this world hang on,
Who for the other folk
A load are and a yoke.

Translated by *Eugene Felgenhauer*

[1] See epic about Kerem and Asli.

Fresh Grass

Emerald grasses and flowers so gay,
Roses so sweet in the wood.

* * *

Pheasants meander the whole of the day,
Thrushes trill songs in the wood.
Dogwood and blackberries, as on display,
Raspberries red in the wood.

* * *

Green-footed mountains with snowy-white peaks
Also are seen in the wood.
Dear old companion who smiles as he speaks,
Forester there in the wood.

* * *

Milk that's the freshest and honey so pure—
All that you wish, in the wood.
Nature, the doctor that always will cure,
Never grows old in the wood.

* * *

Lion so proud and red deer so sweet,
Hart you will see in the wood.
Tell everybody—whoever you meet—
People live long in the wood.

Translated by *Eugene Felgenhauer*

Ali Tude

ALI TUDE was born in 1924 in Baku, and for a time lived in southern, Iranian Azerbaijan. He came back to Baku more than twenty years ago and studied at the University there, in the department of philology. His principal theme is the life and struggle of the people of South Azerbaijan for democracy and freedom and their protest against oppression and destitution. Ali Tude has written many verses about Baku, about Azerbaijanian workers—engine-drivers, carpet weavers and builders.

The Mountain

Once a mountain, none knows why, fell prey to Pride—.
"Look," he said, "how proud I stand, how dignified.
Neither Rain nor Snow can me defeat.
The very Earth lies prostrate 'neath my feet!"
Earth! Old Mother Earth! Long-suffering and mild!
"Mountain, look you underfoot," she called and smiled.
"It is I that spreads before your eyes—
I am the support from which you rise!"

Translated by *Gladys Evans*

The Sword

Awakened from its age-old rest
A city many ages old
Bared the stone layers of its breast. . .
A sword. . .
      They raised it from the mould. . .
It had done its bitter work.
How much blood it caused to flow!
Numberless the foe's lost heads
Slashed in battle by its blow.
On no saddle, on no belt,
As an emblem does it shine.
But. . .
      The history of our land
Mentions it in one short line.

Translated by *Gladys Evans*

The Shusha Mountains ... vibrant-cool the air...
O you creators, gaze on this creation.
And Nature glorify, who made this fair
And awesome sight, that strikes the imagination!

It's sundown ... in the sky hang cumulus—
Piled clouds, like burnished copper shot with
                                                    wine.
Such happy crowds at Djidir Track, such bliss
For those at Isa Spring so crystalline.

I see that even yet upon the grass
Relax the guests who dropped at random in...
Lightly from mountain, gorge, the echoes pass
Back sounds of tympan, viol, mandolin.

Girl of the Mountains

Down sheep and shepherds wind their homeward
                                                    way,
The wind whips on the lilt of piping flute.
To hear the Karabakh melodious lay,
The birds within their nests lie still and
                                                    mute.

Then like a fine white shawl the mountain mist,
Drifts many layers deep into each gorge-vent.
Above the Yalchin summits, amethyst,
The sky is setting up its spangled tent.

Comes evening ... lovely falls the Shusha night!
The moon beyond the mountains climbs uphill—
At every step, the sky another taper lights;
In field and mountain voices raptly still.

Comes evening ... lights in every home flash on,
Each window beams its brilliance at my
                                                    feet.
And in my heart new interest starts to dawn
As I go roaming through familiar streets.

And now a girl with such a lovely voice
Starts singing, singing, singing, somewhere
                                                    near,
So all my heart can not help but rejoice
Such loving kindness in her voice I hear...

"The rose is shaken by her fears,
My patience at an end, I plead:
O dark eyes, dark eyes, dry your tears
And cry no more, there is no need."

As if my feet took root . . . so very long
I stand and listen: O my motherland!
A hundred times I listened to that song
Back in Tauriz from streets on every hand—
Their voices ringing out like muted chimes,
The girls at sunset through the park-gates would flock
                                                    in—

Within my heart, recalling other times,
Breaks wailing the Kemancha violin.

Sing on, dear sister, though it brings me pain,
Sing on, your brother hears, his heart console.
I dearly love that song, that sweet refrain,
As if it were my homeland's tender soul.

Sing on, dear sister! Happiness is yours.
Sing on, may heartbreak never venture near.
This moment, how I wish your voice would soar
So all my folk, my nature land, could hear.

Such homesick love within my heart is borne. . .
Could you but slit my heart and look within! You might
See my love's eyes, clear as early morn,
My love's hair gleaming through as black as night.

A treasured souvenir, her pictured face
I've hung for safety deep within my heart.
This girl that once I held in my embrace,
One moment swift before we had to part.

And so I left my love, Taurizian fair.
Death trailed me shadow-like, an exiled waif.
But still my sweetheart's love has helped me bear
The ache of parting, and my love kept safe. . .

She was a one to sing, the same as you,
O mountain girl, back in her native land—

445

That old sweet song, she often sang it too;
And with her melting voice my heart unmanned.

Where is she now? Look there, how like a snake
Twines the Ara in coils and hooded twist!
While farther from these waters mute, opaque,
The forests thicken dark as midnight mist.

O Karadag! My homeland ever dear!
Land of my fathers, land of Sattarkhan.
And, pondering his lot, to me appeared
In vision a new world for all my clan:

"Attention! Listen! This is free Tauriz!
Welcome, Azerbaijan, where freedom reigns!"
Reaching to all horizons, from Tauriz
In waves the call sweeps continent and main.

Then celebration . . . day of triumph, gay
The hall with flower garlands finely dressed.
O girl from Karabakh! You are today
Among our new-arriving welcome guests.

On stage a crimson banner spreads its wings,
The target of all eyes, where hopes compile.
And there's our Teacher's statue—living thing—
That looks upon us all with such a smile. . .

Lenin! I've known him from my earliest year.
Victorious whatever battle dawned!
Now see that picture! They, too, watch us here—
Erani, Pishevari, Sattarkhan. . .

The meeting opens . . . all with deep concern
Attend the speakers' warm, sincere orations.
O girl from Karabakh! Now its's your turn
To take the floor with glad congratulations.

And while you make your speech, O mountain
                                        Rose,
My heart is washed of grief. At meeting's end
No trace of it remained, and I arose
And went to meet you like an old, old friend.

446

But when you saw the person by my side
You asked me, "who is this, my Poet-brother?"
Eyes on your dark ones, shyly I replied,
"Oh, meet my girl. I hope you like each other."

Translated by Gladys Evans

City

My Pen, you've written of a wealth of things,
Now let your verses to our city sing!
Be quick! Another's words in print may spring
And glorify its valour, work, the song it sings...

A city with Koshkar[1] like heart, and thoughts—skyway.
Embrace its crowds exuberant. Love by day
Its sunshine, and by night its Milky Way—
This city of Copper, Iron, Cobalt-grey.

City where concert-halls themselves surpass,
And tall pavilions preen in ivy and glass,
And stadiums welter ankle-deep in grass,
Steep slopes enlivening the city's level mass.

Its former glory is no vain deceit,
It towers on hills with valleys at its feet.
Its tempo challenges: may cities all compete!
Let cities east and west the challenge meet!

The mountains speak their love to all the sky,
To reach the very stars, their crest-tips try;
And to display it in the whole world's eye
They raise the city on their shoulders heaven-high.

Translated by Gladys Evans

[1] Mountain in Azerbaijanian part of Caucasus.

Bakhtiar Vagabzade

BAKHTIAR VAGABZADE, a well-known poet, dramatist and scholar, was born in 1925 into a working-class family in the ancient city of Nukha. In 1947 he graduated from the Azerbaijanian University, department of philology, took a post-graduate course to receive the degree of Candidate of Science, went on to teach at the University. Three years ago he gained his degree of Doctor of Philology.

His lyric and philosophical poems are alive with the pulse beat of this complex and contradictory age. In his big and small works Vagabzade tries to find an answer to questions of life and death, heroism and immortality, the duty of the planet's citizen and Man's responsibility. He is eager to discover beauty in the commonplace, to record every moment of happiness, and his poetry is addressed to all those who have a warm, sensitive heart.

The merry-go-round like a wheel is turning,
Like our planet through Space so endlessly whirling;
Behind one another, on elephant, steed,
The children ride gaily, with gathering speed.

On the merry-go-round happy moments fly fast,
The little ones loudly clap hands in their mirth.
They think they're not turning around in the least,
That around them is spinning the earth.

So children rejoice, laugh merrily, play—
With the merry-go-round,
Time changes too.
'Tis not you who are spinning round this world today,
But the world which is spinning round you.

The Merry-Go-Round

Then children, be merry, for life is but brief;
'Twill pet and caress you while you are still young.
While you are yet children, the world will forgive,
Though you be capricious and sharp be your tongue.

Oh, the merry-go-round!... A bevy of cranes
Soaring, wheels into line high above in the skies;
And mothers and fathers look on and rejoice
In the happiness beaming from their children's eyes.

A lone urchin stares from afar on their fun,
His eyes are wide open, he's sucking his thumb.
Round and round ride the children...
He looks on in glee,
Excited and thrilled at the view;
He can't keep his eyes from that huge wonder wheel,
And his head spins with visions of wishes come
                                        true.

The urchin looks on and he happily sighs.
"How lovely to ride round like this," say his eyes.
He's here on his own, though, and none can be
                                        found
To give him a ride on this merry-go-round.

But he—he is happy. . .
      I cannot but wonder
At his big little heart. . .
          O my soul,
    Look and wonder!
For he can find pleasure just at the sight
Of somebody else's delight.

                  Translated by *Louis Zellikoff*

My granddad died when he was eighty,
My dad—when he was sixty.
But I am older
In my forties
Than both my dad
And granddad.
Telephones
        Telegraphs
        Radio
        Newspapers
They load the days and load the months
And every hour
        and every minute. . .
Condense the world, whose day is to the
                                right,
And to the left—the night—
Into one tiny room,
With Spring at your head, and Winter—at your
                                feet. . .
Continents, poles
Are united by my speed.
In the heat and the flame
Of this speed,
Of this audacity,
My love
And my very nature
Have changed. . .
The greater the speed,
The shorter the distance.
Yesterday borrows minutes from
                                today
And today—
From tomorrow.
The days are all mixed up,
And so are the months,
We have lost months,
                    economising years.
In a single month I live as much
As my granddad did in a single year.
I'm a river flowing down a mountain,
Skirting the mountain peak,
A stream' muddy in the mountains

I Am Older Than My Grandfather

451

And a clear river in the valley—
A river with hundreds of different moods.
I'm older than my father,
I'm older than my grandfather.

Translated by *Louis Zellikoff*

All are born without a name.
Names are given later on.
First there's one
And later on
A man gets dubbed with many names.
Ranks will come
                    with time. . .
In the home where mothers lie
Their offspring has one name,
However many there may be—
That one name is
Baby.
His eyes are closed.
For him its all the same—
Be it day or night.
He has only one desire
                    and one word alone. . .
Just suppose
          he wants to eat
                    or that he wants to drink,
Or, maybe, wants to sleep—
All that he can do
                    is cry. . .
Crying
Is his only means.
By their crying
Mothers know
What babies need,
                    And what they say.
Perhaps a cry was man's first word,
Primeval tongue,
And weeping first began
The alphabet of art,
                    sophistry,
                         and wisdom. . .
In one building we were born—
All the same in every way.
We were born,
          but of that
We had no idea.
None could tell the difference
Between us by our height,
By our figures, or our faces. . .

One
ilding
e Were Born

453

That means we were all the same
And our name was—
                              baby.
Diapers were our only clothes.
Our only word—a cry.
Our only food was milk.
Things that came much later on,
I do not know who thought them up.
Our names were changed,
Our clothes were changed,
Our faces also changed.
Yet are we not still the same?
Tell me, then, what are they—
All these later changes?

Translated by *Tom Botting*

I

Observatory

Just a small place—
The observatory,
Yet you stand to outface
The Universe!
The end of your probing cannot be found.
You study the infinite.
The field of your search can have no bound.
Your feet on our earth you firmly place,
While your head you thrust through the sky.
And look from the heights of outer space
            Down upon our planet.
There is no bigger window for man's eye
In all the universe than you. . .
"Wait for me," calls Mother Earth,
            "I shall follow through!"
Full of hope,
So proud of your worth!
For she has heard you called
The brains of our old world
Which, predestined,
            through space is hurled.
For you
The daylight
Is dark midnight!
For starlight you reach—
That's your ABC—
Its thread runs through your speech.
At nightfall you see
Curved horizons close—
The heaven's eyelids part,
Astronomers then know
Their day's work will start.
For many years
                on far
They throw light
On some distant, glinting star.
Just a small place—
Yet each night
Your guests—new worlds—
Come face to face. . .
In your confines nigritude
In clarity dissolves.
The window of your building

Revolves upon new dawns. . .
Your edifice stretches out
                    its peaceful hand
To ages yet to come.
On the mountain top you stand
                    a monument to the morrow,
While out there in space,
Star-eyed, there glows
A bright tomorrow.
Confined within your space
The future is born and grows.

Translated by *Tom Botting*

II
The Telescope

Mysteries in the sky,
Mysteries of our earth,
Mysteries through the universe—
How many wonders have you disclosed!
Your eye is fixed upon the heavens
                    It penetrates
Far beyond all reason!
Caught up by the love of man,
You led it out to interminate space—
To the very deepest,
The bottomless
                    void.
You were the ship that first sailed!
You stand between Man and the Universe,
Logic and Hypothesis,
The Known and the Unknown.
The Unfathomed is your course and port of call.
Boundlessness is your golden crown,
And infinity your nearest pale,
Immensity—your starting point.

Translated by *Tom Botting*

An astronomer are you,
                              another—I!
You have your telescope,
                    I my pen.

Both can scan the sky.
Both seek. . .
And we seek—two men.
You a new star born
And I a new world. . .
So we meet the dawn.
In seeking we rise to new
                              heights,

Searching our confines
For new sights,
With success at times.
But new stars,
And new rhymes,
Willingly their secrets never
                              revealed.

Man sought
For thousands of years
                    For what they concealed.
Full of enigmas, the sky is a book
Where for the infinite and boundless
We must look.
Deep, deeper we must sound
The wide unfathomable depths,
Mysteries' bed profound. . .
Beginning with the cipher unity—one,
You rise, your flight from earth begun,
And glide along with dreams enjoyed,
Penetrating deeper probabilities' vast void.
When the heart soars—and halts there can be
                                        none—
A thousand problems rise that the mind must
                                        avoid,

Then, brother, you, like me and everyone,
Become a poet to write of dreams uncloyed.
New is my dream! New is the sorrow that time has
                                        spun!
You work in the heavens. On earth I'm employed,
Let your telescope scan and my pen run,
Probing deepness unalloyed.

III

Astronomer

and Poet

Let the endless universe before us be deployed,
For, brother, when life's course is done
It is best to merge with the void.
The sky displays its ravels still to be undone,
Infinity and boundlessness swim into view.
So down ever deeper! Deep down, undestroyed
Lies all that is new.

Translated by *Tom Botting*

Adil Babayev

ADIL BABAYEV (b. 1925) is the author of many books of verse on different themes, mainly the life of the Caspian oil workers, and the long poem about Sabir, an Azerbaijanian classic. Many of his verses have been set to music. Adil Babayev was born in Nakhichevan, and was educated in Tbilisi and Baku. He was 15 years old when his first poetry appeared in print.

To Mekhti Hussein Zade,
Hero of the Soviet Union,
in Memoriam

Song of Immortality

I think it altogether wrong to measure life in years,
For there are days whose every instant like an age
appears,
And lives each hour of which, indeed, is like a life
entire.
Such lives with pride we call heroic, valiant,
immortal.
And verily, this life of ours is full of wonder!
Some crawl like ugly reptiles on the ground
Yet live, like ravens, to thrice hundred,
While others leave this world not reaching thirty,
Not having loved, not having tasted life's full
virtue.
You, too, departed with a thousand wishes unfulfilled.
You, too, before you breathed your last, when you were
killed
Had visions of Baku's oil-derricks, smelled the smell of
flowers;
Khazar's wild waves were in your heart at the last hour,
The beauty of Gyok-Gyol, Kyapaz, and Spring in
Karabakh.
You dreamed of roaming through the mountains and the
valleys
To borrow colours from the heavens for your pallette.
You knew too well you had to put on soldier's
boots,
To take a gun instead of brushes and to shoot.
Life did not go the way you planned. The fates
ordained
The mountains were to be your canvas, cannonfire your
paint.
And while you fought you thought about your mother-
country's fate.
You had to leave her far behind for her own sake.
A distant land became your last abode, remote and
cold,
And your young life became a legend, still unsung,
untold.

461

You did not live to see Baku on Victory Day,
That cool and happy evening on the 9th of May.
You could not talk with friends about your future or your
                                                              past.
You could not tell us all you went through at the last.
Yet those ill-omened years did not enshrine you in their
                                                              tomb.
You were preserved for us in memory by people whom
You helped to win their freedom, whom you loved like
                                                              brothers dear,
Whom in the fiercest battles you defended without fear.
The Adriatic waters told about you to your people,
The old Carpathian Mountains, and the men of Naples,
The children of Trieste. Your courage rang as a refrain
In battle songs. You were restored to us by the same
                                                              life
For which you fought. The last words that you spoke in
                                                              deadly strife,
Say those who saw you die, were "Mother", "Native land".
In Italy, you were the first man to pronounce "Azerbaijan".
Although you died alone, embraced by rocks, beneath the
                                                              stars,
Your name lives on in songs upon the lips of boys and
                                                              girls,
Those whom you saved from slavery, in their embraces.
Your immortality became embodied in their curls,
Their eyes and faces.... You returned to this proud
                                                              land,
This country from which gloom and poverty have been
                                                              forever banned.

I think it altogether wrong to measure life in years.
Some days there are whose every instant like an age
                                                              appears,
And lives each hour of which is like a life
                                                              entire.
Each day of your life was a victory, inspired
With courage, sacred wrath, a never-dying fire.
You wanted to become an artist but did not.
And yet with pride I name you with the artists of our
                                                              day.

462

For Italy's crimson dawn owes its magnificence to you,
Your country's glory is the work of your hands too.
Let no one think your dreams were unfulfilled.
They did come true and in your heroism were fulfilled.
Your passionate, immortal dreams still inspire men,
Lend ardour to the painter's brush and poet's pen.

Translated by *Dorian Rottenberg*

Okima Billuri

OKIMA BILLURI, a poetess and scholar, was born in 1926 in Baku into the family of a railway worker. For many years she lived in southern, Iranian Azerbaijan. She received education at the University in Baku, and later obtained the degree of Candidate of Science in Moscow for her research in the field of Azerbaijanian poetry. The life of workers and peasants, their hardships and joys, fortitude and staunchness, make the subject of many of her poems. She also has many poems about love and separation. Sometimes this "separation" acquires a social meaning, even a political colouring, implying separation from her native land and her comrades-in-arms.

Come to Me

It was gloomy—you came and dispelled the gloom.
Come again when into the sky comes the moon,
When the dews in the mountains their reign resume.
Come, my love, when the girls pin flowers to their breasts,
When the violet smiles with its head inclined,
When the stars are scattered all over the skies,
When the sky is transparent and blue and wide,
When the streams rush like waterfalls—come to me!
Come, so I'll feel very young and gay,
I'll sing like a blithe, and carefree nightingale.
And you'll be delighted with all I say,
When my dreams strike flames from my soul, come to me.
Come at midday when rivers and lakes are warm,
When the sunshine scorches the stones and the sward.
Sing a song with your heart in every word;
Come to me when I'm longing for you.

The purpose of words is to burn like fire.
Let our hearts not conceal our pure desire.
The thought of our meeting, like a poet's lyre
Thrills me with expectation.

Come in autumn and summer, winter and spring,
Come to me when thick snows to the hillsides cling;
Come, and early spring may your coming bring;
Come to me when the moon looks down from the sky!

Translated by *Dorian Rottenberg*

I Wish

I wish I could live all my life on this planet so
That my warmth like a sun should remain long after I die.
I wish I could live all my life on this planet so
That my love, when I die, should shine like a star on high,
That my trace should remain on this earth just as rainbows
remain
In the cloudless sky after thunder, tempests and rain.
I wish I could live all my life on this planet so
As never to kneel before glory, riches and power.
I wish I could spend all my life on this planet so
As to breathe in the fragrance of every earthly
flower,
So that Mother Nature should keep her smile when I go,
That men should never be hurt by deeds or words.
I wish I could live all my life on this planet so
That my breath should survive in the songs of birds,
That my wishes be blossoms unfolding at break of day,
Thriving and blooming in the torrid breath of the sun.
I wish I could live on this planet in such a way
As to be remembered by all in sorrow and joy,
That lovers should quote me when love holds sway,
That in children's dreams, I, too, should survive and live.
I wish I could live all my life on this planet so
That fragrance and freshness to flowers my spirit would
give,
That they'd whisper to me when in spring they bloom,
That I'd come alive when the swallow's first melody starts,
That my dreams should blossom in dreams nursed by other
hearts.
I wish I could live all my life on this planet so
That my spirit in moonlight should pour down on earth
every night,
That my wishes, my dreams and my thoughts should
continue their life
Flashing like lightning that flares from a thunder cloud.
That brides should remember me on their wedding day,
That girls, when they play the saz, should recite my songs
aloud,
That from soul to soul as a dream I should make my way,
That I'd live on to see the joy of a future day,
To relive my life in pure dreams coming to birth
In hearts that feel all the beauty and joy of this earth.

Translated by *Dorian Rottenberg*

If anyone tells you a gale caught me up in its whirl,
Carried me off and dropped me on the tallest rock in the
world,
Let the thought of my death never enter your mind, for I
Will not perish from tempest or gale: not from any gale
will I die.

If anyone tells you that I have got drowned in the sea
Or have fallen forever asleep 'neath a mountain tree,
Do not believe I have perished, don't believe it, for I
Will not perish in any sea, nor in the hills will I die.

Do Not Believe It

If they tell you the mountains have taken my voice from
me,
That my tears have been taken by brooks, and borne off to
the sea,
Do not believe those words, do not believe them ever,
For I will not shed my tears by any brook or river.

If anyone tells you that my aching heart sings
Sorrowful songs for the autumn winds,
Do not believe those people, for what they say is wrong.
No, not for any autumn wind shall I compose my song.

If anyone tells you that I have forgotten my pledge,
Do not think ill of me and curse me for sacrilege:
"Could her love have burned out, cold as ash in an urn?"
Do believe me, my friend, in no fire will it burn.

If anyone tells you that time has managed to make me old,
That I am forty, fifty, sixty—if that you are told,
Don't believe it, please don't, it never can be.
Neither time nor old age can overcome me.

If anyone tells you I have put up with my lot,
That time has eroded revolt from my bosom—do not,
Do not listen to them, I implore,—they misstate.
Know, my love, I will never become reconciled to my
fate.

If anyone tells you that I have gone out like a light,
That my eyes lost their lustre, becoming as dark as night,

Do not listen to anyone, love, do not ever believe it:
I shan't close life's book so soon, I'm not ready to leave it.

If anyone tells you my eyes have grown faded and cold,
That I have spent my strength, that I am tired and old,
Do not listen—my heart is as ardent, as throbbing with life.
I'm as ready to rush to your side in a battle or strife.

If anyone says to you, "She's ceased to write,
Preferring a life of complacency, dullness and quiet",
Do not listen, my friend, pay no heed to the words of these
                                                    men;
Be assured, I will never take leave of my pen.

If anyone tells you my verse has gone silent as death,
That I'm dead, for my inspiration has breathed its last
                                                    breath,
Then I want you to know that I left this earth
Full of passionate longing to give a new poem birth.

                    Translated by *Dorian Rottenberg*

The Moon and I

The moon has been peeping into my window for years.
How I myself have changed; but not the lunar sphere.
Since childhood I've been gazing at the moon with loving
eyes.
I'd look out from my window and watch it in the skies
And was lured off by fancies arising within my head,
And so every night the moon bore me off from my bed.
Sweet, beautiful dreams filled my soul and I happily
smiled
Seeing dreams that inhabit the pure, cloudless world of a
child.
The moon has not changed in the least, not a line in her
face
Did pitiless time either add to it, change or erase.
Her features are just as they were and her light just as
bright;
Adorning the sky, she still shines in the silence of night.
And never, not once in her life has the moon ever wept or
smiled,
While I've changed completely—no trace of the former
child.
My sight has grown weaker and time has been wrinkling
my brow,
My heart has already been aging since long ago.
And yet I can say that I have not been living in vain,
Songs flowed from my heart all my life—songs of passion
and pain.
My childhood and youth have lived on in those songs till
this day:
They left countless traces that shall not wither away.
At the end of my poem I ask as a final boon,
Shine into my soul as a heavenly beacon, o moon!
Shine always! My heart will forever be true to your love,
For it's warmed by the warmth that you send from above.
Shine into my window, o beacon of nightly skies!
Let me meet every evening still left me and see you rise.
As you share out your light to village and city,
O moon, look into my window at midnight, have pity,
Arise in the night and dispel my loneliness;
I wait for you as I would for the dearest guest!

Translated by *Dorian Rottenberg*

Medina Gyulgyun

MEDINA GYULGYUN (b. 1926) is a poetess from southern, Iranian Azerbaijan. She writes about the brotherhood of peoples, expressing her faith in the power of reason and justice and the ultimate defeat of obscurantism and the triumph of peace on earth. She recites her fiery, incisively publicistic poems at a high pitch of emotionality, like a veritable tribune.

I'm
as formerly
true to you.
Nor ever wandered from your
                              love.
I'm the same, the same as I was.
My heart retains its inner
                        world:
of concern for you,
gentle esteem,
of love,
and constancy.

I'm the same, the same as I was.
My laughter runs all through the
                              room,
lines too
of a loving song,
and dreams
more bold than those I told
                          you of.
Endured, unknown to you,
the heartache of parting, grief...

I'm the same, the same as I
                        was.
Unchanged
in tenderness,
unchanged my love of
                  verse,
esteem for the poet.
Poesy—my treasure on earth,
my dowry to you.
I am wholly unchanged:

I'm the same, the same as
                        I was.
And even were I born again
all the same
I'd live as yesterday I did and do
                              today.
Dearest in life,
you know yourself what way I've changed—

'm the Same,
ie Same
As I Was

471

wrinkles more and more appearing,
calmness leaving my sleep at night,
heartbeat tempo,
shade of hair.
What's changed,
and gone from me
is the world of youth.

Translated by *Gladys Evans*

For a Moment Only...

If I were an eagle in flight over mountain crest,
I should leave my peaks, fly to you as my only nest.
If I were to have a rendezvous full of happiness—
My head on your knee alone would I wish to rest.

If I should become a Parting, with keening thrust
I'd swoop around you, as a whirlwind must.
And should I fall to earth like a shooting star,
For you I'd start to blaze ... till I burnt to dust.

Should a hunter's arrows strike me and fatally
wound,
I'd trace your name in blood out on the ground.
And I would endure with all of my stubborn will
The bitter fury unleashed by a storm unbound.

If Spring should give me her colourful brush to
use,
Your portrait alone to paint I'd choose;
And when sweet Nature would gaze on my work of art,
Her wilding ecstasy would the world confuse.

If I became a song that held not a word
Of grief ... on your lips I'd swing like a bird;
And the sadness and grief that tortured your heart—
They'd be held on a curb-rein, never spurred.

If I could raise a storm as the deep seas do,
I'd dedicate all my polyphony to you.
If I became a garden of rioting colour,
I'd say you gave me each shade and tint and hue.

Could I be the lightning once, or yet the wind,
I'd drive all the shadows away that hang on your mind.
Whenever, wherever, you need me, if at all—
Be sure I will seek you out and search till I find.

Without you, my songs are stilled and as mute as ice;
Without you, all earth and life ... lost paradise.
So live and shine on earth's bosom like a star,
From age to age in undying splendour rise.

Translated by *Gladys Evans*

Gabil Imamberdiev

GABIL IMAMBERDIEU was born in Baku in 1926 into the family of a railway worker, and was educated at the Azerbaijanian teachers' college, in the department of literature. In his poems he sings the beauty of his native land, its pomegranate orchards and mountains. Another favourite theme of his is love and fidelity. His most highly acclaimed work of recent years is "Nasimi", a poem about this Azerbaijanian classic who lived 600 years ago.

However...

Torch infinite,
Monument-granite,
Are not so bad!
The sepulchre
Of marble slab,
A headstone, sir,
With epitaph—
Are not so bad!
Obituaries,
Graveside orations,
Consolations,
Infinitum ad. . .
Are still not bad!
The Service Burial,
And Plaque Memorial,
The sympathy ad—
Are not so bad!
And SHOULD be had!
Not every deceased
Has had as much,
Some will at least
Get overmuch.
However
'Twould be better
To honour the living
A bit of praisegiving
While there's still time—
Much warmer, more fit
Than Torch infinite,
And far more sublime
Than monument-granite.

Translated by *Gladys Evans*

Comparisons

I compare you to a flower—
Though the flower's life
Be only a day
Or only a year.

The likeness lies in
Neither the flower's span
Of life, or that of man.
I compare you to a flower—
In delicacy
And tenderness.

I compare you to a lion—
What likeness here?
The one, a beast of prey—
The other, man.
If you should catch his
Eye, in the heat of rage
He'd tear you all to bits.

I compare you to a lion
In valour,
Courage
And pluck.

I designate you elephant—
Would I come close?
What likeness lies
Between unreasoning
Giant, reasoning man?

I designate you elephant
For strength, for power,
For work that knows
No beginning or end,
For honest merit.

I compare you to a horse—
Yes, even now with
Horses out of date.
Where then

The likeness?
He tolerates saddle,
Harness, flicking whip,
Long roads.
Whereas
Who dares to
Lay a finger
Upon you?
For you're a man,
And he—mere beast.

I compare you to a horse—
For fortitude
When the way ahead is hard
And troubled.

Translated by *Gladys Evans*

"Six and six!"
"Five and five!"
Old men playing Nardi[1]
In the city park,
In autumn time.

"And here's one-one!"
"And there's three-three!"
A misty morning. . .
Damp beads on the Nardi board,
Turns the pieces into stones.

The Leaves Are Falling

Each move a slap—no other sound.
Perhaps they really don't
Enjoy the game. . .
"Five and five!"
"Three and four!"
"Aga-bek, I'm sick of it."
"Give it a rest, then, eh?"
"Don't talk. . ."
And so they sit there
For a space of time.

On their two kindly faces, in their eyes
Beneath the sheltering eyeglass lens—
Yearning, sadness lies.
The leaves are falling:
Yellow, ochred gold.

The leaves are falling
And draw their eyes.
"The leaves fall, Miralyam!"
"I'm not blind!
"But Spring will come,
"The whole world'll smile again."
"And us?"
"Doubt we'll see it.
"First my time will come

[1] Oriental game of ancient origin.

478

"To go, then yours.
"How long do you expect to throw the dice?
"You may cheat yourself, but never time.
"No good hoping, Miralyam."
"I know."
Just then a boy
Came up to them.
And asked the time.
They looked and found
Their watches stopped.

Silent for good—the season
Of deathly stillness closes in.
The leaves are falling:
Yellow, ochred gold.
Buried in autumn leaves
The pieces and the dice.

Translated by *Gladys Evans*

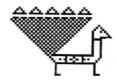

Takhir Sokhrab

TAKHIR SOKHRAB was born in 1926 in the town of Astara, on the Iranian side of the border. For more than twenty years now he has lived in Baku. After graduating from the University in Baku Takhir Sokhrab took a two-year course at the Gorky Literary Institute in Moscow. He writes about life in southern Azerbaijan. In his other poems he reflects on man's place in society and the destinies of the world.

Vietnam

Vietnam is clothed in a blood-smeared
                                        blouse
Of gunpowder-smoke curling in clouds.
The blouse is clasped with exploding shells
Stained with flame from his man-made hells.

Airplanes with wings like enormous scissors
Hack at the necks of forests and cities.
On canvas sheets a tremendous hand
Piles soldiers' bodies. No easy job
To slay a liberty-loving land.

Mountains quiver, and rivers throb:
To slay a whole country—no easy job.
From huts the cry of the dying comes.
Aluminium hawks, bestraddling bombs,
Take a fling. Leaves are shed, though it isn't
                                        winter.
No rice is sowed. But History sows
Vietnam's soil with mines and splinters.
And her rivers, covered all over with wounds,
Bandaged with leaves of yellow and red,
Flow through their blood-flooded beds,
Clasping their dreams to their wounded
                                        breasts.

Uninvited guests, beware of your host!
Vietnam, wreathed with crimson lightning,
Cartridge-necklaced and frightening
To Victory raises her toast!

Translated by *Dorian Rottenberg*

481

Summits

It is my word that reaches you, but not my hand,
O cloud-capped summits, one another higher!
To strive towards summits is the inborn urge of man;
To reach the loftiest of targets we aspire.

Man's mind provides him with the wings he needs for flight,
To test his mighty powers once and yet again.
But why is it that some who reach the heights
After their flight, prefer to live on plains?

I, too, took wing. The stars, without a word,
Watched as I pierced the clouds in my new role.
Though I was born a helpless, wingless bird,
I chose the tallest summit for my goal.

Up I will fly as long as I have breath
And won't maintain that cowardly tradition.
But even if I don't succeed for lack of strength,
I never will go back on my ambition.

At times I lose my way when in the streets.
Friends, do not blame me, for my error is unwonted.
It is because I do not look beneath my feet:
My eyes are on the heights by which I'm haunted.

Translated by *Dorian Rottenberg*

The Child and the Doll

In a land of dauntless heroes
Near a forest dark and wild,
Far off from its native village,
Dead, with a doll in its arms, lay a child.

From a bullet it had perished,
But its doll escaped all harm
For it was securely shielded
By the child's embracing arm.

The foe had dared not touch the doll,
Though of the child's life they took toll.
Stand aside, o ruined city!
Look, humanity, with pity
At a child's adult maturity.

At those adults' childish cruelty
Look, humanity, appalled!
Mourn, mankind! The child has perished.
But, secure in loving arms,
The doll laughs. Its face inherits
All the child's maternal charm.

It laughs at the bullets grimly,
At the flames that caper, dimly
Mirrored in its glassy eyes,
At those who laugh when a child dies,
At those who come to die for lies.

Translated by *Dorian Rottenberg*

Aliaga Kurchaily

ALIAGA KURCHAILY was born in 1928 in the village of Kyurgaragashly, Salsk district, on the banks of the Kura, hence his pen-name. He was educated at the University in Baku. Aliaga Kurchaily has published many books in Baku and also in Moscow, in Russian translation. His poems often appear in magazines and newspapers. His work is notable for its variety of themes, intonations and forms. His style may be true to traditional folk poetry, or else free and modern. His output includes patriotic, love, publicistic, satirical and trenchantly social poems. Aliaga Kurchaily has translated Sergei Yesenin into Azerbaijani, and is at the moment engaged in translating Dante's The Divine Comedy.

* * *

Be you wanderer, pilgrim, tourist or guest,
If you hear a song that sinks deep in your breast,
If you hear a tune coming straight from the soul,
If you meet hospitality in one and all,
If you meet open faces and honest hearts,
It means, my friend, you have come to our parts,
To Shirvan, Mugan, Baku or Mili,[1]
Near the river Kura or the Caspian Sea;
In a word, you have come to Azerbaijan
And, believe me, you are a most fortunate man.

Translated by *Dorian Rottenberg*

* * *

My lunch is wrapped up in a sheet of old newspaper
A hunk of bread and butter...
A pack-lunch to take to work.

Suddenly, my eye lights on some lines from that newspaper:
Somewhere there is a famine,
People suffering hunger.

It is all there in the newspaper: famine, no bread... But
My lunch is wrapped up in it—
A hunk of bread and butter.

With no awareness, no realisation of their need
I shall eat that hunk of bread
And throw away the paper...

It seems to me, if there were not so much indifference
There would be no more famines,
Poverty, or disasters.

Translated by *Avril Pyman*

[1] Azerbaijanian towns and cities.

485

Football and Shakespeare

Excuse me, my friend, but it seems a bit queer
When you say that you envy my stage career.
Such an audience, you say, applauds me each night,
And they keep me bowing, you say, for hours,
And they strew me from head to foot with flowers;
What else could one wish for, what greater
delight?

No, my friend, things are not so bright as you
think.

Matters are such that they make my heart sink.
I was born for the stage—the stage is my home,
The theatre's the only thing I enjoy.
In the theatre I find both sorrow and joy,
To the theatre I look when I'm sad and lone.

There are nights when I look down into the hall;
How empty it is—almost no one at all.
Where are all those people who would break down
doors,

To obtain a ticket by cunning or force?
That was what used to make acting so sweet;
No matter what blizzard there was in the street,—
Even an earthquake could happen—oh yes!
The crowd at the theatre would never grow less.

But nowadays sun-glasses, fancy socks,
Rhymeless poetry, tuneless bougis and rocks,
Tours abroad, miniskirts and beltless breeches,
Themeless and featureless motion pictures
Have become the latest fad and fashion;
They alone can arouse people's passion.

Plaited hair that once gave such charm to our girls
Has now been replaced by synthetic curls. . .
Dark locks are no longer the poet's craze,
A man who recites classic poetry now
Or wears clothes that fashion does not allow
Is ridiculed for his outmoded ways.

Stadiums are packed till they're almost bursting.
Football's the thing for which millions are thirsting.
People keep storming the stadium wickets;

Of all the seventy thousand odd seats
Not a single one's vacant when favourites meet,
Not to mention the sneaks that get in without tickets.

Football has little to do with it, though.
It's just an occasion for drinking, you know,
For howling and yelling and telling tall tales,
For bragging and betting and getting together
Regardless of circumstances and weather,
Boosting sky-high football ticket sales.

Their culture comes spouting from every pore.
They're sportsmanlike—not like we were before.
In gold-rimmed black glasses, like dandies decked out
From any topic to football they'll turn.
If you listen enough you'll be happy to learn
About *penalty, goalkeeper, offside* and *out*.

They can tell you all about soccer and rugger,
But can never distinguish Falstaff from Iago.
If they go to the theatre by some mistake
Or dragged by some theatre-going friend
They will rush to the cloakroom before the end,
Before all the others their coats to take.

Last night, walking home, not a little upset,
A recent acquaintance of mine I met.
He'd been to a football match, so it seemed,
And presented a picture quite strange to see.
His head bounced about on his neck like a ball.
It, too, had no hair and no brains at all.
"They've lost," he exclaimed with a heart-rending
                                                    sigh,
And at thought of the theatre also sighed I.
But he left me, disdainfully, almost at once;
In his eyes I was merely an ignorant dunce.

He wouldn't have sacrificed Pele's one nail
For all that in Shakespeare we, idiots, hail.
Whenever I ventured to speak of the theatre
He'd grimace as if he'd bit off something bitter.

487

To all the complaints that he heard from me
His only reply was *"c'est la vie"*.

There's no one to blame but the times, so he'd say.
Sadly I watched as he swaggered away.
I thought of the theatre the rest of the night.
It certainly is in a sorry plight.
The future before it is gloomy, no doubt,
If football is going to drive Shakespeare out.

Translated by *Dorian Rottenberg*

Beloved, Take Me by the Hand

Beloved, take me by the hand
And let us walk into the wind
I seek no calm or sheltered strand!
Come, let us walk into the wind.

What care we though our cheeks be flailed
Or though our eyes with tears be blind,
Our knees be bent, our footsteps fail:
Our course is set—into the wind.

Though mist and dark about us whirl
And the rough road with ruts is lined
And winds and snows around us whirl. . .
Let us go on—into the wind.

A thousand nights, a thousand dawns
We'll meet, and greet, and leave behind,
And day and night, and on and on
We will walk on—into the wind.

Translated by *Avril Pyman*

Nariman   Hassanzade

NARIMAN HASSANZADE was born in 1931 in Poily, Akstafa district. He was educated at the Gorky Literary Institute in Moscow, and holds the degree of Candidate of Philology. He writes on a great variety of themes, and his poetry reflects a great variety of feelings: happiness, love, anger, meditation and humour. These last few years he has been working on his large lyrico-epic poem "Nariman" in which he painted a true-to-life and charming portrait of Nariman Narimanov, a prominent Azerbaijanian revolutionary and thinker, who was Lenin's friend and comrade and who, like Lenin, was born a hundred years ago, in 1870.

Father Adam,
Mother Eve—
He was ignorant
And so was she—
For eating of the sacred tree
From Paradise to Hell they were driven—
To this world, where we keep on
Increasing with each generation.

And when the Lord of all Creation
Passed his decree,
Old Adam died
And Eve died, too
When they had lived their long days through.
But there remained for us—Temptation.

Temptation

Greed for gold,
For glory, praise,
Greed for power,
Greed for place,
For large estates and—
Greed for other people's land.
We spend our lives 'mong rows of rockets,
We bend beneath the load of rockets.
And live in neither Hell nor Heaven.

When rainy weather gives us blues,
And when the weather's fine,
And when the papers bring bad news,
Buchenwald and Oswiecim come to our minds.

Our spines with cold begin to shiver
As in Mauthausen's furnaces we quiver.

This Earth is Hell in Allah's eyes.
But we—we wish and mean to live
And make our Earth a paradise.

The twentieth century's almost spent.
Again by greed our planet's rent.

Translated by *Louis Zellikoff*

You Will Remember Me

Once you had told me,
You would forget me.
Forget me,
Forget me somehow.
Do, if you can, forget me.

With every meeting
I called you a flower.
Whenever a flower you see,
In garden or market,
You will remember me.

Cars may be racing,
Stars swiftly falling,
Your friend beside you may be.
En route from the meeting,
You will remember me.

Your hair you'll be combing,
Your fingers will tremble,
Once I had combed them for thee.
Your hair will remind you,
You will remember me.

If in the evening
You stroll down the pathway,
Who for you waiting will be,
Who'll see you homeward?
You will remember me.

If at a funeral,
All in black garments,
Someone will ask: who was he?
Then you'll remember,
You cannot but remember,
Then you'll remember me.

Once you had told me,
You would forget me.
Forget me,
Forget me somehow.
Do, if you can, forget me.

Translated by *Eugene Felgenhauer*

492

The bus takes you,
My dreams take me.
Dreams—will they come
                    true?

The seat is soft,
As soft can be,
And all about
Straight streets you see;
The road is smooth,
The highway free.
But rough the pathway
Facing me.

The Two
of Us

We both drive on:
You're driving home,
And I,
Into my dream alone.

On foot proceeds
The one of us,
The other's riding
In a bus.

Your destination—
It is near,
And everything
For you is clear.

But I have very far
                    to go,
And what I'll find,
I do not know.
Within an hour
You'll be home,
My thoughts 'mid death
And woe will roam.

The driver's sitting at the wheel,
And you are calm, you need not
                    fear.
I'm driver, passenger and all,

493

You hurry home,
I to my dream.

You'll be at home,
For sure today.
But as for me,
No one can say.

Translated by *Eugene Felgenhauer*

The Little Girl Who Didn't Want Much

"Please, daddy, buy me coloured socks,
  And that is all I'll ask from you.
  And buy a book about a fox,
  And that is all I'll ask from you.
  A raincoat and a flag—no, two,
  A sunshade (black), a white new hat,
  And that is all I'll ask from you."
"Well, well, my girl—and then what more?"
  "A pen that's green, a ribbon bright—
  And that is all I'll ask you for."

Translated by *Louis Zellikoff*

Picasso's Dove

Born in nineteen forty-two
Between the talons of death,
She became the symbol of life,
She would fly, morning and night,
Where no trenches were in sight.

Neither rifle bayonets
Nor flaming cannon muzzles
Directed at her breast
Could ever destroy her.

In 'fifty, she spread her wings,
Flew as illustrations to books,
Over fences of iron,
Alighted on starched collars
And on slogans. . .

Cleaving the air
In her flight,
She alighted on posters
During world congresses.
She's flying, she's flying now,
She has nests in every clime,
She's at home in every land.

With sputniks made by man
And together with all doves,
Together with the airplanes,
Together with heavy rockets
She flies throughout the world.
And we—we watch the doves
And rockets as they fly;
We watch—Picasso's hopes and dreams
We see with our own eyes.

Translated by *Louis Zellikoff*

Fikret Sadykh

FIKRET SADYKH was born in 1931 in Kyurdamir and is a scholar orientalist by education. His three published collections of poems have been well received by readers. Fikret Sadykh is a poet who believes in taking his time before committing his thoughts to the written page. He works painstakingly to give a perfect finish to his verses, which may be called poetic meditations. Each word of his is as weighty and clear cut as a precious stone.

To Lenin Prize Winner
Kara-Karaev

A single-voiced groan of Auschwitz
                              martyrs
Under a shroud of world-wide mourning,
Then sounds of the sun's footsteps.

A sudden calm before a storm,
The breaking of waves
And the crumbling of rocks.
Dede Korkut relates his tale.

Listening to the Third Symphony

Then emerges the burning soul of Kerem,
Then spouting waters;
The familiar smell of a flower
And—home.

Then arises the question:
Will our world with its tangled
                              hair
Be combed by the warheads of rockets
Or by the shares of ploughs?

Then the picture of Rodin's *Thinker,*
A soul in anxiety,
And at last a final accord:
Hope!

*   *   *

It is rumoured, a map has been found
Of the Antarctic before it froze.
I believe it, and I do not...
They say that long before our civilisation
There existed Atlantis.
I believe it, and I do not.

I have heard it said that fish can
                              speak.
I believe it, and I do not.

497

But what I do believe
Is that if atom-stuffed rockets

From continent to continent begin to fly,
Nothing will remain,
Neither the world nor its maps,
Nor the legends about the Atlantis,
Nor the voices of speaking fish.

Translated by *Dorian Rottenberg*

I could swim across the tempestuous ocean
One single poppy to pluck.
I could cut down impassable woods with one motion
To help my people down on their luck.

I could grope through the curling mists of a gorge
To ascend the highest peak.
Passing star after star, I could fly
To the sun
Through space austere and bleak.

Translated by *Dorian Rottenberg*

I

Songs and poems are brimful of brilliant light.
Full of light are the fairytales I have heard.
Man's road is the road to light, shining bright,
Full of light, as well, is a wise man's word.

Man himself is a splinter chipped off from the sun.
How can you speak of a life without light?
Bread, flowers, hills and rocks their life began
When light came and ended the reign of night.

II

Light

I am enamoured of fire since childhood.
Every evening I searched for the light with my eyes.
When my mother was late in lighting the lamp,
"*Jizza-jizza!*"[1] I whimpered with sobs and cries.

Until now I remember the fires I'd make
In the forest, when we prepared to sup,
And how once the glittering eyes of a snake
I mistook for a firefly and picked it up.

III

I lit up our village's streets with my hands.
Man-made sunshine flooded the out-going roads.
I worked as a gardener: my flowers were lamps
And I tended them just as you tend a rose.

And if somewhere somebody's lamp would
                                    expire
I felt that the light of my soul had gone.
How often my hands would serve as a wire:
I myself burned, and the light went on.

[1] Child's exclamation meaning *fire*.

IV

This new poem of mine also calls for light.
Every line shines forth like a chandelier bright.
No wonder—the place where I came to life
Is Azerbaijan—the birthplace of light.

I grew up and at first believed that I ought
To become an engineer, but changed my decision.
"An engineer only draws blueprints," I thought
And went to work as an electrician.

A star now burns under every roof
And shines instead of the sun at night.
So, the fieriest time of my life—my youth
I burned up, converting it into light.

Translated by *Dorian Rottenberg*

Every cloud holds a mountain stream,
Every cloud hides a waterfall.
        If on the ground
        A whole cloud fell one day
        How unbearably
        On the flowers it would weigh.
                That is why
                Drop by drop
                Rain fell from the sky
To water the poppies and daffodils.
Dew fell on the leaves
And petals
In pearl-like pellets
With which the breeze
Gently started to play.

The Rainbow
Then a rainbow appeared in the sky.
Lost in wonder, stood I;
Had it come from the sky
Or from the rain-sprayed ground?
From the pearl-grey ear of a cloud
Like a crescent-shaped ear-ring it hung.
From the meadows right up to the hills
Its arc it flung,
A trail of many-hued sparks.
Where I stood,
I froze to the spot:
Can it see what wonders it works
Or not?
                From poppy
                To poppy
The rainbow built its radiant bridge
        Blue as the sky,
        Brown as the earth,
        Green as the leaves—
A seven-hued rainbow,
        A luminous rainbow.

It seemed that my own dear globe
        Was a cup
And the rainbow—its crystal handle
By which it was taken up.
        This cup
        Full of cares,

Desires
And joys
The sun holds up in its hands.

And I sipped up a drop of those
        Desires,
        Joys
        And cares;
How well that the rain
Had begun to fall
        Unawares!

How many secrets I could disclose
        In the breeze,
        The dews,
        And the seven hues
Into which the rain's transparency split,
In the wonderful beauty that hid
In the heavy, stone-heavy clouds.

Translated by *Dorian Rottenberg*

Ali Kerim | *ALI KERIM, poet and prose writer, was born in 1931 in Geokchai and graduated from the Gorky Literary Institute in Moscow. His style is laconic and completely modern in spirit and form, and he strives to probe the philosophical meaning of each happening and phenomenon. He is also master of the traditional folk form, mainly using the difficult five-and-seven-syllabled line which makes the poetry dynamic and breathtaking like a gallop down a mountain path. Ali Kerim is the author of* Steps, *a novel about the life of students, the poem* "First Symphony", *and* "Third Rider" *which tells about Lermontov's life in Caucasia.*

Memories of My Father

He was stern. When I hurried away to school
His eyes would secretly follow me.
He never opened his soul to us,
Never showed how anxious for us he could be.

He would only look at us with a smile
And take a puff at his faithful pipe.
He would sooner give up his life for us
Than ever call us "my love" or "my life".

At times he would place his big, calloused hand
Like the hand of Fate, on my shoulder.
Just for a moment his face went alight
With thoughts we did not understand till much older.

His love was chilly as winter snow,
Protecting young shoots from every woe.
While I studied in Moscow, he left me for good.
When the time of eternal parting came
He had wanted to see me, then said he would
Rather I did not know—he was shy
Of the life he had lived. I wish I knew why.
Such was the father that I once had.

Translated by *Dorian Rottenberg*

The Stone

Half-naked
    Primitive man
Threw a stone at his foe
    And spilled his blood.
But the stone did not fall
    On the ground,
It flew farther,
Beyond the horizon.
Don't think that the stone simply vanished.
It turned into an arrow.
It became a sword,
    A bullet,
            A gunshell.
Like thought, it flew on, non-stop,
Till it became an A-bomb.
Disrupting meridians,
Crushing hopes,
Splashing oceans out of their beds,
It flew on. . .
That stone has not stopped to this day.
    Where is it flying?
Turning into neutrons, electrons
    And what not.
Turning into flame,
    Into death,
          Into poison.
O my contemporary,
My brother in the search for truth,
Tell me, can we not stop
That stone,
    Set flying
By half-naked,
    Half-savage
        Primitive man?

Translated by *Dorian Rottenberg*

Mothers Weep

O my Mother,
　　To Mount Sapun[1]
　　　　Your sisters come to weep.
All the grief there is in the world
　　At the foot of that hill
　　　They heap.
All the dirges there are in the world
　　In their hearts
　　　　They seem to keep.
The field of battle is turned
　　Into a field of mourning.
Mothers' laments are heard
　　For miles and miles around,
Where, wedded to Death by bullets,
　　Youths fell on the ground.
How long can mothers keep sobbing
　　For the souls of departed lads
Who have turned into wheaten stubble,
　　Mixed with the earth's hard
　　　　　clods?
One weeps over another's son,
　　Mistaking him for her own;
The other—
　　Over the son of the first,
　　　Thinking the boy was her
　　　　　own.
A third, unsuspecting,
　　sobs: "Oh my son!"
Where there's nought but a rusty shell.
A fourth one grieves over the grave of the
　　　　　foe
　　From whose bullet her only son fell.
Still another, embracing the empty soil,
Shrieks in utter despair:
"My son, my baby, beloved one,
　　Where are you, where, oh where?"
The devouring fire of their grief
Has smelted the tons of lead

---

[1] Hill near Sevastopol, scene of fierce fighting, now memorial cemetery.

That killed their sons on this field,
And have heated the tears they shed.

Mothers on Mount Sapun,
And elsewhere,
     In other parts,
Are weeping over their sons,
     Crying out their hearts.

Translated by *Dorian Rottenberg*

To the Wind of Baku

Wander forever, o wind, in these
                              parts,
Bending, breaking branches.

Calm down at times and be clear as water,
Flowing in waves upon my breast;
Overtake me, whirl me in a crazy vortex,
Whirl me round and round without rest.

But my heart has another request for
                              you,
O cold Hazri, O warm Gilavar,[1]
If life comes back in visions to you,
Remind me about the clamour of war.

Let your gusts, like turbulent waves
Tear me abruptly off the spot.
Rumble and thunder, whirl and rave,
Drive me on, make my breath come fast
                              and hot.

Roar and thunder with all your might,
Toss my hair and strike my chest.
Blow, I say, from the left and right,
Let us grapple again, breast to breast!

The storm dies down, giving way to calm;
Drive calm and complacency out of my home.
O wind of Baku, come, sound the alarm,
Knock at my window, break into my home!

Translated by *Dorian Rottenberg*

[1] Hazri—North wind; Gilavar—South wind.

Jabir Novruz

JABIR NOVRUZ was born in 1933 in Upa, a village in Khizin district, into the family of a peasant. He was educated at the Gorky Literary Institute in Moscow. His poetry is topical and trenchantly publicistic. He is aware of the whole world, and his work carries a strong social message. For several years now Jabir Novruz has been chief editor of the Azerbaijanian youth literary magazine Ulduz, *which means "star".*

I was not born to wealth, but then again
My line was not a race of noble men.
A simpler soul than father you could never meet.
I knew no bed adorned with gold embroidered
                                        sheet.
I was not rocked asleep in soft and rounded arms
In palace halls where life glides by with no
                                        alarms.
My birth took place when skies were leaden autumn-
                                        grey
And in the roughest hut I saw the light of day.
Perhaps I was not wanted here in this wide world!
They wrapped me in a coat and there I snugly
                                        curled.

My Generation

Beside that cot of mine grandmother crooned a song.
The lullabies she sang were ancient, sad and long.
How many things I lacked! In spite of that
                                        I grew.
The world would thrust on me no happiness,
                                        I knew.
I'd watch them milk our old grey cow and stay
To drain a mug of tepid milk each day.
I loved the steppes and mountains basking in the sun.
Throughout the year for coffee I would drink ayrán[1].
In winter cutting winds would slash and stab and
                                        freeze.
In autumn I would wade through mud up to my knees.
Then once I saw misfortune over steppelands ride
And enter in our shack the day my father died.
And all that I was left was just myself alone,
For there was nothing else that I could call my own.
The image of my father faded like a dream,
Then I had no support, while harsh fate ruled
                                        supreme.
It kept me at the run and never let me shirk.
Each little thing I got was earned with sweat and
                                        work.
How many dreams fate shattered! Never did it lack
A stick with which to beat my aching sides and back.
The very smallest things in struggle should be
                                        gained.

[1] Beverage made of dried curds and water.

From my cradle nothing else but love have I attained.
There is no fount of joy that gushes without fail.
For happiness in life I fought with tooth and nail.
Yes, such a man am I and such must be my ways. . .
That this is so I thank those harsh, laborious
days.
No scion was I born of some proud family tree.
I never let that fact depress or worry me.
There were bad people who would make my mother sad,
The kind that stooped to cheat a woman and her lad.
My birth and way of life had served to make me
rough,
But also served to make me unafraid and tough.
This lent me strength and bound me close to earth
and sky.
Both carpenters and shepherds form my family line.
A canal digger was one forefather of mine.
I love my generation and those long gone by
Whose hot blood feeds my heart with throbbing secret
streams,
So I can comprehend each whisper and each sigh,
And I can understand the simple people's dreams.
My generation's stance is always firm and straight.
Companions whom I chose are men of my own fate.
Who form this generation based upon new days?
—The men who stone by stone new edifices raise.
I act and sometimes err, but know in what I do
They'll always stand by me—and I'll stand by them, too.
And when I lose my way along that road of mine,
When I have gone astray, and when I grieve and pine,
When battered by the winds, amid the tempest's strife
I find support in faith that guided all my life.
I'll suffer on my way and errors I shall make,
But, come what may, I know somehow I shall make shift. . .
My happiness in life by tooth and nail I'll take—
But never happiness that's offered as a gift!

Translated by *Tom Botting*

My Mother seems to age before my eyes.
Oh, why must she grow old, dear heart of
mine?
How sad when youth at last takes wing and
flies
Far, far away and leaves behind no sign.

She has no strength. Her eyes are dim with
tears.
What can I do? Her back is bent with years.

No child can help when parents reach that stage...
The last soft light in her dear eyes I see.
I know she'll rise on wings of her great age
And very soon she'll fly away from me.

My Mother Seems to Age

The older folk—the quicker they depart...
They take my thoughts and leave an empty
heart.

Her hands have aged, as have her voice and
sight.
Her maiden name is youth's remaining trace.
Around her head there gleams a cloud of white,
While lines of time are etched upon her
face.

Her stature seems to lessen every day.
She grows so thin she seems to fade
away.

It even seems that age makes her withdraw.
Each day she seems more distant than
before.

When she recalls the past her memory clears...
Those times were best! Now nothing is the
same.

And when she dons a dress of girlhood
years
It hangs in folds upon her wasted
frame.

513

Her beauty fled. Her grace has long departed.
Her wedding ring is slipping from her finger.
In some old world my mother has her place.
The bloom of youth must fade. It cannot
                                    linger.

A lovely girl was she of vital beauty.
The family needed her. Their love was
                                    strong.
She offered joy as if that were her duty
And she was happy as the day is long.

She loved each minute. To the full she lived,
So, like the Araks'[1] fast stream, she'd surge and
                                    race
Or like the Kura.[1] Her bounty sped to give
Her daughter as a bride—to take her place.

So bird-like was my mother, bright and bold,
I loathe to see her droop as she grows old.

She gazed with joy upon her son and heir;
Yet she began to age when I found love.
Perhaps the silver first showed in her hair
When she herself discovered her first love.

And always, in the autumn, winter, spring
We hear a wedding in some house or other.
Young mothers with their children laugh and
                                    sing—
But now there is no laughter for my mother.

Fierce passions rage and new ideals resurge,
Yes, every day we feel their youthful urge.
The children seem to be more young and gay,
Yet my old mother ages every day.

I write this verse to you, my Mother dear.
It is a tale that must ring out each day

[1] Rivers flowing through Azerbaijan.

514

As surely as your children's sons appear,
For time rolls on and age grows every day.

Both joy and sadness in your life you've known.
When you depart you'll see that you are leaving
In this wide world in which you feel alone
Two generations loving you and grieving.

Translated by *Tom Bolting*

Mamed Ibrahim

MAMED IBRAHIM was born in 1933 in Nora, a village in the Nakhichevan Autonomous Republic, an ancient and picturesque land. He was educated at the Azerbaijanian University, the department of geography. He writes as. if he were holding a frank conversation with the reader whom he trusts implicitly. There is not a trace of forced loftiness in his poetry. He delights in good people and the beautiful world, and resents indifference or sordidness. In the main he uses the classical metres and forms of Azerbaijanian poetry, carefully avoiding rhetoric and meticulously polishing every line.

Mother's Age

(n Songs to My Mother)

No more to my ears will my mother's voice come.
Fate has dealt a pitiless blow to me.
I confess, it hurts me when asked by some,
"When your mother died, how old was she?"

"I don't know... Her hair was just turning grey..."
For a long time they haunt me, question and answer.
Can grief for a mother depend on her age?
She was just a mother's age when I lost her.

Translated by *Dorian Rottenberg*

On the Rostrum

Two bosoms were unburdened on the rostrum.
Each cursed the other—for what, doesn't matter.
A third applauded both the second and first one—
And sat down with each to praise and flatter.

Translated by *Dorian Rottenberg*

Whenever paper and pen
Become my tablemates,
Suddenly my desires
Show unusual appetites.

I want to come to grips
With the world-creating force,
I want to make some changes
In Nature's eternal laws.

I want to create new planets
To vie with ours in perfection.
Sometimes I'd make the Earth
turn
In the reverse direction.

**Evening
Meditations**

Perhaps we could then observe
The moon's unseen other side
And see an eternal sunrise
On the face of mankind.

Perhaps then climates would
change,
Vietnam change places with U.S.
Perhaps we'd awake past ages,
Watch humanity in regress.

We'd find out who the creature was
Who first raised a weapon against his
species,
We'd knock it out of his hand,
Chop him up into pieces.

Perhaps then the Negro's lot
Would get a bit richer in pleasure,
And maybe minor nations
Would feel a bit less pressure.
Maybe then bought offices
Would finally find *the* men.

Maybe the worm-eaten props
Sometimes lying around
Would meet with their erstwhile roof

519

And keep it from falling down.
Perhaps along the Araks
Some kind of Cuba might grow?[1]

Perhaps. . .
      Who on earth may know?
Stop that "perhaps", for heaven's sake,
And forgive men their human mistakes.

             Translated by *Dorian Rottenberg*

No Need for Praise

Uncalled-for praise, like the longing to doze
During work, puts the pen in your hand asleep,
For talent resembles the seed that grows
On bare rock, no matter how hard and steep.
Let the glamour of fame not attract your muse.
Living unpraised is worth praise.
                One can bear it.
Self-assertion is needed only by those
Who aren't sure they possess any merit.

             Translated by *Dorian Rottenberg*

---

[1] Araks River dividing Southern and Northern Azerbaijan. Allusion to Cuban revolution.

I look at the mountains and valleys around;
Strange thoughts in my mind they excite.
Avalanches are attractive, I've found,
Though often ungainly at first sight.

Look at the way an avalanche
Abruptly gives life to a cave in a hill;
In aeon-old scenes the eye can catch
New contrasts give way to newer ones still.

From an avalanche streams flow down to the plain,
Livening meadows with the charms of spring.
An avalanche means that something again
Its protest in Nature's face wants to fling.

Avalanches

An avalanche parts a hill from its neighbour,
Melts tears of snow into stream-filling ponds;
An avalanche, wrecking the nest of an eagle,
Turns a hollow into a nest for swans.

All is one to an avalanche—white and black.
It drags off an oak toppled onto an elm.
It carries away the mightiest rock
And hauls off the tiniest pebble as well.

A stonemason with two mighty stone hands:
One hand destroys while the other creates—
It will never flinch when it breaks what is bad,
It seeks no reward when good things it makes.

Translated by *Dorian Rottenberg*

Today I was terribly vexed.
In the morning I looked around
And saw in the district next
Machines levelling out a mound.
It was overgrown with wild mint,
All lovely and gay and green.

O wait, can you wait a minute,
Comrade machine?

But now, the machines wouldn't spare
The mound, for they haven't got hearts.
Like hawks they continued to tear
The mound like a hare into parts.

To a Hill Evicted from the City

The machines just pommelled and
       pommelled
At the poor unresisting earth.
To twin hillocks that mound gave
      birth
Which looked like a two-humped camel.

From the machine's deep shovel
They poured into dum-cars' bellies
The sad stones, turned into rubble,
No longer proud and rebellious.

Torn out of their native beds,
They gathered inside the machines;
Like criminals' chopped-off heads,
They gathered inside the machines.

A bird coming back to its nest—
It carried some down in its beak—
Not knowing where it could rest,
Looked down, disconcerted and weak.

Will they come back to their anthills,
Ants that went off to work at dawn?
Irritatedly panting
Seemed the wind as it blew its horn.

522

Where could it find a refuge?
Where could it rest in the refuse?
Who will unearth the wooden sword
Hidden in the mound by boys?

O noisy theatre of childish wars,
In my ears your voice still roars.
The smiles of the flowers lie supine.
Achean and Cenozoic,
I can't get you off my mind.

Perhaps we've lost—there's no knowing—
Some priceless archeological find?
Who knows if we won't lose even
A whole era's geological museum?

Translated by *Dorian Rottenberg*

Tofik Bairam | *TOFIK BAIRAM was born in 1934 in Baku. His father is an oil-worker. He was educated at the Azerbaijanian teachers' college in the department of history and philology. He writes on various themes, but mainly about his own generation, about the fighters for world peace, about patriotism and friendship.*

The sun ascends into the glowing skies
And the sea lies basking in the warmth it brings,
And like golden fishes the golden rays
Dance carefree upon the sea's blue wings.

The child's plump cheeks like roses glow.
He looks and marvels at the lovely sight.
Towards the sea he wants to go;
As the child comes nearer, the waves gain height.

The wind is tousling his chestnut hair,
Yet his little face from fear is free.
All that moves him now is his one desire
To scoop the gold sunbeams out of the sea.

The Child
and the Sea

The waves come rumbling, fiercer, higher,
As if to devour him just as he stands.
They dash out towards the shore like tigers
And, timid as lambs, roll back from the sands.

Again a gold sunbeam falls on the water;
"Come to me!" cries the child and attempts to snatch
The bodiless light that escapes with laughter.
"What's this fish," he thinks, "that I cannot catch?"

Not frightened at all, he hops and skips,
Laughs gaily in childish joy;
The sea that plays havoc with giant ships
Seems to the child just another toy.

Translated by *Dorian Rottenberg*

A rumour once spread through Azerbaijan
That peasants were going to visit Lenin.
"Let us send him a present, the best that we can,
For the leader lies wounded in bed in the Kremlin."

The news flew like lightning through village and town;
Said the orchards: "Our fruit—let Lenin taste it."
Then the hoary-haired Mount Kyapaz called down:
"Take my silver snow—the purest and chastest."

The meadows spoke up: "Only show us the way,
We will travel with you to the Kremlin too.
Let our beautiful flowers our love display
To the leader, and cure him with sweet, fresh dew."
Then Gyok-Gyol[1] exclaimed: "For its freshness and taste
My water is deemed far better than any."
"My shadow," the plane-tree whispered in haste,
"Will help to cure our beloved Lenin."

Everyone wanted to send as a gift
The best they possessed, the sweetest of fruit.
A hundred trains would have failed to lift
All the people's gifts and set off on their route.

"Now, which is the gift that would suit us best?"
The messengers pondered a whole day long.
White apples from Kuba[2] were chosen at last,
And, to be sure, the choice was not wrong.

Those apples were taken down from their trees
By girls' and women's delicate hands,
And each of them smelled of the gentle breeze—
The live-giving breath of Azerbaijan.

Their freshness the meadows, its fragrance the
                                              rose
Gave to that gift of the people's choice.
All the savour and strength of the soil arose
To be mixed in those apples' wholesome juice.

The Present

[1] Health resort with mineral springs.
[2] Famous fruit-growing region in Azerbaijan.

526

Mothers order the messengers: "Tell the great man,
Every one of us wants him to visit her house.
If only he'd come to Azerbaijan,
And pluck those apples himself from their boughs.

"Perhaps, when our leader receives our present,
Such a joyful journey he really will plan."
And they all believed that one day, fair and pleasant,
He would come to visit Azerbaijan.

Though himself he was barred from coming by fate,
The light of his deathless ideas has arrived.
In our fertile meadows and luscious orchards
The fruit of his life and deeds has thrived.

Translated by *Dorian Rottenberg*

The Old Stone-Hewer

Slowly he walks down the road through the field,
Looking to me like an old Goliath;
A master to whom even rocks would yield,
Now he walks, supported by a chestnut
staff.

The breeze cools his chest, but his breath comes
hard.
His destination isn't yet near.
His forehead is crossed by a purple scar;
Hot sweat trickles down on his silver beard.

How many houses he built out of rocks!
But today he merely passes them by.
He moves, supporting himself on his stick.
Less sure is his hand, less keen his eye.

At every step his heart starts to flutter
Like a fowl that wants to fly from its farm;
The stones which he used to hew with his
hammer
He longs to embrace with a trembling arm.

527

The hoary-haired master thinks as he goes
Of his strength that fails in unequal strife.
He could circle the globe, only that this road
Shouldn't prove the last on his way through life.

The grey-haired master will not be downed.
He loves this life, he wants to live on.
But each time his stick knocks on the ground
The Earth calls out to him loudly: "Come!"

He doesn't demand a monument tall,
The kind built for soldiers who die at their post;
For every fine house, every strong wall,
Are they not monuments suiting him most?

Translated by *Dorian Rottenberg*

A Word to the Stars

For hundreds and thousands of years your light
Was scattered over our waterways.
The sea, overcast by the gloom of night,
Depended for guidance upon your rays.

When you shone, the ships could somehow sail on,
But hit rocks and sank when your light went off.
And the seamen would sigh: "What a blessing is dawn!"
"What good is the night?" the seamen would scoff.

The Khazar took toll of men's hopes and dreams:
Mournful voices each night on its shores would sound.
And the ancient towns swallowed up by the seas,
Were they not night's victims, in darkness drowned?

For ages the rocks would shudder with fright
At the shrieks of people swallowed up by the sea.
Even you, you stars, were powerless to light
Those gloomy waters to let the people see.

The Khazar is no longer gloomy now.
Earthly suns shed their light both near and far.
Every drop of sweat from the toiling man's brow
Has become a star lighting up old Khazar.

Moving in caravans, the milky ways
Come flocking to gaze at the lamplit Khazar.
For towering derricks nowadays
The age-old darkness with floodlights scar.

Tall buildings stand nowadays in the sea.
Broad streets run nowadays in the sea.
There are libraries nowadays in the sea
Where people read books at night—they can see!

The Khazar has found happiness nowadays.
Its songs have circled the world around.
On all of the Earth's great waterways
The Khazar's gay songs and melodies sound.

One's heart gets so much attached to these parts;
This, you think, is the place where your home should be.
And only when, sometimes, a tempest starts
You remember that this is not land, but sea.

Lights and lights, wherever you turn your eye,
Each wave like a glittering golden star.
People forget to look up at the sky
For it seems that both sky and earth are Khazar.

Stars, your time is past, you have lost your worth.
The Khazar no longer has need of you.
With jealousy you look down on the Earth:
New stars shine there—you have nothing to do.

But, stars, I assure you, you needn't be hurt
That the lights of Khazar are brighter than yours.
There are still many gloomier seas in the world:
You can shine upon them—if you like, of course.

Translated by *Dorian Rottenberg*

Fikret Hodja | *FIKRET HODJA, a gifted young poet, was born in 1935 in Akdash. He studied at the railway technical school in Baku and later at the Gorky Literary Institute in Moscow. His favourite theme is "Man and the World", and he writes with passion about the destinies of the world and the responsibility of people for its future. He travels a great deal about the country and has been to Turkmenia, Siberia, Kamchatka and the Altai region. He has also made a trip to Cuba. Fikret Hodja is a Komsomol Prize winner.*

Who Am I?

Taught to walk by my mother,
    A traveller to her grave,
Keeper of Father's ideas,
    And of Mother's lullabies,
      That is who am I.

Translated by Dorian Rottenberg

What a Terribly Long Night!

Each eyelash weighs on my eyes
    Like a heavy burden.
      What a terribly long night!

Sometimes a night
    May be longer than a man's whole life.
    What a terribly long night!

Never before were my thoughts so bitter;
    Never before were my thoughts so sweet.
    What a terribly long night!

My spirit yearns for your presence,
    My eyes are longing for sleep.
    What a terribly long night!

At this moment, I think, in your sleep
    You are smiling, languid and tender.
    Dear, if you only knew
      What a terribly long night it is!

Translated by Dorian Rottenberg

Among the Granite Rocks

High as the sky stand the hills;
On their peaks the sun-spears break
And in golden flakes fall on stone.

Time left its marks—deep folds on the rocks.
When the whip-like winds awake
The rocks like people groan.

The rocks are like guardsmen rousing alarm,
Great monuments of Nature's make
To captive heroes whose names are unknown.

Translated by *Dorian Rottenberg*

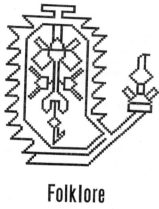

Folklore

Dede Korkut

DEDE KORKUT (Book of My Grandfather Korkut)—is an outstanding monument of Turkic written language, a heroic epic of the medieval Ogouz tribes, related ethnically and linguistically to the three modern Turkic nations—Azerbaijanian, Turkmen and Turkish. The epic is dated 10th-11th centuries, but some parts of it were composed as early as the 9th century. The epic was put in literary shape in the 15th century. There is a short preface and twelve songs written by Korkut, a legendary sage and seer. The epos extolls the courage and fortitude of the Ogouz heroes and their great exploits.

The Book of My Grandfather Korkut
Introduction

In the name of God, the most gracious and the all-merciful, whose aid we beseech! About the time when Allah's prophet, praised be his name, lived on earth, there was born in the tribe of the Bayats a man who was called Debe Korkut (Grandfather Korkut). He was first among the Ogouzes and he knew everything. And all that he prophesied came to pass. He foretold many events of the hidden future, even as the All-Highest put into his mouth. And Dede Korkut said:

"The time is at hand when the kingdom will return to the tribe of the Kayi to be theirs until the Day of Judgement, and none will be found to wrest it from their hands." Those of whom Dede Korkut spake are descendants of Osman; and his words came to pass and so will it ever be. Dede Korkut made many such prophecies; he solved all the difficulties of the Ogouz people for them. Whatever happened, no decisions were made without asking counsel of Dede Korkut; his commands were always obeyed and his advice was always taken.

And Dede Korkut said:
Unless you pray to Allah your deeds will never thrive;
No man will e'er grow rich unless Almighty God provides;
Unless decreed by fate, no harm will e'er befall a servant of the Lord;
Once dead, you cannot come to life again;
Once departed, the soul will never return;
The greedy man heaps treasures as high as lofty mountains;
Yet he gathers and hoards and seeks still more,
Though he cannot eat more than his fill;
Though the rains fall in torrents, they never will fill the seas;
The proud man will find no favour in the eyes of the Lord,
And he who puffs his breast will surely come to grief;
Though you bring up a stranger's son, he never will be a son of your own;
For when he comes of age he will mount his horse and ride away,
Nor will he admit that he ever knew him who fed him;
A molehill will never become a mountain;
Though you bridle a black ass, it will never become a mule;
Though you attire a handmaiden in her mistress's garments, she will never become a lady;
Though the snow falls fast and thick, in spring 'twill disappear;
By autumn the greenest meadow will be bare;
You will never weave cloth from old cotton;
And and old foe will never be a friend;

Unless you mount a swift steed, you will never reach your journey's end;
Unless you deal blows with your own blade of steel,
The blade of your foes on your body you'll feel;
Unless you squander your fortune, you will never gain a reputation for generosity;
Unless her mother sets an example, a daughter will never take advice;
Unless his father sets an example, a son will never give a feast;
A son is for a mother all that she needs; he is like one of her eyes to her;
If a son grows up to be her delight, he is like the fire of her hearth;
But if he grows up a poor man, he is like the ashes in her hearth;
But what is a son to do if his father leaves him no heritage?
But of what avail is his father's legacy if he has no head on his shoulders?
May the Lord preserve you from the malice of the unlucky, O my Khan!
And Grandfather Korkut also said:
A poor horseman who cannot ride a Caucasian horse along steep mountains should better not mount a horse;
It is not worth while attacking cowards with a keen sword;
For the jigit who knows how to wield it, the club is better than a sword or the bow and arrow;
Gloomy houses where wayfarers are not welcomed should better fall to ruins;
Bitter grasses which horses do not eat, should better not grow;
Bitter waters which men do not drink, should better not flow;
A disrespectful son who brings no honour to his father's name, should better not spring from his father's loins;
It were better that such a son should not come from his mother's womb;
It is good to be a son in whom his father delights and who glorifies his father's name;
It were better for false words never to be spoken on this earth;
May the upright live thrice thirty years and ten;
And may you live ten times thirty years and ten;
And may the Lord guard you against all evil, and may your happiness last for ever, O my Khan!
And Grandfather Korkut also said—let us see, O my Khan, what he said:
The wandering deer knows where the best grass grows;
The wild ass knows the flat meadows of the rolling plains;
The camel knows the tracks of many many distant paths;
The fox knows the smell of seven valleys;
The lark knows when the dawn rose on the passing caravan;
Only the mother knows who begat her son;
The steed knows which rider is heavy and which is light;
The mule knows the weight of its load;
Only he who suffers pain knows where it hurts;

The nose bleeds with injury caused by a thoughtless head;
With his kobza[1] in hand, the minstrel wanders from tribe to tribe, and from Bey to Bey;
Only the minstrel knows who is brave, who is a coward;
Let the minstrel, plucking the strings of his kobza, sing your praises among the tribes and among your people.
And may Allah guard you against all wandering griefs, O my Khan!
And Grandfather Korkut said—let us see, O my Khan, what he said:
I will open my lips and sing praises to the Lord above;
To the beloved of the Lord, to the leader of our faith, to Mohammed—Glory!
To Abu Bekr who prays at the right hand of Mohammed—Glory!
To the word "amma"[2] with which the last chapter of the Koran begins—Glory!
To the sura "Yassin"[3] when properly read, syllable by syllable—Glory!
To Ali, Prince of Warriors, who blazed the path for the true faith with his sword—Glory!
To the sons of Ali, grandsons of the Prophet, to Hassan and Hussein, who perished at the hands of the Yezids on the plain at Kerbela—to both brothers—Glory!
To the revelation of God, written, arranged in order and sent down to us from heaven—to the Koran—Glory!
To him who wrote and arranged that Koran so as to give us learned men,
To Osman the son of Affan who cast the false copies of the Koran to the flames—Glory!
To the House of God, built in the low valley, to Mecca—Glory!
To the pilgrim who starts out in good health and who returns in safety and full of righteousness—Glory!
Above all days of the week, to Friday—Glory!
To him who reads the Khutba prayer on a Friday—Glory!
To the community that listens to the reader of the Khutba—Glory!
To the Muezzin who summons the faithful to prayer from the minaret—Glory!
To the lawfully wedded spouses who pray to Allah on their bended knees—Glory!
To the father who has turned white with the passage of time—Glory!
To the mother who spares not her white milk as she suckles her babe—Glory!
To the bride who goes to meet her bridegroom—Glory!
To my beloved brother—Glory!

[1] Stringed instrument.
[2] Glory.
[3] Chapter of the Koran.

To the marriage tent, pitched near the grey goatskin tent—Glory!
To the long tent-rope of the marriage tent—Glory!
To the Incomparable, to the Creator of the Universe, to our Lord—Glory!

May the Lord God in heaven whom we praise, be merciful to us and help us, O my Khan!

Now, the minstrel says: There be four kinds of women.
To the first kind belong the pillars of their home;
To the second kind belong those women who make one turn pale;
To the third kind belong those women who are ever restless, ever meddling;
And to the last belong those for whom no words can be found.

The woman who is the pillar of her home is she who, when a stranger comes from the plains when her husband is away, feeds him, treats him with courtesy and lets him go his ways.

She is of the kind of Ayesha and Fatima,[1] O my Khan! May thousands of such women be born, and may such a woman come to your hearth.

Now, the second kind—the woman who makes one turn pale;

She rises before dawn and, without washing her hands or face, breaks her fast on nine rolls of bread, a pail of sour milk and, stuffing her mouth, fills her belly; after which, smacking her backside, she says:

"Perdition take this tent! Ever since I married, my belly has never been satisfied, my face never wore a smile, my feet have never known shoes or my face a veil; but alas, what can't be cured must be endured. If only this husband died and I married another and he turned out to be better than I expected." May such, O my Khan, never bear any children! May such a woman never come to your hearth.

The next is the ever restless, ever meddling kind of woman. She rises at dawn and, without washing her hands or face, wanders through the camp from tent to tent, from place to place;
She stumbles over everything that's in her way;
She listens in to everything that people say;
She brawls with young and old, insulting everyone;
And only comes back home long after noon is done
To find her tent turned upside down
By the thieving dog, the foal and greedy calf;
That the chickens have not yet returned to their roost;
That the cowcrib is empty, the cow not come home;
She cries to her neighbours: "Zubeida,
Zuleika, my dears, and Ruveida!
Aina-Melik, my dear, Kutlu-Melik, and you—
I only went out for a minute or two,

---

[1] Legendary women, models of wifely virtue.

But who made this mess of my resting place, who?
Could you not have minded my tent a bit, pray?
The rights of a neighbour are sacred, they say!"

And so she goes on. May such women, O my Khan, never bear any children. May such a woman never come to your hearth.

And the next is she whom no words can describe. When an esteemed visitor from the plains comes to her tent, her husband says to her: "Arise, bring forth fresh bread, let us eat and let him eat with us." But she replies: "You have no more baked bread." "But we must feed our guest," says her husband. But this woman replies:

> "Whatever shall I do? This house, may it fall
> upon your head,
> Has neither sieve for sifting flour, nor flour for
> making bread;
> Nor has the camel yet returned with flour from
> the mill;
> And what it brings, may it upon my own backside
> be spilled."

With these words she smacks her behind, and turning her back to her husband, empties the contents of the table cloth before him, on the floor. And though you reproach her with a thousand words, not one will she leave unanswered, nor will she heed a single word of her husband.

Such women are descended from Noah the Prophet's ass; Allah guard you against such a woman, O my Khan, and may such a woman never come near your hearth.

The Lay of Kanturali, the Son of Kanli Kodja

In the days of the Ogouzes, there once lived a wise old man, Kanli Kodja by name, who had a handsome grown-up son called Kanturali. One day Kanli Kodja invited his friends to a feast, and thus addressed his guests:

"My friends, on the death of my sire, as his heir I was named;
He willed all his land and his title to me.
When I die, my son as my heir I proclaim;
And what can be better—my son, come to me—
Than to marry you off while my eyes can yet see?"
Said his son:
"Oh my sire—when did you then decide
To marry me off—have you found me a bride?"
And Kanturali added:

"Oh sire, my bride must rise while I am yet in bed,
My bride must mount her horse ere I have mounted mine;
Ere I ride forth the bloody infidels to fight
My bride must bring an unbeliever's head before my sight."
Kanli Kodja replied:
"My son, it is no maiden you seek, but a strong giant of a woman to do your fighting for you while you eat, drink and make merry."
Kanturali replied:
"Yes, my dear father—such must she be
Else you will go and bring back for me
The first skinny, frail Turkmen maid that you'll see.
Were I to approach her to take my delight
Her womb, it would burst under me out of fright."
Kanli Kodja said:
"My son, it is you who must seek out your bride;
The gold and the wedding feast I will provide."
Whereupon Kanturali, the victorious in battle, arose from his seat, and, with forty jigits, rode off to the land of the Inner Ogouzes. He searched far and wide for a bride but found none to suit his taste; so he returned home. When he came home his father said:
    "Now tell me, my son, have you found you a bride?"
But Kanturali, he only replied:
"Perdition take the Ogouz tribe;
No, I found me no bride, though I searched far and wide."
His father said: "That's not the way to seek for a bride."
"How then, o my father?" asked Kanturali.
His father replied:
"My son—he who sets off at sunrise should never return at noon;
He who sets off at noon should never return with the moon;
I shall go and find you a bride
But the gold and the wedding feast you must provide."
And Kanli Kodja merrily and joyfully rose from his seat and with some of his white-bearded elders rode off to the land of the Inner Ogouzes but could not find a suitable bride there; he turned his horse's head in another direction and rode into the land of the Outer Ogouzes, but there, too, was unable to find a suitable bride for his son; so he took a third direction and came to Trebizond.
Now the Prince of Trebizond had a beautiful daughter; she could draw a two-stringed bow and shoot two arrows—to the left and to the right at one shot—nor did her arrows ever fall to the ground.
He who would win this maiden to wife, and pay for her and her *kaftan*, had to overcome three wild beasts, for the Prince of Trebizond had made a vow:

"To him who these three beasts doth slay
My daugher I will wed;
But he who fails these beasts to slay
Must forfeit his fair head."

And so thirty-two sons of infidel princes lost their heads which now were spiked on his castle battlements.

Now these three beasts were: a fierce lion, a black bull and a black camel, each as large and terrible as a dragon. And these thirty-two youths whose heads were spiked on his castle battlements had met neither the fierce lion nor the black camel—they had all perished on the horns of the black bull before they ever had a chance of setting eyes on them.

Kanli Kodja looked at these heads and at those three wild beasts, and the very skin of his scalp contracted in terror; and he addressed his companions, saying:

"I will return to tell my son the truth,
And if he's brave, he'll win this maid, forsooth;
If not, he must be satisfied
To take a maiden nearer home as bride."

Even the four-legged steed, though strong, limps in his stride—
But the minstrel's song flies swiftly far and wide.

Kanli Kodja left Trebizond and returned to the land of the Ogouzes; and Kanturali heard the news—he was told that his father was on the way home. He called his forty jigits and rode out to meet his father, kissed his hands and thus addressed him:

"Have you found me, O father, a suitable bride?"

"Yes, if you're fearless enough," his father replied.

Said Kanturali:

"Is it silver and gold she desires,
Or mules and Arabian camels as her price she requires?"

"Valour and courage, my son" said his sire.

Kanturali replied:

"I will saddle my black-maned Caucasian steed;
I will fall on the land of the bloodthirsty giaours;
And I'll cut off their heads and I'll spill their vile blood,
And I'll force those proud giaours to vomit their blood;
With men and with women slaves I will return—
Thus will I prove my valour."

But Kanli Kodja replied:

"Not this kind of courage, son, have I in mind—
This maiden is guarded by wild beasts, you'll find;
And he who these three beasts ferocious doth slay

541

This maiden so fair will receive for his wife.
But he who these three beasts so wild fails to slay
Will forfeit his head and with it—his life."
Kanturali made answer:
"O my father, you should not have said these words; but since you have,
I will surely go there, so that I do not have to hide my head or blush for
shame. Fare you well, my noble father, and you, too, my lady
mother."

Then Kanli Kodja said to himself: "O me, what have I done! I will tell
the youth such terrible stories that he will be stricken with fear and maybe,
he will not leave us."

And he said—let me see, O my Khan, what he said:
"The roads into that land, my son, are tortuous and steep,
With quagmires that are perilous to rider and to steed;
The forests there—too dense for speckled snakes to crawl;
The castles there are very tall, they reach into the skies;
The maidens there are very fair—they charm all hearts and eyes;
The headsman strikes without a sound—and heads fall to the
ground;
A heavy shield hangs at the back of that fair maiden's sire;
Upon this earth no other land so evil can be found;
Come back, come back, my son, to us—come back, I beg of you,
Have pity on your hoary sire and your old mother, too."
But Kanturali replied in wrath:
"O father, what is this you say, and what is this I hear?
Can he a jigit really be whose heart is full of fear?
And shame on him who seeks to fill a brave man's heart with fright.
With Allah's help, the winding roads I'll traverse overnight,
The quagmires that are perilous to rider and to steed
I'll fill with sand and over them on my good steed I'll speed;
I'll strike my flint, and set the forests dense alight
So snakes can crawl through them by daylight and by night.
With Allah's aid I'll raze those castles reaching to the skies,
I'll kiss the lips of that fair maid who fascinates all eyes;
What though her father wears a shield between his shoulders broad?
With Allah's aid, his head will fall at one stroke of my sword.
Whether I go or I stay, whether I return, or no—
Or I fall 'neath the terrible camel, or no—
Be I tossed on the horns of the black bull, or no—
Be I torn by the claws of the fierce lion, or no—
Whether I go or remain,
Farewell, my noble parents, till we meet again."
Here his parents understood that his honour brooked of no delay, so

they said: "May fate be merciful to you, O son; go, and may you return safe and sound."

Kanturali kissed his parents' hands, and called his forty noble jigits; for seven days and seven nights they rode until they came to the borders of the land of the unbelievers; there they pitched their tents.

Kanturali spurred his swift steed, played with his mace, tossing it high in the air and catching it ere it fell. And he said:

> "O my forty comrades, forty friends so true,
> I will race against the swift,
> I will battle with the strong,
> The three wild beasts with Allah's aid I'll slay
> And to my parents' tent repair
> With yellow-robed Seljan-Khatun,
> The fairest of all maidens fair.
> Hey, my forty friends, my forty comrades true,
> Let my head fall a sacrifice for you!"

While he was conversing thus with his companions, O my Khan, the news of his arrival was brought to the Prince of Trebizond. He was told: "Kanturali, an Ogouz jigit, has come to woo your daughter."

The Prince of Trebizond sent his unbelievers to meet Kanturali—they met him seven leagues from Trebizond.

"Tell us, O jigit, what brings you to our land," said they.

"We have come to exchange gifts," was the reply. So Kanturali and his forty jigits were received with all honours, bright carpets were spread for them, white sheep were slaughtered for them and seven-year-old red wine was poured for them; after which they were escorted to the Prince of Trebizond.

The Prince sat on his throne, which was placed in the centre of a large field; he was guarded by one hundred armoured warriors, all unbelievers. And the spectators stood seven deep around the field; Seljan-Khatun, his daughter, had ordered a tall tower to be built in the centre of this field; all her maids-in-waiting were dressed in red—she alone wore a yellow robe, and she sat in her tower, watching the spectacle from on high.

Kanturali was brought before the Prince of Trebizond, and made a speech in greeting; the Prince, who wore a black hat, replied to his greeting and commanded many-coloured carpets to be spread, and they sat down. Then he said:

"Tell me, O jigit, whence come you?"

Kanturali rose to his feet, approached him proudly, uncovered his handsome head, rolled up the sleeves on his lily-white arms and said:

543

"To climb your tall mountain that stands against us, my Lord, have I come;

"To cross your wide river, its swift-running waters, my Lord, have I come;

"To seek your protection and friendship 'neath your shadow have I come;

"By Allah's command, at our Prophet's behest, your daughter to wed have I come."

The Prince of Trebizond said: "This jigit has a ready tongue, but does he possess a valiant arm? Strip him naked as he was when his mother bore him." This was done, and Kanturali wrapped a thin, golden-coloured robe about his loins, and thus he was led to the field.

Now Kanturali was handsome to perfection, and among the Ogouz tribes only four jigits wore such a loincloth. These were: Kanturali, Kara-Chyukgur and his son Kyrk-Konik, and Beirek—he who rode the grey horse.

And as Kanturali wrapped his robe around his loins, the maiden watched him from her tower; she thrilled as she looked at him and felt a weakness in all her body; her mouth began to water like that of a sick calf. She exclaimed to her maids-in-waiting:

"If God the All-Highest but softened the heart
Of my father, and made him name a price for me,
And let me as bride of this jigit depart!
If he died by these beasts, what a shame it would be!"

Just then, the bull was led into the lists by a chain of iron; bending its knees, it pierced a slab of marble with its horns like a piece of cheese, and the unbelievers murmured:

"Now it will gore that jigit to death
And trample and tear him, and all in one breath;
Perdition take the Ogouz tribe!
Why should these forty jigits and their Bey's only son
Die for one maiden, when all's said and done?"

Hearing these words, the forty jigits lifted up their voices and wept. Kanturali looked to his right, and saw his forty jigits weeping; he cast his eyes to his left, and again he saw his forty jigits weeping. And he said:

"O my forty jigits, my forty companions!
Wherefore do you mourn for me?
Bring me my kobza and sing me my praises."

544

Whereupon the forty jigits began to sing his praises—let us see, O my Khan, how they praised him:

"O Kanturali, O Our Sultan and Chief!
Did you not depart from your tent,
And did you not then speed
On your swift-footed, black-maned Caucasian steed?
As over the snow-covered mountains you sped,
As over the steep snowy hillsides you sped,
The beasts and the birds from your shadow they fled;
As you passed by your father's white-crested tent,
The milkmaids on milking the kine were intent.
And he who was named 'little bull', tell us now,
Is he not the calf of the black horned cow?
Are brave men afraid of death?
Seljan-Khatun yellow-robed looks at you from her
                                                                      tower,
On whom she looks, in her love's flame will be surely
                                                                      devoured.
So for love of this yellow-robed maiden, take heart,
O Kanturali."

And Kanturali said: "Lead out your bull,
Let your bull come to me."
So they led the bull by its chains to Kanturali and let it loose. The bull turned its horns, like two pointed spears of steel, at Kanturali, but praising Mohammed, blessed be his name, he smote it on the forehead, forcing it to its haunches; then, with its head in one fist and its tail in the other, he dragged it to the edge of the field. Long did they struggle, the victory leaning neither to the bull nor to Kanturali. But the bull, its jaws foaming white, slowly began to weaken. Then Kanturali exclaimed:

"Man conquered this world with his brain.
To run from this bull I shall feign
And behind this black bull my valour display."

He praised Mohammed, blessed be his name, and retreated from the bull's head, whereon it dashed forward and fell, so that its horns pierced the earth; Kanturali lifted it thrice by the tail, and thrice did he throw it to the ground; and all its bones were shattered. He then placed his right foot on the bull's spine piercing it with his sword; withdrawing his blade, he skinned the bull; leaving its flesh on the ground, he offered its hide to the Prince of Trebizond, saying:

545

"Tomorrow at dawn you will give me your daughter as bride."
"O give him the girl, let him take her and go," the Prince replied.
But the Prince of Trebizond's nephew said:

"The lion is monarch of beasts, so let the young Khan
Prove he can play with the lion as well, if he can.
And then we will give him the maid."

So the lion was led into the field. It roared so loud that all the horses standing there pissed blood.
Kanturali's jigits whispered to each other:

"He slew the bull indeed, but now—
This lion—will he slay it, and how?"

And they started weeping. Kanturali, seeing them weeping, exclaimed:

"Take my kobza, one of you, and sing my praise.
I, who love the yellow-robed maid,
Will I fear with the lion to fight?"

And his companions said—let us see, O my Khan, what they said:

"He who slays the young foals
Among the green reeds;
Who, tearing out the heart of his prey
Drinks its warm blood;
Who retreats not before the keen sword's heavy blow—
He who fears not the mighty birchen bow,
Who retreats not before the keen white-feathered shaft;
He who slays the royal lion, monarch of the beasts,
Will he permit the pup of a piebald cur
To snap at him?
Do brave jigits spare their foes in battle?
Seljan-Khatun yellow-robed looks at you from her tower,
He on whom she looks will in the flame of her love be devoured,
So for love of this yellow-robed maiden, take courage."
"Listen, giaour," said Kanturali:
"Loosen your lion and lead him to me;
I would cleave him in twain, did I have my good sword,
But in thee do I trust, upon thee, my good Lord,

Magnanimous Allah, dispenser of wealth—
Hearken, and come to my aid!"

The lion was let loose; it galloped towards Kanturali, who wrapped a piece of woollen cloth around his fist and, praising the Prophet, blessed be his name, dealt the lion such a blow that he broke its jaw; seizing the lion by its mane, he broke its back and then, lifting it, cast it to the ground so that all its bones were shattered. Then he approached the Prince of Trebizond and said:

"Tomorrow you'll give me your daughter to wed."
"Fetch the maiden and give her to him," the Prince said.
"For he has found favour in our royal sight,
And gazing on him, my heart takes delight.
Let him stay, if he wishes, with us; but if no—
He is free to depart where'er he may go."
Once more the Prince's nephew protested and he said:
"The camel is king of the beasts, so let the young Khan
Play with the camel as well, if he can.
And then we will give him the maiden."

By the mercy of Allah, and in answer to the prayers of the Beys and Pashas, the Prince of Trebizond commanded his servants to bind the camel's jaw with seven knots; but the envious infidels did not obey his command; they let the camel loose and unbound, thinking: "Kanturali will surely perish; the camel will crush him to death and only then will it release him from its embraces." But our brave jigit, who had already vanquished two beasts, stumbled and dropped to the ground, fatigued with battle. And six headsmen with drawn swords approached him from behind, whereupon his forty companions lifted up their voices, saying—let us see, O my Khan, what they said:

"Kanturali, you mounted your black-maned Caucasian
steed,
You called your bold jigits and rode off with speed;
But yesterday you climbed the snowy mountain steep,
But yesterday you swum the torrent, swift and deep,
But yesterday you crossed into
The blood-thirsty giaours' land;
And when the black bull rushed at you,
You shattered its bones;
When the fierce lion attacked you,
You shattered its bones;
But when the black camel comes to attack,

Why in defence are you tardy to act?
Rumours will climb the tall mountains so steep,
Rumours will cross the bloodstained rivers so deep,
The Ogouz tribe, hearing these rumours, will say:
'Know you what Kanturali's done and,
Kanturali, Kanli Kodja's young son?
When the black bull attacked him,
He shattered its bones;
When the fierce lion attacked,
He shattered its bones;
But when the black camel came to attack,
Why in defence was he tardy to act?'
Young and old, great and small, they will lift up their
        voice,
The old men and old women will hold you in scorn,
Your grey-bearded sire will be stricken with grief,
Tears of blood will fall fast from your old mother's eyes;
Open your eyes, O my Khan, and arise!
See, six cruel headsmen behind you, with drawn sword
        in hand
Are ready to strike off your head, young and fair
Ere you of its loss will be ever aware.
Oh won't you look up at the skies?
A grey goose is flying at you—can't you see?
Then let loose your falcon, O Kanturali!
Seljan-Khatun the yellow-robed is beckoning to you,
O can you not see?
The camel will crush you, they say, with its nose.
Seljan-Khatun the yellow-robed looks at you from her
        tower.
On whom she looks, in her love's flames will surely he
        be devoured,
And the yellow-robed maiden, in her love for you, bids
        you arise!"

Kanturali sprang up and said:

"Listen! When I smite that camel's nose,
People will say:
'He smote that camel at that maiden's command.'
Tomorrow, word will reach my native land.
The Ogouz people will say:
'The camel fell by his hand
And he won that fair maiden to wife.'

548

Come, strike my kobza, sing my praise!
In God Almighty, who created me,
I place my trust.
So will a mere camel make me retreat?
God willing, I will cut off its head."

Then Kanturali's forty jigits commenced singing his praises, saying—let
us see, O my Khan, what they said:

"The eagle is the Sultan of all the birds that fly,
It builds its nest on rocky peaks that reach right to
the sky;
And in its flight its pinions brush Almighty Allah's
throne.
And from the heights, with folded wings, it falls just
like a stone.
It swoops upon the fowl that on the placid lakes do
swim.
In passion fierce it tears its prey to pieces, on the
wing;
And when by hunger moved, it flies in search of prey.
Will it the magpie then permit to strike it with its
wing?
Do brave jigits e'er think of death when rushing to
the fray?
Seljan-Khatun the yellow-robed looks at you from her
tower.
On whom she looks, in her love's flame will surely be
devoured.
So for love of this yellow-robed maiden, take heart!"

Kanturali praised Mohammed, blessed be his name, and smote the camel
once with his foot; the camel roared, and he smote it again; the camel,
unable to stand, fell to its knees. Kanturali, standing on its back, killed it
with two strokes of his sword; then he cut out two strips from its hide and
threw them to the Prince's feet, saying: "They will do for repairing your
warriors' stirrups or quiver straps."
Here the Prince of Trebizond exclaimed;

"By God, this jigit has found favour in my sight,
His prowess fills my heart with delight."

And he commanded tents to be set up in forty places; forty many-coloured
wedding tents did he command to be pitched. The maiden was brought

549

before Kanturali and they were both led inside the marriage tent. A minstrel came and sang love songs for them; but Kanturali the Ogouz jigit, breathing deeply, unsheathed his sword, and smiting the ground, clove it and said:

> "May I be cloven like this earth,
> My ashes—scattered like the dust;
> May my own arrow wound me to death;
> My sword may it cleave me in two.
> May I never beget a son; if I do,
> May he not live ten days
> If I enter this marriage tent
> Before I see my noble father's face,
> Before I see my lady mother's face."

He struck his tent, loaded his camels and his horses, making them roar and neigh. When night fell he set forth on his way. He rode for seven days and seven nights, until he reached the borders of the land of the Ogouz tribe. There he pitched his tent, and said:

> "O listen, my forty friends and forty comrades true,
> May my own head be sacrificed for you!
> Our God on high has shown to me the way;
> I took his path; those three wild beasts I slew
> Seljan-Khatun the yellow-robed I won.
> Now bring this news unto my sire, and let him meet his son!"

And Kanturali looked around him and he saw swan-birds and cranes, hazel-hens and partridges flying high and low in the air; he saw ice-cold streams and lakes; meadows and shady groves did he see. Seljan-Khatun found this very beautiful and approved of the site of the camp; they laid them down to rest and ate, drank and made merry.

In those days, if misfortune befell a jigit of the Ogouz tribe, it was usually during his slumber. Kanturali fell into a deep sleep. And as he slept, his bride said:

> "There be many who declare they love me.
> I fear that they may try to catch us by surprise
> And capture my jigit as fast asleep he lies.
> I fear that they will slay him, and bind my lily hands,
> And bring me to my parents' house, back to my native land."

So she harnessed Kanturali's steed in armour, and donned armour herself; with spear in hand she ascended the top of a nearby hill and looked around. And you should know, O my Khan, that meanwhile the Prince of Trebizond had changed his mind, saying:

"Because he slew my three beasts he has ridden off with my one and only daughter." And he selected six hundred infidels all arrayed in black robes and in armour of burnished steel. A whole day and a whole night did they march, and unexpectedly they came to where Kanturali had encamped; but the maiden was standing on guard. She looked and saw that the foe had arrived to attack them. She spurred her horse and sped to Kanturali and thus addressed him; let us see, O my Khan, what she said:

> "Beware, lift your black head, O jigit!
> Open your handsome black eyes, O jigit!
> Open your eyes ere they bind your white hands!
> Open your eyes ere they smite your white brow
> Against the black earth!
> Open your eyes ere they cut off your handsome head,
> Ere you utter a sound!
> Ere they spill your red blood all over the ground!
> The enemy's here, your foes have arrived!
> Say—why are you lying inactive?—arise!
> Though the hills have not trembled, the whole earth
> is rent;
> The old Beys have not died, and yet all are confused
> And the people in crowds have descended the hills,
> And your foe to attack you has marshalled his ranks.
> Is this, then, the best place to rest?
> For setting up house—is this place the best?
> What has happened to you, O my Kanturali?"

Thus did she loudly address him. Kanturali stirred in his sleep, opened his eyes, arose and said: "What are you talking of, my fairest?" She replied:

> "Arise, my jigit, for the foe has arrived;
> To arouse you is my duty;
> To go into battle, your prowess to show—
> That is your duty."

Here Kanturali raised his brows and saw that Seljan-Khatun had galloped off, spear in hand. He kissed the earth, saying:

"Inspired with our faith, we place our trust in the words of our Prophet, And God the All-Highest has granted our wishes in his secret halls."
He washed his face and hands in clear water from a stream, bent his lily-white brow to the earth and, bowing twice, performed his prayer; then he mounted his horse, praised Mohammed, blessed be his name, and spurring his steed, rode forth to meet the black-robed infidels.

Seljan-Khatun spurred her horse and overtook Kanturali, who said: "My fairest, whither are you hurrying?" And she answered:

> "O Prince of jigits, if but the head be whole
> Will not a headgear for this head be found?
> These infidels are many.
> We will join them in battle and fight against them;
> If one of us two in this battle must die—
> So let it be;
> And he of us who from this battle comes through,
> Be it you, be it me,
> Let him haste and return to our tent."

And, spurring her steed, Seljan-Khatun rushed into the fray, causing grievous loss to the foe.

Those who fled, she pursued not;
Those who begged quarter—she slew not.
Thinking that the enemy was routed, she rode back to the tent, her bared sword dripping with blood. But Kanturali was nowhere to be seen.

Meanwhile, Kanturali's mother and father had arrived; They saw a maiden holding a bloodstained sword, but no sign of their son. They asked her if she knew where he was—let us see, O my Khan, what they said:

> Kanturali's mother said:
> "Oh tell me, my daughter, my fair maiden, say,
> When early this morning you rose from your bed,
> Did you bid your servants to bear off my son,
> Did you bid your servants my son to behead
> Before he could open his handsome dark eyes?
> Did you make him groan and with mournful cries say,
> Where are you, mother? Where, father, are you?
> I can see you, but no sign of my son,
> No sign of my Bey; say, what have you done?
> O tell me the truth and say where is my son!
> My heart grieves me sorely; say one word, but one!
> And on my poor head may all your sorrows fall."

And here Seljan-Khatun understood that these were her father-in-law and mother-in-law. Pointing her horsewhip to the tent, she said:

> "Go, rest inside that tent, while I
> Will seek him where the ravens fly
> In croaking circles o'er the slain
> And dust clouds rise to fall again."

Spurring her steed, Seljan-Khatun rode to the top of a nearby hill. Gazing around her, she noticed clouds of dust thickening and dispersing in a distant ravine. She rode fast and saw that Kanturali's horse was wounded by an arrow; that an arrow had grazed Kanturali's brow, and that his face was all covered in blood; he, however, never curbed his horse for a moment —he only wiped the blood from his brow, and, while the treacherous unbelievers sought to surround him, with bared sword drove them before him.

At this sight Seljan-Khatun's heart was consumed with fire and, as a falcon swoops down upon a flock of geese, so did she spur her horse into the thick of the unbelievers, smiting them hip and thigh as she rushed through their broken ranks.

Kanturali looked round and saw a stranger driving his enemies before him; he knew not that this was Seljan-Khatun; he waxed wroth and said —let us see, O my Khan, what he said:

> "You arose and you left your own tent, O jigit,—
> What kind of a jigit are you?
> You've mounted your black-maned Caucasian steed,
>
> jigit,
> What kind of a jigit are you?
> You're attacking my foes without asking my leave,
> And you're slashing their heads off before they can
>
> breathe;
> And this, by my tribe, is deemed shameful and
>
> base;
> So begone before I, like a falcon, swoop down
> And cut off your head before you can turn round;
> Ere I spill your heart's blood all over the ground
> And tie to my saddle your head with your beard!
> O jigit, whose last hour has come!
> What kind of a jigit are you?
> Return while yet you are alive."

At this, Seljan-Khatun replied—let us see, O my Khan, what she said:

"My jigit, my Prince of jigits!
Do camels desert their young?
Do Caucasian mares kick their foals?
Do ewes ever butt their own lambs?
Do fearless jigits ever slay
Those whom they call their beloved ones, pray?
O my jigit, my Prince of jigits!
One flank of these unbelievers will be mine
And the other flank, thine!"

Here Kanturali understood that it was Seljan-Khatun who was overcoming and dispersing his foes; he fell upon one flank and, sword in hand, pounced upon the unbelievers, sweeping off head after head. The enemy was vanquished, the foe was scattered, and Seljan-Khatun, lifting Kanturali on to the croup of her steed, sped from the battlefield.

As they rode back, Kanturali said to Seljan-Khatun:

"You mounted your black-maned Caucasian steed;
The land of your forefathers you left behind
With me, a new home and new parents to find
In the shade of my own father's white-crested tent.
But in summer when you and our bright-eyed young brides
Gather round to make merry and shorten long nights,
Then you, when your turn comes a story to tell
Will rise to your feet as you boastingly say:
'When Kanturali in the battle grew faint
I lifted him on to my steed, and with speed
We both from the battlefield then rode away.'
I can't bear the sight of you, Seljan-Khatun,
I love you no longer, O Seljan-Khatun,
And now with my own hand you I will slay."

But Seljan-Khatun understood full well how he felt and answered him, saying—let us see, O my Khan, what she said:

"O my Prince of jigits, my Kanturali—
When it's time to boast
Let men do the boasting.
For they are like lions
But she who boasts is a liar;
For boasting will never turn
A woman into a man.
I never sported with you

554

Under your many-coloured blanket;
I never kissed your honey-sweet lips;
My scarlet lips
No vows exchanged with you.
Quickly did you fall in love with me
And as quickly your love did expire,
You worthless son of a worthless sire!
God Almighty knows
How true I am to you.
So slay me not, my friend."

But Kanturali replied: "No—you must die without fail, and I will slay you."

Seljan-Khatun waxed wroth and said:

"O you worthless son of a worthless sire!
Who refuses to listen to reasonable words!
You worthless son of a worthless sire—
Shall we fight with our bows and our arrows
Or shall we do battle with swords?"

And spurring her steed, she rode to the top of a nearby hill. There she emptied her quiver of its ninety arrows and removed the iron tips from two of them. One she put away and the other grasped in her hand—she could not bring herself to shoot an iron-tipped arrow at him. And she said: "Shoot your arrow, jigit";

But Kanturali replied:

"No—maidens first—you shoot." So with her first shot she grazed his scalp, without even drawing blood. Thereupon he ran to Seljan-Khatun, embraced her warmly and they kissed each other.

Kanturali then said—let us see, O my Khan, what he said:

"My fairest one, whose slender waist
The cypress doth outdo;
Whose footstep light upon the grass
Rests lighter than the dew;
Whose rosy cheeks are like unto
Red blood drops on the snow;
Between whose tiny lips so fair
Two almonds cannot pass;
Whose brows, so black and delicate,
None but a scribe could trace,

555

Whose jet-black tresses sweep the ground
Just like a royal train!
O Sultan's daughter, lion's breed!
I never could have slain you!
I sooner would have killed myself!
I never thought to slay you—
I only meant to try you!"
Seljan-Khatun replied—let us see, O my Khan, what she said:
"I mounted my black-maned Caucasian steed,
The land of my fathers behind me I left,
Forsaking the white-crested tent of my sire;
I have chased the wild game, the wild goat I have
                                        chased;
On the slopes of steep snow-covered hills I have raced.
When but one shaft I shot, I knew what I did,
When I shot that arrow with no iron tip—
I was only testing you, jigit!
I could never slay you, my jigit!"

Then they ran swiftly to each other and embraced one another; they kissed each other's honey-sweet lips and, mounting a grey horse, rode off to Kanli Kodja Bei, Kanturali's noble father.

When he saw his son, Kanli Kodja gave thanks to the Lord. Together with his son and daughter-in-law Kanli Kodja returned to the land of the Ogouz people; there he pitched his tent on a green, flowery meadow. He bade his servants slaughter the fattest horses, cames and sheep, and celebrated his son's wedding. He feasted the other Ogouz Beys and set up his golden canopy. Kanturali entered his marriage tent and attained all his desires.

My grandfather Korkut was also invited. He sang a merry song and recounted the adventures that befell those brave warriors who fought in defence of our faith.

"Where are those heroes now today
Of whom I spoke, who said:
'The world entire is mine'?
All carried off by Death!
They all lie hidden in the earth.
Who will inherit this mortal world?
O mortal life, you come and go
And end in death.
May Allah, when your hour of death arrives
Keep you in the true faith
And may the Almighty keep you

From asking evil-doers for aid.
May your God-given hope be never betrayed.
For the sake of your lily-white face,
We have composed a prayer of five words;
May it be accepted by the Most High
And may those who say 'Amen' see God's face.
May all our prayers be joined in one, and be firm
And my God forgive you your sins
For the sake of Mohammed his chosen,
Whose name be praised, O my Khan!"

Translated by *Louis Zellikoff*

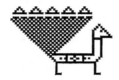

Asli and Kerem

ASLI AND KEREM is a folk love story, composed in the 16th-17th centuries, although some scholars hold the opinion that it should be dated 13th-14th centuries (M. G. Tahmasib). Unlike the majority of such poems this one has a tragic ending—the lovers die. And also it has just this one version. The songs of this poem are still sung by the people and are invariably included in the repertoire of the ashugs. The famous opera "Asli and Kerem" by Uzeir Gajibekov, the founder of Azerbaijanian opera, is based on this love story.

Book of the Wise

Fragments from *ASLI AND KEREM*

People, well-bred, go their way, and are courteous, polite,
 Folk who are decent and true, those—life's honour retain.
Never confide cherished secrets to strangers who pass,
Beauties, if flirts, make bad wives, and are worse than the plain.

* * *

Honoured are those who will never reproach, in no way,
Those who don't steal, who will never in honesty sway;
Sons who will often their fathers' wise words disobey—
Honour those never retain, nor wipe out this dark stain.

* * *

Rams from your fold you shall sacrifice, sins to atone,
Clothes you shall wear, of your woollen cloth honestly sewn,
Fruits you shall eat from the orchard you work in, and own—
Stealing leaves always a stain, and in theft there's no gain.

* * *

Barber Murad, do not grieve for the quick passing day,
Nobody stays here forever, but all go away,
Fortune is reaper, the world is the corn-field, they say,
Corn-fields, if vast like the main—give no cause for the birds to
complain.

* * *

Sages have sayings, they utter them once in a while,
Twice we'll pronounce our saying in exquisite style:
"Sometimes we rise to the sky and forget every trial,
Sometimes we're hurled down again—from the hill to the
plain."

559

Happen it might you'll ascend a mountain like hapless
                                                    Medjnun,

Or in an ocean of sorrows immersed you'll be soon,
Or maybe hundreds of fires will leave you immune—
Or if a fatal time came you will burn in the flame.

Times may be near, Mohammed, that to work will inspire,
Or it may happen for work you will have no desire,
Times may to iron or stone change your body entire,
Fate may destroy you like glass, and your name soil and maim.

* * *

Sages utter their sayings not twice, but three times.
We shall also pronounce our sayings three times. Let our
                                                    foe go blind
                                                            with spite.

Do not entrust with an errand any stranger you meet,
 He may decline your fair offer, or brand you with shame.
Do with your own hands your work—it is more dignified,
Doing you best in your strivings to follow your aim.

* * *

Do not go wandering from hamlet to hamlet, my soul,
Hearing the truth spoken, do not resent it, my soul,
Do not go burning in treacherous flames, o my soul!
Guides are not needed, I say, if you take the right way.

Beads, decorating a saddle, are rubies—he'll lie,
Tell the bare truth and your words, in offence, he'll deny,
Failing his self to assert, his prestige he'll belie,
Lose his great influence he may, and respect, anyway.

Things that by theft and by stealth the dishonest procure,
Bring no well-being in life, and are most insecure,
Things you have stolen will bring you misfortune, for sure,
Keeping piratical prey proves one's moral decay.

560

Do not chop heads on the way when the helpless you meet,
Hear their complaints of the beks and the shahs, how they
torture and beat,
How the poor suffer—with torment their lives are replete. . . .

* * *

My friends, what shall I tell you, what shall we talk about? Well, let me tell you about the city of Ganja. And if I speak of the city of Ganja, then of what man is it to be? Of Ziyad-Khan, of course. The noble man had no heir who would inherit his riches, his property. He was preoccupied with the thought of having a child. This thought weighed heavily upon him, so Ziyad-Khan never smiled.

Ziyad-Khan had a vizier by the name of Kishish, who was a very cruel man. As the saying goes—water seeks a pit. In this case the two became drawn together, being birds of a feather. They were people of one and the same lot. Kishish also had no children.

One day Ziyad-Khan sat in the garden of Kishish, and together with him they discussed the past and the future. Ziyad-Khan said: "Kishish, you have no children, neither have I. After our death there will be nobody to kindle the lights in our houses. Let us give food to the poor, to the beggars, and say prayers and turn sacrifices to God the Almighty. Then, perhaps, he will be merciful to us and send us children. Let us agree to it beforehand."

Kishish answered: "I agree to anything, as long as we have children. I agree to what you say."

Ziyad-Khan said: "If a daughter is sent to me and to you a son, I shall marry my daughter to your son. If you have a daughter and I a son—you will give your daughter in marriage to my son."

Kishish agreed to this. The proposal of his sovereign struck him to the heart.

Next day Ziyad-Khan gathered around him all the poor and all the beggars of Ganja—the grown-ups and the children. He gave them food and clothing, to some who were very old, the poor, and sick—he gave money, and then sent them all home to enjoy what he had given them, and to pray for him.

It often happens that the prayers of the people are heard. God heard the prayers of the two, deprived of their joy in life, as he heard the prayers of the beggars.

Nine months, nine days, nine hours and nine minutes passed since that moment. To Ziyad-Khan a son was born, and to Kishish a daughter.

Ziyad-Khan gave a magnificent banquet, and invited to it lords and

561

nobles. The boy was named Mahmud, and the girl—Maryam. Nurses were engaged to take care of the children.

Years passed, months flew by, the children grew up. Now they both reached the age of eight. Ziyad-Khan appointed the mullah as teacher for his son, whereas Kishish took upon himself the teaching of his daughter.

There is a saying that the tongue of a sage outmarches time. Months flew by, years passed. Maryam and Mahmud reached the age of fifteen. But during all these fifteen years the girl and the boy never met. The boy spent all his time in the company of his tutor—Sofi.

It happened one day that Mahmud and his tutor Sofi went hunting. The falcon, set free for catching the game, flew into the garden of Kishish. Mahmud ran to the garden of Kishish and saw his falcon imprisoned in the hands of his father's vizier.

Mahmud took the saz which was slung over his shoulder. Let us hear what he said to Maryam:

> My falcon has flown to your garden by chance,
> O fair, noble maiden, return me my bird!
> Great beauties surround you, your beauty shines best—
> Fair maid, hear my word and return me my bird!

Maryam took a saz into her hands and spoke as follows:

> O youth, your fine bird to our garden has flown,
> Be Kerem,[1] come and capture the falcon, your own,
> A slave of your eyes I have suddenly grown,
> Kerem, hear my word and recapture your bird!

Mahmud:

> The Goddess of Fortune brought joy to my heart,
> At first made me weep, now she softens my smart,
> Your father will kill me, won't let me depart,
> Pure maid, hear my word and return me my bird!

Maryam:

> You stand there before me, we stand face to face,
> All gardens I'd like to give up for your grace,

---

[1] Kerem in Arabic means generous, gentle.

562

There's nought to forbid to a youth of your race...
I pray you, Kerem, come, recapture your bird!

Mahmud:

In spring we shall all hear the nightingale's trill,
Your eyes are so lovely, they charm me, and thrill!

Maryam:

You've changed my first name, it's Asli, at your will,
Kerem, hear my word, come, recapture your bird!

And that is how Maryam and Mahmud came to love each other at first sight, with all their heart and soul, and because they did not want to give any cause for gossip, and for the sake of intimacy, they decided to change their names.

So Mahmud became Kerem, and Maryam—Asli.

Kerem couldn't endure being parted from Asli. He thought of her day and night. His father saw his son's distraction and became puzzled and disturbed. What could be the reason of Mahmud's ailment?

Then Ziyad-Khan asked his son the reason of his state, that caused his father so much anxiety. Kerem answered:

Kishish has a daughter, a maid whom I love,
Her beauty's enthralled me, O what shall I do?
Her clustering curls fall in picturesque waves,
My love is sincere, but what course to pursue?

Kishish's fair daughter, the best ever born,
She's lovely, she's perfect, she's Venus at dawn,
The daughter of lakes, like a swan in the morn,
I love her, I'm true, but what course to pursue?

The wretched Kerem speaks: I sorrow indeed,
Sad partings are knives that to agony lead,
Armenian is she, and this makes my heart bleed,
Her flames scorch anew, but what course to pursue?

The fact that Asli was the daughter of an Armenian worried Ziyad-Khan. He doubted that Kishish would consent to the marriage of his daughter with Kerem, and he was convinced that Kishish was going to break his word and be false to what they had agreed upon, before the birth of Mahmud and Maryam.

563

Ziyad-Khan met Kishish and broached the subject. The latter consented to marry his daughter to the Khan's son, but he begged for a three-months respite to prepare for the wedding.

When the term was over, Ziyad-Khan, accompanied by his retinue, set out for the house of Kishish. But he was not at home. It became clear that Kishish, an Armenian, was against the marriage of his daughter with a Moslem, and had secretly abandoned the precincts of Ganja and carried off his daughter in an unknown direction.

Kerem refused to believe this. He searched for Asli everywhere. At last he came to the place where they had first met. He questioned the cypress under whose branches they had vowed eternal fidelity to each other.

> O cypress, long months for Asli have I searched,
> Say, beautiful cypress, o where is your hind?
> My eyes shed hot tears which are streamlets of blood,
> Fine cypress, be kind, say, o where is your hind?
> If false your reply, may branches go dry!
> Let winds bend your trunk if my tears you defy,
> If false your reply, may your leafage fall dry!
> Fine cypress, be kind, say, o where is your hind?
> You answer no word, I'm in doubt and in pain,
> I'll call to the clouds on you sorrows to rain,
> My cries reach the sky with a doleful refrain—
> Fine cypress, be kind, say, o where is your hind?

Kerem searched for Asli everywhere, but nowhere could he find her. Now he had no doubt that Kishish had departed and taken his daughter with him. Then he appealed to the mountains:

> My sweetheart, my beauty has fled from Zangi,[1]
> Be bars on her ways, mountains, wrapped in a haze!
> She fled with her parents, my lovely gazelle,
> Be bars on their ways, mountains, wrapped in a haze!
> The guests all were ready to come to the feast,
> The numbers of visitors quickly increased,
> My sweetheart I've lost, tears to flow have not ceased,
> Be bars on their ways, mountains, wrapped in a haze!
> Because of his love has Kerem lost his mind,
> He'll sacrifice world his fair sweetheart to find,
> Asli and Kishish left their homestead behind,
> Be bars on their ways, mountains, wrapped in a haze!

Ziyad-Khan implored him and admonished him. But all was in vain. Then Kerem appealed to all the people gathered around him:

[1] Town in Armenia.

I want to ascend now the snow-covered mount,
I shed bitter tears while her image I keep,
No drug can be found for my sufferings keen,
Her image I keep and, with thoughts of her, weep.
The birds on the mountain trill gaily above,
My hind has escaped, no one knows where's my dove,
Kishish cannot fathom the depth of my love,
Her image I keep, and, with thoughts of her, weep.
The wretched Kerem says: My sufferings abound,
The voice of my love does not cease to resound,
We read scores of lessons and none that are sound,
Her image I keep and, with thoughts of her, weep.

Kerem implored his parents not to hinder him in his search for Asli. To Ziyad-Khan nothing remained but to give his consent. Kerem pressed the saz to his breast. The strings began to sing, and he addressed himself to his friends and acquaintances with the following words:

My body's consumed by this passionate love,
For her, my sweet friend, I shall search without end,
I may or I may not return to my home,
For her, my sweet friend, I shall search without end.

What intrigues dame Fortune is wont to devise:
I weep bitter tears, they have blinded my eyes,
My close boon companions, give ear to my cries,
For her, my sweet friend, I will search without end.
Good-bye to my country, I'll go like the wind,
I'll roam throughout lands, leaving many behind,
If death only spears me, my sweetheart I'll find,
For her, my sweet friend, I will search without end.

In the company of his tutor Sofi, he made the rounds of many countries, passing through many a village and farm, mixing with most different folk, telling them of his grief, of the sorrow that exhausted him.

Not only people did he question, but appealed also to animals, nay, also to trees. They all sympathised with him, shared his great sorrow, and cursed the stubborn Kishish. They all did what they could to help Kerem in his inconsolable grief.

So they passed through many towns and villages. There was hardly a place that they didn't visit. After long wanderings they came to a Georgian village. The youths and girls of the village surrounded him and plied him

565

with questions—who he was, where he came from and where he was bound for. Kerem gave the following answer:

> Fate made me a florist to tend a fair bloom,
> The lily, the rose and the corn-flower weep,
> The snow-storms come sweeping the dead leaves
> around,
> Through gardens they sweep making everyone weep.
>
> My country, my people I left far behind,
> Some hand stole my rose still a bud, scarce defined,
> To find her I roam throughout realms like the wind,
> My land's grief is deep, people, villages weep.
> From river to lake I flew down like a drake,
> From there, like a stag for the fields I did make,
> Kerem says: my name and my honour's at stake!
> The passers-by weep, and the endless roads weep.

Sofi told the Georgians who Kerem was and all about his sorrowful fate. It was only with the greatest difficulty that the Georgians succeeded in leading Kerem to a table where a fine meal was served. They invited him to partake of the good food. But though they insisted and pleaded, everything was in vain: Kerem remained adamant to their entreaties, and didn't touch a single course. He hardly conversed with the people. After long questionings, Kerem at last said:

> Dear people, o what is the state of a man,
> And what does he feel if his sweetheart is lost?
> Through distances great will he search for his love—
> To find the one lost, by his passion thus forced.
>
> No pink can be grafted by hands that don't care,
> No rose without thorns can be found anywhere,
> No work can be done, even if it's your share—
> When your sweetheart is lost and your purpose crossed.
>
> The falcons sweep high in the shimmering air,
> The cranes seek the lake for their nests over there;
> At fifteen, sometimes, you may have greying hair—
> When your sweetheart is lost, and your purpose crossed.
>
> Kerem may grow old in his young years, they say,
> He'll die in these turbulent places, they say,

And silent and numb he will grow, as they say—
When your sweetheart is lost and your purpose crossed.

One of the Georgians said: "Since Kishish refused to marry his daughter to you, and the girl submitted to her father's order, left you, and followed her sire, you ought to give up searching for her. What is the use of continuing this search? Remain here with us in Georgia, we will find you a girl still more beautiful than Asli." He pointed out one of the girls who was present there and said: "Look, what a lovely maiden. She is worth a thousand Aslis, whom you are hopelessly searching for!"

Kerem looked at the Georgian maid and said:

A beautiful maiden I've met in this land,
Like sunshine, her beauty sets Georgia alight,
She sings like a nightingale, trilling till dawn,
Her lips are alluring—a perfect delight!

Our Maker endowed her with beauty most rare,
The one whom she loves has for others no care,
She's graceful and slim, and seems walking on air,
Her slenderness light vies with cypresses slight.

Each tooth is a perfect, a wonderful pearl,
Her eyebrows are bow-strings, adorning the girl,
Her tresses are long and are thick—curl to curl,
Though plaited quite tight—they're a wonderful sight!

The Georgians were convinced that in reality Kerem was a true, genuine bard. Sofi and Kerem, after long inquiries learnt that Kishish and his daughter Asli were at that time residing in Tiflis. So the Georgians, together with Kerem, set out to find Kishish. They said to him: "If you don't marry the girl to Kerem, we shall abduct her!"

Kishish said to Kerem: "Kerem, I have acted unjustly, and have now repented. In Ganja I was obliged to give her to you. Well, I give my consent. Tomorrow morning we shall return to Ganja, and there celebrate your wedding."

The Georgians, who sympathised with Kerem, were overjoyed at such a happy issue. In the night they arranged a banquet in honour of Kerem. Then they began preparing for the wedding. Next day Kerem, accompanied by the Georgians, came to Kishish, but didn't find him at home. He had departed and carried off his daughter in an unknown direction. Kerem said:

567

O dear and kind people, I've lost my Asli,
Again I'm to languish—o what a sad plight!
You hear the sad notes in the nightingale's song—
The rose says "good night", she is dead to my sight!

I stopped being watchful, believing his lies,
In parting such terrible suffering lies,
In parting with her the tears blinded my eyes,
I'm burning in fire, o my sorrowful plight!

Kerem again went off on his wanderings. He again roamed about villages and towns. And, at last, he found himself in Armenia. And here he met a group of girls at the well, where they had come to draw water. Kerem approached them to ask for a drink of water and to question them about Asli. But he had become such an object of ugliness to look at with his hideous, untended beard, that the girls shrank away from him in fear. Kerem said:

O soft-hearted sisters, you tremble with fear!
Don't shrink from the roadway, your path is quite right!
I languish in sorrow, I live without love,
Let dreams be my lot and let yours—be delight.

I pass as a traveller on many a road,
And carry of love in my heart a great load,
I'm tortured by thirst, let me drink on my road,
To soften my plight while I trudge through the night!

The wretched Kerem yearns for lovely Asli,
My heart is in wounds with my tears flowing free,
In mourning for her I am dressed, as you see,
For me the black night, while for you—morning bright.

Sofi told the maidens the history of the love of Kerem for Asli. The maidens showed them the house where Kishish lived. Kerem and Sofi passed many hours near the house in the hope of catching a glimpse of the people inside, but it was all in vain, nobody came out in answer to their calls. The doors were locked and barred, and there were no other means of getting into the house. But Sofi questioned the neighbours, and learnt that Asli's mother was working as a barber-surgeon in the town. She tore out teeth for all those who suffered from toothache.

As soon as Kerem heard this news he ran up to the house and began beating on the door with all his strength. Asli's mother didn't recognise Kerem. She asked: "Who are you, and what is it you want?" Kerem answered: "You know, I have a terrible toothache, it is beyond bearing, I can't stand it." Asli's mother led him into the house. She sat down at her appointed place and asked: "Which tooth is it?" Kerem showed her one of his sound teeth.

She began drawing out the tooth; and when it became loose she, at last, pulled it out.

Seeing that Asli didn't appear, he addressed the woman with the following words: "Aunty, you have drawn the wrong tooth. The one next to it is the one that aches!" The woman pulled out this tooth too. And in such a way she pulled out all his teeth. When she was drawing the last one, Kerem couldn't bear the pain any longer, and fainted.

When he came to himself, he saw Asli bending over him. He got up and said:

> I thank the Almighty, I've seen my Asli!
> I dreamt in the next world to meet her again!
> I know, they will never, Love, give you to me,
> I've gone through great agony, suffered much
> pain.
>
> I see you're indifferent, your love has gone dead,
> Come, let me embrace you with love that has bled,
> One night, in the fall, I'll come round to your
> bed,
> Find peace there again, may my sufferings wane!

The wife of Kishish recognised Kerem and ran off to warn her husband. Asli said:

> As soon as I saw you my heart gave way,
> I burn, and your words are to me bitter bane,
> I beg in the name of my forebears: be kind!
> I burn, I suffer unbearable pain!

Kerem:

> In search of my love this far road did I
> make,
> What tortures I bore, o Asli, for your sake!
> In oceans of suffering my heart sorely ached,
> Great cups full of pain for your sake I did drain!

Asli:

> I crept to no garden to rest for a while,
> No rose did I pluck in my terrible trial,

569

Since both we were parted, not once did I smile,
I burn, I suffer unbearable pain!

Kerem:

I shed bitter tears when thus parted from you,
You led me to lands that are strange to my view,
My teeth by your mother were drawn—thirty-two!
Great cups full of pain for your sake I did drain!

Asli:

You forced me to flee to a far alien shore,
My grief's hundredfold, nay, it's even much more,
I ought to have died, you'd be free as before,
I burn, I suffer unbearable pain!

Kerem:

Long years have I roamed in the mountains alone,
My breast aches with longing, I cry and I moan,
I call you, Asli, with a sad, pleading tone—
Great cups full of pain for your sake did I drain!

Kishish again deceived Kerem. He went to consult a patriarch, and they came to the following decision: Asli must get married at once. Then they found a bridegroom for her: a rich Armenian merchant sent his match-makers to her father. But Asli turned them back with empty hands:

You masters and beks, who come urging your suit,
I claim a rich ransom, first rate it must be,
Five hundred *tumani* for father's new clothes,
And also a thousand *tumani* for me!

I ask for a castle of glass, fair and fine,
For jewellers to silver that castle of mine,
The bridegroom must youth and male beauty combine,
Talk sweetly to me, play the saz at my knee.

The autumn is bringing the fall of leaves near,
['T were better that suitors were not to appear!]
I want forty servants of beauty and cheer,
They all ought to be—tender-voiced, full of glee.

The bridegroom with beauty my heart should disarm,
His lips should be sweet, and his speech full of charm,
Asli speaks the truth and her words do no harm:
Kerem let it be, and no other for me!

Kishish realised that there was no other way out than to take his daughter
with him and disappear once more. As soon as it was night he vanishes
together with Asli. In the morning Kerem discovers that Kishish has again
deceived him. He presses the saz to his breast and sings:

My heart is in flames, it is burnt to the core,
I burn and I weep and my sufferings grow,
Kishish has deceived me again, as before,
I've learnt of his plot, and my bitter tears flow.

My soul is athirst for her nobleness great,
I cannot be free from this terrible weight,
Asli left her hearth, I believe her, I'll wait,
I trust her in woe, and my bitter tears flow.

No doctor is here to see clear that I ail,
My heart is in blood and I know that I fail,
Kerem soon will die in this fiery gale,
I burn, I'm aglow, and my bitter tears flow.

The young Armenian men, maidens, brides, old men and women admonished Kerem to give up his love. They advised him to remain with them and
to marry from among their women any beauty that would catch his fancy.
Kerem said:

Dear friends, I'm perplexed, and I feel very
                                          sad,
My love I'd give up, but my heart will resent!
My heart loves the beauty, and won't give her
                                          up!

I'd want to assent, but my heart won't consent!

She trips like a pheasant, a bird of a kind,
Her robe is in patterns, so quaintly designed,
Her glances remind me of those of a hind,
My passions relent, but my heart won't consent!

I gave her my life, spent in languishing sighs,
The tears flow in torrents of grief from my eyes,

571

Kerem loves Asli—this unparalleled prize—
To leave her I'm bent, but my heart won't consent!

Once again Kerem, accompanied by Sofi, started on a journey. They went to different places, and, while crossing the mountains of Laleli-dag, they were caught in a terrible snow-storm. They wandered about for a long time, but could not find the road. And at last Kerem exclaims:

My Maker, I pray you, don't let me succumb
And die in this cold, o give ear to my prayer!
Have pity and save me, take hold of my hand,
And lead me to her, me, bent low in despair.

The snow-storm and gales rage in fury around,
By icy-cold grips are my members all bound,
If death closes in, put my soul on safe ground,
I cannot find safety or peace anywhere.

To me, to Kerem, no assistance has come,
Asli is untrue, to my cries deaf and dumb,
And life, spent in grief, makes my heart cold and numb,
I searched everywhere, but found fortune nowhere.

Barely had Kerem time to finish what he was saying, when behold! the prophet Khizir appeared, and in no time carried the two travellers, who had lost their way in the mountains, to an exotic country, where reigns lovely, enchanting weather, and all is bliss.

And again Kerem, together with Sofi, crossed valleys, ravines, hills, and again questioned the hinds, hunters, and travellers about where Kishish and his beloved Asli might be residing.

Kerem passed through incredible difficulties. He fell ill, but never gave up his efforts to search for his beloved Asli. On a certain day he chanced to pass a burial ground, and came across a human skull. He picked it up and turned it over in his hands. Then he said:

"Sofi, do you see this skull? I wonder how many years it has lain in the ground? And mind, this same fate awaits us both. Now what shall I do? I think I'll ask him a few questions." These are the questions he put to the skull, pressing his saz to his breast:

I want you to answer some questions of mine:
Say, skull, did you live here and breathe this same air,
And were you a man, or a beast in this world?
Of fruits, rich and ripe, did you eat your full share?

He had barely time to finish his sentence, when the skull replied:

Now listen, I'll tell you my story, dear man:
I was a great Khan and my country was fair,
But grief and misfortune befell me one day—
Let sages know all of my case, and beware!

Kerem:

Say, skull, when you lived in this world we behold,
And laboured, as others, for riches and gold,
Then were you a youngster, and twenty years old?
Or man full of care and with iron-grey hair?

The Skull:

The melon-fields raised me to prosper and rise,
Lochmàn[1] was I then, and would sit with the wise,
Long years I grew roses to gladden the eyes,
For all I would dare—glory's crown was my share.

Kerem:

Say, skull, were you eminent, grand in your days?
Did riches attract you, and well-being daze?
Or were you a tyrant in numerous ways?
Or money and fare with the poor you would share?

The Skull:

My riches were countless, of gold I was fond,
Thought not of the torments that held the beyond,
The death-cup I drank, broke with life every bond,
I was old, I declare, and was crowned with white hair.

Hardly had the Skull finished saying these words, when it rolled down a hill and fell into a grave. Kerem and Sofi continued on their way. Questioning right and left as to the whereabouts of Asli, they came to the Arzrum Mountains. A snow-storm overtook them. The sorrows of Kerem augmented. Visions of death in an alien country and of poverty, arose before him. Then he took his saz. Now let us hear what he told us:

Three moments in life are three things that I shun:
Sad parting, great poverty, death drawing near,
These things cannot bring any joy to the heart—
Sad parting, great want, and death's bier drawing near.

[1] Sage.

Great numbers of Solomons fell from the throne,
And many a rosy cheek ashen has grown,
And those—into pits irrevocably thrown—
By parting, great want, and death's bier drawing near.

Rich castles were burnt to a ruinous pile,
And poisons made foodstuffs and liquors go vile,
To premature age was brought youth's sunny smile—
By parting, great want, and death's bier drawing near.

And then the snow-storm became more fierce. It grew dark, pitch dark. But Kerem never halted, but continued on his way, without turning back. Surmounting great difficulties and terrible sufferings, he reached the town of Arzrum. But here, too, he could learn nothing. When they decided to leave this town, they saw that the road led in three directions. At the cross-roads Kerem pressed his saz to his breast. Let us hear what he sang:

On leaving the town, at the cross-roads I halt,
I pray unto God: o, what road should I take?
An answer of God day and night I implore—
To make no mistake, o which road should I take?

Kind people, o tell me, o tell me, I pray,
O where is my country, my kin, where are they?
The lake is deserted, the ducks flown away....
To make no mistake, o which road should I take?

So spoke Kerem. The road stretched before him and both Kerem and Sofi cried: "The Lord be with us!" They said these words and took to the road pointed out to them by God. A shepherd they met on the road showed them the house where Kishish was residing.

Kishish who had made friends with the Pasha Gaissar, lived here in Kaisari. After searching for some time, Kerem wandered into a melon-field belonging to the parents of Asli. Here he noticed several girls playing and singing, and among them—Asli. At once she recognised Kerem, but showed no sign of recognition. After that, very soon, the girls found out that Kerem was an ashug. They called to him to approach. But now Asli saw that Kerem was dressed in rags. She handed him a handful of coins, saying:

"Take this money, go and dress the way the local ashugs do."

Oh! How those words made Kerem's wounds bleed! He pressed his saz to his breast and began thus:

The clothes that I wore were of richest design,
Now naked I stand, laugh, Asli, at my state!
Of yore I liked jewels that glittered and shone,
My anguish is great, laugh, Asli, at my fate!

I looked at your face and I felt such delight,
In secret I grieved of my sad, hopeless plight!
I crowned you with diadems, dazzlingly bright...
Your alms have no weight, I need none at this date!

For love of my sweetheart by sorrow I'm bound,
In whom to confide on this alien ground?
I'm son of a Khan who is rich and renowned,
And slavelings of late, on my pleasure would wait.

Asli was not stone-hearted, she repented of what she said to her suitor,
and handed him a rose with the words: "Bard, take this rose, bards love
roses and all kinds of flowers."

Kerem:

Your treachery opened a precipice deep,
No rose do I need, your sweet words come too late!
And, laughing, you ruined my hearth and my home,
You, ready to hate, your sweet words have no weight...

But Asli interrupted Kerem with the following words: "Bard, you are in
an alien country, and so am I. My beloved one has remained in my native
land, he is shedding bitter tears. But this is neither here nor there. You
ought to know that in this country the bards have clothes of a different
make. Do not be offended, take this money, if you don't fancy new clothes,
then you will need it for your journey."

Kerem answered:

In anguish for you I burned up in the flame,
Repeating your name with unhappiness great,
A slave of a Christian—the son of a Khan!
A slave in this state—a deplorable fate!

The life of Kerem you dispersed in the wind,
And God you denied both in heart and in mind,
You made me a griever, the worst of his kind;
But care comes too late! and your alms have no weight!

575

Asli could not bear his words any longer. She fainted. The girls got angry with Kerem and told him to go away, without understanding anything. When Asli regained consciousness, she realised that Kerem was gone. She asked the girls where Kerem was, but the girls answered that they had grown angry with the ashug, and had sent him away.

Kerem reached the bazaar. There he bought some clothes of good quality. He had a bath, changed his garments and shaved. Then he again set out for the country house of Kishish. But lo! on the way the servants of the Pasha arrested him, and bound his arms with ropes. It appeared that Kishish had calumniated Kerem.

Kerem told the Pasha how his soul longed for Asli and how he had suffered in searching for her. The Pasha had a wise vizier who said:

"My good Pasha! Kerem is a true bard. He is right, and has suffered so much, and all to no purpose. We must take Asli away from this stubborn Kishish and give her to Kerem."

Kishish was in a way about this decision, and insisted that Kerem was no true bard. Then they decided to submit Kerem to a test: He had to guess the names of the girls without seeing them. A true bard must also be a wizard. The girls in the group were all dressed in the same kind of clothes, and their faces were veiled. Asli was arrayed in the same kind of clothes as the rest, and her face was also veiled. She took her stand among the disguised girls. Kerem was blindfolded. The girls, one by one, were led past Kerem. Kerem played the saz, sang and pronounced the name of each girl. He guessed it, and guessed right. After this, Kerem underwent some other tests. After these were over, all those present said he was indeed a true bard. Then the Pasha spoke to Kishish:

"We have no doubt that Kerem is a real bard. It's not the time for subterfuges of any kind. You must give your daughter in marriage to Kerem." Kishish was forced to listen to reason, and he was given three days to prepare his daughter for the wedding. In the night, when all the people were plunged in deep sleep, Kishish took his daughter Asli and disappeared from the town. He came to the town of Khaleb.

The people of this town knew Kishish was staying in the house of the Chief of the Guards. Kerem and Sofi had no difficulty in finding this house. Kerem stood near the fence of the house of the Chief of the Guards and sang a doleful lay. The passers-by began sympathising with his grief. A kind-hearted old woman tried to comfort him by saying:

"I shall tell your Asli that you are just here, near the fence." Yet she had her misgivings. She came up to Asli and asked her whether she really loved Kerem:

"He is a Moslem, while you are a Christian, you are so different. . . ."

Asli, shedding bitter tears, answered in the following strain:

Dear Granny, don't judge or condemn me, I pray,
My nightingale sings mid the roses I rear,
But fate sent me sorrows and grief to endure:
A tyrant severe, an existence austere.

I've donned a black robe on my body pure, white,
O, doctor my wounds, be a help in my plight,
Kerem passes by with his arms bound up tight,
I shed tear for tear, I was cruel to my dear.

My duty, my word are dispersed in the air,
I burn in the flames that, surrounding me, flare,
The merciful Lord rejects my prayer.
My love is not here, we are parted, o dear!

The old woman felt boundless pity for both of them, and she said, loudly sobbing: "The numbers of people these elders have ruined, just think! Destroying their hearths and homes! See to what the stubborn Kishish has brought his daughter, tender as a rose; he now wants to marry her to a man whom she does not love. He does not want to wed her to a handsome, slender youth, only because he is a Moslem. How unreasonable!"

Asli asked the old woman to carry her petition to the Pasha.

The old crone felt boundlessly sorry for Asli. She handed her letter to the Pasha's vizier. The latter read the petition, and reported it to the Pasha. The affair was made public. The Pasha ordered Kishish to arrange the marriage of Asli and Kerem. Kishish consented and made preparations for the wedding. When the hour of the wedding approached, Kishish dressed his daughter in her wedding clothes. As soon as Asli was brought before Kerem, he pressed his saz to his breast and sang as follows:

In scarlet my sweetheart is richly arrayed,
She looks oh! so lovely and wondrously chaste,
A glittering sash of opalescent tints
Adorns her fine waist with an exquisite taste.

Her father and mother—both parents are here,
She's fair as a swan on the sprays of a mere,
Fine jewels, bright glittering, hang from each ear,
She stands, proud and chaste, as in rubies encased.

Live, sweetheart beloved, for great gladness and joy,
What fate has ordained—this no force can destroy,
Your cheek has two birthmarks that make you look coy,
To you, sweet and chaste, to sing praises I haste.

But the wedding gown in which Kishish had dressed his daughter, began to suffocate Asli. In vain did Kerem try to unbutton the dress, the button-holes would not yield. It appeared that Kishish had bewitched the wedding gown. Kerem lost his presence of mind, not knowing what to do, he began to sing:

> Dame Fortune, I curse you for being so vile:
> Unbutton her dress, I implore, don't delay!
> She's choking, I'm burning, you see what we feel?!
> The buttonholes, pray, let them give up their prey!
>
> Kishish has great wealth, earned by others' distress,
> He's stubborn, his actions you never can guess,
> Her collar is choking her—cut them, unless
> It strangles her—o, do relieve her, I pray!
>
> Let spring come again, and the snow disappear,
> Kerem is quite ready to die, and right here,
> Who fashioned those buttons—I curse, without fear!
> Unbutton them, pray, with my life I shall pay!

Both Kerem and Asli tried their utmost to get rid of the buttons. In despair Kerem heaved a deep sigh. While they were struggling with the last button, from Kerem's mouth burst a flame of fire, which enveloped his body. He began to burn. Asli ran and brought a pitcher with water, and poured it over him. But it appeared that Kishish put oil instead of water in the pitcher, and so Kerem burned like dry wood. Hearing their cries and wailings, people came running in crowds. Asli addressed her mother with the following words:

> My youth you have blemished, now hear Asli weep,
> You've both wrecked my life, o my parents, for shame!
> The ashes of ruin I heap on your heads!
> I cry for Kerem, it is you whom I blame!
>
> You made me be silent, you muddled my mind,
> By crushing my rose, is my youth left behind,
> My eyes see his ashes, he's gone like the wind!
> He's burnt, but his name I repeat, all the same!

Asli took the ashes of Kerem, scattered them over her head, and wept. A spark smouldering in the ashes, fell on Asli's tresses and they caught fire. And so she, too, burned up in the flames leaving nothing but ashes.

Asli's and Kerem's ashes were buried side by side. Kishish, dying, expressed the wish to be buried between their two graves.

And now there is a popular belief that every spring on each of their graves there grows a bush of roses. But when the roses on the two bushes sway toward each other and try to unite, then from the grave of Kishish appears a bush of thorns which hinders the roses of the two bushes from coming together.

A wise bard retold the tragedy of the two lovers, concluding the legend with the following words:

O world, your first people were Adam and Eve,
They sinned and were banished their hard lot to share,
Then Abel was killed—and thus bloodshed arose,
And spread in red streams over all the world fair.

The names of great chieftains and shahs then we see:
Dzhamshidì-Dzham, and also Nushiravanì,
Khulakù, Genghiz-Khàn, Tamerlàne—all were free
To carry great conquests . . . now where are these, where?

O world inconsistent, and covered with blight,
Magnificent castles you ruined in fight,
You flourished death cudgels and clubs, of a night,
The strong Rustam-Zàl gone, I'd care to know where?

And scores of physicians were torches of light:
Hagàni, Aristotle were pillars of might,
And Plato, they all went with illness to fight,
Lochman did his share, for himself had no care.

Khosrov, Zuleikha and Khassan Yusuf too,
Asli and Kerem and avra-Valigù,
Sheikh Sanàn loved as no one, and gave love its due,
I want to know where are their deeds, where? o where?

Hafiz and Djalil, Fisuli, Navoi,
Nizami, Hilali and the Sheik Saadi—
They all graced the world; and the bard Firdousi—
His soul is somewhere, but I'd like to know—where?

The wheel of dame Fortune turns ever ahead,
My last hour's striking to lay down my head,
And when Valekhì Natavàn's soul has fled—
To know the truth bare, would they ask: his work—where?

Translated by *Olga Moisseyenko*

Köroglu

KÖROGLU, the outstanding popular-heroic saga, holds a place of honour in the treasure-house of Azerbaijanian culture.

Composed in the 16th-17th centuries, during the powerful peasant movement in Azerbaijan, the saga describes the struggle of the people against the local feudal lords and foreign invaders. Köroglu, the popular hero, embodies the finest qualities of the people—he is fearless in battle and tender in love, he is brave, resourceful, and ready to die for a friend. The plot and imagery of Köroglu have found a reflection in other literatures, and there are versions of this poem in Turkmen, Uzbek, Tajik, Georgian and Armenian. The basic idea of the poem is revolt against slavery and tyranny, for freedom. The image of Köroglu has become a symbol of fearlessness and courage. An opera of the same name by Uzeir Gajibekov has won lasting popularity in Azerbaijan.

Research done by scholars specialising in this field shows that the poem, although it has its elements of fiction, is based on historical facts related to the struggle of the Trans-Caucasian peoples against the oppression of Iranian-Turkish invaders and local lords.

Crane Feathers

A Chapter from *KÖROGLU*

When Eivaz returned to Chanlibel, Nigyar Khanym forgot her anxiety. With a husband like Köroglu and a son like Eivaz—with two brave men at her side—how else could she feel but calm and secure? If anyone was really happy in the world, it was Nigyar Khanym. Yet Köroglu was even happier than Nigyar Khanym. To him Eivaz was not only a son, but a friend who would help him to weather the vicissitudes of fate, a worthy assistant in all affairs. For his courage and gallantry Eivaz had earned a good name and wide fame among the brave men of Chanlibel, excelling many of his coevals.

Köroglu used to spend his free time training his braves. He taught them how to ride, fence, wield the sword, use the shield and the bow and arrows. The exercises would go on all day, far into the evening.

On one such day the brave warriors, dividing up into groups, were performing military exercises. Eivaz put on his armour and together with one of the groups of horsemen rode out into the field.

Köroglu and Damirchioglu sat on a rise, watching the men. Suddenly they saw a group of riders galloping to the fields with Eivaz at their head. Prancing on his horse, he looked like a young eagle. Proudly he sat his Arab steed, the Egyptian sword hanging from his belt, reminding Linka Choglok[1] about to slay a thousand enemies. His horse flew straight on, like an arrow sent from a bow. With crane feathers adorning his fur hat, he was like the son of Caesar with a diadem on his head.

Nigyar Khanym watched her son with adoration and, turning to Köroglu, exclaimed:

"Köroglu, look, do you see who gallops yonder?" In reply to Nigyar, Köroglu pressed his saz to his bosom and said:

> Nigyar Khanym, I will tell you who rides there;
> It is our Eivaz, it is our Eivaz.
> On his body a suit of steel armour he wears.
> It is our Eivaz, it is our Eivaz.
>
> My son Eivaz is fifteen years old.
> With his brush, the Creator painted his eyebrows.

[1] Legendary warrior.

On his head he wears the feathers of a crane.
It is our Eivaz, it is our Eivaz.

In the battlefield he's the boldest of the bold.
A better man than he never was;
He will charge at the foe like a camel enraged;
It is our Eivaz, it is our Eivaz.

In his hand an Egyptian sword he holds,
The steed he rides—more handsome n'er was.
He is ready to fight—death itself he defies.
It is our Eivaz, it is our Eivaz.

Bravest of all the bravest men,
He can fight as well as I play the saz.
The valiant son of Köroglu,
It is our Eivaz, it is our Eivaz.

Telli Khanym was among the onlookers, too. Damirchioglu, her husband, had recovered his health, and she was in the best of spirits.

"Nigyar Khanym, how well the crane feather becomes Eivaz," Telli Khanym said. "If it's so becoming to men, imagine how it would look on you and me. Let us send the lads to get some more feathers."

At that moment, Eivaz galloped right up to them. He dismounted, bowed to Nigyar Khanym, Köroglu, Damirchioglu and all the women, and then addressed Köroglu:

"Do you hear, father? The Khanyms wish to have crane feathers like mine. Allow me to go and get them."

At first Köroglu would not give his consent. Eivaz would be going alone and something might happen to him. But then he changed his mind; it would be better to let him go. A brave man must get used to dangers and misadventures. Let him learn to surmount hardships and obstacles.

So Köroglu turned to Nigyar Khanym and asked:

"What do you say, should he go or not?"

Nigyar looked at Eivaz. She saw that Eivaz was watching her with tense expectation. His eyes implored her not to deny him this pleasure. His mother's heart gave in. She could not bear to disappoint him, and so she agreed.

Damirchioglu then stepped forward and said:

"Köroglu, let me go with him."

Kosa Safar interfered:

"You have just got back on your feet, you are not strong enough yet."

582

Damirchioglu did not let him finish, and said:

"No, Kosa Safar, I shall go in spite of everything. There is no use talking."

Köroglu asked: "What is the cause of such insistency?"

Damirchioglu said: "For one thing, Eivaz is still very young. He cannot go alone. And then, it was Telli Khanym who asked for the feathers. It is her whim. Does it befit me to sit at home while not I, but another goes to fulfill her desire?"

Köroglu gave him his consent, and then Belli Ahmed stepped out of the ranks of warriors and said:

"Köroglu, allow me to accompany them as well."

Köroglu allowed Belli Ahmed to go also.

There was a long road ahead of them. Eivaz rode Gyrat, and Damirchioglu and Belli Ahmed the horses they had chosen. They rode across ravines and gullies, going straight on till they reached the outskirts of Baghdad. Here they saw as many cranes as there are pebbles in the mountains. They put their horses to graze, took their bows and arrows and went hunting for cranes. They killed one, then five, then fifteen of the birds. In less than half an hour they had shot down a whole heap of them. Then they sat down to pluck the feathers, putting them away in their saddlebags, and after that they roasted the birds and sat down to eat under the date-palms. The crane shashlyk was so filling and the cool shade of the palms so nice to relax in after their strenuous exercise, that their meal over, all three fell fast asleep.

One of the guards of Baghdad's ruler Aslan Pasha had been watching all their actions. As soon as they fell asleep, he rushed off as fast as he could to report to his master. Three strangers, he told him, of such-and-such description, wearing such-and-such clothes, were at the moment sleeping like logs near such-and-such a spring. And one of them looked like Köroglu.

The guard had hardly finished when Aslan Pasha thought of the Sultan's latest firman.[1] Köroglu's raid on Turkmenia, his battle with Arab Reikhan,[2] the rescue of Eivaz were on everyone's lips. On hearing the news, the Hotkar[3] had again sent firmans to every Pasha in his domains, promising a gift from his own hands to anyone who killed Köroglu or one of his men, and the gallows to anyone who saw them and failed to report it. One such firman had been addressed to Aslan Pasha. And so, as soon as the guard mentioned the name of Köroglu, Aslan Pasha ordered the commander of his army to prepare to march. The troops were alerted to the beating of drums, the soldiers put on armour and set off.

---

[1] Firman—royal prescript.
[2] Arab Raikhan—ruler of Persia and other countries.
[3] Hotkar—Sultan, Sovereign.

Gyrat, the faithful steed of Eivaz, beat the earth with his hoofs, and neighed in alarm. Damirchioglu and Belli Ahmed awoke and saw that the troops of Aslan Pasha had surrounded them on all four sides. Belli Ahmed gripped the handle of his sword, but Damirchioglu stayed his hand.

"What are you doing? Don't you see Eivaz is still asleep? Until he awakes, we cannot enter into combat. If we lose each other, Eivaz may fall into the enemy's hands."

Having said this, Damirchioglu began to rouse Eivaz, but however he tried, Eivaz would not wake up. They shook him, called out his name, but all in vain. Meanwhile, enemy troops were arriving in ever greater numbers, like locusts. Damirchioglu was in despair. At last, he took up his saz and plucking the strings, intoned:

> Foes are surrounding us on all sides.
> Awake, do not sleep so fast, Eivaz.
> The foes are surrounding us on all
> sides.
> Awake or they will destroy us, Eivaz.
>
> Do not believe any traitor's words;
> It is only I who tell you the truth.
> Arise and show an undaunted face,
> Shine like the sun, Eivaz, brave youth.
>
> Would you let Belli Ahmed be captured,
> His strong hands bound behind his
> back,
> And Damirchioglu to be sold into
> slavery?
> Be a worthy son of Köroglu, Eivaz.

Only the sounds of the saz succeeded in awakening Eivaz, who saw at once that the enemy had beleaguered them on all sides. And their horses had been lassoed by Aslan Pasha's men. Damirchioglu, Belli Ahmed and Eivaz were left to fight on their feet. Aslan Pasha ordered his troops to advance and seize them alive. When the troops came into motion, Damirchioglu gave a blood-curdling whoop and drew his sword. The three men slashed out at the enemies to the left and right of them. But the more men they felled, the more came up, and there was no retreat to safety. They had no horses, and the enemy pressed on and on. The brave men were exhausted to the limit. Finally Aslan Pasha's soldiers managed to part the three from one another, after which they were taken prisoners and together with their horses delivered to Baghdad.

Now for a time we must leave the three captives to themselves. Meanwhile, I will acquaint you with a man named Haji Aziz.

Köroglu had once made friends with a merchant by the name of Haji Aziz, and their friendship had been going strong for many years. By a lucky coincidence, Haji Aziz happened to be in Baghdad when Eivaz and his brave comrades were brought there as prisoners. He had come there to sell his goods in the market, and it was there he heard the news that three robbers had been seized just outside the city and were being led to the gallows for execution. All the people in the market poured out into the street to look at them. Haji Aziz, too, came out to see what was happening. The crowd stood waiting about for a long time. At last the headmost troops came marching into the street. Aslan Pasha himself rode in front, after him came his comrades, and then the rank-and-file horsemen. And now everyone saw the group of soldiers escorting the captives. Imagine the feelings of Haji Aziz when he saw them. The world went dark before his eyes. He did not know what to do. How rescue them? This would be much harder than trading in the Baghdad market, where he could hoodwink a thousand buyers at one go. Here he would have to use the sword, not his tongue. Supposing he went poste-haste to Chanlibel and informed Köroglu? But Chanlibel was a whole week's journey from Baghdad. By the time he reached it and gave warning, by the time Köroglu got here, the three would already be hanged.

While Haji Aziz tried to decide what to do, he noticed three horses led along at a short distance from the captives. He looked again and recognised Köroglu's famous horse Gyrat. "O my dark heart, I have found a way out of this calamity," he said to himself. "I must get hold of Gyrat and ride to Chanlibel, to let Köroglu know what has happened." Haji Aziz then set off after the troops escorting the captives, and the horses, and followed them all the way to the palace of Aslan Pasha.

Aslan Pasha spoke thus:

"Let the captives be put in prison and the horses brought here."

The guards led off Eivaz and his brave comrades to the dungeon, and the Pasha's chief groom brought the horses. Aslan Pasha ordered him to mount Damirchioglu's horse first and try its paces. The chief groom rode the horse back and forth several times, then stopped before Aslan Pasha, who seemed to be quite pleased. Then the chief groom mounted Belli Ahmed's horse and put it through its paces too. Aslan Pasha was pleased with it as well. After that came the turn of Gyrat. Haji Aziz was nervous and impatient: he did not know what to do, how to act. "Even if it means losing the whole of my fortune," he thought, "I must get hold of Gyrat." Meanwhile, the chief groom had climbed into the saddle. But the horse refused to stir. Nothing would make Gyrat budge. At last the chief groom lost his temper and lashed the horse with all his might. But the horse only dropped its head still lower. The chief groom whipped it again, but Gyrat only tucked its tail between its

585

legs, closed its eyes and made a few limping steps. Aslan Pasha sneered and said:

"It seems two of the captives are high-ranking men, and the third is their attendant. Yes—there he is, just look at his face! And this must be the attendant's horse." Then, turning to the chief groom, he said: "Let these two horses join my herd. And that nag—give it to the guard. Let him keep it for himself. At any rate, it will lift his feet off the ground."

The guard was cut to the quick. After all it was he who had informed the Pasha of the enemies' presence near the city, and he expected to get the promised reward—a new gown. Instead he got nothing but a worthless nag. He felt terribly angry and injured.

On seeing this, Haji Aziz thanked Gyrat from the bottom of his heart. Pushing his way through the crowd, he approached the guard and said:

"How much would you like for that clumsy nag?"

The words of Haji Aziz only added to the guard's irritation. He cursed and swore at the merchant, but Haji Aziz came closer and began coaxing him:

"Dear man, why do you scold me so? What have I done?" Haji Aziz used all his sugary eloquence and finally pacified the guard. No wonder our ancestors used to say the tongues of those haggling traders could lure a snake out of its hole. In the end, Haji Aziz paid the guard a small sum of money, and Gyrat was his.

Haji Aziz quickly led Gyrat to the yard of the house where he was staying. He filled the horse's manger with a good helping of barley and hurried back to the market. There he bought one *batman* of pitch and a whole length of cotton, and took his purchases home. He waited until dusk, then made a fire and put an iron cauldron on it. The pitch melted and became as soft as wax. This he smeared on the cotton and wound it round the horse. Now he mounted Gyrat, the pitch gluing him so firmly, he seemed to be bound to it with ropes. Haji Aziz made sure he would not fall off and slightly eased the bridle. Gyrat started off at a gallop, flying like an arrow short from a bow, as if it had a foal waiting at Chanlibel. Haji Aziz was so shaken by the ride that he forgot he was Haji Aziz. Finally, he fell into a swoon. What distance Gyrat covered he did not know. How fast Gyrat ran he did not know either. But before long he was suddenly roused by the shrill neighing of the horse. Haji Aziz opened his eyes and saw that he was already in Chanlibel.

When the warriors heard Gyrat neighing, they rushed out to meet it. They saw the horse galloping at top speed; another moment, it seemed, and its hoofs would split in two. No rider could be seen on its back—neither Eivaz nor anybody else. When the horse came closer, they saw a dark bundle on its back. What could it be, they wondered. In another moment Gyrat had come level with them, galloped up to Köroglu and stopped before him as if frozen to the spot. Gyrat turned round towards the road along which it had come and gave such a loud neigh that it set all the hills and gullies trembling. Turning back to Köroglu again, it looked at him and started beating the earth with its hoofs. Köroglu put his arms round the neck of his faithful horse and kissed its face. One of his warriors saw that what was thought to be a bundle, was in fact the body of a man. He was alive but unconscious. They took him by the hand to get him off, but however they pulled, he would not stir. At last they saw he had glued himself to the saddle with pitch.

To cut a long story short, they took him off at last, together with the cloth and the saddle, and laid him down on the ground. Köroglu recognised his old friend Aziz. Immediately, he called for hot water and everything else that might be necessary. Haji Aziz at last recovered his senses.

"Tell me, what happened to you?" Köroglu asked him. Haji Aziz replied:

> Courageous Köroglu, first I must ask you,
> Are you informed of what befell your son Eivaz?
> If not, there are some tidings I must share,
> And will inform you what befell your son Eivaz.

> Does the courageous ever ask for quarter?
> He faces the Pasha and his dread hangmen.
> So do Belli Ahmed and Damirchioglu.
> Now I will tell you what befell your son Eivaz.

> Haji Aziz has been the victim of men's fury;
> Your son Eivaz, who is the boldest of them all,
> I saw him with hands bound tight behind his back.
> Now I have told you what befell your son Eivaz.

After this introduction, which he sang to the strains of a saz, Haji Aziz told Köroglu the whole story.

"O Köroglu! Eivaz, Damirchioglu and Belli Ahmed have all been captured by Aslan Pasha and cast into prison. If you don't fly to their rescue, you will never see their faces again."

The news startled the brave warriors. All the women sat with downcast heads. Köroglu turned and looked at Nigyar Khanym. Her despair was so utter, she was so stricken with grief, he saw, that she seemed about to faint. Words could not describe her state of mind. She had turned pale as Samarkand paper. Her brown eyes filled with tears, like spring clouds. Her lovely, ruby-red lips were bloodless, like a poppy smitten by frost. Köroglu was about to speak, when Nigyar Khanym rose to her feet. Looking neither at Köroglu nor at the brave warriors, she walked with slow steps to the edge of the hill on which they were assembled. She cast a look at the road by which Eivaz had departed, then glanced at the mountains whose tall peaks were covered with snow. Plucking three hairs from her locks, she pressed them to her marble bosom and said:

> O mountains propping the skies with your heads,
> O mountains, where have you hidden Eivaz?
> O mountains, you who devoured three braves,
> O mountains, where have you hidden Eivaz?
>
> If I curse you, your stones will crumble.
> Nothing will save you from blizzards and tempests.
> Your stones will fall out, baring your carcass.
> O mountains, where have you hidden Eivaz?
>
> Thinking of my son, I will start to weep
> And wash off your slopes with tears of distress.
> I will set you on fire with my scorching wrath.
> O mountains, where is my son, confess?
>
> I, Nigyar, with my searing sighs
> Will topple your summits into the river,
> And in your place I will build a tower.
> Where is my son? Is he lost forever?

The whole world went dark before Köroglu's eyes. And Chanlibel seemed to spin around him. Raising his hand, he took Gyrat by the bridle. He leapt into the saddle with such fury, that if it were another horse and not Gyrat, he would have broken its back. Then, addressing Kosa Safar, he said:

> Tell my brave warriors to awake.
> My Eivaz has fallen into enemy hands.
> Only blood on my sword my wrath will slake.
> My Eivaz has fallen into enemy hands.
>
> I slept and saw my doom in my dreams.
> Yet I know—ahead of us victory gleams.
> Saddle my travel-worn horse, o friends,
> My Eivaz has fallen into enemy hands.

After these words Köroglu shouted:

"I am off. Follow me, my brave warriors. I will await you in the gardens of Baghdad. The one who comes first and greets me early in the morning, I will reward with a hundred gold coins."

Having said this, Köroglu let go the horse's bridle. Gyrat reared and galloped off in the direction of Baghdad. The brave warriors quickly got ready for the journey, put on their armour and set off on their way. How long and how fast they rode, I cannot say, but early next morning Köroglu saw Deli-Mehtar, Kosa Safar, Chöpur Mehti, Isabala, Topdagydan, Tokhmageuran, Halayposan, Tanrytanymys and Dilbilmez, who reined in their horses before him, putting their hands on their swordhandles. Köroglu looked down the road leading to Chanlibel—it would be easier to count the dates in the orchards of Baghdad than the numbers of his brave soldiers.

"My bold men, you have arrived in time," Köroglu said. "But it is still too early to march on the city. We must wait a while: perhaps we can find out what is going on in Baghdad. If all of us armed men break into the city, Aslan Pasha and his henchmen may kill the prisoners at once."

At that very moment a horseman, galloping from the city, came into view.

Köroglu said to Kosa Safar: "This man comes from the city. Stop him, maybe he can tell us something useful."

Kosa Safar spurred his horse to intercept the unknown rider. In less than a second he had caught him up. The man was dressed in a *chukha*,[1] on his feet he wore Baghdad slippers, and on his head a silk turban. He was a stout, broad-shouldered man.

"Listen, friend, can you wait a minute?" Kosa Safar said to him. "Where are you going in such a hurry?"

The stranger replied: "Yes, I am in a hurry. I must be quick. My reapers are waiting for me in the field. I bring them bread for their lunch. Then I must return to the city as fast as possible."

"What is happening in the city?" Kosa Safar then asked. "Nothing bad, I hope."

"Aslan Pasha has captured three of Köroglu's warriors," the stranger replied. "They are all to be hanged today. There will be great festivities and merry-making to mark the occasion. I must hurry back to the city to be present at the execution. Afterwards, when they are hanged, I shall throw

---

[1] Chukha—a short coat.

a black stone into each of their graves to earn a reward from God in the next world."

The stranger had no sooner finished speaking than Kosa Safar pounced on him like a bird of prey and seized him by the throat. When he threw him on the ground, Köroglu who had come up saw that the man was already dead.

"Why did you kill him?" Köroglu asked.

Kosa Safar told him everything, Köroglu turned to his brave men and said:

"Get off your horses and each throw one black stone on his corpse. Let him get as much of God's blessings as he wanted."

Seven thousand seven hundred and seventy brave warriors dismounted and each threw a black stone on the corpse. So many were the stones that they formed a great pile. And it is still said to exist, that pile of black stones grown into a mountain. It has come down to us from our grandsires that anyone passing that pile threw a black stone on to it, for it was believed to be a deed of virtue.

So this was how Köroglu learned that his son and his brave friends were to be hanged that day. He immediately ordered his men to mount.

At a slow trot, they moved off towards the city. On their way they met an old man reaping wheat. The man was weeping bitterly, the tears running down his face.

"Worthy man, why are you weeping?" Köroglu asked, riding up to him.

Without raising his head, the old man replied: "What is it to you? You can never cure my wounds or soothe my grief. Go, wherever you are bound."

The old man did everything to get rid of him, but Köroglu would not be shaken off. At last he said: "Since you're so set on getting your own way, will you be so good and tell me who you are and what is that band of men following you?"

"I come from the district of Muradbeili, and am here to purchase goods," Köroglu replied. "The roads are unsafe, so I came with my armed men. Who knows what might happen on the way?"

When the old man heard him mention Muradbeili, he thought a little and said:

"Very well, you say you are from the district Muradbeili. Tell me then, do you know Köroglu?"

Köroglu guessed that the old man had some secret.

"Of course I do."

The old man said:

"If you know him, tell me, are you his friend or not?"

"Of course I am his friend. But why are we wasting words? Why do you ask me about these things?"

"My son," the old man replied, "to tell the truth, I was neither Rustam Zal nor Giziroglu Mustafabek,[1] nor am I a match for Köroglu. But in my time, I was worth something too. Yes, I was a man of courage and skill and never showed my back to the enemy."

Here the old man paused, wiped off a tear with his sleeve and continued: "Baghdad is ruled by Aslan Pasha. He is a very wicked man, a traitor who knows no equal in all the world. Moreover, he is a very cunning man. Three days ago he seized three of Köroglu's brave men and cast them into prison. Yesterday he sent heralds to proclaim to the people that they were to be hanged today. My son, to tell you the truth, I cannot bear the thought that such bold lads will die at the hands of this ruthless madman. If he fought them one by one in honest battle, as befits a man, I would not be so vexed. Tell me, what can I do? My age is my greatest handicap. I am already a hundred years old. Too old to fight injustice. As our forebears used to say when a man can no longer use his hands he resorts to his tongue. But when his tongue is locked, when he is under the yoke of beks and khans, all he can do is shed tears. And so now all I can do is to writhe in the fire of grief and weep."

When the old man had finished, Köroglu bade his brave men help him with his work. In less than an hour they had mowed, sheathed and stacked the old man's wheat. The old man looked on in bewilderment, thinking to himself, "Who can they be and what are they going to do?" At first it occurred to him that they might be Aslan Pasha's henchmen, come with orders to burn his wheat. But then he saw he was wrong: they were helping him out of generosity. Their behaviour little resembled an act of lawlessness customary to the Pasha.

As soon as the brave men had finished their work, Köroglu told the old man:

"Well, Father, now I can tell you who I am. I am Köroglu. Today I will light a fire in the heart of Aslan Pasha which will smoulder until his dying day. We are going to break into his city. Take a big sack and wait for me near the treasury of Aslan Pasha." Köroglu was about to order his warriors to march, when the old man spoke.

"Wait, Köroglu," he said. "I see Aslan Pasha has driven you into a rage. Your eyes flash fire and lightning and cannot see clearly. You must not enter the city just as you are. You will be instantly recognised. Enter the city alone, then let your men filter in by fives and tens, and be sure they mix with the city dwellers to go unnoticed."

Kosa Safar said:

---

[1] Legendary outlaws, heroes of popular tradition.

To the summits of far-off mountains
Winter comes and spring comes in time,
All in my mouth is trembling,
My tongue to the left, my teeth to the right.

What shall we do, brave men,
To tear out the enemy's heart,
To help Eivaz, to save him?
Run four to the left, five to the right!

Ah, how angry I am!
Fury boils in my heart.
As soon as you see the enemy,
Beat him, give him no quarter.

Köroglu has no other course
But to fight to the very last man.
When he draws his Egyptian sword,
Heads fly to the left, bodies to the right.

The commanders began to divide their men into groups. When Köroglu saw everything was ready, he said:

"My brave men, I will divert the enemy's attention, while you take up your positions. Mix with the people and surround the square in such a way that when you draw your swords none should be able to move from the spot."

Köroglu finished speaking. Over his own clothes he put the garments of an ashug, then hung a saz on his shoulder and set forth into the city.

Now let Köroglu walk off to the city square in an ashug's garments, let his brave men mix with the people and occupy their posts, and let the old man go home after his sack. What we must speak of now is Aslan Pasha.

His heralds had informed the people about the execution and summoned them to the city square. The square looked so gay and was decorated so festively that one might think a holiday or a great wedding was in preparation. Aslan Pasha's hangmen brought in Köroglu's brave men and stopped them at the foot of the gallows. Aslan Pasha was in high spirits. He sat in state on his throne mounted on a dais in the middle of the square. Every now and then he addressed the Sadr-Azam,[1] saying:

"Wait a little and you will see what a present I have for the Sultan. Up to now not a single Pasha could as much as blow into the eye of one

[1] Sadr-Azam—Turkish sultan's chief vizier.

592

of Köroglu's bold men. Now the Sultan will know the name of Aslan Pasha!"

The hangmen smeared the nooses with oil, ready to tighten them round the necks of their victims. Aslan Pasha ordered the drums to beat a tattoo. The Sadr-Azam stepped forward and gave his orders. Several *askérs* marched in and stationed themselves around the square in case there were any troublemakers in the crowd. When all the preparations had been completed, the hangmen led Eivaz up to the gallows.

Blood rushed to Damirchioglu's head. He strained with all his might but could not tear the ropes binding his hands. With every new effort, the ropes cut deeper into his flesh. Damirchioglu understood that his hands were bound with a waxed bowstring. The thought upset him and he said:

> Where are you, valiant Köroglu?
> Would that you broke into this square;
> When your Egyptian sword you draw
> It is stained with blood to the
> > handle.

> Were Gyrat to gallop by
> This wicked land would be destroyed.
> Were Köroglu to gallop here,
> The foes would take to their heels.

Then, addresing Aslan Pasha, he said:

> Torture Damirchioglu,
> That he may confess his sins,
> Order only us two to be hanged
> But spare Eivaz, for his youth.

At that very moment Köroglu appeared in the square. Aslan Pasha noticed an ashug with a saz enter the forbidden circle.

"Hey, ashug!" the Pasha cried.

"Yes, I am an ashug. What can I do for you?"

"Do you know any of Köroglu's couplets?" Aslan Pasha asked.

Köroglu replied: "Allow me to sing you a better song whose words have some meaning, at least. Who is Köroglu for his words to be sung in your presence?"

"Oh no, I see you have misunderstood me," the Pasha said. "My troops have seized three of Köroglu's men. That's why I am holding today's celebrations. Here they are, standing by the gallows. Sing one of Köroglu's couplets to cheer them up."

Köroglu turned round, looked at Eivaz, Damirchioglu and Belli Ahmed, then glanced at his men standing among the crowd, pressed his saz to his breast and plucked the strings with such force that the sounds were heard all over the square. Like a bird of prey, he circled around the square, singing:

> My men, today is the day of battle.
> The land of the wicked must be destroyed.
> Wounds are a sign of a warrior's courage.
> The enemy's blood is sweet as sherbet.
>
> Soldiers must show their courage in battle,
> Swooping upon their foe like hawks.
> The Egyptian sword has to whirl in the air,
> The enemies' guts must twine round their bodies.
>
> Köroglu will drink of the enemy's blood,
> Let the heavens echo his battle cries.
> Slay the viziers, take the khans captive,
> Let corpse upon corpse in a mountain rise.

"Splendid, Ashug," Aslan Pasha said, applauding. "You sing as well as Köroglu himself."

Köroglu turned round, looked at his son and the two brave men, and saw they had recognised him. Damirchioglu fixed his eyes on one gallows, Belli Ahmed on the other. Köroglu guessed that they were only waiting for their hands to be untied, to tear up all the gallows and then settle accounts with the enemy. Then Köroglu looked at Eivaz. He stood beside the gallows, his eyes set on Köroglu, tears of joy ready to spill over from his eyes. Seeing Eivaz in such a state, Köroglu burst into song:

> My dear Pasha, light of my eyes,
> Release Eivaz and let him go home.
> Pasha, I beg you, be kind and wise,
> Release Eivaz and let him go home.
>
> I'll bid the sky pour down its lightning,
> I'll plant a garden round your house.
> I'll sing your praise as high as the mountains,
> Release Eivaz and let him go home.
>
> Here where Pashas and beks confer
> I humbly stand, unarmed, alone.
> Köroglu implores you, great Pasha,
> Release Eivaz and let him go home.

594

But now let Köroglu continue his singing, let the Pasha sit listening to his songs, and let the brave men stay waiting the outcome. At present we have another man to speak of—Giziroglu Mustafa bek.

In the Baghdad district there lived a celebrated warrior named Giziroglu Mustafa bek. In the past his father had been a vizier,[1] but then he rebelled against the sultan and was hanged on the gallows. After that fatal day Mustafa bek and forty of his followers withdrew into the mountains. Ever since then they had been waging war on all pashas without exception. From time to time Giziroglu made raids on one of the high-ranking enemies of his father, seized and hanged him on the spot, after which he again retreated to the mountains.

Giziroglu Mustafa bek had long wished to meet Köroglu face to face and settle accounts. As the saying goes, "two rams' heads cannot stew in one cauldron". True to this proverb, Giziroglu often said: "Fame can't be shared: it's either Köroglu or myself. There is not enough for us both." Köroglu had also heard a good deal about Giziroglu Mustafa bek. He had never seen him, but knew all about his might and prowess, and looked for a chance to meet him.

To cut a long story short, rumours reached Giziroglu Mustafa bek that Aslan Pasha had seized three of Köroglu's brave warriors and was going to hang them that day. Giziroglu Mustafa bek summoned his men and said:

I am setting off to the city of Baghdad.
Who wants to follow me, let him come.
Seven arts and a thousand handicrafts;
Who would slay the enemy, let him come.

Can you see how worried I am?
Every second drags on like a year.
Who can cut seven heads with a single sword,
Let him come with me, do you hear?

Where is the rose that adorned the garden?
No nightingale makes it his home.
Three of Köroglu's bold men are held captive.
We must save them. All who are brave must
come.

Giziroglu first spoke to the strains of the saz, then he repeated it in plain words.

"It is true that I have accounts to settle with Köroglu. When this affair

[1] Official post at the sultan's court.

595

is past, we will have a chance to straighten things out. But just now I feel nothing but anger at the treachery of Aslan Pasha. Köroglu's bold men did not raid him, nor did they harm his men. All the witnesses say that they were peacefully and quietly hunting cranes on the plain. Aslan Pasha wants to hang these innocent men only to win the favour of the Sultan. Aslan Pasha wags his tail before the Sultan. I shall cut off that tail and stick it in his eyes. Let it be a warning to all other toadies and despots. I will not allow him to hang these innocent men."

Giziroglu's horsemen approved the decision of their leader and praised him for his noble heart. Then they all armed themselves, put on their mail suits and set off to Baghdad. Not far from the place of execution there was a small hill. Giziroglu rode up the hill to see what was happening. He saw Köroglu in ashug's disguise singing in the middle of the square. Giziroglu was astonished. Indeed, he said to himself, Köroglu is a remarkably brave man. Turning to his men, he said:

"Let us wait and see how all this ends. I refuse to believe that he can rescue his bold men with all those troops around them. I swear I will wait here till the end. All this is quite amazing. If I see that his strength is running low, I will come to his aid. But if he does have the power to rescue his men, I will follow after him. And as soon as he leaves the city, I will settle accounts with him. God help either me or him. So let it be."

Meanwhile Köroglu, quick and agile, circled around the square, and sang his songs. He was playing for time to let his men take up their positions. Giziroglu waited for a long time, surprised that Köroglu was taking so long before going into battle with his enemies. At first he thought Köroglu's men had not come yet and he did not want to risk battle alone. So he decided to let Köroglu know that he and his men were here, ready to help him.

Giziroglu had a six-foot club with a double end, which was known to everyone in and around Baghdad. When women scolded their children, they would say: "Be quiet, or I'll call Giziroglu and he'll teach you a lesson with his club."

Now Giziroglu raised that club above his head, swung it round twice and flung it upward with all his might. The club hit the dome of the mosque near the square striking it so hard that sparks went flying.

"What's that? Is it fire coming down from the skies?" Aslan Pasha cried, jumping down from his throne.

Köroglu saw something huge and heavy drop on the ground at his feet. He guessed that it was the double-ended club of Giziroglu Mustafa bek and realised that he must be somewhere near.

"Pasha," Köroglu said, "that fire is indeed coming down from the sky. Heavenly wrath is always hanging over your head. Be sure you make good note of it."

Köroglu had not finished when he noticed that the Sadr-Azam was about to make off. Köroglu pressed his saz to his chest and sang:

> Do not waste words, Aslan Pasha,
> Sadr-Azam, your high guest, is leaving
> you.
> The bird of paradise is on the wing,
> Soon it will flee and abandon you.

Aslan Pasha looked quickly over his shoulder. Only now he noticed that the Sadr-Azam was really trying to slip away.

Only now, too, Aslan Pasha began to doubt the identity of the ashug. The Sadr-Azam had probably guessed that the ashug was Köroglu himself. He resumed his seat when he saw the Pasha looking about him worriedly.

"What has happened?" Aslan Pasha asked turning to him: "What was that noise from the sky?"

The Sadr-Azam bent down to Aslan Pasha's ear and said:

"Pasha, may you ever prosper! This ashug doesn't seem worth trusting. He is too much like Köroglu."

Köroglu realised that the Sadr-Azam had guessed his secret. To allay his suspicions, he took up his saz and began to sing another couplet:

> You on the square have shown yourself fearless.
> No one has come, though the sun is setting.
> Giziroglu threw his club on the square.
> It was his club that struck the earth.

Köroglu finished and looked at his braves. He saw they were ready, and only waiting for his signal. They were biting their lips and moustaches in fury. Köroglu made another round of the square and then, turning to Damirchioglu, Belli Ahmed and Eivaz, he said:

> Be prudent, you three bold men.
> Now your fearless friend comes forth.
> Your chains and ropes will be torn;
> Now your fearless friend comes forth.

> A falcon has flown from Chanlibel.
> Open your eyes, for he has come.
> Disperse, do not let yourselves be caught.
> Now your fearless friend comes forth.

The hangman led Eivaz to the gallows. He waited for the ashug to finish singing before putting the noose round Eivaz's neck. Köroglu, circling round the square, came up to him and said:

> Don't look so haughtily, hangman, at me:
> An owl would not dare to pounce on a siren.
> Soon I will make you swallow your blood,
> The square will be swamped in a bloody flood.

Köroglu made another round of the square, took his saz and sang the next couplets:

> My bold men, line up and close your ranks,
> We have laid a snare for the enemy troops.
> Chop off the stupid heads of the fools.
> Turn the square into a sea of blood.
>
> After my whoop you must hasten in pairs.
> When I call you, rush and join in the fray.
> It is I, Köroglu, now you all must know.
> Blood must be mixed with blood today.

The ranks of Köroglu's bold men came into motion. Köroglu gave a blood-curdling whoop. He said:

> It is time, my bold men, the hour has come.
> Rush out into the square.
> Like falcons, swoop from the heavens above,
> Spring forward to taste red blood.
>
> Let pure-blooded horses neigh in their wrath.
> Let Egyptian swords sow death.
> One of you cut the ropes on our friends.
> Others fly at the foe.
>
> When Köroglu gives a whoop again,
> Let the beks look and tremble with fear.
> I myself will deal with Aslan Pasha,
> And you take care of Sadr-Azam.

Köroglu, continuing his song, stroked his moustache. His bold men dashed out on the square. At one leap, Köroglu was at the side of Aslan

Pasha. The Egyptian sword had hardly flashed in the air, when the head of Aslan Pasha flew off. In the twinkling of an eye the bold men cut the ropes, releasing Eivaz, Damirchioglu and Belli Ahmed. Köroglu noticed that the three gallows at the different ends of the square were going up and down. And each time they came down, a dozen or two of Aslan Pasha's soldiers were turned into pulp. Köroglu looked again and saw that Damirchioglu, Belli Ahmed and Eivaz had uprooted the gallows and, using them as clubs, were fighting in the thick of the enemy forces.

Cutting his way through with his Egyptian sword, Köroglu reached the doors of Aslan Pasha's treasury and saw the old man he had met the day before standing there. With his faithful club he dealt such a hearty blow at the treasury door, that it flew into splinters. Then he called out to the old man: "Come here!"

When the old man came Köroglu asked him: "Where is that sack of yours?"

"My son, I was so overjoyed that I forgot all about it," the old man answered.

Köroglu said, "Never mind. Come into the treasury." Köroglu gave him a sack of gold, charging two of his men to see him safely home and then come back.

But now we will tell you what happened between Köroglu and Giziroglu Mustafa bek. As soon as Köroglu had passed his hand across his moustache, all hell broke loose in the square. At first Giziroglu could not understand anything, but then it all became clear to him.

"Hark you, my men, there is nothing for us to do here," he said to his horsemen. "Now I am convinced of his might and skill. All that remains is for me to settle my private accounts with him. Come on."

Saying this, Giziroglu galloped home with his riders. When the battle was over, Köroglu looked round and saw that Giziroglu was no longer there. He immediately understood the reason. Giziroglu would not fail to intercept him on his way back. He had gone away on purpose, so that the warriors should not witness the duel between them.

Köroglu's brave men were in high spirits. At Köroglu's orders they mounted their horses and prepared to set off for Chardakli Chanlibel.

"Kosa Safar, how many roads lead from here to Chanlibel?" Köroglu asked.

"There are two roads from here to Chanlibel," Kosa Safar said. "One of them we took when we came here. But there is another road leading through the mountains, over there, beyond those hills. It's a very difficult road. Moreover, it takes much longer."

That was exactly what Köroglu wanted. Turning to his brave men, he said:

"You go along the straight road. I myself will ride home through the mountains. If you reach Chanlibel first, you may consider that you have rescued the lads without my help. The whole of Aslan Pasha's treasury is yours then. If I come before you, the treasury is mine."

Saying this, Köroglu rode off, without waiting for an answer. Whipping Gyrat he crossed the hills in a trice. The brave men knew nothing about his secret intention, and mounting their horses they started homeward.

Köroglu turned his horse back and ascended the hill. When he was sure the braves were out of sight he went back and, pushing his hat down on his eyebrows, rode at a slow trot along the riverbank. He had not gone far when suddenly Gyrat pricked up its ears and reared. It had heard the far-off neighing of another horse. Köroglu turned round and saw Giziroglu galloping on his Alapacha so fast that the dust behind him got mixed with the fog and the fog got mixed with the dust. Gyrat, on hearing Alapacha's neighing, froze to the spot. However hard Köroglu urged Gyrat on with his stirrups, the horse would not stir. Köroglu turned round to see if Giziroglu was still far off. Suddenly, Giziroglu's club came down on his head with full force. Köroglu lost his balance, toppled head down from the horse and rolled into the river. Giziroglu flung his club away and took out his sword, intending to cut off Köroglu's head. But Köroglu suddenly sprang to his feet, picked up Giziroglu's club and brought it down on the man's head with all the strength he could muster. Giziroglu went rolling down into the river. However, he got up quickly and tried to climb onto the bank but could not do it. Köroglu gave him his hand and helped him out, then grasped the handle of his sword to continue the battle. But Giziroglu said:

"Wait, Köroglu! Do you bear me malice?"

"I don't feel hostile towards you, it is you who wish me ill," Köroglu replied.

"I have no more cause for hostility now," Giziroglu then said. "I only wanted to see who was the stronger, you or I. Now I am satisfied. It would be stupid to go on fighting. Give me your hand, and let us be friends."

Köroglu and Giziroglu shook each other by the hand, embraced, kissed and parted as friends. Now let Köroglu continue on his way, while we shall see what Giziroglu did next.

Giziroglu rode straight back to his horsemen, and they asked him: "Where is the head of Köroglu? Where is your promise?"

Giziroglu told them everything, the whole truth. Some of his men began whispering among themselves. They said that Giziroglu was telling lies,

600

that he had not even shown himself to Köroglu. However hard Giziroglu tried to convince them, they refused to believe him. At last Giziroglu lost his patience and said:

"If you want to accuse me of lying, let us go straight to Chanlibel. Ask Köroglu himself. If he is an honourable man, he will tell you the truth, but if he proves base, I will challenge him to fight before your eyes, and you can judge for yourselves from a safe distance."

The horsemen agreed to Giziroglu's proposal. They mounted their horses and set off for Chanlibel.

Let Köroglu ride on to Chanlibel, with Giziroglu following him along the same road. Listen, I shall now tell you about Köroglu's followers.

The brave men rode their horses hard and reached Chanlibel in the morning, when dawn had just broken. All the women came out to meet them. Seeing Nigyar Khanym from a distance, Kosa Safar called out to her:

"Nigyar Khanym, tell us please, has Köroglu arrived or not?"

Nigyar Khanym replied: "No, he has not."

"Very well," Kosa Safar said, "for this once, at least, we have won our wager with him. We have come home earlier than he."

At that very moment they heard the neighing of Gyrat. They turned round and looked in the direction of the sound. Gyrat was grazing on the forbidden land of Yagigorugu, and Köroglu lay on his side on the green grass.

"Where have you been?" he said, smiling. "I have worn out my eyes staring down the road, waiting for you to appear".

"Again you have won the wager!" Kosa Safar said.

"Yes, I have," Köroglu replied. "But I must remind you about an old tradition of ours. It is the custom that whoever first gives me salaam in the morning at the entrance to our camp, I reward him with a hundred gold coins. In accordance with this custom, I must give each of you a hundred gold coins. Today seven thousand seven hundred and seventy brave men came up to me all together. Aslan Pasha's treasury contains just that amount of gold coins. In other words, the entire treasury is yours. Go now, and divide the gold among yourselves just as you think right."

A great feast was held that day in Chanlibel. But let them eat and drink, sing and make merry, while I tell you about the band of Giziroglu Mustafa bek. He and his men arrived in Chanlibel when the brave warriors were feasting.

"They are making merry, celebrating their victory, and it would be unjust to upset their mood," Giziroglu Mustafa bek said. "Let us wait until they finish."

So Giziroglu and his men kept out of sight, mustering their patience.

The cupbearer made a round of the tables and filled everyone's cup with wine. Nigyar Khanym laughed together with all the rest.

"Now, Köroglu, please tell us all about the way you went to Baghdad and released our brave men," she begged.

Köroglu began from the very beginning and told everything to the women and brave men that had remained behind in Chanlibel. He neither added anything, nor left anything out. The only thing he did not mention, was his encounter with Giziroglu Mustafa bek. Nigyar gazed at him with her lovely brown eyes, and then looked around. She cast a sly glance at Köroglu and said:

"My dear Köroglu, you are a man of great wisdom, courage and prowess. I wonder if in all the great universe there is another like you, or were you the only one, born to be like this, and there is no one to equal you in all the world?"

Köroglu did not answer her question directly, but calmly got up from his place, took the saz from the ashug Junun, pressed it to his chest and said:

A noble mother once gave birth
To a man so strong and brave,
The only one of his kind, I know—
Giziroglu Mustafa bek.

The tip of his spear shines with enemy blood,
His brave men wear armour of steel,
His fame resounds far, he is brave and bold,
Giziroglu Mustafa bek.

A steed he has called Alapacha
Which my Gyrat can never outrace.
His mighty club has a double end;
Such is Giziroglu Mustafa bek.

If we were born of one father both
Neither one would be dearer to you.
We would be brothers, I and he,
Giziroglu Mustafa bek.

If you are asking me for the truth
Then among friends I must confess,
Köroglu was once thrown into the river
By Giziroglu Mustafa bek.

As soon as Köroglu had finished singing, Giziroglu Mustafa bek left his hiding place and came up to the merry company.

"Köroglu, you are indeed the noblest of the noble. But one thing you do wrong. You exaggerate the merits of other men and diminish your own. You should never do that. Now I will tell the honest company everything as it really was."

And so Giziroglu began to tell them everything as it really was. And not a word did he add or leave out.

Köroglu and Giziroglu again embraced, kissed and took the pledge of brotherhood. Giziroglu's men then came up and joined the company.

The feast was resumed.

Translated by *Dorian Rottenberg*

Kachag Nabi

KACHAG NABI, a heroic 19th-century epic poem, describes the struggle of the Azerbaijanian poor against the local landowners and tsarist officials. Kachag Nabi, a labourer who led the anti-feudal movement, is not a fictitious character. Ashug songs describing his exploits have many variants and versions. Everywhere, however, Nabi and his wife Hajar symbolise fearlessness and fortitude. The epic has inspired playwrights, poets and prose writers.

The Battle of Arakli

Fragment from the *KACHAG NABI*

The enemies stepped up their attacks, the beks and khans giving Nabi no respite on either bank of the Araks. They spared neither money nor energy to kill Nabi and followed hot on his heels.

Hardly had Nabi and his men forded the river, than the khans and government officials at once reported his coming to the Governor-General and the beks in the neighbourhood.

"Keep your eyes open," they warned. "Nabi and his men have slain two officers and many soldiers. He is coming your way."

The High Sheriff, Jafarkulibek Javanshir, dispatched messengers to every quarter to run Nabi to earth.

While they were looking for him, one rich man came to Goris to complain that Nabi had broken into his granaries and had given all the grain to the poor.

"Where did Nabi go himself?" the High Sheriff asked.

"To Kafan," said the rich man.

The High Sheriff was about to dispatch a posse to Kafan, when another rich man came from Hoznavar to complain that Nabi had also broken into his granaries and had given all the wheat and grain to the poor.

The High Sheriff was about to dispatch his men to Hoznavar, when a warden came to say:

"Nabi and his men have collected the tax in coins of gold from the people of Kechili. Here are the receipts he gave."

The High Sheriff was utterly confused. He did not know which way to turn.

At that very moment Aliagabek Javanshir, an officer from another district, arrived.

"The peasants of landlord Haji Hussein-aga have risen up against the bek. Nabi came to their aid and slew Haji and burned his estate down."

There was such news every day. The High Sheriff was beside himself. He was horrified. In low spirits, he penned despatches to the Tsar, Viceroy, and Governor-General.

Then at the head of a large force and to the roll of drums, he set off for Kechili. At the time Nabi and his men were resting on Mt. Kechili. Nabi was warned that the High Sheriff was coming.

"Let him come," he said. "As God wills, either he or I will win."

While the force of the High Sheriff was approaching the foot of the mountain, the rebels dug trenches. Nabi looked at them and said:

"What could be better than that? What can they do to us now?"

Like ants the troops of the High Sheriff surrounded the mountain and shots were exchanged. In the very first skirmish Nabi and his men shot down five enemy soldiers. In a panic, they retreated in disarray to Kechili. They had achieved nothing and had left five dead behind.

Nabi and his men came down from the mountain and marched to the farmstead of Molla where Nabi spent three days with his mother and brothers. On the fourth day he and his men saddled their horses and galloped to Arhashan. They had hardly come there when the High Sheriff approached with two hundred mounted troopers.

When they learned that the High Sheriff was near, Nabi and his men retreated along secret paths to Garachyngyl. The High Sheriff and his troopers sped through Arhashan towards Garachyngyl, but when they entered it, they learned that Nabi was hiding in the Garagush mountains. The High Sheriff led his force to Garagush, where one bek told them that Nabi and his rebels had made for Arakli.

Thinking that Nabi was fleeing in fright, they took heart and began to storm Mt. Arakli. They pressed on in a seemingly endless file, desirous of killing Nabi's rebels to the last man.

Goja, one of Nabi's brave comrades, lay in ambush behind a cliff that was surrounded by the enemies from every side. Goja made his every shot tell. But he was open on the flanks and could neither retreat nor hide from the hail of bullets. Suddenly, he was struck down with a grievous wound. And now hear how the wounded Goja called Nabi to his succour:

> To the roll of drums they lined up for the fray.
> Crack, crack, went my gun, as I held them at bay.
> But faint grows my heart now that you're far away.
> Pray speed fast to my side, O Kachag Nabi!
> Come to me with Hajar, O dauntless Nabi!
>
> The sight of the foe makes me sick to the heart,
> And both eyes so true has the mist made to smart,
> And I know full well from this Earth I'll
> > depart.
> Pray speed fast to my side, O Kachag Nabi!
> Come to me with Hajar, O dauntless Nabi!
>
> Reloading my gun, I fired sure and true,
> To strike the foe down, my every shot flew.
> O angel of Death, I did not wait for you.
> Pray speed fast to my side, O Kachag Nabi!
> Come to me with Hajar, O dauntless Nabi!

And here as I lie, all bespattered with gore,
O Gach Mehti dear, I shall see you no more.
My life ebbs full fast, but the battle still roars.
Pray speed fast to my side, O Kachag Nabi!
Come to me with Hajar, O dauntless Nabi!

Again and again did I fire at the foe,
Again and again did I see them down go,
But then came the bullet that lay me low.
Pray speed fast to my side, O Kachag Nabi!
Come to me with Hajar, O dauntless Nabi!

O where are my comrades, avenge me they must,
When I am departed, my bones put to dust.
My dear mother tell how kept Goja his trust.
Pray speed fast to my side, O Kachag Nabi!
Come to me with Hajar, O dauntless Nabi!

Nabi heard Goja's cries and made his way to Goja's trench, to find him already dead, clasping tight the stock of his rifle. Nabi kissed his bloody unseeing eyes, and shouting: "O my brave Goja", shot dead one trooper after another. However, the situation was disastrous. The rebels feared that every man would fall. When the foe laid low another two of Nabi's brave comrades, he waxed furious and cried out so loudly as to make earth and sky tremble. He dashed out at the enemy like a lion. The enemy ranks broke and fled. The rebels sent trooper after trooper toppling over into the gorge. They killed and slew without mercy. Following fast on the heels of the foe, Nabi plucked at the strings, and now hear what he sang:

Come, rise up like lions, men, rise up and fight,
And strike at the enemy with all your might!
Come, scatter the foe helter-skelter in flight!
Come, pile up the corpses of enemy slain,
On this field today Nabi glory will gain!

Avenge our dead comrades, who so staunchly fought!
For brave men and true will the foe's fire mean naught.
Against the cursed foe shall now havoc be wrought
Come, pile up the corpses of enemy slain,
On this field today Nabi glory will gain!

Come, aim your guns true, not a single shot waste,
Get the foe 'twixt your sights and fire not in haste.

Come, rise up in fury, the enemy chase.
Come, pile up the corpses of enemy slain,
On this field today Nabi glory will gain!

Nabi and his men chased the foe away and returned to Arakli. They carried the dead bodies of their slain comrades to the village of Arafsa and gave them a fitting funeral. Vast crowds came to pay tribute. The rebels donned black in mourning and held a week-long wake.

Nabi was overwhelmed with grief at the death of his three comrades, all men as staunch as Goja. Gloomy, he foundered in a sea of sorrow.

Clothed in mourning, he spent some time roaming in the neighbourhood of Nakhichevan. There he met a worker.

"Kishi[1], where are you going?" he asked.

"To Baku. And may all your woes be mine," the other said.

"Why are you going to Baku?" Nabi wanted to know.

"I have taken leave of absence at my work and wish to see my relatives."

"How do the workers live?" Nabi asked.

"Like dogs. We are made to work fourteen hours a day and are paid only a few coppers. All the workers have empty pockets and bellies."

Nabi shook his head and asked:

"What do you do?"

"I am an oilman, I draw the oil out of a well. I have spoiled my eyes watching the gusher all night long. I am drenched in oil from head to foot, as if it were so much water."

"Have you at least got a house of your own?"

"No. We live in barracks, a hundred or more in each, right out on the oil fields. The walls are all begrimed with soot and the roof leaks. Nabi, it will only pain you to hear how we live. The wicked villains subject us to the tortures of the damned."

And Nabi said:

"I wonder when at last will we throw off the yoke of our harsh masters and beks? God neither kills them nor shows us the way out. They tell me to come out of hiding and make peace with the gentry. Can one ever make peace, though, with tyrants? We must fight them to the last man!"

"What can you do alone? They have the power and the soldiers. What can you, poor Nabi, do?"

"If I do that and you do that and others do that, we can succeed," Nabi said, giving the worker a hundred-ruble bill. "Take this money, you will find a use for it."

[1] Friend.

Nabi and his men went from Goris to Uchtep. On the way he saw some reapers weeping and pulling their hair. He rode up and asked:

"Brothers, why are you crying? What is the matter?"

"Nabi," they said, "we spent a whole month harvesting to earn some money. Then two robbers fell upon us and took all our money away. What are we to tell our families?"

Nabi knitted his eyebrows, and pulling a wad of banknotes out of his pocket, gave the money to the reapers with these words:

"Is there enough here to make up for what was stolen from you?"

"There is twice as much," the reapers said. "May the holy Ali not forget you."

And the reapers went on their way, saying prayers for Nabi.

Meanwhile, Nabi and his men set off for Ganlyji in the direction of Kechaldag. On the way they encountered the High Sheriff and his force. There was some heavy firing, but as the rebels were running short of ammunition, they resolved to retreat right up to the top of the mountain.

As night fell, Nabi left his men encamped on Mt. Shyh, and himself with two comrades rode right up to Jafarkulibek's house in Goris. He was not at home at the time and when his wife saw Nabi she was greatly affrighted. However, Nabi told her:

"Please, don't be afraid, Khanym. We won't do anything to you. We need ammunition. Give us some rounds of ammunition."

Jafarkulibek's wife led them into the ammuntion dump and said: "Here, take as much as you like."

Nabi took many rounds of ammunition and went back to Mt. Shyh. Here they saw that the High Sheriff was about to capture Hajar and the other rebels. They opened fire from the rear, dispersed the High Sheriff's troops and set out for Mt. Suleimandagy.

In the villages at the foot of this mountain the rebels saw many hungry, ragged peasants and cripples. Nabi looked at them with pain in his eyes and swore that he would not leave the place until he had done something for them.

They fell on a landlord's estate, broke open the granaries and gave the grain to the starving. After that, they made straight for Mt. Demirdag.

The sheriff went with a large force to this mountain to engage Nabi. But hardly did the battle begin in earnest than the sheriff's troops fled, the rebels chasing them back to the foot of the mountain. The enemy retreated in flight to Ordubad. Nabi and his men also set out, and, going through Sisnan, and Zangezur and crossing the two rivers of Bershad and Heker, came to the Glijan Gorge. The beks, rich men and the wardens amassed a big force and marching upon the Glijan gorge, opened fire at the rebels from every quarter. Nabi waxed wroth and cried:

"This day, brothers, we must give them such a thrashing that they never forget it to their dying day. Glijan Gorge must run with their blood!"

As the rebels attacked the foe, Nabi plucked at the strings, and hear now what he told his comrades true:

> In Gorge of Glijan we shall our mettle show,
> 'Tis here, my friends, we give battle to the foe.
> Give them no quarter, let their blood forth flow!
> So, lads, fire your rifles, recharge and fire well,
> And let us blast the foe all the way to hell!
>
> Against the khans and beks has Nabi sworn to fight,
> All the cruel and grasping has he vowed to smite,
> On them has he fallen with his crushing might!
> So, lads, fire your rifles, recharge and fire well,
> And let us blast the foe all the way to hell!
>
> Fearless Kachag Nabi, none so brave as he,
> As his loving Hajar, as lion-hearted she.
> Friends of all the poor and foes of rich they be.
> So, lads, fire your rifles, recharge and fire well,
> And let us blast the foe all the way to hell!

And then and there Nabi and his comrades mounted their horses and dashed at the foe. The rebels indeed made the Glijan Gorge run red with their blood. The few survivors fled for their lives.

The news of the heroism Nabi and his men had displayed in the Glijan battle reached every ear. Friends were jubilant, foes were terrified. Nabi and his comrades then set out for Goris. On their way there, going through the village of Saitas, they heard loud cries. Nabi checked his mount, and, cocking an ear, said:

"Let us take a look at what can be going on there."

They say that the warden Mehtibek had lashed an old man to a post and was whipping him. Nabi jumped down off his horse, and grabbing the warden by the scruff of his neck, cried:

"You dog, why are you beating this venerable old man?"

"He wants the old man to work in the fields, but he is too weak to go," someone explained.

"You despot, and son of a despot, he is old enough to be your father! Haven't you any heart?" Nabi cried.

Nabi had the old man untied and Mehtibek lashed to the post in his place. The old man had been so badly beaten that he could hardly move.

Supporting him under the arm, Nabi took him aside and sat him on the grass.

"Sit here and watch," he said.

He gave his comrades a wink, and they, catching up two big sticks walloped Mehtibek so soundly that his body grew as black as felt. When the old man saw Mehtibek beaten, he felt sprier. Leaving the warden bound to the post, Nabi and his men went away.

Mehtibek's flogging made the sheriffs feel bad. The Governor-General himself ordered them to go about the matter in earnest and have Nabi killed as soon as possible.

Nabi and his followers circumvented Grakyol and reached Mt. Guluz-dag. They had ridden a long way and were dog-weary. They had thought they would have some respite, but this was not to be. The High Sheriff attacked Nabi and the fighting began in earnest. With his very first shot, Nabi killed the steward of Warden Aliaga. The troops were about to turn, when the High Sheriff cried:

"Stand or die! There is no retreating!"

The rebels cared little for the enemy's threats. They went straight on to Ellij, the foe following on their heels. In Ellij there was some very heavy firing and in the space of but one hour the rebels killed twelve of the High Sheriff's troopers. Nabi looked to see his comrades fighting like lions. His eyes smiled. The heroism of his gallant comrades multiplied his own powers a hundredfold. Hajar glanced at Nabi and caught his delight. She brandished her gun, then clasped it to her bosom, and now hear what she cried:

And Nabi did say: Here in Ellij I stand,
My whiskers a-curled and my gun in my hand,
With my first shot, the Sheriff's steward I brand.
Let all around leave the outlaw Nabi;
Hajar the brave by his side will be!

Riders few has he, a mere dozen or so,
But like hawk swooping down, he charges the foe,
In panic beks flee, like whipped curs they go,
Let all around leave the outlaw Nabi;
Hajar the brave by his side will be!

A brave heart my Nabi, a staunch heart and true,
For Hajar the brave, the one man she would woo.
The day his foes meet him, they ever will rue.
Let all around leave the outlaw Nabi;
Hajar the brave by his side will be!

611

Barely had Hajar finished than the rebels leaped onto their horses and rushed at the enemy. Hajar's steed pranced, as she fired her gun. They chased the enemy all the way to the village of Engelavud and then returned. During the engagement peasants lined the road to watch and meanwhile did everything they could to help Nabi by giving him word of the enemy's movements.

When the enemy force had dispersed, there came cries from all around, imploring God on high to help Nabi.

In another five villages in Sisian he collected the tax in gold coin. Neither government nor peasants suffered—only the rich. Both peasants and tax collectors addressed God with grateful prayers for Nabi.

One day the rebels came to Gyrkhlarakh. The Governor had roundly reproached the High Sheriff. The latter with Mamedbek gathered a large troop of horsemen and set off for Gyrkhlarakh and opened fire at the mountain from every side. The rebels felt fine, as they had dug in well. Then one of Nabi's comrades, Zaman by name, was shot dead because of his own rashness. Nabi waxed wroth, he was about to mount his horse Bozat and charge the enemy, when a bullet wounded the animal. Nabi kissed the wound and the horse pranced as if it were not wounded at all. Nabi was downhearted because when he had his horse under him, he felt as if he were leading a whole regiment. He turned around and saw his good comrade Zaman drop behind the bushes. Hear now what Nabi cried:

> On Mount Gyrkhlarakh a fierce engagement was fought,
> The bullets flew fast, and great havoc was wrought.
> In the heat of the fray was Nabi unhorsed.
> Now will they seize me, put chains on my feet,
> And in dungeon dire dishonour will meet.
>
> The mountains loomed high, but no paths could I find.
> My horse shot from under me, O fate unkind!
> My powder all spent, and the foe close behind.
> Now will they seize me, put chains on my feet,
> And in dungeon dire dishonour will meet.
>
> The foe they were strong and they pressed on apace,
> Good Zaman was killed, as they gave us the chase.
> O evil the day, sad and sorrowful grace!
> Now will they seize me, put chains on my feet,
> And in dungeon dire dishonour will meet.

It was a dark and moonless night. Nabi could hardly make out the faces of his comrades as he said:

"My dear brothers, my horse Bozat has been wounded and I feel as if my wings had been cropped. Let us avail ourselves of the cover of darkness and retreat."

Nabi mounted another man's horse and led Bozat by the reins. They swooped down on the enemy's right flank and broke through to gallop straight on to the summer grazing grounds of Kechili. After a little rest they came to the villages of Uchtep and Korunzur. It was autumn, as I well remember. Here Nabi wrote the sheriff a letter in which he said:

"I have collected the tax in gold coin in eight villages of Zangizur, five villages of Sisian, six villages of Kafan and twelve villages of Ordubad. You may not collect the tax in gold coin there again."

Several hours later the High Sheriff and his force overtook the rebels who had encamped on the Bow Goris and opened fire at them. Nabi and his men leaped onto their horses and rushed into the attack. Within an hour they had chased the enemy troop into Goris. This exploit that Nabi and his comrades accomplished lent inspiration to Samed the Bard and this is what he said:

> That day on Mount Goris there massed a large force,
> From every quarter came the enemy's horse.
> When from the place where they lay hid in the gorse
> Cried Nabi: "To horse!" and the foe they attacked.
> Their blades gleamed and flashed as they chopped and they
> hacked.

> The foe's ranks were broken and put to the flight,
> As Nabi and his men struck with all their might.
> With rifle and sword did they good work that night.
> Cried Nabi: "To horse!" and the foe they attacked.
> Their blades gleamed and flashed as they chopped and they
> hacked.

> Ismail from Ganja did ride with head high,
> While proud Selimbek beat his breast with deep sigh,
> And Husein-Aga slunk off back to his sty.
> Cried Nabi: "To horse!" and the foe they attacked.
> Their blades gleamed and flashed as they chopped and they
> hacked.

After he had finished, he came down and approached Nabi. The rebels gave him many presents. Then they filled their empty cartridge belts and as midnight struck set out for Gajihun.

Translated by *Arthur Shkarovsky*

Ashug Kurbani

ASHUG KURBANI was a famous 16th-century folk poet. His goshmas—short lyrical poems or else ones carrying a socio-philosophical message—were handed down as gems of oral art from generation to generation, and came to us in the form of folk songs. The famous folk poem entitled "Kurbani" is compiled from the poet's verses.

Violet

O my dearest, my love, my beautiful peri,
Custom bids us pluck violets when spring days begin.
With your tender white hand gather a nosegay,
Pin it under your dainty chin.

* * *

Your beauty, a gift of the powers above,
Has driven me almost insane with love.
Were you plucked by an angel masked as a dove?
O violet, he should pluck more of your kin.

* * *

Kurbani's poor heart is your captive for aye.
Why punish me with separation, pray?
You too, my love, are wasting away;
Tell me, when will happier days begin?

Translated by *Dorian Rottenberg*

Ah, I saw you sway as you walked, Salatin;
Do not sway or bad men may do harm to you.
Do not stand by the window in your pink dress,
Or some evil eye may do harm to you.

Stay a while, let me ask whose daughter are you,
Or what happy mortal's true sweetheart are you:
You were born in the shade—shaded snow are you;
Beware, the warm sun may do harm to you.

Kurbani says, let no one extoll my love,
Button your collar tighter, my love.
Let your plaits not touch ground; tie them higher, love,
Or the roadway dust may do harm to you.

Translated by *Dorian Rottenberg*

How Can You?

O beauty, with such a wide choice in the world,
You prefer a stranger, my foe! How can you?
You who were titled *Eagless* by men
Have destroyed your renown with one blow! How can you?

I have looked for you everywhere; where do you hide?
My passion devours me day and night.
You yourself set that flame of passion alight;
Will you quench it and leave me in woe? How can you?

May Allah in heaven protect you from woes,
May your soul be serene and untroubled, sweet rose.
Ah, my love, how I wish I could hold you close.
Will you leave me to burn alone? How can you?

How sweet are the words you pronounce for my ear.
I am perishing, slain by your eyes, my dear.
Women always make fools of men, I fear.
Do you, darling, also do that? How can you?

How I wish, o my love, you'd take pity on me,
For the agony suffered by poor Kurbani.
The moon longs your beautiful face to see,
Yet your face you refuse to show; how can you?

Translated by *Dorian Rottenberg*

Ashug Abbas Divarganly

ASHUG ABBAS DIVARGANLY is reputed to have lived in the 17th century, in the reign of Shah Abbas I. The romantic love story "Abbas and Gulkez" which has preserved for us the ashug's wonderful goshmas is based on his numerous verses.

When you set off on the way to your love,
Be sure you leave her with no grudge against you.
Plant soft kisses on her honey-sweet lips.
Let those honey-sweet lips bear no grudge against you.

The harvest is gathered, the garden is bare.
If the heart is not satisfied, it will despair.
Dear, arrange the ends of your kerchief down there
So your pomegranates bear no grudge against you.

The nightingale voices his grief for the rose.
Pomegranates on a beauty's breast lie close.
Come and go through her garden upon your toes,
So the nightingale and rose bear no grudge against you.

Let Her Bear No Grudge

Among beauties you are a rose deep-red;
A nightingale circles over your head,
O breeze, do not blow, waft gently instead,
So the lock on her brow bear no grudge against you.

Says Abbas: when the weeping break into laughter,
When a beauty becomes aware that you love her,
When she honours you by coming soon after,
Embrace her, let her bear no grudge against you.

Translated by *Dorian Rottenberg*

Oh, brothers and sisters, what have we come to:
The jay hates the eagle as never before.
Sons hate their fathers, daughters—their mothers,
And daughters-in-law hate their mothers-in-law.

Some people like vagabonds roam in the mountains,
Some wear clothes of leather—a sin in effect.
Some people know nothing of tact and good manners,
While others pay sultans and khans no respect.

Some people wander all day doing nothing.
Some people do not hold Allah in awe.
Some people do not believe in praying.
Some people refuse to obey the law.

There are people who walk over hill and valley,
There are people to whom a rose won't appeal.
There are people who can't buy cloth for their garments,
There are those who wear silk, but won't wear a veil.

There are some who possess the power to work wonders.
There are some who can never achieve their aims.
There are some who cannot buy bread for their children,
And some who eat butter, but honey disdain.

There are people whom you would present with flowers.
There are people who change their eyebrows' hue.
O Abbas Turfaghan, what have you come to:
Your old woman declares she doesn't like *you*!

Translated by *Dorian Rottenberg*

Peri You are laughing, laughing, peri, at my grief,
As if my grief were something funny, peri.
Wealthy suitors your house and garden surround,
And you laugh with lips sweet as honey, peri.

Ever since we have walked with you in Tauris,
I've been daily wounded anew for my bliss.
I would rather be chained, cast in jail, than bear this.
How much grief you have brought me, my cunning peri!

Poor Abbas is already awaited above
Since his sweetheart tramples upon his love,
For you songs and talent are not enough:
At a moneyless lover you laugh, peri!

Translated by *Dorian Rottenberg*

Ashug Khasta Kasum

ASHUG KHASTA KASUM was one of the most popular 18th-century folk poets. Khasta, which he chose for a pen-name, means "one in pain". And indeed his goshmas are full of pain caused by the injustices, deceits and betrayals of the day. Many of his goshmas are didactic—teaching people how to live, and begging for honesty, truth, reason and humaneness. Khasta Kasum's goshmas are still performed today by the modern ashugs.

Partridges

Now that I'm going, to whom shall I leave you
With your perch on the rooftop, partridges?
Adorned with blue silk, kerchiefs on your heads,
Change your clothes, let the hunters waste cartridges.

The tops of the rocks are the partridges' home.
They cluck, call their mates when they feel alone.
And when near the nest sounds a hunter's horn
They take to the sky, poor partridges.

Singing songs on the rocks sit partridge-mothers,
Clucking, competing with one another.
And you holding a feast or mourning your brothers,
Smearing your feathers with blood, o partridges?

If you have any sorrow, tell it to me.
Let me share it, whatever it happens to be.
Bear Kasum no ill, for he has to see
His kin in far-off Daghestan, dear partridges.

Translated by *Dorian Rottenberg*

Sanam,[1] Come Too

All famous beauties have come to the feast.
In the best of your dresses, Sanam, come too.
You're afraid, like a deer that sees the bow.
With your raven-black tresses, Sanam, come too.

I am not an ashug if I can't sing your charms.
All the world dreams of bliss in your snowy arms.
Your speech like sweet balsam comforts and calms.
With lips sweet as molasses, Sanam, come too.

Says Khasta Kasum: I can see on your face
Two moles that enhance your beauty and grace.
No, nothing I see in you is out of place.
Made for love and caresses, Sanam, come too.

Translated by *Dorian Rottenberg*

[1] Sanam—beauty; often used as a female's name.

623

Go Away

Go away, beauty, go and be cursed.
May your life till the last be nothing but woe.
May your black tresses be turned into snakes
And not fall in dark waves to the ground below.

May you always weep when all others feel joy.
May you burn on a fire, you're so wayward and coy.
Let faithful beauties your service employ;
May you be their slave, and before them bow low.

I would give all my soul for a woman who's true.
I would worship her beauty all my life through.
But I wish that no children be born to you,
That no flowers—just thorns—in your garden should grow.

O you girl, no one knows your real nature but me.
Then be punished at doomsday for treachery.
Let a viper bite you while sleeping you be.
May all ears be deaf when you groan with woe.

But Khasta Kasum is so lonely and sad,
If you come and embrace him, he will be glad.
To all I have said, I have this to add;
Come to me, and I'll wish you good fortune; so!

Translated by *Dorian Rottenberg*

All Is Well

O turbulent soul, never say to yourself:
"To live I desire, in life all is well."
Some day may your brothers turn alien and strange,
Say not: "I have brothers", say not: "all is well!"

When people surround you don't swagger with cheek,
Don't give joy to Satan—ne'er of friends vilely speak,
If stronger yourself—do not bully the weak,
No soul must you tell that you're strong, and all's well.

If brave parents bore you, be valiant and brave,
Beware of the tempests that thunder and rave,
Behave as a generous bard must behave,
Say not: "I live well, I am rich, and all's well!"

To whom must Khasta Kasum go to complain?
It serves Kasum right to bear suffering and pain;
A good lad will keep his fair name from a stain,
Called cad—that's your knell! better die—'twill be well!

Translated by *Olga Moisseyenko*

Ashug Alesker

ASHUG ALESKER (1821-1926) was born in Ak-Kilsa, a village in the Basar-Kechar district of Armenia. He is known throughout Transcaucasia. His poems are classics of ashug art, written with remarkable skill, elegance and sheer virtuosity. He extolled courage and honesty, and condemned hypocrisy and bigotry. Besides the verses he himself had composed in the course of his long life, Ashug Alesker is said to have known some sixty tales and poems by heart, performing them at celebrations which, in Azerbaijan, invariably feature the singing of ashugs.

You Must Have

To be a bard and wander far from home
You knowledge and a thinking head must have.
How you are to behave, you too must know,
Politeness, erudition you must have.

To quell the devil in you you must seek,
About the truth with people learn to speak,
Be honest, true, obedient and meek.
Respect of all the people you must have.

And know the price of every word you say,
In metaphors you should your thoughts convey.
Before you speak, you every word should weigh.
The gift to daze and puzzle you must have.

Be quick to understand a hint, howe'er,
Of strangers you should, as a rule, beware,
And like a clock advance to what is fair.
True heart and word of honour you must have.

So, Alesker, give alms unto the poor,
That angels would a place for you ensure.
Your glance should be both resolute and pure,
A pathway clear before you you must have.

Translated by *Eugene Felgenhauer*

The Wicked World

O listen, friends, and I'll reveal to
you
Of what duplicity the world does smack,
For mercy's gone, and justice is curtailed.
It seems that every Kazi[1] is a quack.

Cold winds of evil all about us play,
And life is getting harder every day,
The mollas, kerbalans, akhunds,[2] betray,
The souls of all Meshadis[3] are black.

[1] Kazi—confessor.
[2] Molla and akhund—clerical functionaries.
[3] Meshadi, kerbalan—pilgrims to holy places.

The atamans and bandits all advance,
At poor and helpless they all look askance,
They simply kill, whene'er they have the chance,
And all about one hears their rifles crack.

And when police or overseers come,
Throughout the villages one hears a moan.
For debts the poor are skinned down to the bone.
Beneath the whip they bend their aching back.

The lords desire with supercilious pride,
The common folk into their graves to ride.
So, Ashug Alesker, we need not hide
That simple decency the thieving headmen lack.

Translated by *Eugene Felgenhauer*

In Trouble You Will Get

Now, do not boast and say you perfect are,
There is a chance in trouble you will get.
You are a mote, you still a baby are,
You'll lose your head, in trouble you will get.

Begin below, if you would reach the height,
If you're a fox, with bear you should not fight.
Don't lift a stone because you think it's light,
For if you fail, in trouble you will get.

Do not be proud and do not raise your nose,
You do not know which way the wind now blows,
For I may strip you of your gaudy clothes,
With tail plucked short, in trouble you will get.

Don't wag your tongue—your tongue it is your foe.
Now, Alesker has met such long ago,
And with his hands he'll knead you into dough;
You'll take a fall, in trouble you will get.

Translated by *Eugene Felgenhauer*

She Is Killing Me

O woe is me, and question not, my friends!
A beauteous doe I know is killing me,
Without a sword, without a firearm,
And no one knows that she is killing me.

I'd like to know what I to her have done,
That she my very company should shun.
I'd sacrifice my soul, though I've but one.
I'd like to know why she is killing me?

I, Alesker, have visited the same,
While I'm alive, I hardly can refrain;
And death's bright angel, mother, do not blame:
It is her piercing glance that's killing me.

Translated by *Eugene Felgenhauer*

Ashug Hussein Bozalganly

ASHUG HUSSEIN BOZALGANLY (1872-1949) was born in Ashagi-Bozalganly, a village in the Tavuss district of Azerbaijan. He had a brilliant knowledge of the great epic poem Köroglu *and other folk sagas, and won many a contest even against the recognised champion of "poetic battles" Ashug Alesker.*

I Recall

When I embraced my beloved's slender neck,
Deep in her locks my fingers hid, I recall.
I wanted to place my hand on her breast,
When coyly a button she undid, I recall.

Languidly she came up and I saw her desire;
Laughing, clapping her hands, full of charm and fire!
She hid in my home, an angel in earthly attire,
Her sweet words spiced with love and wit, I recall.

Then, by the mirror, an image of girlish grace,
She combed her locks and arranged them around her face.
Then she came to me and we lay in a hot embrace;
Closer and closer to me she clung, I recall.

How her eyelashes fluttered and pierced my breast!
The scent of musk arose from her vest,
Then she went away and left me distressed,
She did not care, but pretended she did, I recall.

Oh, how hard I suffered at my sweetheart's hands!
Before me her pitiless image still stands.
Yet I doubt that her cruelty she understands.
But how clearly her fiery caress I recall!

Translated by Dorian Rottenberg

631

My Jeyran

O strength of my sinews, light of my eyes,
I'm in love with you, source of my woes, my jeyran!
I would take all your troubles upon myself;
How your hair down your shoulders flows, my jeyran!

Ah, your beauty has turned me into a dove.
How I long for you, how you torture me, love!
Tell me what drug is strong enough
To cure me—I suffer, God knows, my jeyran!

I need no riches, no castles, no money;
I'd be satisfied with your lips' sweet honey,
Your wit, your perfection and your smile so sunny,
Your dimpled chin, your face like a rose, my jeyran!

Translated by *Dorian Rottenberg*

She Left

I do not know what I said, but she took offence;
Like a turbulent river that overflows, she left.
She frowned and measured me with her glance;
Looking at me in a spirit morose. She left.

I couldn't hold her: I scared off my game;
My arrow missed the jeyran, its aim,
Long I pursued her, but all in vain.
Bringing my life to a close, she left.

Refusing to tell him her secret, she left Hussein,
She left Hussein and Hussein is now lying slain.
She looked at me, her eyes overfilled with disdain,
Her lashes pierced me like arrows from bows. She left!

Translated by *Dorian Rottenberg*

Ashug Shamshir

ASHUG SHAMSHIR (b. 1893) is a prominent modern folk poet, a member of the Union of Soviet Writers. He lives in Akdabanly, a village in the Kelbejar district of Azerbaijan, where he was born. His father was the well-known ashug Kurbani. Shamshir started out in life as a hired labourer, and was then a shepherd. He has used practically all the forms of ashug poetry in his numerous works. His poems are incisive, unpredictable in imagery and change of mood, imbued with a profound philosophical meaning and an unobtrusively didactic humane message.

O beauty asking about my life,
Fairer than anyone I have known,
How totally happy must he be
Who calls you his very own.

Nature gave you both beauty and grace;
Be inaccessible, pure and chaste;
If you are wise, avoid disgrace,
And your plight you will ne'er bemoan.

Pay no heed to the foul and base,
Do not copy their evil ways,
Don't give your body to him who plays
With women. Better remain alone.

Be well-behaved, inaccessible stay,
Do not forget tomorrow today.
Honestly work to pay your way,
Then you will have no cause to groan.

To worthy persons bow your head,
Ask about their affairs when met.
When others quarrel, do not get
Involved, nor assume a haughty tone.

Let my words not be lost in vain;
Wisdom from elders try to gain.
Don't reject advice with disdain,
You are young, there is much to you unknown.

All Shamshir has said you must heed
For he gives you advice you will need;
Ignorance may to evil lead;
Knowledge to good is a stepping stone.

Translated by *Dorian Rottenberg*

Oppressor

This cannot continue, the day must arrive
When justice will come upon you, oppressor.
You plunder the people of village and town;
Where is your conscience, your honour, oppressor?

What is my fault that you torture and plague me?
No one attempts to protect and save me,
Yet I don't weep in vain, for time will avenge me;
I suffer, but who'll be your mourner, oppressor?

A pity my words do not touch your heart;
But our woes are recorded ere we depart;
You will suffer bitterly, aye, you will smart
For the merciless slaughter of poor men, oppressor.

This old universe saw off many a lord;
The memory of tyrants is cursed and abhorred;
Hangman, you will die from the avenging sword;
Before it's too late, stop your plunder, oppressor.

Don't boast of your strength, don't be proud of your power,
Don't think it is far off, your fatal hour.
For Shamshir's fortune is yet to flower,
While you have good cause to tremble, oppressor!

Translated by *Dorian Rottenberg*

The Beauty and I

Said I: Whence, O beauty, your gait so fine?
Said she: From the swan that swims on the brine.
Said I: Is it henna that makes your hair shine?
Said she: It is Nature—my beauty is mine.

Said I: The sweet sound of your speech turns my head!
I'm sorry for you, poor man, she said.
Said I: Let us walk to that flowerbed.
Said she: Your offer I must decline.

Said I: Your lashes have pierced my breast.
Said she: My victims with bliss are blessed.
Said I: Tell me, where can a lover find rest?
Said she: On your mistress's bosom recline.

Said I: O beauty, a man's sole wealth is love!
Said she: Only beggars think love is enough.
Said I: Your breasts are pomegranates sent from above!
Said she: O man, you are out of your mind!

Said I: Poor Shamshir has been smitten by you.
Said she: In your words there's nothing new.
Said I: Your lips shine with honey-like dew.
Said she: It is medicine for men of your kind.

Translated by *Dorian Rottenberg*

Don'ts

Of a man who is scholarly, wise and good
Nothing bad must be said when he is dead.
Of him who enriches the world with his thoughts
Nothing degrading or base must be said.

Politeness and breeding give beauty to man;
They make him happier than anything can.
If a man does good throughout his life's span,
To offend or insult or debase him is bad.

O Shamshir, remember kind deeds done to you.
Joy awaits all those who wise ways pursue;
Do no evil to those who come to you,
He who goes can't be chained to remain, it is said.

Translated by *Dorian Rottenberg*

Musts

We must stop the mouth of the indolent knave
Who will sneer when others are doing good deeds.
He who spreads nonsensical rumours about,
Should be thrashed and beaten until he bleeds.

* * *

Show restraint with the knowing, mature and wise;
Do not raise your eyebrows or play with your eyes.
Think before you utter requests and replies.
Who respects his listener, in all succeeds.

* * *

A man who is reasonable and clever
His knowledge will perfect forever;
If you'd turn words to pearls—endeavour
To spread them, if they're wise indeed.

* * *

O Shamshir, do not ruin your life with grief
Because of men who don't deserve belief.
But to the man who's true and will never deceive
Give all you possess—whate'er he may need.

* * *

Let a skilful teacher give guidance to you;
It may be hard, but you will get your due.
Poet, craftsman, whatever trade you pursue,
A good name you must leave and sow good seeds.

Translated by *Dorian Rottenberg*

Ashug Hussein Djavan

ASHUG HUSSEIN DJAVAN (b. 1916) is one of the more
outstanding modern folk poets of southern, Iranian
Azerbaijan. He lives in Baku, and is a member of the Union
of Soviet Writers. Djavan means "young", and his poetry
is indeed full of youthful enthusiasm, optimism and cheer.
He has published five collections of verse.

Sattarkhan

O courageous son of Azerbaijan,
You fell a martyr to the freedom of man.
You pledged faith to your country, bold Sattarkhan,
And were loyal to her since your manhood began.

You fought with the foes of your country so dear;
Wherever on horseback you would appear
The enemies' faces went yellow with fear,
And to rescue their treacherous hides, they ran.

You fought for the coming of happy times
And look—the sun into heaven climbs.
In Tabriz the roses blossom, sublime;
You were their gardener, fearless man.

You became a bright beacon for sightless eyes.
You give strength to the strong, wisdom to the wise,
In our laughing eyes as a sun you arise.
Hope of the pure in heart, peerless man!

Translated by *Dorian Rottenberg*

I Fell Into Sorrowful Meditation

As I viewed my misery-stricken nation
I fell into sorrowful meditation.
My people's weeping and loud lamentation
Set my spirit on fire—so sad was I.

My land's in the hands of hangmen cold-hearted;
Even mothers with little children are parted.
When I heard my people weeping I started
To roam with bowed head, so sad was I.

I will smile when my people escape from their chains,
When no more misery or sorrow remains;
When Tabriz is free from the tyrant that reigns
No one will say that with grief mad am I.

The murderous foe may wait till he die:
We free men as slaves at his feet will not lie.
When the South hoists the crimson banner on high
Then Hussein will at last say, "How glad am I!"

Translated by *Dorian Rottenberg*

Who Taught You, Dear?

Who was it that taught you, dear,
To tread the earth like a deer,
To wear on your brow that lock of hair,
Tell me, who taught you, dear?

To awake with the rising sun,
A crimson silk gown to put on,
To move and to dance like a swan,
Tell me, who taught you, dear?

I adore my sweet Zanishan;
Like a rose she looks to a man.
To pluck flowers as no one else can
Tell me, who taught you, dear?

To move like a bird, swift and free,
Like a lithe gazelle, young and fleet,
Like a duck floating on the sea,
Tell me, who taught you, dear?

Like the moon your sweet face glows bright;
Like the morning star after night
Your brown eyes shed a tender light.
Tell me, who taught you, dear?

Translated by *Dorian Rottenberg*

Ever since the great universe was created
You have witnessed infinite woe, Garadag,
Each fold on your brow is a century's trace.
How old you are no one can know, Garadag!

Many times with sorrow and grief you were seized
For your sons whose lives on your flanks had ceased.
Every rock of yours was a fortress besieged:
Every stone on your soil tells me so, Garadag!

Wicked rulers silenced you year after year.
Your bosom bears wounds from the enemy's spear.
Your heart often ached and your eyes shed tears;
On your face their signs clearly show, Garadag.

Garadag[1]

With cruel shahs we fought for your liberty;
The blood that we spilled could fill a whole sea.
From the world's beginning you yearned to be free—
In anguish your head bent low, Garadag.

Tabriz is your mother and you are her son.
You were faithful to her since time began.
With us all, you mourn for her son Sattarkhan,
That is why your head's white as snow, Garadag.

Azerbaijan today is a country of light.
Your name fills her valiant people with pride;
Sarab, Urmia[2] quake at your thunder's might;
Kurdistan is your brother, you know, Garadag.

The sun will arise once again and its warmth
Will make peaches in your orchards bloom forth.
A triumphant banner that knows no defeat
In your countrymen's hands will glow, Garadag.

It will light up all nations throughout the East;
On its beauty and glory all eyes will feast
As they do on your girls, so lovely and sweet;
In a tirma[3] shawl as they go, Garadag!

[1] Mountain in the Azerbaijanian part of the Caucasus.
[2] Sarab—city in Iran; Urmia—formerly, Resaiah.
[3] Silken gaily ornamented shawl worn in the Caucasus.

644

Your warriors will raise their triumphant voices
And you will look on as your land rejoices,
Adorned by the sun with blossoms choicest
On the Day of Victory, O Garadag!

Full of courage and strength Garadag's sons stand.
Led by bold Sattarkhan, the pride of our land.
Hussein Djavan, too, holds a gun in his hand.
Do not fear, though the world's rife with foes, Garadag.

Translated by *Dorian Rottenberg*

Bayat | *BAYAT is a form of folk poetry, a quatrain. It is sung to the tune of folk songs. It is mainly written in lines with a definite rhyming pattern and the main idea stated in the last two lines. Of the known forms there are love bayats, lamentations, lullabies, shepherd songs, philosophical bayats, and puns with homonymic rhymes. A bayat is a finished work of poetry with a clear-cut pattern and composition.*

My friend, what grievous troubles wake
While people sleep, what troubles wake—
The poor endure more misery
Than raging seas bring in their wake.

* * *

Friend, no one knows much happiness,
Not one but lives a life of stress:
You'll see injustice, wound and
                            wrong
From shahs, but never their largesse.

* * *

Poor bard, I groan eternally;
Long doomed to fight adversity
Since I became a hopeless slave
They sell and buy and barter me.

* * *

You bury a foreigner should he die,
But through back-streets he's carried by;
You hardly mark his death at all—
But do his mother notify!

* * *

My friend, if beggared, alms demand;
Beg door-to-door, beg on every hand:
Better at home a pauper be
Than wealthy khan in a foreign land.

* * *

I've only a sheepskin hat left to wear,
My heart is aching with despair:
Our eyes met, and I fell in love—
Am I to blame she was so fair?

647

A beaten servant's piercing screams,
Disturbed some people's nightly dream.
But that day tumbled, brick by brick—
His life's castle, all his dreams.

* * *

Churn and churn so butter comes,
Drink with a will to work that hums:
Here's to our collective farm!
Here's to our chairman and working
                                    chums!

* * *

Oh, rue is holy, rue is blest,
Of healing properties possessed—
Where this herb in plenty grows,
By disease are none distressed.

* * *

I picked red roses, filled a tray,
Till morn beside me let them stay—
When you come to see your love,
She'll rise to meet you, fragrant, gay.

* * *

My love, come where the melons grow
In the garden row on row—
One smile from you, and I'll my
                                    heart
Upon your burning altar throw.

* * *

A hawk into our garden flew,
His prey intending to pursue.
Even though I lay here dead,
I'd come alive at a kiss from you.

Let's seek our garden, so discrete
Our lips may passionately meet:
We'll be like nightingales and sing,
Nor feel the earth beneath our feet.

* * *

Come, love, into our mountain bower,
Our garden where the melons flower—
Over the wall and come to me
For one happy, joyous hour.

* * *

The moon is sliding down to rest,
By sleeplessness I am possessed—
My lonely hands are languishing
To touch my loved one's tender
breast.

* * *

The moon is setting, sad and frail,
To find relief in sleep I fail:
Where melons grow, the rose is cool
Before the love-sick nightingale.

* * *

I plucked a rose so red and deep,
Until tomorrow I will keep:
My love invites me then to call—
Before me dainties she will
heap.

* * *

In the heart of Ganji town
A wedding candle's burning down—
Oh, in the arms of this fair youth,
May God your life with blessings crown.

O love, the hive is for the bee;
Bees swarm, and hives there have to be:
When lovers true are joined as one,
Then angels hold a jubilee.

✢ ✢ ✢

My rival gave a heavy sigh;
And, cup in hand, sat blank of eye;
Of course, his thoughts are all on
                                       her—
He caught a better glimpse than I.

✢ ✢ ✢

My stockings are of patterned threads,
The pattern is with roses spread—
If you love me truly, meet
Me near my neighbour's flowerbeds.

✢ ✢ ✢

I'd go, if only someone showed
The way, and joined me on the road.
A letter for my love—won't someone
Take it to her far abode?

✢ ✢ ✢

My baby's gone to bye-lo,
So that he may grow.
I won't let them wake him up:
Sweet is morning sleep, you know.

✢ ✢ ✢

Grown birds may fly both east and
                                       west,
But nestlings keep within their nest.
I pray and pray and pray for you:
My fears give me no rest.

My lullaby is sweet as sweet,
My baby's sleep is light and fleet—
One thing alone I ask of God:
One day your wedding guests to meet.

* * *

The mullah calls, the morn is here,
So rise and dress, my little dear—
I want to look and look at you,
To feast my eyes on yours so clear.

* * *

Bye-lo, bye-lo, my little one,
You're my bread and salt alone—
I wait to see what help you'll be
To Mother, when you're grown.

* * *

What happened to my babykin?
Sonny, you're so pale and thin;
Time to open up your eyes—
I've lots of milk for babykin.

* * *

Hushabye, lullabye, don't you cry,
Don't bring me heart-ache by and by:
When you grow, be brave and strong—
On me, you'll never need rely.

* * *

Bye-lo, O bye-lo, little babykins,
To break your Mummy's heart a sin;
Sleep in bye-lo-land so deep—
You'll not steal sleep from Mummykins.

Before the flags of dawn unfurl,
Let's walk in vales with dew empearled;
Lowland vales will bless our love—
We'll have a boy, and not a girl.

       *   *   *

With apple gold, with apple white,
I'll strew your pathway for delight—
Wed not beauty, but noble heart;
Nor wed an ignoble though pretty sprite.

       *   *   *

Mother-in-law, cook pilaff and rice,
Put wood on the fire, we'll wed in a trice!
You've lost a son, and now he's mine—
Lie down, and on your brow put ice!

       *   *   *

She piles wood on the roof to
                  dry!
Hayfork, spade they simply fly—
When her married son comes
                  home,
Mother-in-law is smart and spry!

       *   *   *

On poppy and on mountain fall
No sun, nor any light at all—
Sisters must live for brothers'
                  children,
No life have they their own to call.

       *   *   *

Poor child—see that the fire won't dim,
Put on the wood and the hearth keep
                  trim—

May a poor orphan girl ignore
Her stepfather's selfish whim?

* * *

The tribe packs up to move away,
The birds fly north and cannot stay:
Nothing's lasting, hard the lesson—
Yet ignore it no one may.

* * *

A jolly place is Khanabad,
My friend went off to Khanabad—
Say one word to a tyrant and...
They'll ship you off to Khanabad.

* * *

My friend, upon the mountain here,
The nightingale sings loud and clear:
A buzzard circled, came to rest—
Now all the mountain shakes with fear.

* * *

Motionless, the gentle doe—
Seeking shelter from her foe;
Hunter, withered be your hand
The moment arrow's loosed from bow!

* * *

The garden with roses I set out,
Where we with laughter used to shout;
You'd start laughing, I'd laugh too—
Now what have I to laugh about?

* * *

My friend, I'm thinking of a sea,
About a ship becalmed at sea;
Because I shed so many tears—
A sea is now surrounding me.

653

* * *

A bitter foe came to my door,
It was my blood he thirsted for:
But I was back from a foreign land,
My strength returned to me once more.

* * *

At a stranger people look askance,
The strange land led him a sorry dance:
The moment the exile came back home—
Happiness was his inheritance.

* * *

O see the snow on the mountain crag,
And the hawk with wings like a floating
                                    flag—
Should all the world turn Paradise,
My joy would still be Garadag!

* * *

I believed: their words were sweet—
Naked, I trod through the desert's heat;
I sought my own, my tribal kin,
My countrymen I longed to meet.

* * *

As minstrel, I love my Garabakh,
My own Sheki, Shirvan, and Garbag...
If Teheran turned into heaven—
I'd never forget dear Garabakh.

* * *

Fog! throughout the mountains rise,
Drive the sheep where fresh pasture
                                    lies.
I'll follow the sheep till I find my
                                    love—
And deafen the mountains with my cries!

The falling leaves pile up waist high,
The garden burns in the sun's brighty eye;
The nightingale looks for his rose,
From bush to bush, he flutters by.

* * *

Above Tabriz—Mount Marag's crest,
Her thick locks the comb arrest—
Of my dear love, no news at all;
I ask all round—a useless quest.

* * *

I go and stand upon the road,
My words come tumbled, speech is
                        slowed:
I thirst and ache to meet my love—
My eyes are fixed upon the road.

* * *

When stars are flashing in the skies,
When hearts are fused with loving ties,
It's hard to part, surrender up
All that's familiar to the eyes.

* * *

Nightingales fly to and fro,
Younder where the roses grow.
But where are you, where can you be?
Searching the road, my glances go...

* * *

These fortresses my heart appal,
Such mounds of stone with buttressed
                        wall—
I fear to die in a foreign land,
My sweetheart's bitter tears will
                        fall.

I took the road to Khalkhal town:
But all the way my heart was down;
If I go and stay there, I'm afraid—
Another will my darling own.

Let's go on to the upper spring,
Such water, your very blood will sing!
But you'll say this, and I'll say that—
Our tears will mingle with the spring.

O bard, the days and months will run!
I pace the days, count one by one:
I'll build a wall around your
                    grave
And stay by you in the blazing sun.

O noble father, I've come hence
To your dear grave, to seek defence:
You may be dead, but in this world
Your name still calls forth deference.

Misfortune in its train,
My dear, brings lasting pain—
Isn't it like this world to take
The good ones first, while the bad
                    remain?

The melons, rotting, scent the air;
No pomegranate left, no pear.
Confusion rages if you die,
Your sweetheart's harvest is despair.

Can gardens to licorice be reconciled?
Or would the rose-bush feel defiled?
Has anybody sympathy
For her who cannot bear a child?

* * *

Rises the moon, and sets away—
But does it reach the Milky Way?
How can a mother, without her child,
With rest or sleep her fears allay?

* * *

You, O master, I entreat
Don't humble me in your conceit:
A friend looks always in your eyes,
An enemy only at your feet.

* * *

This road takes you to Ordubad,
From Salmas through to Ordubad—
Our troops will meet no ambush if
Our chief with wisdom's ironclad.

* * *

Pick a pretty sash to wear,
Tie a ribbon in your hair,
But don't believe the artful one,
Nor to a stranger secrets bare.

* * *

I'll keep my sheaf of arrows nigh,
I must go and don't you cry—
Perhaps I won't come back, who knows?
But don't you trust the traitor-spy!

The Shah sits on his throne in state,
At times he too complains of fate:
The cock crows just to hear himself,
But morning comes at its own gait.

* * *

Each slope of Mount Kyapez, its crest,
To many a secret might attest—
While you're so busy winning friends,
An enemy's perched within your nest.

* * *

Let them tell the questing stranger:
My sleeping soul shall wake to danger—
Reveal no secrets to a traitor:
He'll give them away to any stranger.

* * *

Huge slabs of ice our roadway bar...
Who'll use an axe that can hardly scar?
He's stupid as the sated dog
Who howls by night at moon and star.

* * *

Bring in some wood, and let it
                              bide;
Fill your hookah—put aside.
If they won't hear what you've to say—
Ignore them, in your heart all hide.

* * *

Behold the pomegranate tree!
Pomegranates I love to see.
But peer deep into his secret heart—
Who to your face says: Friend I be.

* * *

Bard am I for all of ye
Who approve and value me—
No gunfire can smash our friendship's ties
If we maintain our unity.

* * *

The cranes fly on in filed array,
Harsh voices streaming far away—
If we separate or lag,
The enemy will have his way.

* * *

As bard, I see the fogs that creep
Through lowland, up the mountain steep—
Shut your ears to enemy wiles,
Or a fool's harvest you will reap.

* * *

I love our bright and happy days,
This radiant life the past outweighs.
While Lenin's teaching leads us on
To a happy life by freedom ways.

Translated by *Gladys Evans*

Glossary

Agamamed—khan, ruler of Persian province

akhund—Islamic religious office

ashug—folk singer

asker—soldier

bayat—ditty, four-line poetic form with fixed rhyming pattern, widely used by folk-singers and poets

Bairam—Islamic religious feast

bei—nobleman, official

Black Stone—meteorite built into the wall of the sanctuary at Mecca, symbol of faith

chukha—long coat worn by men

Dede Korkut—narrator of one of the most ancient Azerbaijanian epics bearing his name (see p. 534)

div—evil spirit

Firdousi—Iranian poet

Fisuli—Azerbaijanian poet (see p. 106)

gassyda, g'ita—poetic forms

giaour—infidel

Hatai—Azerbaijanian poet (see p. 98)

Jamshid, Jami-Jam—mythical Persian king, possessor of a magic cup in which he described the destinies of men

jigit—brave youth, warrior, horseman

kaaba—chief moslem sanctuary at Mecca

Kajjar—Persian dynasty

Kerbala—city, place of pilgrimage

Kerem—epic hero

khanum (khanym)—lady, madam

Khassan—relative of Mohammed

Khazar—Caspian Sea

Khizir—Islamic saint, patron of wayfarers

khoja—respectful form of address, honorary title

Khosrau—king, character in Nizami's poem *Farhad and Shirin*

khuda—prayer

kobza—stringed instrument

Kubbas, Key-kubbad—Persian king

Leili—beloved of Medjnun, character in many oriental poems and legends

Linka Choglok—legendary outlaw

Lokhman (Lukman)—legendary sage, physician, any wise, knowing person

Medjnun—literally, insane; legendary hero often figuring in oriental poetry as ideal lover

molla—polite form of address

mufti—head of Islamic clergy

Nofel—Islamic religious leader

Novshad—oriental deity

Nushiravan—kingdom in Persia

Osman—founder of Turkish dynasty

Ogouzes—forerunners of Azerbaijanians

peri—fairy

Sabukhee—member of religious sect

Sattarkhan—leader of uprising in early twentieth century

saz—stringed instrument

seid—religious official

shaitan—devil

Sham—kingdom in Iran

Shariat—collection of Islamic laws

shiites—religious sect

sunnites—religious sect

sura—chapter of the Koran

tuman—Persian coin

tar, tara—stringed instrument

Varga—oriental epic hero, model of true love

yatagan—scimitar

Yussuf—St. Joseph

Zuleika—beautiful heroine of oriental poetry

REQUEST TO READERS

Progress Publishers would be glad to have your opinion of this book, its translation and design and any suggestions you may have for future publications.

Please send your comments to 21, Zubovsky Boulevard, Moscow, U.S.S.R.